THE COLLECTED WORKS OF
G. K. CHESTERTON

I

THE COLLECTED WORKS OF G. K. CHESTERTON

I

HERETICS
ORTHODOXY
THE BLATCHFORD CONTROVERSIES

with Introduction and Notes by
David Dooley, Editor

IGNATIUS PRESS   SAN FRANCISCO

© 1986 Ignatius Press, San Francisco
All rights reserved
ISBN 0–89870–077–9 (HB)
ISBN 0–89870–079–5 (SB)
Library of Congress catalogue number 85–081511
Printed in the United States of America

CONTENTS

CONTENTS

THE BLATCHFORD CONTROVERSIES

INTRODUCTION

By David Dooley

According to Chesterton's own account, Victorian religion and ethics were wearing thin by the time of his birth in 1874. Typically, his own family was "not stiff with orthodox religion" but "reverently agnostic or latitudinarian".[1] His school days at St. Paul's did little to encourage him in religious belief or practice. He did begin appearing in print, especially through poems written for a student magazine called *The Debater*; and he began his long career as an amiable controversialist by helping to found the Junior Debating Society and becoming its chairman. In his last year at school, he won a prize for a poem on a set subject, and the subject was Saint Francis Xavier. In imitation of Browning, one of his favorite authors, he took for his theme the idea that apparent failure on earth may still mean success in God's eyes. Before that, when he was only sixteen, he had written a poem entitled "Adveniat Regnum Tuum" which described weak and miserable humankind as crying out, "How long, oh Lord, how long?" and praying, "Father, Thy Kingdom come."[2] Still he was something of a youthful iconoclast; some of his poems, as Garry Wills points out, suggest the dawn of a new era in which human history will no more be stained by the antics of those who "struggle for a name and slaughter for a sign".

> We love who had done with the churches, we worship who may not believe.

The pretensions of jealous priests and exclusive dogmas are destroyed, to be replaced by a Rousseauean humanitarianism; for all faiths are as symbols, and man is divine.[3]

The period after his school days, the years from 1892 to 1895, when he was at the Slade School of Art, forms the subject of the

---

[1] G. K. Chesterton, *Autobiography* (London, 1937), 27.
[2] Quoted in Maisie Ward, *G. K. Chesterton* (London, 1944), 45.
[3] Garry Wills, *Chesterton: Man and Mask* (New York, 1961), 15–16.

fourth chapter of his autobiography, "How to be a Lunatic". It was marked by pessimism and despair: "As Bunyan, in his morbid period, described himself as prompted to utter blasphemies, I had an overpowering impulse to record or draw horrible ideas and images; plunging deeper and deeper as in a blind spiritual suicide." When he had been for some time in "the darkest depths of the contemporary pessimism", his whole being revolted against it. He invented a rudimentary theory of his own: "It was substantially this: that even mere existence, reduced to its most primary limits, was extraordinary enough to be exciting. . . . In fact, I had wandered to a position not very far from the phrase of my Puritan grandfather, when he said that he would thank God for his creation if he were a lost soul. I hung on to the remains of religion by one thin thread of thanks."[4]

According to his brother Cecil, Gilbert read the Gospels partly because he was not forced to read them; religious terms and imagery came more and more into his notebooks in this period (1892–1895). But Gilbert's biographer, Maisie Ward, says that it did not occur to him to question the assumption of the time: that official Christianity had travestied the original intention of Christ.[5] A strong influence upon him from 1896 on, however, was Frances Blogg, whom he was to marry in 1901. He observed in his autobiography that, acting on a perverse principle, she actually practiced a religion, the Anglo-Catholicism in which she had been brought up. Years later he wrote to her,

> Therefore I bring these rhymes to you
> Who brought the Cross to me.[6]

There were other influences as well, such as Conrad Noel, a somewhat eccentric Anglican clergyman with a penetrating mind, and the writer with whose name Chesterton's was so often to be linked, Hilaire Belloc. "So, under the probably unconscious influence of Mr. Belloc," Cecil Chesterton was to write, "Mr. Chesterton was drawn towards the Catholic faith."[7]

---

[4] Chesterton, *Autobiography*, 93–94.
[5] Maisie Ward, 63.
[6] Ibid., 76.
[7] *G. K. Chesterton: A Criticism* (London, 1908), 99.

The remark came in the critical study which Cecil published anonymously in 1908. In it he declared that his brother had become a Catholic: "Growing up in an atmosphere of theological liberalism [he] has slowly thought himself out of it and become the avowed champion of a strict Catholic orthodoxy." Referring to the odd circumstance of his brother's being a regular columnist for the *Daily News*, with whose readers he had little in common, Cecil wrote that "Thousands of peaceful semi-Tolstoian Nonconformists have for six years been compelled to listen every Saturday morning to a fiery apostle preaching consistently the praise of the three things which seem to them most obviously the signs-manual of Hell — War, Drink and Catholicism." He also said, "Mr. Chesterton stands for Anti-Imperialism and for much else besides, for Catholicism with its back to the wall, for the hunger of a perplexed age, for the more lucid life of the Ages of Faith, for the revolt against Modernity — in a word, for what may legitimately be called 'reaction'."[8]

Later critics of Chesterton will protest that Cecil made many mistakes in chronology and in the interpretation of his brother's intellectual and spiritual development. After all, G. K. was to become a Catholic convert only in 1922, long after Cecil himself had done so, long after Cecil's death. The term "fiery apostle" may also seem inappropriate for one who was going to be accused of frivolity in his approach to religious questions. Margaret Clarke would say, for example, that Chesterton avoided the serious content of his faith and used his religion for the spinning of pleasant fancies, that his early writings were not truly Christian but gnostic in their insistence on results.[9]

Others question Cecil's declaration in different ways. Before she becomes paradoxical, Garry Wills comments, Miss Clarke brings forward evidence which has real import; she sees obvious facts which many have overlooked. He then goes on to give his own estimate of Chesterton's religious position at the time under discussion:

> It is true that *Heretics* and *Orthodoxy* are not examples of Christian apologetic. *Orthodoxy* is, on one level, personal apologia and defence;

[8] Ibid., 162–63, 60, xi–xii.
[9] Margaret Clarke, "Chesterton the Classicist", *Dublin Review*, 229 (1955), 51–67, discussed in Wills, 3 and 87.

its further aim, along with *Heretics*, is to help re-establish certitude and philosophical realism against the flux of progressivism and scientific relativism. Chesterton's Christian apologetic was written much later.[10]

In spite of the brilliance of his book, Wills too can be paradoxical: he calls Chesterton more French than English, Hilaire Belloc more English than French, and Belloc not an orthodox Catholic but "pagan metal in a Christian mould". But is he correct in his view that Chesterton's Christian apologetic was going to come long after *Heretics* and *Orthodoxy*?

Heretics appeared in 1905. For some time before that, Chesterton had been involved in a long-running argument about religion with the editor of the *Clarion*, in the pages of that weekly paper and elsewhere. Commenting on the controversy, Dudley Barker writes,

> This was said by Cecil Chesterton to be his brother's first public declaration of faith in the orthodox system of Christian dogmas, and it has usually been taken as Chesterton's declaration of belief in the divinity of Christ. In fact, it was not. Blatchford, certainly, was attacking Christianity; he had made a series of assaults upon it, in his book *God and My Neighbour*, and in the *Clarion*. But the view that Chesterton disputed with him was his Determinism; and for this Chesterton required, as he himself showed, only a limited definition of Christianity.[11]

Barker is alluding to four questions concerning his religious position which Blatchford put to Chesterton and which the latter answered in the *Daily News*. The second question was "What do you mean by the word *Christianity*?" Chesterton replied,

> A belief that a certain human being whom we call Christ stood to a certain superhuman being whom we call God in a certain unique transcendental relationship which we call sonship.[12]

The careful distinction between "human being" and "superhuman being", Barker says, is indicative of Chesterton's reservations at the time. Garry Wills agrees: "The answer is as carefully worded as it is brief, and we must therefore take as intended the opposition

[10] Wills, 87.
[11] Dudley Barker, *G. K. Chesterton: A Biography* (London, 1973), 169.
[12] Ibid.

between 'human being' and 'superhuman being'." Though Maisie
Ward claims that the articles Chesterton wrote for the *Clarion* express clearly his belief in Christ's divinity and provide a sketch of
some elements of Christian theology, Wills denies this and claims
support from Chesterton's autobiography:

> It was not a question of some abstract theological thesis, like the
> definition of the Trinity or the dogmas of Election or Effectual Grace.
> I was not yet so far gone in orthodoxy as to be so theological as all
> that. What I was defending seemed to me a plain matter of ordinary
> human morals. Indeed it seemed to me to raise the question of the very
> possibility of any morals. It was the question of Responsibility,
> sometimes called the question of Free Will.[13]

To the problem of whether this statement means that the dispute
was "about" free will exclusively we shall have to return.

In her *Outline of Sanity* Alzina Dale is partly indebted to Barker
but gives a slightly different emphasis to Chesterton's religious position. "When dealing with Chesterton, the approach to politics is
misleading in almost every instance", Garry Wills declares, but Miss
Dale intrepidly confuses his religion with his politics, declaring that
in the *Clarion* contention for the first time Chesterton "publicly used
'liberalism' as 'orthodoxy' ". "Paradoxically," she continues, "in
defending liberalism he found he was defending Christianity, and
vice versa — although he was talking about a rational way of life, not
a faith, because he had not yet subscribed to many creedal [sic]
elements of Christianity." *Orthodoxy* tied together his religious convictions and his political concerns: in defending classical liberalism
from within and without, he discovered Christian tradition.[14]

If these various critics leave us confused about Chesterton's
religious position at the time he wrote *Heretics*, one point is easy to
establish: that they themselves are very confused about the *Clarion*
controversy. Alzina Dale says that Chesterton was writing as a
liberal and that all liberals accept the doctrine of progress. On the
other hand, Cecil Chesterton writes that his brother had rejected the

---

[13] Chesterton, *Autobiography*, 181–82; Wills, 84–85.
[14] Wills, 67; Alzina Stone Dale, *The Outline of Sanity: A Biography of G. K. Chesterton* (Grand Rapids, Michigan, 1982), 118–21.

doctrine of progress by this time and was writing as a reactionary, an old-fashioned Tory in fact. Both of these opinions cannot be correct. Barker refers to Blatchford as a "staunch old Socialist". This becomes in Miss Dale's book "one of the Socialist old guard". Christopher Hollis describes Blatchford as "a very decent old man". Blatchford often *seems* very old, definitely one of the old guard, but since he was born in 1851, he was only in his early fifties at the time of the controversy. Hollis says that Chesterton used his weapon of paradox "in a little composite book called *The Doubts of Democracy* to which he contributed an essay"—contriving to make three mistakes in less than one sentence, since Chesterton contributed more than one essay to a book which was not really "little" and which appeared under a different title. Garry Wills complains that Maisie Ward cut the four articles Chesterton wrote to three; he does not realize that three appeared in the *Clarion,* and one was divided in two in the book. Barker says that Blatchford had made a series of assaults upon Christianity "in his book *God and My Neighbour,* and in the *Clarion*". This gives a wrong impression, since the articles in the *Clarion* came first, and out of them came the book. Alzina Dale says that "the first Blatchford-Chesterton 'debate' was about free will." This is misleading, however, since in Chesterton's first *Daily News* column on Blatchford's attacks he welcomed discussion of religious differences, declared that the greatest of all the triumphs of science was the method of hypothesis and said as well that many young men such as himself were returning to a spiritual view of existence because it provided a more satisfactory view of things than the scientific or materialistic hypothesis. So he did not begin by dealing with determinism at all. Chesterton would have had many a chuckle at these paradoxical and contrary interpretations of what he said in the *Clarion* controversy. Evidently it is desirable to examine that controversy, to see what actually was said and what the dispute tells us about Chesterton's religious opinions at the time it occurred.[15]

[15] A. Dale, 86–87; Cecil Chesterton, 172–89; Barker, 168–69; Christopher Hollis, *The Mind of Chesterton* (London, 1970), 64; Wills, 84.

The Clarion Controversy

A friend of Robert Blatchford declared that in his "fighting period" between 1890 and 1920 this crusading journalist did more to improve the lot of the British people than almost any other man. Though he himself came from an impoverished background, he still had his whole outlook on life changed by the slums of Manchester, on which he wrote a number of newspaper stories. He became a Socialist, was fired by a publisher who would not publish Socialism in his paper, and started his own paper, the *Clarion*, in 1891. During its first ten years, he claimed, it had a greater influence on English life than any other newspaper, including the *Times*. His pamphlet on English social conditions, *Merrie England* (1893), sold over a million copies and did more to awaken England to Socialism than anything else.

Even his enemies paid tribute to his honesty and sincerity. Chesterton, not an enemy but a genial adversary, gave him generous praise: "Very few intellectual swords have left such a mark on our time, have cut so deep or remained so clean. . . . His triumphs were triumphs of strong style, native pathos, and picturesque metaphor; his very lucidity was a generous sympathy with simple minds. . . . For the rest, he has triumphed by being honest and by not being afraid."[16] Referring to him by a pseudonym he used, Shaw gave him a similar tribute: "There are very few men who can write as Nunquam does, with conscience and strong feeling; and yet without malice. . . . Nunquam keeps his temper, and treats the heathen as fellow-men to be converted, not as reptiles to be scotched."[17]

On January 23, 1903, Blatchford reviewed Haeckel's *The Riddle of the Universe*, translated by Joseph McCabe, in enthusiastic terms. He declared that the book demolished the entire structure upon which the religions of the world were built: "There is no escape from that conclusion. The case for science is complete." His subsequent articles attacking Christianity, and the book entitled *God and My Neighbour* which came out of them, attracted a great deal of attention; the

[16] Quoted by Alexander M. Thompson in his preface to Robert Blatchford, *My Eighty Years* (London, 1931), x.

[17] Quoted by Alexander M. Thompson in his "In the Library" column, *Clarion* (June 24, 1904), 3.

controversy lasted not just months but years. To protests that he was diverting his socialistic paper from the work which it was called upon to do, he answered, "My object is not so much to help to destroy an obsolete religion, as to help to build up a better religion in its place." The old religion forgot about the "neighbor" part of the commandment to love: "To build a cathedral, and to spend our tears and pity upon a Saviour Who was crucified nearly two thousand years ago, while women and little children are being crucified in our midst, without pity and without help, is cant, and sentimentality, and a mockery of God."[18]

As part of his campaign, he had to show that social failure is not a result of individual culpability but of heredity and environment: "Before we can propagate our religion of Determinism and Humanism, we must first clear the ground of Free Will, of sin against God, and of the belief in the divine inspiration of the Bible."[19] His views on philosophy and religion complemented his views on society and politics.

Occasionally in his *Clarion* articles he took note of protests and rejoinders. On March 27, he referred to a column by Chesterton in the *Daily News* on him and his rationalism, saying that it amounted to little more than a statement that Chesterton believed in some form of spiritual life because nearly all other men did. His article was clever and witty, in fact brilliant, but he might just as well have let off a catherine wheel (pinwheel): "Pretty, sparkling, and surprising as a catherine wheel may be, it cannot be regarded as a contribution to a theological debate."

Of course, it *was* a more serious contribution to a theological debate than Blatchford realized, even though it did not argue about particular scriptural passages or the like. Whereas Blatchford had declared that no honest person could deny Haeckel's proof of evolution, Chesterton blandly referred to the Darwinian hypothesis — saying that evolution was something no one tried to prove but everyone took for granted. He and others preferred the spiritual to the materialistic hypothesis, he continued, not because of specific

[18] Quoted by Thompson, ibid.
[19] Ibid.

doctrinal arguments but "because it gave an intelligible picture of the world. We have returned to it because, by the rejection of rationalism, the world suddenly became rational."[20] Besides revealing Chesterton's penchant for turning an opponent's argument upside down through use of a witty paradox, the statement shows his central contention in his quarrel with Blatchford. As he was to put it in his autobiography, it was not a question of some abstract theological thesis. The secularists drove him to Christianity because their positions were so clearly untenable — particularly when they denied human responsibility.

Nevertheless, though the issue was in large measure determinism versus responsibility, many related questions of a doctrinal nature did come in; critics like Wills contend that the discussion was very theoretical in nature, dealing with metaphysical and philosophical questions, but Chesterton did discuss God's creation of the world and of Adam, the fall of Adam, predestination, the responsibility of Christians — and indeed of all men for torture and cruelty — and many other matters of theology and religious history.

While Blatchford continued his attacks, Chesterton continued his rebuttals, in the *Daily News* and also in six articles in the monthly *Commonwealth* between July and December 1903. He also wrote letters to the *Clarion*, all long, some very long. In one, which appeared on August 7, he pointed out that Blatchford was contradicting himself: while maintaining that no one but God could be praised or blamed for any human act, he still said that man could be unjust and cruel toward his fellow man. If there is no free will, Chesterton observed, you cannot even say, "Please pass the mustard", because the word *please* implies a choice. Maintaining once again that the strength of Christianity has nothing to do with controversial ingenuity, he said that it is simply indispensable: those who attack it wind up in positions which no sane mass of people have ever held, like Schopenhauer saying that life itself is a delusion, or Nietzsche that charity is a delusion, or Nunquam that human goodness and badness are delusions. So Christianity guards, through the ages, an eternal sanity.

[20] Chesterton, "The Return of the Angels", London *Daily News* (March 14, 1903), 8.

This is one of his best contributions to the controversy, and it came in a letter. Whether or not he was a disillusioned Liberal at this time, or a Tory reactionary, or a radical populist, this busy journalist was prepared, not only to devote whole articles to the defense of Christianity, but to write long letters to the newspapers on the topic, even though these letters took him away from his gainful employment.

He was a more staunch defender of Christianity at this time than many of his critics seem to believe. On August 28 he compared Blatchford to an Oriental mystic; Christianity, he said, has always seen afar off this fatalistic Blatchford, who freezes all human effort and insults all human dignity, and with great difficulty it drove him back across the Danube and the Straits of Gibraltar, leaving us progress and free will. When Blatchford accused him of undue haste, he responded, "I do not know that it is much more of a proof of hurry in me that I defend Christianity once a month than it is in you that you attack it once a week."[21]

The facetiousness of his replies, however, often masked their seriousness. In the third of his answers to Blatchford, when he was asked what he believed, one part of his reply was "That Mr. Blatchford is an honest man, for instance." In the fourth—to the question: "Why do you believe it?"—his response was, "Because I perceive life to be logical and workable with these beliefs and illogical and unworkable without them." Barker calls this a pragmatic answer, clear indication of the reservations which Chesterton had about Christianity at this time.[22] The reply is that his starting point was indeed personal experience—as was Newman's. The latter's *Grammar of Assent* asserted the right of the man in the street to give assent to religious propositions, which in the nature of things he cannot prove. Religious assent has never been a deduction from what we know but an assertion of what we are to believe; religious truth is not scientific demonstration. Chesterton was saying virtually the same thing. He was able to give assent, not only to the proposition

[21] Chesterton, letter headed "Mr. Blatchford, Persecution, and Other Things", *Clarion* (Nov. 20, 1903), 3.

[22] Barker, 169.

that Blatchford was an honest man and (less certainly) to the existence of Japan, but also to a number of things he could never have established pragmatically, "ranging from the mystical dogma that man is the image of God to the mystical dogma that all men are equal and that babies should not be strangled."

At the end of the column in which he put forth his four questions (on December 4), Blatchford invited the champions of Christianity to step forward and put their case in his newspaper: "They shall have a fair field if they will come forward. I will find good men to answer them, and one side shall have the same space as the other, and no member of the *Clarion* Staff shall interfere." Out of this fair offer came the series of defenses of Christianity which ran from January to August of 1904 and the selection of these articles which George Haw edited under the title *The Religious Doubts of Democracy*. Haw began the series with four articles on Christianity and Socialism, followed by three on God and Man. In the *Clarion* for June 24, Haw wrote a concluding note to the series—before it had concluded—commending Blatchford for his astonishing magnanimity in allowing the opposition three of the best columns of his newspaper for nearly half a year without interference. He also listed the remaining contributors—Professor Moulton, Father Adderly, Dr. Fry, George Lansbury "and then, finally, Mr. G. K. Chesterton will wind up the discussion in one or two articles."

The debate between Blatchford and Chesterton had been going for sixteen months, therefore, before the first of Chesterton's pieces appeared in the *Clarion*, on July 22, 1904. It was entitled "Christianity and Rationalism". In it he argued paradoxically that Blatchford's arguments against Christianity in *God and My Neighbour* were his own reasons for believing in it; he persisted in treating this primer of agnosticism as a textbook in theology. The next week's article was headed "We are all Agnostics until we discover that Agnosticism will not work". In it he contended that Christianity, though it is a very mystical religion, has been the religion of the practical part of mankind: "The Christian has a triune God, 'a tangled Trinity', which seems a mere capricious contradiction in terms. But in action he bestrides the earth, and even the cleverest Eastern can only fight him by imitating him first." Complete agnosticism is the obvious attitude for man; we are all agnostics until we find that it will not work. The Christian mystery, by its darkness, illumines all things.

Instead of writing one or two articles, Chesterton wrote three, the last of which was divided in two in *Religious Doubts of Democracy*. It appeared under the heading "Mr. Blatchford's Religion. Is Nobody to Be Responsible for Anything?" on August 5; Haw found it easy to divide it into "Miracles and Modern Civilisation" and "The Eternal Heroism of the Slums" for purposes of his book. Chesterton's defense of miracles, including the miracle of the Resurrection, rests on the inadequacy of the case against them, together with the conviction that the existence of a world of spirits is part of the common sense of all mankind. Responding to an attack on Christianity for its alleged cruelties, he declared that, if the gory past of an institution is going to damn it, Blatchford ought not to point his finger at the Church but at the State, the Mother of all whips and thumbscrews, "the very thing which Mr. Blatchford and his socialistic following would make stronger than it has ever been under the sun."

In the second part of his article, he argued that when Blatchford said that sin arises from vile environments, he was falling back "upon the old contemptible impertinence which represents virtue to be something upper-class, like a visiting card, or a silk hat." "Is it Nunquam", he asked pointedly, "who denied the eternal heroism of the slums? The thing is almost incredible, but so it is." Whatever their circumstances, men have always thought they were at least free in their own minds. But this strange comforter tells them that their thoughts are the inevitable result of heredity and environment: they are not free men but machines.

In spite of his much-praised magnanimity, Blatchford was not going to let the Christian responses to him go unanswered. On August 12, he announced that he had asked some of the ablest of the freethinkers to reply. First came Joseph McCabe, an ex-priest who had already written *Why I Left the Church of Rome* and was to direct many more attacks at Catholicism, including *The Pope Helps Hitler to*

World Power in 1941. He began by attacking Haw's arguments, but on October 21, in an article entitled "Christianity Defended by Sleight of Hand", he mounted a devastating attack on Chesterton's method of argumentation. He tried to "strip Mr. Chesterton's case for Christianity of all its literary tinsel and its sparkling paradoxes"; he argued that Chesterton could not defend his reckless statements and sweeping generalities, that in defending the concept of free will he was ignoring the findings of modern psychologists, and that he was deserting serious methods of conducting enquiry.

The answer to this slashing attack was to come in the sixteenth chapter of Chesterton's *Heretics*, "Mr. McCabe and a Divine Frivolity". Chesterton did appear in the *Clarion* columns once more on December 23, with a letter headed "The Inconsistency of Robert Blatchford", in which he argued again that Blatchford could not reproach men and urge them to a nobler choice if he denied free will. "As long as you continue, in the face of every actual problem," he concluded, "to act in flat contradiction to all your principles, you will continue to be the very jolly person you are. But the world might contain some day a logical Determinist: and he would be a lunatic."

The controversy continued long after December 1904, but we need follow it no farther. This analysis of it is far from complete; it has taken little account of Chesterton's *Daily News* and *Commonwealth* articles on Blatchford, of the responses by the freethinkers (which were published as a book under the title *Christianity and Rationalism on Trial*), and of the many articles and books inspired by the dispute, some of them with titles like *Clarion Fallacies: A Reply to Mr. Robert Blatchford's Strictures . . .* and *Anti-Nunquam: An Examination of the Book "God and My Neighbour"*.

Our main interest here, however, is in what the debate tells us of Chesterton's development. He wrote as a convinced and orthodox Christian — long before G. S. Street, in a review of *Heretics*, asked him to define his own standpoint and thus led him to write *Orthodoxy*. He wrote as one who believed that life had to have a spiritual dimension and who accepted the doctrines of the Fall, the Incarnation, the Redemption, the Resurrection, the Trinity and many other essentials of Christian belief. He did not expect to "prove" the truth of these doctrines to the satisfaction of someone like Blatchford. In the nature of the case, Chesterton maintained, proof is impossible. Religion is a matter of faith, not of demonstration; it cannot be proved empirically. Though it provides a reasonable explanation of human existence by accounting for dimensions of experience for which materialism has no explanation, it contains mysteries which are entirely beyond the range of human thought.[23]

If Chesterton was not "the avowed champion of a strict Catholic orthodoxy" in 1903 and 1904, therefore, he was certainly an avowed champion of Christianity.[24]

Heretics

In an article on "The Making of Chesterton's 'Heretics' ", David Evans has shown that in the period between 1900 and 1910, when he wrote many of the books by which he is best remembered, Chesterton's journalism allowed him to "air" the materials which he would

[23] A similar view of the importance of the *Clarion* controversy in Chesterton's development is taken by Stanley L. Jaki in "Chesterton's Landmark Year: the Blatchford-Chesterton Debate of 1903–1904", *Chesterton Review*, 10 (1984), 409–23. Though we reached the same conclusion independently of each other, Father Jaki's was the earlier work.

[24] At least one reader of the *Daily News* became tired of the controversy and wished that Chesterton would turn to other subjects. In a letter, "H. S. S." wrote as follows:

Stern Blatchford, *thou* hast dashed the glee
   of our Omniscient Babe:
Thy name alone now murmurs he,
   Or that of dark McCabe.

All vain his cloudy fancies swell,
   His paradox all vain.
Obsessed by that malignant spell
   Of Blatchford on the brain.

(Quoted in Leo Anthony Hetzler, C.S.B., "The Early Literary Career of G. K. Chesterton: His Literary Apprenticeship and an Analysis of His Thought, 1874–1914", Ph.D. thesis, Cornell University, 1964, 102.)

soon incorporate into a coherent and unique view of life. Very few
of the *Daily News* articles which he wrote before 1905 have been
reprinted; yet some of these were used as material for his first important polemical work, *Heretics*, published on June 6, 1905.[25]

On February 18, 1905, in "Bigotry versus Intolerance", he expounded the theme of *Heretics*:

> The modern world . . . is bigoted. It is not bigoted to abuse a heretic,
> so long as this is strictly understood, that you abuse him as a heretic
> . . . I think, for instance, that the only thing wrong about Mr.
> Blatchford is his being wrong. That is, I disapprove of him as a
> heretic.

The very same point was made in the "Introductory Remarks" to
Heretics a few months later, except that Kipling was used as an example instead of Blatchford. Many of Chesterton's essays from the
previous three years were incorporated into the book, some of them
with hardly any revision. Evans points out that two very recent
essays, "The Butterfly Again" and "A note on a Satirist", were put
together to make chapter seventeen of *Heretics*, "On the Wit of
Whistler". Chapter three of *Heretics*, "On Mr. Rudyard Kipling",
had its origin in a book review written in November 1902. Chapter
eight, "The Mildness of the Yellow Press", derived its theme as well
as its examples from "The Mildness of the Journalist" (written in
May 1903) and "The Battle of the Standard" (which appeared in
November 1904). Chapter six of *Heretics*, "Christmas and the
Aesthetics", which deals in passing with Auguste Comte, is partly
based on "Man on an Altar", which appeared on May 30, 1903.
Evans does not discuss all the borrowings and echoes found in
Heretics. He does establish that there were many such borrowings,
and he does give illustrations of how Chesterton carried out the process of revision, tidying up slight awkwardnesses of expression,
pruning his more extravagant images and suppressing material
which did not contribute to the effect he was seeking.

Heretics contains some of the best things Chesterton ever wrote;
the brief chapter on Shaw is an example. At first his approach to a

[25] David Evans, "The Making of Chesterton's 'Heretics' ", *Yearbook of English
Studies*, 5 (1975), 207–13.

subject may strike the reader as odd and perhaps even perverse; out of the seeming perversity, however, will emerge an entirely new perspective on the subject he is discussing. In the third chapter, for instance, he describes Kipling as a man of the world—which ordinarily would be interpreted as a commendation of him. But it is not a commendation for Chesterton: the man of the world regards one place as much the same as another; he has not the time to get attached to one particular locality; he has not the patience to become part of anything. If we wish to understand Arabia or China, Chesterton says, it must not be as tourists or inquirers but with the loyalty of children and the patience of poets. So Kipling becomes an example not of large-mindedness but of small-mindedness because of his failure to attach himself sufficiently to anything.

As we have seen, the opinion that Chesterton was not writing Christian apologetic in these years had to be modified when we looked at the *Clarion* controversy; presumably, therefore, it will not apply to *Heretics* either, since the book came out of the articles Chesterton had been writing, largely between 1902 and 1905. Garry Wills writes that Chesterton's aim in *Heretics* was to help reestablish certitude and philosophical realism; his Christian apologetic was to be written much later. There are many types of Christian apologetic, however, and *Heretics* is an example of one of them. By showing what heresy implies, Chesterton illustrates what orthodoxy implies.

He comments initially on the modern pride in being heterodox. Even atheism is too theological for us today, he writes; general theories are everywhere condemned. Shaw says that "The golden rule is that there is no golden rule." This was certainly not the idea of those who introduced our freedom, says Chesterton: "When the old Liberals removed the gags from all the heresies, their idea was that religious and philosophical discoveries might thus be made." The ironic result has been, not that we settle on a certain number of received ideas, but that we settle on none; heresy triumphs. Even blasphemy depends upon belief and is fading with it.

Objecting to the prevailing spirit of negation, he refers to the increasing morbidity of modern ethics, the absence of vivid pictures of purity and spiritual triumph. In Ibsenism, there are no cardinal virtues; Ibsen pounces on something which he perceives to be a root of evil, some convention, some deception, some form of ignorance, but he does not profess to know how virtue and happiness are brought about. We are face to face with the problem of a human consciousness filled with very definite images of evil but none of good: "To us, as to Milton's devils in *Pandaemonium*, it is darkness that is visible."

With this basically religious perspective in mind, Chesterton discusses some of the leading figures and tendencies of his world. The great failure of Kipling is that he has not attached himself definitely to any cause or community but to the world, meaning all the miscellaneous interests to which a Christian refers when he quotes the admonition to him to keep himself "unspotted from the world". Bernard Shaw, far from being inconsistent as his critics maintain, is entirely consistent—remarkably so. The trouble with him is that he will not be content to accept man as God made him; he is always comparing human beings with some form of superman. When Christ at a symbolic moment was establishing His great society, He chose for its leader a shuffler and a coward, in a word a man—"And upon this rock He has built His Church, and the gates of Hell have not prevailed against it." Wells also does not allow for the stuff or material of man, and he longs for Utopia; for him, everything is becoming, there is no being, nothing abides. His romances foresee men like gods or giants; the whole secret of the practical success of Christendom, however, lies in its humility, however imperfectly fulfilled, so that its wonder is for the gift of things which man cannot possibly deserve.

In each case, in other words, a theological perspective is being employed. Having analyzed his heretics and their heresies one by one, Chesterton concludes with an assertion of the importance of orthodoxy. The vice of the modern notion of progress, he suggests, is that it is concerned with the breaking of bonds and the casting away of dogmas. But if there be such a thing as mental growth, it means the growth into more and more definite convictions, more and more dogmas. In fact, man can be defined as an animal that makes dogmas. When he drops one doctrine after another in a refined scepticism, when he sits as God—holding no form of creed but contemplating all—he sinks slowly backwards into the vagueness of animals and the unconsciousness of grass.

In his last few paragraphs Chesterton makes it very clear that he is discussing the place of religion in our lives: "Religion is exactly the thing which cannot be left out—because it includes everything." He comes back to a point he has made elsewhere, that the very man who utters a doubt helps define a religion: "We who are Christians never knew the great philosophic common sense which inheres in that mystery until the anti-Christian writers pointed it out. . . . It is a reasonable position to deny the stones in the street; it will be a religious dogma to assert them. It is a rational thesis that we are all in a dream; it will be a mystical sanity to say that we are all awake." For man to be truly awake and truly alive, he must not abandon himself to pessimism and scepticism but affirm the place of religion and dogma in his life: "We shall be of those who have seen and yet have believed."

The reader of *Heretics* may see other lines of discussion in it besides the one described above. Nevertheless, it is obvious that, even though he is not explaining the specific articles of his religion in the book, Chesterton is arguing the need for faith, for dogma, for Christian belief.

Maisie Ward writes that *Heretics* aroused animosity in many minds. Reviewers who had been extending a friendly welcome to a beginner changed their tune when they found him attacking landmarks in the world of letters, venturing to detest Ibsen and to ask Ibsen's translator William Archer whether he hung up his stocking on Ibsen's birthday and accusing Kipling of lack of patriotism. One reviewer said that it was "unbecoming to spend most of his time criticising his contemporaries". Another said that "his sense of mental perspective is an extremely deficient one", another that "the manufacture of paradoxes is really one of the simplest processes conceivable." Curiously, most of the reviewers did not seem to understand Chesterton's position. Even after he had shown how he disagreed with Shaw, one critic called him Shaw's disciple—just as another discerned the influence of Shaw in Chesterton's novel *The Napoleon of Notting Hill*, "but without a trace of Shaw's wonderful humour and perspicacity".[26]

In his analysis of the reviews, Father Leo Hetzler disagrees with Maisie Ward's assessment of them. He finds that, rather than stressing the angry dissent to what Chesterton said about some of England's leading literary figures, the reviewers tended to quote the judgments which seemed especially penetrating and with which they agreed. The *Westminster Gazette* said in fact that the book "comes like a gale into a stuffy room". A controversy of sorts did arise, however, concerning Chesterton's style and degree of seriousness in controversy. Some reviewers spoke of him as a mere witty jester or sophist, generally interesting, often amazing, but seldom convincing. Some considered that he dealt with sacred subjects with irreverence or lack of dignity. Indeed, "denouncing G. K. C." was mentioned in a *Daily News* editorial as one of the common activities of the ordinary citizen, along with racing for the train and gambling on the stock exchange.

Nevertheless, he had his defenders. The *Saturday Review* argued that his paradoxical inversions were never there simply to startle but "for the greater part are forcible, illuminating and eminently serious", and the "perversity" of which some accuse him "is never sought for its own sake, but is always a happy accident incidental to his being so conspicuously in the right." Similarly Stanton Coit, an atheist who had opposed Chesterton in the past, defended his style on the grounds that he had to express new ideas and relations in old words; he also said that Chesterton's playing with words rid them of their accretions and showed forth their all-important inner meaning.[27]

In his introduction to *Heretics* Chesterton gave an amusing definition of a heretic as "a man whose view of things has the hardihood to differ from mine". The obvious retort, especially by those who did not read his book carefully, was that if orthodoxy was simply his standpoint and heterodoxy somebody else's, the terms were not worth bothering about. G. S. Street was not alone in saying that it would be time for him to consider whether Chesterton's heretics were really heretics or not when he was given some clear idea of what standard Chesterton was measuring his subjects against. Chesterton was not slow to respond to this complaint or demand; he wrote *Orthodoxy*. The tremendous success of that book has tended to put its predecessor in the shade. Christopher Hollis believes that the earlier book deserves little consideration: "We therefore can turn to the positive book and need not consider in great deal the negative."[28] Nevertheless, *Heretics* is a very good book in its own right, even if *Orthodoxy* is a better one. Also, as we have seen, there is much more than negation present in *Heretics*; the standard against which contemporary negativism and pessimism are measured is clearly present, even if it is given a fuller exposition in the later book.

Orthodoxy

Just as David Evans sees the origins of *Heretics* in articles which Chesterton wrote for the *Daily News*, A. L. Maycock sees the main interest of the essays which Chesterton wrote for the *Clarion* as lying in the fact that they were first drafts of ideas that were to be expounded five years later in *Orthodoxy*. When he wrote this, it was half a century after *Orthodoxy* had first appeared, and he had to admit that it was not much read at that time. But he stressed the impact it made when it first came out and for some years later:

> But in the ten or twenty years following its publication, its influence was incalculable. At what may be called the popular level *Orthodoxy* was the pioneer of a completely new approach to the proclamation of Christian truth. It wrested the initiative from the sceptics and presented the historic faith upon a note of triumphant challenge. That in itself was something quite new. The book was a trumpet-call, a *sursum corda*; and it was as exciting as a voyage of discovery.[29]

The reference to a voyage is very much to the point, since Chesterton says in his second paragraph that he has often had a fancy

[28] Hollis, 62.

[29] A. L. Maycock, ed., *The Man Who Was Orthodox: A Selection from the Uncollected Writings of G. K. Chesterton* (London, 1963), 57–58.

for writing a romance about an English yachtsman "who slightly miscalculated his course and discovered England under the impression that it was a new island in the South Seas". A little farther on he says that he has a peculiar reason for mentioning the yachtsman: "For I am that man in a yacht. I discovered England." In this book, which he refers to as "not an intellectual treatise but a sort of slovenly autobiography", he describes the intellectual voyage he undertook in search of spiritual truth. The pattern of his voyage is clear: he comes back again and again to the fact that when he discovered some new island, some new position, he invariably thought that he was its sole discoverer, and he always learned in time that Christianity had been there before him. Maycock writes, "This idea of all journeying as a homeward journey and all vision as a recovery of surprise occurs again and again in Chesterton's thought. . . . It haunted his mind to the end of his life."[30]

One way of distinguishing *Orthodoxy* from *Heretics* is by saying that there is more of the *Clarion* controversy in the later book. The reasons for belief are brought forward much as they were in Chesterton's controversy with Blatchford and with frequent use of the latter's name and reference to his ideas. In the book Chesterton had scope to provide a more detailed and satisfactory exposition than in the Blatchford dispute to say why it was possible for an intelligent modern to believe in Christianity. Nevertheless he made it clear at the end of his first chapter that he was not writing a work of systematic theology and not setting forth the claims of any one branch of the Christian Church for special recognition:

> These essays are concerned only to discuss the actual fact that the central Christian theology (sufficiently summarized in the Apostles' Creed) is the best root of energy and sound ethics. They are not intended to discuss the very fascinating but quite different question of what is the present seat of authority for the proclamation of that creed. When the word "orthodoxy" is used here it means the Apostles' Creed, as understood by everybody calling himself Christian until a very short time ago. . . .

"When I was engaged in a controversy with the *Clarion* on the

[30] Ibid., 41.

matter of free will", Chesterton writes in the first chapter following his introduction, "that able writer Mr. R. B. Suthers said that free will was lunacy, because it meant causeless actions, and the actions of a lunatic would be causeless." He proceeds to recapitulate the arguments which he used in the previous dispute, demonstrating again the absurdity of using free thought to destroy free will and concluding that "the determinists come to bind, not to loose." Whereas he had formerly said that the determinists cannot even say "Please pass the mustard", here he says that they are not free to say "Thank you" for the mustard. Moving to another point, he declares that the man who cannot believe his senses and the man who cannot believe anything else are both insane; this leads him to a contention strongly maintained in one of his *Clarion* essays, that mysticism keeps men sane.

Near the beginning of the next chapter, he behaves with typically paradoxical generosity to Blatchford when he says the latter attacks Christianity because he is mad on one Christian virtue:

> . . . the merely mystical and almost irrational virtue of charity. He has a strange idea that he will make it easier to forgive sins by saying that there are no sins to forgive. Mr. Blatchford is not only an early Christian, he is the only early Christian who ought really to have been eaten by lions. For in his case the pagan accusation is really true: his mercy would mean mere anarchy. He really is the enemy of the human race—because he is so human.

As he goes on to discuss modern fashions of thought which have the effect of destroying thought itself, Chesterton stresses two of the concepts central to Blatchford's position, evolution and a theory of progress which virtually takes change as an ideal.

Over against Blatchford's demand for rational explanations, Chesterton insists in chapter four, "The Ethics of England", on magic and mystery and the wonder of existence. But the whole modern world, he complains, is in the grip of scientific fatalism. Again he returns to the subject of miracles and to the workings of a Divine Will over against the materialist's position which shows us nothing except "more and more infinite corridors of space lit by ghastly suns and empty of all that is divine".

In chapter five, "The Flag of the World", Chesterton contrasts the optimist with the pessimist, maintaining—as Suthers had once ridiculed him for doing—that only the Christian has genuine grounds for joy. In chapter six, "The paradoxes of Christianity", he again describes the effect of the great agnostics on him: "I never read a line of Christian apologetics. I read as little as I can of them now. It was Huxley and Herbert Spencer and Bradlaugh who brought me back to orthodox theology. They sowed in my mind my first wild doubts of doubt." In chapter seven "The Eternal Revolution", he confronts Blatchford's faith in science with the assertion that we cannot take our principles from nature because no such thing as a concept of the good can be found in it. He points to the irony which occurs when the Socialist, with a beaming face, proves that the poor cannot be trustworthy. "On the basis of Mr. Blatchford's view of heredity and environment," he writes, "the case for the aristocracy is quite overwhelming." Only the Christian Church, he continues, can offer any rational objection to a complete confidence in the rich, for she has always maintained that the danger is not in man's environment but in man himself. In fact the whole case for Christianity rests in the fact that the man who is dependent on the luxuries of life is a corrupt man.

In one of his most significant chapters, "The Romance of Orthodoxy", Chesterton discusses the alleged spiritual identity of all human religions, noting that "students of popular science, like Mr. Blatchford, are always insisting that Christianity and Buddhism are very much alike. . . ." His answer is that they are very different: "To the Buddhist or the eastern fatalist existence is a science or a plan, which must end up in a certain way. But to a Christian existence is a *story*, which may end up in any way." The Western energy which dethrones tyrants has been directly due to the Western theology which says, "I am I, thou art thou."

In the final chapter, "Authority and the Adventurer", Chesterton confutes three converging convictions of modern men—that men are merely animals, that religion arose in ignorance and fear and that priests have blighted societies. He asserts as well that orthodoxy is the only safe guardian of morality or order, and also of true liberty, innovation and advance. In an extended summary of his grounds for belief, he brings forward a whole list of propositions which he defended in the *Clarion* controversy — that it is exactly where biology leaves off that religion begins, that religion rests on a primary intellectual conviction rather than on demonstration, that correspondences between pagan beliefs and legends do not disprove the truth of Hebraic and Christian beliefs, that there are better grounds for believing in religious phenomena such as miracles than in disbelieving in them, that religion requires authority and dogmas and that, for the agnostic, joy is contracted to one corner of the world, whereas the Christian has expansive grounds for mirth.

The Queen called *Orthodoxy* a very dull book, consisting of "vapourings upon deep subjects, concerning which Mr. Chesterton's mind is in a haze." R. A. Scott-James, like many another, considered it Chesterton's masterpiece; in an unsigned review in *The World* it was called "a work of quite extraordinary intellectuality, earnestness and power." Others denied the intellectuality or found the method of argumentation defective. The *Nation* said: "The very brilliance of his antithetical reasoning, though it forces attention and even admiration, is apt to raise suspicions which are not without some justification." It also complained that the author's procedure was too confident — "every objection he sets up he demolishes in a telling phrase; no opponent has a grain of truth." Nevertheless it called the book an astonishing achievement, likely to be regarded as an important modern bulwark of the faith.

The *Observer* said that Chesterton's "orthodoxy" is founded upon a comprehensive distrust of reason: "But, as a poetic fantasy, the thing is splendid, and one can almost forgive the sophistry for the fineness of its expression. . . ." The *Westminster Review* likewise complained about Chesterton's logic, saying that we are perpetually escaping from one half-truth into another half-truth. It also criticized Chesterton for not defining *orthodoxy* or *Christianity*, two terms which certainly needed defining. Yet it praised the work for being full of edification in the truest sense of the word and said that "Behind it is a fine and buoyant spirit, as well as an intelligence that really illuminates."

The *Times Literary Supplement* was much more hostile, saying that as journalism Chesterton's work seemed to have permanent value, but in book form it became ephemeral. It called his motives in philosophy not rational but wholly aesthetic, and went beyond this to deny any Christian emphasis in the book:

We think, therefore we are; but if Mr. Chesterton began to think he would cease to exist; so he writes instead, and we are all the richer for it. He praises Christianity for all the characteristics which do not belong to it, and fancies himself orthodox for toying with beliefs which have nothing to do with Christianity. . . . He congratulates himself that he is Orthodox because he maintains a Christianity in which there is no Christ and no redemption nor any Sermon on the Mount. . . .[31]

The criticism is severe; but it is factually wrong, in regard to the omission of Christ. As we have already noticed, Chesterton stated in his introductory chapter that by *orthodoxy* he meant the doctrine stated in the Apostles' Creed, a basic statement of Christian belief. At the end of his third chapter, he denounces what the moderns have done to Christ:

There is a huge and heroic sanity of which moderns can only collect the fragments. There is a giant of whom we see only the lopped arms and legs walking about. They have torn the soul of Christ into silly strips, labelled egoism and altruism, and they are equally puzzled by His insane magnificence and His insane meekness. They have parted His garments among them, and for His vesture they have cast lots; though the coat was without seam woven from the top throughout.

The force of this passage is reminiscent of the account which Canon Barnett gave of an evening in 1905 when, after someone had spoken discourteously of Christ, Chesterton,

slipping off his indifference like a loose coat, sprang to his feet and, with glorious eloquence and rapidity, told of his own faith, stripped the incidents of time and circumstance from the Character which has

[31] These reviews are reprinted in D. J. Conlon, ed., *G. K. Chesterton: The Critical Judgments*, part I 1900–1937 (Antwerp, 1976), 159–77. The quotation from the *Times Literary Supplement* is on 171.

transfigured history, and declaimed that reverence and humility were the paths all men should keep open, for they alone led to the evolution of the true. I never now read anything by Mr. Chesterton without seeing him on that platform defending, in a physical elephantine rage, his spiritual angelic surety.[32]

In his chapter on "The Paradoxes of Christianity", Chesterton again writes that orthodox theology has specially insisted that Christ was not a being apart from God and man but both things at once and both things thoroughly, "very man and very God". And the last paragraph of *Orthodoxy* consists of little except a tribute to Christ, except for the comment that there was one thing He concealed from all men — His mirth.

Catholic reviewers of *Orthodoxy* treated its author almost as one of themselves. In a long review in the *Bookman*, the Reverend William Barry reckoned it a notable sign of the times "when Fleet Street discovers that the celebrated unbelievers who for half a century ruled press and public opinion were the deadliest of enemies to our race, and the heroes of the modern Dunciad."[33] Wilfrid Ward, Newman's biographer, wrote a long article for the *Dublin Review* in which he said that he was puzzled by reactions to the book. He himself classed Chesterton's thought, though not his manner, with that of such men as Burke, Butler and Coleridge, whereas others refused to take him seriously at all; although he considered *Orthodoxy* a triumphant confirmation of his own view, the others regarded it as a confirmation of theirs. He found the chapter on "The Paradoxes of Christianity" especially valuable; in it, he said that Chesterton

> gives us a rough and unphilosophical expression of the line of reasoning in a book which he has, perhaps, never read — Cardinal Newman's *Essay in Aid of a Grammar of Assent*. He tells us, in popular language, that it is by the cumulative argument, by the "illative sense", which cannot express all the latent reasons which influence its decision, that he, like others, really reached his conclusions. . . .[34]

---

[32] *Canon Barnett*, by his wife, vol. 2, 101–2, quoted in Maisie Ward, *Return to Chesterton* (New York, 1952), 81.

[33] Conlon, 189.

[34] Wilfrid Ward, "Mr. Chesterton among the Prophets", *Dublin Review*, 144 (1909), 15.

In his opinion *Orthodoxy* had to be taken very seriously indeed:

> and if even half of what he says needs qualification and correction, that will not prevent the book giving us as a permanent legacy more of original and practically helpful suggestions than perhaps anything which has appeared in our own day on Chateaubriand's theme, "the genius of Christianity".[35]

Ward described Chesterton's position as "Christianity with a strong Catholic bias"; he noted the emphasis on authority as against the emphasis on private judgment which the Reformation introduced. A Jesuit priest, Father Joseph Keating, wrote a long article, "Faith Found in Fleet Street", in which he referred to a rumor that Chesterton had become a Catholic. Even if the rumor does not prove to be true, he said, Chesterton's contribution to modern thought is not unworthy of our consideration, "for he has done much to upset the smug self-complacency of those who pride themselves on having outgrown Christianity, the After-Christians of our age."[36] He also "placed" *Orthodoxy* in very clear fashion: "If it be urged that acceptance of any set of doctrines on the ground of their felt suitability to human conditions is mere pragmatism and not the theological virtue of faith, it may be answered that Mr. Chesterton is treating rather of the *praeambula fidei*, those various considerations and arguments which should lead a reasonable man to the conclusion that Christianity is true."[37] And he concluded by wishing that Chesterton could spend some time away from Fleet Street in order to do some high and concentrated thinking: "Had we the power we should banish him to Monte Cassino for a year there to work through the *Summa* of Saint Thomas, with Dante as his only relaxation. On his return, we fancy, he would astonish the world."[38]

Chesterton never would spend the year of leisure, reading and contemplation at Monte Cassino which Father Keating wished him to have. Still he would eventually write a book on the author of the *Summa*, St. Thomas Aquinas — and that book would win praise

[35] Ibid., 31.
[36] Joseph S. Keating, S.J., "Faith Found in Fleet Street", *Month*, 112 (1908), 486.
[37] Ibid., 494.
[38] Ibid., 497.

from a distinguished historian of medieval philosophy, Etienne Gilson. But Gilson also praised *Orthodoxy*—described it, in fact, as Chesterton's most stimulating book:

> When it came out I hailed it as the best piece of apologetic the century had produced. In a sense all his later works are a variation on the same theme. I was interested in the biography of the conversion of a well-known American financial expert whose conversion was brought about by reading in succession Chesterton's "Orthodoxy", Fulton Sheen's "God and the Intelligence", and Karl Adam's "Spirit of Catholicism". I don't wonder—they would convert the Devil if he had a sense of humor, an open mind, and could pray for grace![39]

[39] Quoted in Cyril Clemens, *Chesterton as Seen by His Contemporaries* (New York, 1972 [1939]), 149–50.

A NOTE ON THE TEXTS

According to John Sullivan's *G. K. Chesterton: A Bibliography*, the first edition of *Heretics* was published by John Lane: The Bodley Head on June 6, 1905. It was dedicated "To My Father". The text used here, taken from a 1911 edition printed in the United States, contains very few variations from the 1905 edition.

Orthodoxy, dedicated "To My Mother", appeared on September 25, 1908, according to Sullivan; it is misdated 1909 on the title page. An American edition dated 1908 has a preface by Chesterton which does not appear in the English edition. The present text, based on the American edition, again contains very few variations from the first English edition, mainly a few differences in punctuation.

The notes are intended to be sparse rather than full; they are based on the presumption that some of the more eminent personages of the Boer War period are now virtually unknown and that American readers especially will benefit from the identification of some English place names where these have special significance in their contexts.

HERETICS

1905

I

INTRODUCTORY REMARKS ON THE IMPORTANCE OF ORTHODOXY

Nothing more strangely indicates an enormous and silent evil of modern society than the extraordinary use which is made nowadays of the word "orthodox." In former days the heretic was proud of not being a heretic. It was the kingdoms of the world and the police and the judges who were heretics. He was orthodox. He had no pride in having rebelled against them; they had rebelled against him. The armies with their cruel security, the kings with their cold faces, the decorous processes of State, the reasonable processes of law—all these like sheep had gone astray. The man was proud of being orthodox, was proud of being right. If he stood alone in a howling wilderness he was more than a man; he was a church. He was the centre of the universe; it was round him that the stars swung. All the tortures torn out of forgotten hells could not make him admit that he was heretical. But a few modern phrases have made him boast of it. He says, with a conscious laugh, "I suppose I am very heretical," and looks round for applause. The word "heresy" not only means no longer being wrong; it practically means being clear-headed and courageous. The word "orthodoxy" not only no longer means being right; it practically means being wrong. All this can mean one thing, and one thing only. It means that people care less for whether they are philosophically right. For obviously a man ought to confess himself crazy before he confesses himself heretical. The Bohemian, with a red tie, ought to pique himself on his orthodoxy. The dynamiter, laying a bomb, ought to feel that, whatever else he is, at least he is orthodox.

It is foolish, generally speaking, for a philosopher to set fire to another philosopher in Smithfield Market[1] because they do not agree in their theory of the universe. That was done very frequently in the

---

[1] London's central meat market.

last decadence of the Middle Ages, and it failed altogether in its object. But there is one thing that is infinitely more absurd and unpractical than burning a man for his philosophy. This is the habit of saying that his philosophy does not matter, and this is done universally in the twentieth century, in the decadence of the great revolutionary period. General theories are everywhere contemned; the doctrine of the Rights of Man is dismissed with the doctrine of the Fall of Man. Atheism itself is too theological for us to-day. Revolution itself is too much of a system; liberty itself is too much of a restraint. We will have no generalizations. Mr. Bernard Shaw has put the view in a perfect epigram: "The golden rule is that there is no golden rule." We are more and more to discuss details in art, politics, literature. A man's opinion on tramcars matters; his opinion on Botticelli matters; his opinion on all things does not matter. He may turn over and explore a million objects, but he must not find that strange object, the universe; for if he does he will have a religion, and be lost. Everything matters—except everything.

Examples are scarcely needed of this total levity on the subject of cosmic philosophy. Examples are scarcely needed to show that, whatever else we think of as affecting practical affairs, we do not think it matters whether a man is a pessimist or an optimist, a Cartesian or a Hegelian, a materialist or a spiritualist. Let me, however, take a random instance. At any innocent tea-table we may easily hear a man say, "Life is not worth living." We regard it as we regard the statement that it is a fine day; nobody thinks that it can possibly have any serious effect on the man or on the world. And yet if that utterance were really believed, the world would stand on its head. Murderers would be given medals for saving men from life; firemen would be denounced for keeping men from death; poisons would be used as medicines; doctors would be called in when people were well; the Royal Humane Society would be rooted out like a horde of assassins. Yet we never speculate as to whether the conversational pessimist will strengthen or disorganize society; for we are convinced that theories do not matter.

This was certainly not the idea of those who introduced our freedom. When the old Liberals removed the gags from all the heresies, their idea was that religious and philosophical discoveries might thus be made. Their view was that cosmic truth was so important that every one ought to bear independent testimony. The modern idea is that cosmic truth is so unimportant that it cannot matter what any one says. The former freed inquiry as men loose a noble hound; the latter frees inquiry as men fling back into the sea a fish unfit for eating. Never has there been so little discussion about the nature of men as now, when, for the first time, any one can discuss it. The old restriction meant that only the orthodox were allowed to discuss religion. Modern liberty means that nobody is allowed to discuss it. Good taste, the last and vilest of human superstitions, has succeeded in silencing us where all the rest have failed. Sixty years ago it was bad taste to be an avowed atheist. Then came the Bradlaughites,[2] the last religious men, the last men who cared about God; but they could not alter it. It is still bad taste to be an avowed atheist. But their agony has achieved just this — that now it is equally bad taste to be an avowed Christian. Emancipation has only locked the saint in the same tower of silence as the heresiarch. Then we talk about Lord Anglesey[3] and the weather, and call it the complete liberty of all the creeds.

But there are some people, nevertheless — and I am one of them — who think that the most practical and important thing about a man is still his view of the universe. We think that for a landlady considering a lodger, it is important to know his income, but still more important to know his philosophy. We think that for a general about to fight an enemy, it is important to know the enemy's numbers, but still more important to know the enemy's philosophy. We think the question is not whether the theory of the cosmos affects matters, but whether, in the long run, anything else affects them. In the fifteenth century men cross-examined and tormented a man because he preached some immoral attitude; in the nineteenth century

[2] Charles Bradlaugh (1833–1891) waged a long campaign for free thought and against religion. He won the right to take a seat in Parliament without taking an oath on the Bible.

[3] The first Marquess of Anglesey, who died in 1854, he commanded the Allied cavalry at Waterloo.

we fêted and flattered Oscar Wilde because he preached such an attitude, and then broke his heart in penal servitude because he carried it out. It may be a question which of the two methods was the more cruel; there can be no kind of question which was the more ludicrous. The age of the Inquisition has not at least the disgrace of having produced a society which made an idol of the very same man for preaching the very same things which it made him a convict for practising.

Now, in our time, philosophy or religion, our theory, that is, about ultimate things, has been driven out, more or less simultaneously, from two fields which it used to occupy. General ideals used to dominate literature. They have been driven out by the cry of "art for art's sake." General ideals used to dominate politics. They have been driven out by the cry of "efficiency," which may roughly be translated as "politics for politics' sake." Persistently for the last twenty years the ideals of order or liberty have dwindled in our books; the ambitions of wit and eloquence have dwindled in our parliaments. Literature has purposely become less political; politics have purposely become less literary. General theories of the relation of things have thus been extruded from both; and we are in a position to ask, "What have we gained or lost by this extrusion? Is literature better, is politics better, for having discarded the moralist and the philosopher?"

When everything about a people is for the time growing weak and ineffective, it begins to talk about efficiency. So it is that when a man's body is a wreck he begins, for the first time, to talk about health. Vigorous organisms talk not about their processes, but about their aims. There cannot be any better proof of the physical efficiency of a man than that he talks cheerfully of a journey to the end of the world. And there cannot be any better proof of the practical efficiency of a nation than that it talks constantly of a journey to the end of the world, a journey to the Judgment Day and the New Jerusalem. There can be no stronger sign of a coarse material health than the tendency to run after high and wild ideals; it is in the first exuberance of infancy that we cry for the moon. None of the strong men in the strong ages would have understood what you meant by working for efficiency. Hildebrand[4] would have said that he was working not for efficiency, but for the Catholic Church. Danton[5] would have said that he was working not for efficiency, but for liberty, equality, and fraternity. Even if the ideal of such men were simply the ideal of kicking a man downstairs, they thought of the end like men, not of the process like paralytics. They did not say, "Efficiently elevating my right leg, using, you will notice, the muscles of the thigh and calf, which are in excellent order, I——" Their feeling was quite different. They were so filled with the beautiful vision of the man lying flat at the foot of the staircase that in that ecstasy the rest followed in a flash. In practice, the habit of generalizing and idealizing did not by any means mean worldly weakness. The time of big theories was the time of big results. In the era of sentiment and fine words, at the end of the eighteenth century, men were really robust and effective. The sentimentalists conquered Napoleon. The cynics could not catch De Wet.[6] A hundred years ago our affairs for good or evil were wielded triumphantly by rhetoricians. Now our affairs are hopelessly muddled by strong, silent men. And just as this repudiation of big words and big visions has brought forth a race of small men in politics, so it has brought forth a race of small men in the arts. Our modern politicians claim the colossal license of Caesar and the Superman, claim that they are too practical to be pure and too patriotic to be moral; but the upshot of it all is that a mediocrity is Chancellor of the Exchequer. Our new artistic philosophers call for the same moral license, for a freedom to wreck heaven and earth with their energy; but the upshot of it all is that a mediocrity is Poet Laureate. I do not say that there are no stronger men than these; but will any one say that there are any men stronger than those men of old who were dominated by their philosophy and steeped in their religion? Whether bondage be better than

[4] Saint Gregory VII, who reigned as pope from 1073 to 1085, reformer of abuses and defender of papal prerogatives, was one of the greatest of medieval popes.

[5] Georges Jacques Danton (1759–1794), one of the leaders of the French Revolution, came into conflict with Robespierre and went to the guillotine in 1794.

[6] Christian Rudoph De Wet (1854–1922), a Boer general, achieved great success in guerilla warfare against the British, as he recounted in *The Three Years' War* (1902).

freedom may be discussed. But that their bondage came to more than our freedom it will be difficult for any one to deny.

The theory of the unmorality of art has established itself firmly in the strictly artistic classes. They are free to produce anything they like. They are free to write a "Paradise Lost" in which Satan shall conquer God. They are free to write a "Divine Comedy" in which heaven shall be under the floor of hell. And what have they done? Have they produced in their universality anything grander or more beautiful than the things uttered by the fierce Ghibbeline Catholic,[7] by the rigid Puritan schoolmaster?[8] We know that they have produced only a few roundels. Milton does not merely beat them at his piety, he beats them at their own irreverence. In all their little books of verse you will not find a finer defiance of God than Satan's. Nor will you find the grandeur of paganism felt as that fiery Christian felt it who described Faranata[9] lifting his head as in disdain of hell. And the reason is very obvious. Blasphemy is an artistic effect, because blasphemy depends upon a philosophical conviction. Blasphemy depends upon belief, and is fading with it. If any one doubts this, let him sit down seriously and try to think blasphemous thoughts about Thor. I think his family will find him at the end of the day in a state of some exhaustion.

Neither in the world of politics nor that of literature, then, has the rejection of general theories proved a success. It may be that there have been many moonstruck and misleading ideals that have from time to time perplexed mankind. But assuredly there has been no ideal in practice so moonstruck and misleading as the ideal of

[7] In the late Middle Ages, the Guelphs were the party of the Pope and the Ghibellines the party of the Emperor. Chesterton's description seems paradoxical, since Dante, a White Guelph, was fined and forced into exile from Florence when the Black Guelphs gained ascendancy in the city. But it is a good description of him in his later years.

[8] Milton was not a schoolmaster in the ordinary sense; he acted as tutor to his sister's two sons, and, as his treatise *Of Education* shows, he must have been a very demanding instructor.

[9] Chesterton's spelling of the name is wrong. In Canto X of the *Inferno*, Dante meets Farinata degli Uberti, leader of the Ghibellines in Florence and, after he had been banished, victor over the Florentine Guelphs when his army ambushed them in 1260.

practicality. Nothing has lost so many opportunities as the opportunism of Lord Rosebery.[10] He is, indeed, a standing symbol of this epoch — the man who is theoretically a practical man, and practically more unpractical than any theorist. Nothing in this universe is so unwise as that kind of worship of worldly wisdom. A man who is perpetually thinking of whether this race or that race is strong, of whether this cause or that cause is promising, is the man who will never believe in anything long enough to make it succeed. The opportunist politician is like a man who should abandon billiards because he was beaten at billiards, and abandon golf because he was beaten at golf. There is nothing which is so weak for working purposes as this enormous importance attached to immediate victory. There is nothing that fails like success.

And having discovered that opportunism does fail, I have been induced to look at it more largely, and in consequence to see that it must fail. I perceive that it is far more practical to begin at the beginning and discuss theories. I see that the men who killed each other about the orthodoxy of the Homoousion[11] were far more sensible than the people who are quarrelling about the Education Act.[12] For the Christian dogmatists were trying to establish a reign of holiness, and trying to get defined, first of all, what was really holy. But our modern educationists are trying to bring about a religious liberty without attempting to settle what is religion or what is liberty. If the old priests forced a statement on mankind, at least they previously took some trouble to make it lucid. It has been left for the modern mobs of Anglicans and Nonconformists to persecute for a doctrine without even stating it.

[10] The fifth Earl of Rosebery (1847–1929) succeeded Gladstone as Prime Minister in 1894 but was forced to resign in 1895 because of a split in his party. As leader of the Liberal imperialists, he was diametrically opposed to Chesterton's position. He retired from politics in 1905 when Sir Henry Campbell-Bannerman, also a Liberal, was chosen Prime Minister.

[11] Literally "same substance"; a term used to express the dogma that the essence or substance of God the Father and the Son is the same. The suitability of the term was bitterly contested in the fourth century.

[12] An act of 1902 which established a comprehensive system of local government for elementary and higher education. It had a long and stormy passage through Parliament.

For these reasons, and for many more, I for one have come to believe in going back to fundamentals. Such is the general idea of this book. I wish to deal with my most distinguished contemporaries, not personally or in a merely literary manner, but in relation to the real body of doctrine which they teach. I am not concerned with Mr. Rudyard Kipling as a vivid artist or a vigorous personality; I am concerned with him as a Heretic—that is to say, a man whose view of things has the hardihood to differ from mine. I am not concerned with Mr. Bernard Shaw as one of the most brilliant and one of the most honest men alive; I am concerned with him as a Heretic—that is to say, a man whose philosophy is quite solid, quite coherent, and quite wrong. I revert to the doctrinal methods of the thirteenth century, inspired by the general hope of getting something done.

Suppose that a great commotion arises in the street about something, let us say a lamp-post, which many influential persons desire to pull down. A grey-clad monk, who is the spirit of the Middle Ages, is approached upon the matter, and begins to say, in the arid manner of the Schoolmen, "Let us first of all consider, my brethren, the value of Light. If Light be in itself good——" At this point he is somewhat excusably knocked down. All the people make a rush for the lamp-post, the lamp-post is down in ten minutes, and they go about congratulating each other on their unmediaeval practicality. But as things go on they do not work out so easily. Some people have pulled the lamp-post down because they wanted the electric light; some because they wanted old iron; some because they wanted darkness, because their deeds were evil. Some thought it not enough of a lamp-post, some too much; some acted because they wanted to smash municipal machinery; some because they wanted to smash something. And there is war in the night, no man knowing whom he strikes. So, gradually and inevitably, to-day, to-morrow, or the next day, there comes back the conviction that the monk was right after all, and that all depends on what is the philosophy of Light. Only what we might have discussed under the gas-lamp, we now must discuss in the dark.

II

ON THE NEGATIVE SPIRIT

Much has been said, and said truly, of the monkish morbidity, of the hysteria which has often gone with the visions of hermits or nuns. But let us never forget that this visionary religion is, in one sense, necessarily more wholesome than our modern and reasonable morality. It is more wholesome for this reason, that it can contemplate the idea of success or triumph in the hopeless fight towards the ethical ideal, in what Stevenson called, with his usual startling felicity, "the lost fight of virtue."[13] A modern morality, on the other hand, can only point with absolute conviction to the horrors that follow breaches of law; its only certainty is a certainty of ill. It can only point to imperfection. It has no perfection to point to. But the monk meditating upon Christ or Buddha has in his mind an image of perfect health, a thing of clear colours and clean air. He may contemplate this ideal wholeness and happiness far more than he ought; he may contemplate it to the neglect or exclusion of essential things; he may contemplate it until he has become a dreamer or a driveller; but still it is wholeness and happiness that he is contemplating. He may even go mad; but he is going mad for the love of sanity. But the modern student of ethics, even if he remains sane, remains sane from an insane dread of insanity.

The anchorite rolling on the stones in a frenzy of submission is a healthier person fundamentally than many a sober man in a silk hat who is walking down Cheapside.[14] For many such are good only through a withering knowledge of evil. I am not at this moment claiming for the devotee anything more than this primary advantage, that though he may be making himself personally weak and miserable, he is still fixing his thoughts largely on gigantic strength

---

[13] "Still obscurely fighting the lost fight of virtue, still clinging, in the brothel or on the scaffold, to some rag of honour, the poor jewel of their souls!" Robert Louis Stevenson, "Pulvis et Umbra", in *Across the Plains* (1892).

[14] A street in the City (the financial district) of London.

and happiness, on a strength that has no limits, and a happiness that has no end. Doubtless there are other objections which can be urged without unreason against the influence of gods and visions in morality, whether in the cell or street. But this advantage the mystic morality must always have—it is always jollier. A young man may keep himself from vice by continually thinking of disease. He may keep himself from it also by continually thinking of the Virgin Mary. There may be question about which method is the more reasonable, or even about which is the more efficient. But surely there can be no question about which is the more wholesome.

I remember a pamphlet by that able and sincere secularist, Mr. G. W. Foote, which contained a phrase sharply symbolizing and dividing these two methods. The pamphlet was called "Beer and Bible," those two very noble things, all the nobler for a conjunction which Mr. Foote, in his stern old Puritan way, seemed to think sardonic, but which I confess to thinking appropriate and charming. I have not the work by me, but I remember that Mr. Foote dismissed very contemptuously any attempts to deal with the problem of strong drink by religious offices or intercessions, and said that a picture of a drunkard's liver would be more efficacious in the matter of temperance than any prayer or praise. In that picturesque expression, it seems to me, is perfectly embodied the incurable morbidity of modern ethics. In that temple the lights are low, the crowds kneel, the solemn anthems are uplifted. But that upon the altar to which all men kneel is no longer the perfect flesh, the body and substance of the perfect man; it is still flesh but it is diseased. It is the drunkard's liver of the New Testament that is marred for us, which we take in remembrance of him.

Now, it is this great gap in modern ethics, the absence of vivid pictures of purity and spiritual triumph, which lies at the back of the real objection felt by so many sane men to the realistic literature of the nineteenth century. If any ordinary man ever said that he was horrified by the subjects discussed in Ibsen or Maupassant, or by the plain language in which they are spoken of, that ordinary man was lying. The average conversation of average men throughout the whole of modern civilization in every class or trade is such as Zola would never dream of printing. Nor is the habit of writing thus of these things a new habit. On the contrary, it is the Victorian prudery and silence which is new still, though it is already dying. The tradition of calling a spade a spade starts very early in our literature and comes down very late. But the truth is that the ordinary honest man, whatever vague account he may have given of his feelings, was not either disgusted or even annoyed at the candour of the moderns. What disgusted him, and very justly, was not the presence of a clear realism, but the absence of a clear idealism. Strong and genuine religious sentiment has never had any objection to realism; on the contrary, religion was the realistic thing, the brutal thing, the thing that called names. This is the great difference between some recent developments of Nonconformity and the great Puritanism of the seventeenth century. It was the whole point of the Puritans that they cared nothing for decency. Modern Nonconformist newspapers distinguish themselves by suppressing precisely those nouns and adjectives which the founders of Nonconformity distinguished themselves by flinging at kings and queens. But if it was a chief claim of religion that it spoke plainly about evil, it was the chief claim of all that it spoke plainly about good. The thing which is resented, and, as I think, rightly resented, in that great modern literature of which Ibsen is typical, is that while the eye that can perceive what are the wrong things increases in an uncanny and devouring clarity, the eye which sees what things are right is growing mistier and mistier every moment, till it goes almost blind with doubt. If we compare, let us say, the morality of the "Divine Comedy" with the morality of Ibsen's *Ghosts*, we shall see all that modern ethics have really done. No one, I imagine, will accuse the author of the "Inferno" of an early Victorian prudishness or a Podsnapian[15] optimism. But Dante describes three moral instruments—Heaven, Purgatory, and Hell, the vision of perfection, the vision of improvement, and the vision of failure. Ibsen has only one—Hell. It is often said, and with perfect truth, that no one could read a play like *Ghosts* and remain indifferent to the necessity of an ethical self-command.

[15] Mr. Podsnap, in Dickens' *Our Mutual Friend*, is a type of self-satisfaction and self-importance.

That is quite true, and the same is to be said of the most monstrous and material descriptions of the eternal fire. It is quite certain that realists like Zola do in one sense promote morality — they promote it in the sense in which the hangman promotes it, in the sense in which the devil promotes it. But they only affect that small minority which will accept any virtue as long as we do not ask them for the virtue of courage. Most healthy people dismiss these moral dangers as they dismiss the possibility of bombs or microbes. Modern realists are indeed Terrorists, like the dynamiters; and they fail just as much in their effort to create a thrill. Both realists and dynamiters are well-meaning people engaged in the task, so obviously ultimately hopeless, of using science to promote morality.

I do not wish the reader to confuse me for a moment with those vague persons who imagine that Ibsen is what they call a pessimist. There are plenty of wholesome people in Ibsen, plenty of good people, plenty of happy people, plenty of examples of men acting wisely and things ending well. That is not my meaning. My meaning is that Ibsen has throughout, and does not disguise, a certain vagueness and a changing attitude as well as a doubting attitude towards what is really wisdom and virtue in this life — a vagueness which contrasts very remarkably with the decisiveness with which he pounces on something which he perceives to be a root of evil, some convention, some deception, some ignorance. We know that the hero of *Ghosts* is mad, and we know why he is mad. We do also know that Dr. Stockman is sane; but we do not know why he is sane. Ibsen does not profess to know how virtue and happiness are brought about, in the sense that he professes to know how our modern sexual tragedies are brought about. Falsehood works ruin in *The Pillars of Society*, but truth works equal ruin in *The Wild Duck*. There are no cardinal virtues of Ibsenism. There is no ideal man of Ibsen. All this is not only admitted, but vaunted in the most valuable and thoughtful of all eulogies upon Ibsen, Mr. Bernard Shaw's "Quintessence of Ibsenism." Mr. Shaw sums up Ibsen's teaching in the phrase, "The golden rule is that there is no golden rule." In his eyes this absence of an enduring and positive ideal, this absence of a permanent key to virtue, is the one great Ibsen merit. I am not discussing now with any fulness whether this is so or not.

All I venture to point out, with an increased firmness, is that this omission, good or bad, does leave us face to face with the problem of a human consciousness filled with very definite images of evil, and with no definite image of good. To us light must be henceforward the dark thing—the thing of which we cannot speak. To us, as to Milton's devils in Pandemonium,[16] it is darkness that is visible. The human race, according to religion, fell once, and in falling gained the knowledge of good and of evil. Now we have fallen a second time, and only the knowledge of evil remains to us.

A great silent collapse, an enormous unspoken disappointment, has in our time fallen on our Northern civilization. All previous ages have sweated and been crucified in an attempt to realize what is really the right life, what was really the good man. A definite part of the modern world has come beyond question to the conclusion that there is no answer to these questions, that the most that we can do is to set up a few notice-boards at places of obvious danger, to warn men, for instance, against drinking themselves to death, or ignoring the mere existence of their neighbours. Ibsen is the first to return from the baffled hunt to bring us the tidings of great failure.

Every one of the popular modern phrases and ideals is a dodge in order to shirk the problem of what is good. We are fond of talking about "liberty;" that, as we talk of it, is a dodge to avoid discussing what is good. We are fond of talking about "progress;" that is a dodge to avoid discussing what is good. We are fond of talking about "education;" that is a dodge to avoid discussing what is good. The modern man says, "Let us leave all these arbitrary standards and embrace liberty." This is, logically rendered, "Let us not decide what is good, but let it be considered good not to decide it." He says, "Away with your old moral formulae; I am for progress." This, logically stated, means, "Let us not settle what is good; but let us settle whether we are getting more of it." He says, "Neither in religion nor morality, my friend, lie the hopes of the race, but in education." This, clearly expressed, means, "We cannot decide what is good, but let us give it to our children."

Mr. H. G. Wells, that exceedingly clear-sighted man, has pointed

[16] The "high capital of Satan and his peers" in Milton's *Paradise Lost* (I, 756). In Hell there is no light, but "darkness visible" (I, 63).

out in a recent work that this has happened in connection with economic questions. The old economists, he says, made generalizations, and they were (in Mr. Wells's view) mostly wrong. But the new economists, he says, seem to have lost the power of making any generalizations at all. And they cover this incapacity with a general claim to be, in specific cases, regarded as "experts," a claim "proper enough in a hair-dresser or a fashionable physician, but indecent in a philosopher or a man of science." But in spite of the refreshing rationality with which Mr. Wells has indicated this, it must also be said that he himself has fallen into the same enormous modern error. In the opening pages of that excellent book "Mankind in the Making," he dismisses the ideals of art, religion, abstract morality, and the rest, and says that he is going to consider men in their chief function, the function of parenthood. He is going to discuss life as a "tissue of births." He is not going to ask what will produce satisfactory saints or satisfactory heroes, but what will produce satisfactory fathers and mothers. The whole is set forward so sensibly that it is a few moments at least before the reader realizes that it is another example of unconscious shirking. What is the good of begetting a man until we have settled what is the good of being a man? You are merely handing on to him a problem you dare not settle yourself. It is as if a man were asked, "What is the use of a hammer?" and answered, "To make hammers;" and when asked, "And of those hammers, what is the use?" answered, "To make hammers again." Just as such a man would be perpetually putting off the question of the ultimate use of carpentry, so Mr. Wells and all the rest of us are by these phrases successfully putting off the question of the ultimate value of the human life.

The case of the general talk of "progress" is, indeed, an extreme one. As enunciated to-day "progress" is simply a comparative of which we have not settled the superlative. We meet every ideal of religion, patriotism, beauty, or brute pleasure with the alternative ideal of progress — that is to say, we meet every proposal of getting something that we know about, with an alternative proposal of getting a great deal more of nobody knows what. Progress, properly understood, has, indeed, a most dignified and legitimate meaning. But as used in opposition to precise moral ideals, it is ludicrous. So far from it being the truth that the ideal of progress is to be set against that of ethical or religious finality, the reverse is the truth. Nobody has any business to use the word "progress" unless he has a definite creed and a cast-iron code of morals. Nobody can be progressive without being doctrinal; I might almost say that nobody can be progressive without being infallible—at any rate, without believing in some infallibility. For progress by its very name indicates a direction; and the moment we are in the least doubtful about the direction, we become in the same degree doubtful about the progress. Never perhaps since the beginning of the world has there been an age that had less right to use the word "progress" than we. In the Catholic twelfth century, in the philosophic eighteenth century, the direction may have been a good or a bad one, men may have differed more or less about how far they went, and in what direction, but about the direction they did in the main agree, and consequently they had the genuine sensation of progress. But it is precisely about the direction that we disagree. Whether the future excellence lies in more law or less law, in more liberty or less liberty; whether property will be finally concentrated or finally cut up; whether sexual passion will reach its sanest in an almost virgin intellectualism or in a full animal freedom; whether we should love everybody with Tolstoy, or spare nobody with Nietszche;—these are the things about which we are actually fighting most. It is not merely true that the age which has settled least what is progress is this "progressive" age. It is, moreover, true that the people who have settled least what is progress are the most "progressive" people in it. The ordinary mass, the men who have never troubled about progress, might be trusted perhaps to progress. The particular individuals who talk about progress would certainly fly to the four winds of heaven when the pistol-shot started the race. I do not, therefore, say that the word "progress" is unmeaning; I say it is unmeaning without the previous definition of a moral doctrine, and that it can only be applied to groups of persons who hold that doctrine in common. Progress is not an illegitimate word, but it is logically evident that it is illegitimate for us. It is a sacred word, a word which could only rightly be used by rigid believers and in the ages of faith.

III

ON MR. RUDYARD KIPLING
AND MAKING THE WORLD SMALL

There is no such thing on earth as an uninteresting subject; the only thing that can exist is an uninterested person. Nothing is more keenly required than a defence of bores. When Byron divided humanity into the bores and bored, he omitted to notice that the higher qualities exist entirely in the bores, the lower qualities in the bored, among whom he counted himself. The bore, by his starry enthusiasm, his solemn happiness, may, in some sense, have proved himself poetical. The bored has certainly proved himself prosaic.

We might, no doubt, find it a nuisance to count all the blades of grass or all the leaves of the trees; but this would not be because of our boldness or gaiety, but because of our lack of boldness and gaiety. The bore would go onward, bold and gay, and find the blades of grass as splendid as the swords of an army. The bore is stronger and more joyous than we are; he is a demi-god—nay, he is a god. For it is the gods who do not tire of the iteration of things; to them the nightfall is always new, and the last rose as red as the first.

The sense that everything is poetical is a thing solid and absolute; it is not a mere matter of phraseology or persuasion. It is not merely true, it is ascertainable. Men may be challenged to deny it; men may be challenged to mention anything that is not a matter of poetry. I remember a long time ago a sensible sub-editor coming up to me with a book in his hand, called "Mr. Smith," or "The Smith Family," or some such thing. He said, "Well, you won't get any of your damned mysticism out of this," or words to that effect. I am happy to say that I undeceived him; but the victory was too obvious and easy. In most cases the name is unpoetical, although the fact is poetical. In the case of Smith, the name is so poetical that it must be an arduous and heroic matter for the man to live up to it. The name of Smith is the name of the one trade that even kings respected; it could claim half the glory of that *arma virumque*[17] which all epics

---

[17] "Arms and the man I sing", the opening of Virgil's epic, *The Aeneid*.

acclaimed. The spirit of the smithy is so close to the spirit of song that it has mixed in a million poems, and every blacksmith is a harmonious blacksmith.

Even the village children feel that in some dim way the smith is poetic, as the grocer and the cobbler are not poetic, when they feast on the dancing sparks and deafening blows in the cavern of that creative violence. The brute repose of Nature, the passionate cunning of man, the strongest of earthly metals, the weirdest of earthly elements, the unconquerable iron subdued by its only conqueror, the wheel and the ploughshare, the sword and the steam-hammer, the arraying of armies and the whole legend of arms, all these things are written, briefly indeed, but quite legibly, on the visiting-card of Mr. Smith. Yet our novelists call their hero "Aylmer Valence," which means nothing, or "Vernon Raymond," which means nothing, when it is in their power to give him this sacred name of Smith—this name made of iron and flame. It would be very natural if a certain hauteur, a certain carriage of the head, a certain curl of the lip, distinguished every one whose name is Smith. Perhaps it does; I trust so. Whoever else are parvenus, the Smiths are not parvenus. From the darkest dawn of history this clan has gone forth to battle; its trophies are on every hand; its name is everywhere; it is older than the nations, and its sign is the Hammer of Thor.

But as I also remarked, it is not quite the usual case. It is common enough that common things should be poetical; it is not so common that common names should be poetical. In most cases it is the name that is the obstacle. A great many people talk as if this claim of ours, that all things are poetical, were a mere literary ingenuity, a play on words. Precisely the contrary is true. It is the idea that some things are not poetical which is literary, which is a mere product of words. The word "signal-box" is unpoetical. But the thing signal-box is not unpoetical; it is a place where men, in an agony of vigilance, light blood-red and sea-green fires to keep other men from death. That is the plain, genuine description of what it is; the prose only comes in with what it is called. The word "pillar-box"[18] is unpoetical. But the thing pillar-box is not unpoetical; it is the place to which

---

[18] The standard English letter box, in the shape of a pillar and painted red.

friends and lovers commit their messages, conscious that when they have done so they are sacred, and not to be touched, not only by others, but even (religious touch!) by themselves. That red turret is one of the last of the temples. Posting a letter and getting married are among the few things left that are entirely romantic; for to be entirely romantic a thing must be irrevocable. We think a pillar-box prosaic, because there is no rhyme to it. We think a pillar-box unpoetical, because we have never seen it in a poem. But the bold fact is entirely on the side of poetry. A signal-box is only *called* a signal-box; it *is* a house of life and death. A pillar-box is only *called* a pillar-box; it *is* a sanctuary of human words. If you think the name of "Smith" prosaic, it is not because you are practical and sensible; it is because you are too much affected with literary refinements. The name shouts poetry at you. If you think of it otherwise, it is because you are steeped and sodden with verbal reminiscences, because you remember everything in *Punch* or *Comic Cuts* about Mr. Smith being drunk or Mr. Smith being henpecked. All these things were given to you poetical. It is only by a long and elaborate process of literary effort that you have made them prosaic.

Now, the first and fairest thing to say about Rudyard Kipling is that he has borne a brilliant part in thus recovering the lost provinces of poetry. He has not been frightened by that brutal materialistic air which clings only to words; he has pierced through to the romantic, imaginative matter of the things themselves. He has perceived the significance and philosophy of steam and of slang. Steam may be, if you like, a dirty by-product of science. Slang may be, if you like, a dirty by-product of language. But at least he has been among the few who saw the divine parentage of these things, and knew that where there is smoke there is fire — that is, that wherever there is the foulest of things, there also is the purest. Above all, he has had something to say, a definite view of things to utter, and that always means that a man is fearless and faces everything. For the moment we have a view of the universe, we possess it.

Now, the message of Rudyard Kipling, that upon which he has really concentrated, is the only thing worth worrying about in him or in any other man. He has often written bad poetry, like Wordsworth.

He has often said silly things, like Plato. He has often given way to mere political hysteria, like Gladstone. But no one can reasonably doubt that he means steadily and sincerely to say something, and the only serious question is, What is that which he has tried to say? Perhaps the best way of stating this fairly will be to begin with that element which has been most insisted by himself and by his opponents — I mean his interest in militarism. But when we are seeking for the real merits of a man it is unwise to go to his enemies, and much more foolish to go to himself.

Now, Mr. Kipling is certainly wrong in his worship of militarism, but his opponents are, generally speaking, quite as wrong as he. The evil of militarism is not that it shows certain men to be fierce and haughty and excessively warlike. The evil of militarism is that it shows most men to be tame and timid and excessively peaceable. The professional soldier gains more and more power as the general courage of a community declines. Thus the Pretorian guard[19] became more and more important in Rome as Rome became more and more luxurious and feeble. The military man gains the civil power in proportion as the civilian loses the military virtues. And as it was in ancient Rome so it is in contemporary Europe. There never was a time when nations were more militarist. There never was a time when men were less brave. All ages and all epics have sung of arms and the man; but we have effected simultaneously the deterioration of the man and the fantastic perfection of the arms. Militarism demonstrated the decadence of Rome, and it demonstrates the decadence of Prussia.

And unconsciously Mr. Kipling has proved this, and proved it admirably. For in so far as his work is earnestly understood the military trade does not by any means emerge as the most important or attractive. He has not written so well about soldiers as he has about railway men or bridge builders, or even journalists. The fact is that what attracts Mr. Kipling to militarism is not the idea of courage, but the idea of discipline. There was far more courage to the square mile in the Middle Ages, when no king had a standing army, but

[19] The bodyguard of Roman emperors, which was disbanded in 312 A.D. after its influence had become so great that it could make and remove emperors.

every man had a bow or sword. But the fascination of the standing
army upon Mr. Kipling is not courage, which scarcely interests him,
but discipline, which is, when all is said and done, his primary
theme. The modern army is not a miracle of courage; it has not
enough opportunities, owing to the cowardice of everybody else.
But it is really a miracle of organization and that is the truly Kiplingite ideal. Kipling's subject is not that valour which properly belongs
to war, but that interdependence and efficiency which belongs quite
as much to engineers, or sailors, or mules, or railway engines. And
thus it is that when he writes of engineers, or sailors, or mules, or
steam-engines, he writes at his best. The real poetry, the "true
romance" which Mr. Kipling has taught, is the romance of the division of labour and the discipline of all the trades. He sings the arts of
peace much more accurately than the arts of war. And his main contention is vital and valuable. Everything is military in the sense that
everything depends upon obedience. There is no perfectly epicurean
corner; there is no perfectly irresponsible place. Everywhere men
have made the way for us with sweat and submission. We may fling
ourselves into a hammock in a fit of divine carelessness. But we are
glad that the net-maker did not make the hammock in a fit of divine
carelessness. We may jump upon a child's rocking-horse for a joke.
But we are glad that the carpenter did not leave the legs of it un-
glued for a joke. So far from having merely preached that a soldier
cleaning his side-arm is to be adored because he is military, Kipling
at his best and clearest has preached that the baker baking loaves and
the tailor cutting coats is as military as anybody.

Being devoted to this multitudinous vision of duty, Mr. Kipling
is naturally a cosmopolitan. He happens to find his examples in the
British Empire, but almost any other empire would do as well, or,
indeed, any other highly civilized country. That which he admires
in the British army he would find even more apparent in the German
army; that which he desires in the British police he would find flour-
ishing in the French police. The ideal of discipline is not the whole
of life, but it is spread over the whole of the world. And the worship
of it tends to confirm in Mr. Kipling a certain note of worldly wisdom, of the experience of the wanderer, which is one of the genuine
charms of his best work.

The great gap in his mind is what may be roughly called the lack of patriotism—that is to say, he lacks altogether the faculty of attaching himself to any cause or community finally and tragically; for all finality must be tragic. He admires England, but he does not love her; for we admire things with reasons, but love them without reasons. He admires England because she is strong, not because she is English. There is no harshness in saying this, for, to do him justice, he avows it with his usual picturesque candour. In a very interesting poem, he says that—

> *"If England was what England seems"*

—that is, weak and inefficient; if England were not what (as he believes) she is—that is, powerful and practical—

> *"How quick we'd chuck 'er! But she ain't!"*

He admits, that is, that his devotion is the result of a criticism, and this is quite enough to put it in another category altogether from the patriotism of the Boers, whom he hounded down in South Africa. In speaking of the really patriotic peoples, such as the Irish, he has some difficulty in keeping a shrill irritation out of his language. The frame of mind which he really describes with beauty and nobility is the frame of mind of the cosmopolitan man who has seen men and cities.

> "For to admire and for to see,
> For to be'old this world so wide."

He is a perfect master of that light melancholy with which a man looks back on having been the citizen of many communities, of that light melancholy with which a man looks back on having been the lover of many women. He is the philanderer of the nations. But a man may have learnt much about women in flirtations, and still be ignorant of first love; a man may have known as many lands as Ulysses, and still be ignorant of patriotism.

Mr. Rudyard Kipling has asked in a celebrated epigram what they can know of England who know England only. It is a far deeper and sharper question to ask, "What can they know of England who know only the world?" for the world does not include England any more than it includes the Church. The moment we care for anything deeply, the world — that is, all the other miscellaneous interests — becomes our enemy. Christians showed it when they talked of keeping one's self "unspotted from the world;" but lovers talk of it just as much when they talk of the "world well lost." Astronomically speaking, I understand that England is situated on the world; similarly, I suppose that the Church was a part of the world, and even the lovers inhabitants of that orb. But they all felt a certain truth — the truth that the moment you love anything the world becomes your foe. Thus Mr. Kipling does certainly know the world; he is a man of the world, with all the narrowness that belongs to those imprisoned in that planet. He knows England as an intelligent English gentleman knows Venice. He has been to England a great many times; he has stopped there for long visits. But he does not belong to it, or to any place; and the proof of it is this, that he thinks of England as a place. The moment we are rooted in a place, the place vanishes. We live like a tree with the whole strength of the universe.

The globe-trotter lives in a smaller world than the peasant. He is always breathing an air of locality. London is a place, to be compared to Chicago; Chicago is a place, to be compared to Timbuctoo. But Timbuctoo is not a place, since there, at least, live men who regard it as the universe, and breathe, not an air of locality, but the winds of the world. The man in the saloon steamer has seen all the races of men, and he is thinking of the things that divide men — diet, dress, decorum, rings in the nose as in Africa, or in the ears as in Europe, blue paint among the ancients, or red paint among the modern Britons. The man in the cabbage field has seen nothing at all; but he is thinking of the things that unite men — hunger and babies, and the beauty of women, and the promise or menace of the sky. Mr. Kipling, with all his merits, is the globe-trotter; he has not the patience to become part of anything. So great and genuine a man is not to be accused of a merely cynical cosmopolitanism; still, his cosmopolitanism is his weakness. That weakness is splendidly expressed in one of his finest poems, "The Sestina of the Tramp Royal," in which a man declares that he can endure anything in the way of hunger or horror, but not permanent presence in one place.

In this there is certainly danger. The more dead and dry and dusty a thing is the more it travels about; dust is like this and the thistle-down and the High Commissioner in South Africa. Fertile things are somewhat heavier, like the heavy fruit trees on the pregnant mud of the Nile. In the heated idleness of youth we were all rather inclined to quarrel with the implication of that proverb which says that a rolling stone gathers no moss. We were inclined to ask, "Who wants to gather moss, except silly old ladies?" But for all that we begin to perceive that the proverb is right. The rolling stone rolls echoing from rock to rock; but the rolling stone is dead. The moss is silent because the moss is alive.

The truth is that exploration and enlargement make the world smaller. The telegraph and the steamboat make the world smaller. The telescope makes the world smaller; it is only the microscope that makes it larger. Before long the world will be cloven with a war between the telescopists and the microscopists. The first study large things and live in a small world; the second study small things and live in a large world. It is inspiring without doubt to whizz in a motor-car round the earth, to feel Arabia as a whirl of sand or China as a flash of rice-fields. But Arabia is not a whirl of sand and China is not a flash of rice-fields. They are ancient civilizations with strange virtues buried like treasures. If we wish to understand them it must not be as tourists or inquirers, it must be with the loyalty of children and the great patience of poets. To conquer these places is to lose them. The man standing in his own kitchen-garden, with fairyland opening at the gate, is the man with large ideas. His mind creates distance; the motor-car stupidly destroys it. Moderns think of the earth as a globe, as something one can easily get round, the spirit of a schoolmistress. This is shown in the odd mistake perpetually made about Cecil Rhodes. His enemies say that he may have had large ideas, but he was a bad man. His friends say that he may have been a bad man, but he certainly had large ideas. The truth is that he was not a man essentially bad, he was a man of much geniality and many good intentions, but a man with singularly small views. There is nothing large about painting the map red; it is an innocent game for children. It is just as easy to think in continents as to think in cobble-stones.

The difficulty comes in when we seek to know the substance of either of them. Rhodes' prophecies about the Boer resistance[20] are an admirable comment on how the "large ideas" prosper when it is not a question of thinking in continents, but of understanding a few two-legged men. And under all this vast illusion of the cosmopolitan planet, with its empires and its Reuter's agency, the real life of man goes on concerned with this tree or that temple, with this harvest or that drinking-song, totally uncomprehended, totally untouched. And it watches from its splendid parochialism, possibly with a smile of amusement, motor-car civilization going its triumphant way, outstripping time, consuming space, seeing all and seeing nothing, roaring on at last to the capture of the solar system, only to find the sun cockney and the stars suburban.

[20] Rhodes had called the Boers' military strength "the greatest unpricked bubble in existence".

IV

MR. BERNARD SHAW

In the glad old days, before the rise of modern morbidities, when genial old Ibsen filled the world with wholesome joy, and the kindly tales of the forgotten Emile Zola kept our firesides merry and pure, it used to be thought a disadvantage to be misunderstood. It may be doubted whether it is always or even generally a disadvantage. The man who is misunderstood has always this advantage over his enemies, that they do not know his weak point or his plan of campaign. They go out against a bird with nets and against a fish with arrows. There are several modern examples of this situation. Mr. Chamberlain,[21] for instance, is a very good one. He constantly eludes or vanquishes his opponents because his real powers and deficiencies are quite different to those with which he is credited, both by friends and foes. His friends depict him as a strenuous man of action; his opponents depict him as a coarse man of business; when, as a fact, he is neither one nor the other, but an admirable romantic orator and romantic actor. He has one power which is the soul of melodrama—the power of pretending, even when backed by a huge majority, that he has his back to the wall. For all mobs are so far chivalrous that their heroes must make some show of misfortune—that sort of hypocrisy is the homage that strength pays to weakness. He talks foolishly and yet very finely about his own city that has never deserted him. He wears a flaming and fantastic flower, like a decadent minor poet. As for his bluffness and toughness and appeals to common sense, all that is, of course, simply the first trick of rhetoric. He fronts his audiences with the venerable affectation of Mark Antony—

> "I am no orator, as Brutus is;
> But as you know me all, a plain blunt man."

[21] Joseph Chamberlain (1836–1914), English politician and Secretary of State for the colonies from 1895 to 1903. An ardent advocate of Imperial federation, he was wrongly blamed for precipitating the Boer War, but he did support it without question.

It is the whole difference between the aim of the orator and the aim of any other artist, such as the poet or the sculptor. The aim of the sculptor is to convince us that he is a sculptor; the aim of the orator is to convince us that he is not an orator. Once let Mr. Chamberlain be mistaken for a practical man, and his game is won. He has only to compose a theme on empire, and people will say that these plain men say great things on great occasions. He has only to drift in the large loose notions common to all artists of the second rank, and people will say that business men have the biggest ideals after all. All his schemes have ended in smoke; he has touched nothing that he did not confuse. About his figure there is a Celtic pathos; like the Gaels in Matthew Arnold's quotation, "he went forth to battle, but he always fell." He is a mountain of proposals, a mountain of failures; but still a mountain. And a mountain is always romantic.

There is another man in the modern world who might be called the antithesis of Mr. Chamberlain in every point, who is also a standing monument of the advantage of being misunderstood. Mr. Bernard Shaw is always represented by those who disagree with him, and, I fear, also (if such exist) by those who agree with him, as a capering humorist, a dazzling acrobat, a quick-change artist. It is said that he cannot be taken seriously, that he will defend anything or attack anything, that he will do anything to startle and amuse. All this is not only untrue, but it is, glaringly, the opposite of the truth; it is as wild as to say that Dickens had not the boisterous masculinity of Jane Austen. The whole force and triumph of Mr. Bernard Shaw lie in the fact that he is a thoroughly consistent man. So far from his power consisting in jumping through hoops or standing on his head, his power consists in holding his own fortress night and day. He puts the Shaw test rapidly and rigorously to everything that happens in heaven or earth. His standard never varies. The thing which weak-minded revolutionists and weak-minded Conservatives really hate (and fear) in him, is exactly this, that his scales, such as they are, are held even, and that his law, such as it is, is justly enforced. You may attack his principles, as I do; but I do not know of any instance in which you can attack their application. If he dislikes lawlessness, he dislikes the lawlessness of

Socialists as much as that of Individualists. If he dislikes the fever of patriotism, he dislikes it in Boers and Irishmen as well as in Englishmen. If he dislikes the vows and bonds of marriage, he dislikes still more the fiercer bonds and wilder vows that are made by lawless love. If he laughs at the authority of priests, he laughs louder at the pomposity of men of science. If he condemns the irresponsibility of faith, he condemns with a sane consistency the equal irresponsibility of art. He has pleased all the bohemians by saying that women are equal to men; but he has infuriated them by suggesting that men are equal to women. He is almost mechanically just; he has something of the terrible quality of a machine. The man who is really wild and whirling, the man who is really fantastic and incalculable, is not Mr. Shaw, but the average Cabinet Minister. It is Sir Michael Hicks-Beach[22] who jumps through hoops. It is Sir Henry Fowler[23] who stands on his head. The solid and respectable statesman of that type does really leap from position to position; he is really ready to defend anything or nothing; he is really not to be taken seriously. I know perfectly well what Mr. Bernard Shaw will be saying thirty years hence; he will be saying what he has always said. If thirty years hence I meet Mr. Shaw, a reverent being with a silver beard sweeping the earth, and say to him, "One can never, of course, make a verbal attack upon a lady," the patriarch will lift his aged hand and fell me to the earth. We know, I say, what Mr. Shaw will be saying thirty years hence. But is there any one so darkly read in stars and oracles that he will dare to predict what Mr. Asquith[24] will be saying thirty years hence?

The truth is, that it is quite an error to suppose that absence of definite convictions gives the mind freedom and agility. A man who believes something is ready and witty, because he has all his weapons

[22] A Conservative politician (1837–1916), Colonial Secretary from 1878 to 1880 and Chancellor of the Exchequer during the South African War.

[23] A leader of the Liberal Party (1830–1911), who had been critical of British policy in South Africa but called the Boer War "just and inevitable".

[24] Herbert Henry Asquith (1852–1928) served as Home Secretary in two Liberal administrations of the 1890s. Since he approved of the Boer War but not of the way it was conducted, there were perhaps grounds for Chesterton's comment.

about him. He can apply his test in an instant. The man engaged in conflict with a man like Mr. Bernard Shaw may fancy he has ten faces; similarly a man engaged against a brilliant duellist may fancy that the sword of his foe has turned to ten swords in his hand. But this is not really because the man is playing with ten swords, it is because he is aiming very straight with one. Moreover, a man with a definite belief always appears bizarre, because he does not change with the world; he has climbed into a fixed star, and the earth whizzes below him like a zoetrope. Millions of mild black-coated men call themselves sane and sensible merely because they always catch the fashionable insanity, because they are hurried into madness after madness by the maelstrom of the world.

People accuse Mr. Shaw and many much sillier persons of "proving that black is white." But they never ask whether the current colour-language is always correct. Ordinary sensible phraseology sometimes calls black white, it certainly calls yellow white and green white and reddish-brown white. We call wine "white wine" which is as yellow as a Blue-coat boy's legs.[25] We call grapes "white grapes" which are manifestly pale green. We give to the European, whose complexion is a sort of pink drab, the horrible title of a "white man"—a picture more blood-curdling than any spectre in Poe.

Now, it is undoubtedly true that if a man asked a waiter in a restaurant for a bottle of yellow wine and some greenish-yellow grapes, the waiter would think him mad. It is undoubtedly true that if a Government official, reporting on the Europeans in Burmah, said, "There are only two thousand pinkish men here," he would be accused of cracking jokes, and kicked out of his post. But it is equally obvious that both men would have come to grief through telling the strict truth. That too truthful man in the restaurant; that too truthful man in Burmah, is Mr. Bernard Shaw. He appears eccentric and grotesque because he will not accept the general belief that white is yellow. He has based all his brilliancy and solidity upon the hackneyed, but yet forgotten, fact that truth is stranger than fiction. Truth, of course, must of necessity be stranger than fiction, for we have made fiction to suit ourselves.

[25] Those of a student at Christ's Hospital, the famous London charity school where Coleridge and Lamb were students. It moved to Horsham, Sussex, in 1902.

So much then a reasonable appreciation will find in Mr. Shaw to be bracing and excellent. He claims to see things as they are; and some things, at any rate, he does see as they are, which the whole of our civilization does not see at all. But in Mr. Shaw's realism there is something lacking, and that thing which is lacking is serious.

Mr. Shaw's old and recognized philosophy was that powerfully presented in "The Quintessence of Ibsenism." It was, in brief, that conservative ideals were bad, not because they were conservative, but because they were ideals. Every ideal prevented men from judging justly the particular case; every moral generalization oppressed the individual; the golden rule was there was no golden rule. And the objection to this is simply that it pretends to free men, but really restrains them from doing the only thing that men want to do. What is the good of telling a community that it has every liberty except the liberty to make laws? The liberty to make laws is what constitutes a free people. And what is the good of telling a man (or a philosopher) that he has every liberty except the liberty to make generalizations. Making generalizations is what makes him a man. In short, when Mr. Shaw forbids men to have strict moral ideals, he is acting like one who should forbid them to have children. The saying that "the golden rule is that there is no golden rule," can, indeed, be simply answered by being turned round. That there is no golden rule is itself a golden rule, or rather it is much worse than a golden rule. It is an iron rule, a fetter on the first movement of a man.

But the sensation connected with Mr. Shaw in recent years has been his sudden development of the religion of the Superman. He who had to all appearance mocked at the faiths in the forgotten past discovered a new god in the unimaginable future. He who had laid all the blame on ideals set up the most impossible of all ideals, the ideal of a new creature. But the truth, nevertheless, is that any one who knows Mr. Shaw's mind adequately, and admires it properly, must have guessed all this long ago.

For the truth is that Mr. Shaw has never seen things as they really are. If he had he would have fallen on his knees before them. He has always had a secret ideal that has withered all the things of this world. He has all the time been silently comparing humanity with something that was not human, with a monster from Mars, with the Wise Man of the Stoics, with the Economic Man of the Fabians, with Julius Caesar, with Siegfried, with the Superman. Now, to have this inner and merciless standard may be a very good thing, or a very bad one, it may be excellent or unfortunate, but it is not seeing things as they are. It is not seeing things as they are to think first of a Briareus with a hundred hands, and then call every man a cripple for only having two. It is not seeing things as they are to start with a vision of Argus with his hundred eyes, and then jeer at every man with two eyes as if he had only one. And it is not seeing things as they are to imagine a demi-god of infinite mental clarity, who may or may not appear in the latter days of the earth, and then to see all men as idiots. And this is what Mr. Shaw has always in some degree done. When we really see men as they are, we do not criticize, but worship; and very rightly. For a monster with mysterious eyes and miraculous thumbs, with strange dreams in his skull, and a queer tenderness for this place or that baby, is truly a wonderful and unnerving matter. It is only the quite arbitrary and priggish habit of comparison with something else which makes it possible to be at our ease in front of him. A sentiment of superiority keeps us cool and practical; the mere facts would make our knees knock under us with religious fear. It is the fact that every instant of conscious life is an unimaginable prodigy. It is the fact that every face in the street has the incredible unexpectedness of a fairy-tale. The thing which prevents a man from realizing this is not any clear-sightedness or experience, it is simply a habit of pedantic and fastidious comparisons between one thing and another. Mr. Shaw, on the practical side perhaps the most humane man alive, is in this sense inhumane. He has even been infected to some extent with the primary intellectual weakness of his new master, Nietzsche, the strange notion that the greater and stronger a man was the more he would despise other things. The greater and stronger a man is the more he would be inclined to prostrate himself before a periwinkle. That Mr. Shaw keeps a lifted head and a contemptuous face before the colossal panorama of empires and civilizations, this does not in itself convince one that he sees things as they are. I should be most effectively convinced that he did if I found him staring with religious astonishment at his own feet. "What are those two beautiful and industrious beings," I can imagine him murmuring to himself, "whom I see everywhere, serving me I know not why? What fairy godmother bade them come trotting out of elfland when I was born? What god of the borderland, what barbaric god of legs, must I propitiate with fire and wine, lest they run away with me?"

The truth is, that all genuine appreciation rests on a certain mystery of humility and almost of darkness. The man who said, "Blessed is he that expecteth nothing, for he shall not be disappointed," put the eulogy quite inadequately and even falsely. The truth is, "Blessed is he that expecteth nothing, for he shall be gloriously surprised." The man who expects nothing sees redder roses than common men can see, and greener grass, and a more startling sun. Blessed is he that expecteth nothing, for he shall possess the cities and the mountains; blessed is the meek, for he shall inherit the earth. Until we realize that things might not be, we cannot realize that things are. Until we see the background of darkness we cannot admire the light as a single and created thing. As soon as we have seen that darkness, all light is lightening, sudden, blinding, and divine. Until we picture nonentity we underrate the victory of God, and can realize none of the trophies of His ancient war. It is one of the million wild jests of truth that we know nothing until we know nothing.

Now this is, I say deliberately, the only defect in the greatness of Mr. Shaw, the only answer to his claim to be a great man, that he is not easily pleased. He is an almost solitary exception to the general and essential maxim, that little things please great minds. And from this absence of that most uproarious of all things, humility, comes incidentally the peculiar insistence on the Superman. After belabouring a great many people for a great many years for being unprogressive, Mr. Shaw has discovered, with characteristic sense, that it is very doubtful whether any existing human being with two legs can be progressive at all. Having come to doubt whether humanity can be combined with progress, most people, easily pleased, would have elected to abandon progress and remain with humanity. Mr. Shaw, not being easily pleased, decides to throw over humanity with all its limitations and go in for progress for its own sake. If man, as we know him, is incapable of the philosophy of progress, Mr. Shaw asks, not for a new kind of philosophy, but for a new kind of man. It is rather as if a nurse had tried a rather bitter food for some years on a baby, and on discovering that it was not suitable, should not throw away the food and ask for a new food, but throw the baby out of the window, and ask for a new baby. Mr. Shaw cannot understand that the thing which is valuable and lovable in our eyes is man — the old beer-drinking, creed-making, fighting, failing, sensual, respectable man. And the things that have been founded on this creature immortally remain; the things that have been founded on the fancy of the Superman have died with the dying civilizations which alone have given them birth. When Christ at a symbolic moment was establishing His great society, He chose for its cornerstone neither the brilliant Paul nor the mystic John, but a shuffler, a snob, a coward — in a word, a man. And upon this rock He has built His Church, and the gates of Hell have not prevailed against it. All the empires and the kingdoms have failed, because of this inherent and continual weakness, that they were founded by strong men and upon strong men. But this one thing, the historic Christian Church, was founded on a weak man, and for that reason it is indestructible. For no chain is stronger than its weakest link.

V

MR. H. G. WELLS AND THE GIANTS

We ought to see far enough into a hypocrite to see even his sincerity. We ought to be interested in that darkest and most real part of a man in which dwell not the vices that he does not display, but the virtues that he cannot. And the more we approach the problems of human history with this keen and piercing charity, the smaller and smaller space we shall allow to pure hypocrisy of any kind. The hypocrites shall not deceive us into thinking them saints; but neither shall they deceive us into thinking them hypocrites. And an increasing number of cases will crowd into our field of inquiry, cases in which there is really no question of hypocrisy at all, cases in which people were so ingenuous that they seemed absurd, and so absurd that they seemed disingenuous.

There is one striking instance of an unfair charge of hypocrisy. It is always urged against the religious in the past, as a point of inconsistency and duplicity, that they combined a profession of almost crawling humility with a keen struggle for earthly success and considerable triumph in attaining it. It is felt as a piece of humbug that a man should be very punctilious in calling himself a miserable sinner, and also very punctilious in calling himself King of France. But the truth is that there is no more conscious inconsistency between the humility of a Christian and the rapacity of a Christian than there is between the humility of a lover and the rapacity of a lover. The truth is that there are no things for which men will make such herculean efforts as the things of which they know they are unworthy. There never was a man in love who did not declare that, if he strained every nerve to breaking, he was going to have his desire. And there never was a man in love who did not declare also that he ought not to have it. The whole secret of the practical success of Christendom lies in the Christian humility, however imperfectly fulfilled. For with the removal of all question of merit or payment, the soul is suddenly released for incredible voyages. If we ask a sane man how

71

much he merits, his mind shrinks instinctively and instantaneously. It is doubtful whether he merits six feet of earth. But if you ask him what he can conquer—he can conquer the stars. Thus comes the thing called Romance, a purely Christian product. A man cannot deserve adventures; he cannot earn dragons and hippogriffs. The mediaeval Europe which asserted humility gained Romance; the civilization which gained Romance has gained the habitable globe. How different the Pagan and Stoical feeling was from this has been admirably expressed in a famous quotation. Addison makes the great Stoic[26] say—

> "'Tis not in mortals to command success;
>   But we'll do more, Sempronius, we'll deserve it."

But the spirit of Romance and Christendom, the spirit which is in every lover, the spirit which has bestridden the earth with European adventure, is quite opposite. 'Tis not in mortals to deserve success. But we'll do more, Sempronius; we'll obtain it.

And this gay humility, this holding of ourselves lightly and yet ready for an infinity of unmerited triumphs, this secret is so simple that every one has supposed that it must be something quite sinister and mysterious. Humility is so practical a virtue that men think it must be a vice. Humility is so successful that it is mistaken for pride. It is mistaken for it all the more easily because it generally goes with a certain simple love of splendour which amounts to vanity. Humility will always, by preference, go clad in scarlet and gold; pride in that which refuses to let gold and scarlet impress it or please it too much. In a word, the failure of this virtue actually lies in its success; it is too successful as an investment to be believed in as a virtue. Humility is not merely too good for this world; it is too practical for this world; I had almost said it is too worldly for this world.

The instance most quoted in our day is the thing called the humility of the man of science; and certainly it is a good instance as well as a modern one. Men find it extremely difficult to believe that a man who is obviously uprooting mountains and dividing seas, tearing down temples and stretching out hands to the stars, is really

[26] From Addison's *Cato* (1713), act I, sc. ii, lines 44–45.

a quiet old gentleman who only asks to be allowed to indulge his harmless old hobby and follow his harmless old nose. When a man splits a grain of sand and the universe is turned upside down in consequence, it is difficult to realize that to the man who did it, the splitting of the grain is the great affair, and the capsizing of the cosmos quite a small one. It is hard to enter into the feelings of a man who regards a new heaven and a new earth in the light of a byproduct. But undoubtedly it was to this almost eerie innocence of the intellect that the great men of the great scientific period, which now appears to be closing, owed their enormous power and triumph. If they had brought the heavens down like a house of cards their plea was not even that they had done it on principle; their quite unanswerable plea was that they had done it by accident. Whenever there was in them the least touch of pride in what they had done, there was a good ground for attacking them; but so long as they were wholly humble, they were wholly victorious. There were possible answers to Huxley; there was no answer possible to Darwin.[27] He was convincing because of his unconsciousness; one might almost say because of his dulness. This childlike and prosaic mind is beginning to wane in the world of science. Men of science are beginning to see themselves, as the fine phrase is, in the part; they are beginning to be proud of their humility. They are beginning to be aesthetic, like the rest of the world, beginning to spell truth with a capital T, beginning to talk of the creeds they imagine themselves to have destroyed, of the discoveries that their forbears made. Like the modern English, they are beginning to be soft about their own hardness. They are becoming conscious of their own strength—that is, they are growing weaker.

But one purely modern man has emerged in the strictly modern decades who does carry into our world the clear personal simplicity of the old world of science. One man of genius we have who is an artist, but who was a man of science, and who seems to be marked above all things with this great scientific humility. I mean Mr.

[27] Having published *The Origin of Species* in 1859, Darwin did not take an active part in the controversy arising out of it. Thomas Henry Huxley did and won for himself the nickname "Darwin's bulldog".

H. G. Wells. And in his case, as in the others above spoken of, there must be a great preliminary difficulty in convincing the ordinary person that such a virtue is predicable of such a man. Mr. Wells began his literary work with violent visions—visions of the last pangs of this planet; can it be that a man who begins with violent visions is humble? He went on to wilder and wilder stories about carving beasts into men and shooting angels like birds. Is the man who shoots angels and carves beasts into men humble? Since then he has done something bolder than either of these blasphemies; he has prophesied the political future of all men; prophesied it with aggressive authority and a ringing decision of detail. Is the prophet of the future of all men humble? It will indeed be difficult, in the present condition of current thought about such things as pride and humility, to answer the query of how a man can be humble who does such big things and such bold things. For the only answer is the answer which I gave at the beginning of this essay. It is the humble man who does the big things. It is the humble man who does the bold things. It is the humble man who has the sensational sights vouchsafed to him, and this for three obvious reasons: first, that he strains his eyes more than any other men to see them; second, that he is more overwhelmed and uplifted with them when they come; third, that he records them more exactly and sincerely and with less adulteration from his more commonplace and more conceited everyday self. Adventures are to those to whom they are most unexpected— that is, most romantic. Adventures are to the shy: in this sense adventures are to the unadventurous.

Now, this arresting mental humility in Mr. H. G. Wells may be, like a great many other things that are vital and vivid, difficult to illustrate by examples, but if I were asked for an example of it, I should have no difficulty about which example to begin with. The most interesting thing about Mr. H. G. Wells is that he is the only one of his many brilliant contemporaries who has not stopped growing. One can lie awake at night and hear him grow. Of this growth the most evident manifestation is indeed a gradual change of opinions; but it is no mere change of opinions. It is not a perpetual leaping from one position to another like that of Mr. George Moore.[28] It is a quite continuous advance along a quite solid road in a quite definable direction. But the chief proof that it is not a piece of fickleness and vanity is the fact that it has been upon the whole an advance from more startling opinions to more humdrum opinions. It has been even in some sense an advance from unconventional opinions to conventional opinions. This fact fixes Mr. Wells's honesty and proves him to be no *poseur*. Mr. Wells once held that the upper classes and the lower classes would be so much differentiated in the future that one class would eat the other. Certainly no paradoxical charlatan who had once found arguments for so startling a view would ever have deserted it except for something yet more startling. Mr. Wells has deserted it in favour of the blameless belief that both classes will be ultimately subordinated or assimilated to a sort of scientific middle class, a class of engineers. He has abandoned the sensational theory with the same honourable gravity and simplicity with which he adopted it. Then he thought it was true; now he thinks it is not true. He has come to the most dreadful conclusion a literary man can come to, the conclusion that the ordinary view is the right one. It is only the last and wildest kind of courage that can stand on a tower before ten thousand people and tell them that twice two is four.

Mr. H. G. Wells exists at present in a gay and exhilarating progress of conservatism. He is finding out more and more that conventions, though silent, are alive. As good an example as any of this humility and sanity of his may be found in his change of view on the subject of science and marriage. He once held, I believe, the opinion which some singular sociologists still hold, that human creatures could successfully be paired and bred after the manner of dogs or horses. He no longer holds that view. Not only does he no longer hold that view, but he has written about it in "Mankind in the Making" with such smashing sense and humour, that I find it difficult to believe that anybody else can hold it either. It is true that his chief

[28] George Moore (1852–1933), who had a substantial reputation as a novelist at the time Chesterton was writing, had been brought up as a Roman Catholic and become the Church's bitter antagonist.

objection to the proposal is that it is physically impossible, which seems to me a very slight objection, and almost negligible compared with the others. The one objection to scientific marriage which is worthy of final attention is simply that such a thing could only be imposed on unthinkable slaves and cowards. I do not know whether the scientific marriage-mongers are right (as they say) or wrong (as Mr. Wells says) in saying that medical supervision would produce strong and healthy men. I am only certain that if it did, the first act of the strong and healthy men would be to smash the medical supervision.

The mistake of all that medical talk lies in the very fact that it connects the idea of health with the idea of care. What has health to do with care? Health has to do with carelessness. In special and abnormal cases it is necessary to have care. When we are peculiarly unhealthy it may be necessary to be careful in order to be healthy. But even then we are only trying to be healthy in order to be careless. If we are doctors we are speaking to exceptionally sick men, and they ought to be told to be careful. But when we are sociologists we are addressing the normal man, we are addressing humanity. And humanity ought to be told to be recklessness itself. For all the fundamental functions of a healthy man ought emphatically to be performed with pleasure and for pleasure; they emphatically ought not to be performed with precaution or for precaution. A man ought to eat because he has a good appetite to satisfy, and emphatically not because he has a body to sustain. A man ought to take exercise not because he is too fat, but because he loves foils or horses or high mountains, and loves them for their own sake. And a man ought to marry because he has fallen in love, and emphatically not because the world requires to be populated. The food will really renovate his tissues as long as he is not thinking about his tissues. The exercise will really get him into training so long as he is thinking about something else. And the marriage will really stand some chance of producing a generous-blooded generation if it had its origin in its own natural and generous excitement. It is the first law of health that our necessities should not be accepted as necessities; they should be accepted as luxuries. Let us, then, be careful about the small things, such as a scratch or a slight illness, or anything that can be managed with care. But in the name of all sanity, let us be careless about the important things, such as marriage, or the fountain of our very life will fail.

Mr. Wells, however, is not quite clear enough of the narrower scientific outlook to see that there are some things which actually ought not to be scientific. He is still slightly affected with the great scientific fallacy; I mean the habit of beginning not with the human soul, which is the first thing a man learns about, but with some such thing as protoplasm, which is about the last. The one defect in his splendid mental equipment is that he does not sufficiently allow for the stuff or material of men. In his new Utopia he says, for instance, that a chief point of the Utopia will be a disbelief in original sin. If he had begun with the human soul — that is, if he had begun on himself — he would have found original sin almost the first thing to be believed in. He would have found, to put the matter shortly, that a permanent possibility of selfishness arises from the mere fact of having a self, and not from any accidents of education or ill-treatment. And the weakness of all Utopias is this, that they take the greatest difficulty of man and assume it to be overcome, and then give an elaborate account of the overcoming of the smaller ones. They first assume that no man will want more than his share, and then are very ingenious in explaining whether his share will be delivered by motor-car or balloon. And an even stronger example of Mr. Wells's indifference to the human psychology can be found in his cosmopolitanism, the abolition in his Utopia of all patriotic boundaries. He says in his innocent way that Utopia must be a world-state, or else people might make war on it. It does not seem to occur to him that, for a good many of us, if it were a world-state we should still make war on it to the end of the world. For if we admit that there must be varieties in art or opinion, what sense is there in thinking there will not be varieties in government? The fact is very simple. Unless you are going deliberately to prevent a thing being good, you cannot prevent it being worth fighting for. It is impossible to prevent a possible conflict of civilizations, because it is impossible to prevent a possible conflict between ideals. If there were no longer our modern strife between nations, there would only be a strife between Utopias. For the highest thing does not tend to union only; the highest thing tends also to differentiation. You can often get men to fight for the union; but you can never prevent them from fighting also for the differentiation. This variety in the highest thing is the meaning of the fierce patriotism, the fierce nationalism of the great European civilization. It is also, incidentally, the meaning of the doctrine of the Trinity.

But I think the main mistake of Mr. Wells's philosophy is a somewhat deeper one, one that he expresses in a very entertaining manner in the introductory part of the new Utopia. His philosophy in some sense amounts to a denial of the possibility of philosophy itself. At least, he maintains that there are no secure and reliable ideas upon which we can rest with a final mental satisfaction. It will be both clearer, however, and more amusing to quote Mr. Wells himself.

He says, "Nothing endures, nothing is precise and certain (except the mind of a pedant). . . . Being indeed!—there is no being, but a universal becoming of individualities, and Plato turned his back on truth when he turned towards his museum of specific ideals." Mr. Wells says, again, "There is no abiding thing in what we know. We change from weaker to stronger lights, and each more powerful light pierces our hitherto opaque foundations and reveals fresh and different opacities below." Now, when Mr. Wells says things like this, I speak with all respect when I say that he does not observe an evident mental distinction. It *cannot* be true that there is nothing abiding in what we know. For if that were so we should not know it all and should not call it knowledge. Our mental state may be very different from that of somebody else some thousands of years back; but it cannot be entirely different, or else we should not be conscious of a difference. Mr. Wells must surely realize the first and simplest of the paradoxes that sit by the springs of truth. He must surely see that the fact of two things being different implies that they are similar. The hare and the tortoise may differ in the quality of swiftness, but they must agree in the quality of motion. The swiftest hare cannot be swifter than an isosceles triangle or the idea of pinkness. When we say the hare moves faster, we say that the tortoise moves. And when we say of a thing that it moves, we say, without need of other words, that there are things that do not move. And even in the act of saying that things change, we say that there is something unchangeable.

But certainly the best example of Mr. Wells's fallacy can be found in the example which he himself chooses. It is quite true that we see a dim light which, compared with a darker thing, is light, but which, compared with a stronger light, is darkness. But the quality of light remains the same thing, or else we should not call it a stronger light or recognize it as such. If the character of light were not fixed in the mind, we should be quite as likely to call a denser shadow a stronger light, or *vice versa*. If the character of light became even for an instant unfixed, if it became even by a hair's-breadth doubtful, if, for example, there crept into our idea of light some vague idea of blue-ness, then in that flash we have become doubtful whether the new light has more light or less. In brief, the progress may be as varying as a cloud, but the direction must be as rigid as a French road. North and South are relative in the sense that I am North of Bournemouth and South of Spitzbergen. But if there be any doubt of the position of the North Pole, there is in equal degree a doubt of whether I am South of Spitzbergen at all. The absolute idea of light may be practically unattainable. We may not be able to procure pure light. We may not be able to get to the North Pole. But because the North Pole is unattainable, it does not follow that it is indefinable. And it is only because the North Pole is not indefinable that we can make a satisfactory map of Brighton and Worthing.

In other words, Plato turned his face to truth, but his back on Mr. H. G. Wells, when he turned to his museum of specified ideals. It is precisely here that Plato shows his sense. It is not true that everything changes; the things that change are all the manifest and material things. There is something that does not change; and that is precisely the abstract quality, the invisible idea. Mr. Wells says truly enough, that a thing which we have seen in one connection as dark we may see in another connection as light. But the thing common to both incidents is the mere idea of light — which we have not seen at all. Mr. Wells might grow taller and taller for unending aeons till his head was higher than the loneliest star. I can imagine his writing a good novel about it. In that case he would see the trees first as tall things and then as short things; he would see the clouds first as high and then as low. But there would remain with him through the ages in that starry loneliness the idea of tallness; he would have in the awful spaces for companion and comfort the definite conception that he was growing taller and not (for instance) growing fatter.

And now it comes to my mind that Mr. H. G. Wells actually has written a very delightful romance about men growing as tall as trees; and that here, again, he seems to me to have been a victim of this vague relativism. "The Food of the Gods" is, like Mr. Bernard Shaw's play, in essence a study of the Superman idea. And it lies, I think, even through the veil of a half-pantomimic allegory, open to the same intellectual attack. We cannot be expected to have any regard for a great creature if he does not in any manner conform to our standards. For unless he passes our standard of greatness we cannot even call him great. Nietzsche summed up all that is interesting in the Superman idea when he said, "Man is a thing which has to be surpassed." But the very word "surpass" implies the existence of a standard common to us and the thing surpassing us. If the Superman is more manly then men are, of course they will ultimately deify him, even if they happen to kill him first. But if he is simply more supermanly, they may be quite indifferent to him as they would be to another seemingly aimless monstrosity. He must submit to our test even in order to overawe us. Mere force or size even is a standard; but that alone will never make men think a man their superior. Giants, as in the wise old fairy-tales, are vermin. Supermen, if not good men, are vermin.

"The Food of the Gods" is the tale of "Jack the Giant-Killer" told from the point of view of the giant. This has not, I think, been done before in literature; but I have little doubt that the psychological substance of it existed in fact. I have little doubt that the giant whom Jack killed did regard himself as the Superman. It is likely enough that he considered Jack a narrow and parochial person who wished to frustrate a great forward movement of the life-force. If (as not unfrequently was the case) he happened to have two heads, he would point out the elementary maxim which declares them to be better than one. He would enlarge on the subtle modernity of such an equipment, enabling a giant to look at a subject from two points of view, or to correct himself with promptitude. But Jack was the champion of the enduring human standards, of the principle of one man one head and one man one conscience, of the single head and the single heart and the single eye. Jack was quite unimpressed by the question of whether the giant was a particularly gigantic giant. All he wished to know was whether he was a good giant — that is, a giant who was any good to us. What were the giant's religious views; what his views on politics and the duties of the citizen? Was he fond of children — or fond of them only in a dark and sinister sense? To use a fine phrase for emotional sanity, was his heart in the right place? Jack had sometimes to cut him up with a sword in order to find out.

The old and correct story of Jack the Giant-Killer is simply the whole story of man; if it were understood we should need no Bibles or histories. But the modern world in particular does not seem to understand it at all. The modern world, like Mr. Wells, is on the side of the giants; the safest place, and therefore the meanest and the most prosaic. The modern world, when it praises its little Caesars, talks of being strong and brave: but it does not seem to see the eternal paradox involved in the conjunction of these ideas. The strong cannot be brave. Only the weak can be brave; and yet again, in practice, only those who can be brave can be trusted, in time of doubt, to be strong. The only way in which a giant could really keep himself in training against the inevitable Jack would be by continually fighting other giants ten times as big as himself. That is by ceasing to be a giant and becoming a Jack. Thus that sympathy with the small or the defeated as such, with which we Liberals and Nationalists have been often reproached, is not a useless sentimentalism at all, as Mr. Wells and his friends fancy. It is the first law of practical courage. To be in the weakest camp is to be in the strongest school. Nor can I imagine anything that would do humanity more good than the advent of a race of Supermen, for them to fight like dragons. If the Superman is better than we, of course we need not fight him; but in that case, why not call him the Saint? But if he is merely stronger (whether physically, mentally, or morally stronger, I do not care a farthing), then he ought to have to reckon with us at least for all the strength we have. If we are weaker than he, that is no reason why we should be weaker than ourselves. If we are not tall enough to touch the giant's knees, that is no reason why we should become shorter by falling on our own. But that is at bottom the meaning of all modern hero-worship and celebration of the Strong Man, the Caesar, the Superman. That he may be something more than man, *we* must be something less.

Doubtless there is an older and better hero-worship than this. But the old hero was a being who, like Achilles, was more human than humanity itself. Nietzsche's Superman is cold and friendless. Achilles is so foolishly fond of his friend that he slaughters armies in the agony of his bereavement. Mr. Shaw's sad Caesar says in his desolate pride, "He who has never hoped can never despair." The Man-God of old answers from his awful hill, "Was ever sorrow like unto my sorrow?" A great man is not a man so strong that he feels less than other men; he is a man so strong that he feels more. And when Nietzsche says, "A new commandment I give to you, 'be hard,'" he is really saying, "A new commandment I give to you, 'be dead.'" Sensibility is the definition of life.

I recur for a last word to Jack the Giant-Killer. I have dwelt on this matter of Mr. Wells and the giants, not because it is specially prominent in his mind; I know that the Superman does not bulk so large in his cosmos as in that of Mr. Bernard Shaw. I have dwelt on it for the opposite reason; because this heresy of immoral hero-worship has taken, I think, a slighter hold of him, and may perhaps still be prevented from perverting one of the best thinkers of the day. In the course of "The New Utopia" Mr. Wells makes more than one admiring allusion to Mr. W. E. Henley.[29] That clever and unhappy man lived in admiration of a vague violence, and was always going back to rude old tales and rude old ballads, to strong and primitive literatures, to find the praise of strength and the justification of tyranny. But he could not find it. It is not there. The

[29] Poet and journalist (1849–1903). In one phase of his writing, he adopted Kipling's swashbuckling vein and praised the virtues of colonial adventurers.

primitive literature is shown in the tale of Jack the Giant-Killer. The strong old literature is all in praise of the weak. The rude old tales are as tender to minorities as any modern political idealist. The rude old ballads are as sentimentally concerned for the under-dog as the Aborigines Protection Society. When men were tough and raw, when they lived amid hard knocks and hard laws, when they knew what fighting really was, they had only two kinds of songs. The first was a rejoicing that the weak had conquered the strong, the second a lamentation that the strong had, for once in a way, conquered the weak. For this defiance of the *status quo*, this constant effort to alter the existing balance, this premature challenge to the powerful, is the whole nature and inmost secret of the psychological adventure which is called man. It is his strength to disdain strength. The forlorn hope is not only a real hope, it is the only real hope of mankind. In the coarsest ballads of the greenwood men are admired most when they defy, not only the king, but what is more to the point, the hero. The moment Robin Hood becomes a sort of Superman, that moment the chivalrous chronicler shows us Robin thrashed by a poor tinker whom he thought to thrust aside. And the chivalrous chronicler makes Robin Hood receive the thrashing in a glow of admiration. This magnanimity is not a product of modern humanitarianism; it is not a product of anything to do with peace. This magnanimity is merely one of the lost arts of war. The Henleyites call for a sturdy and fighting England, and they go back to the fierce old stories of the sturdy and fighting English. And the thing that they find written across that fierce old literature everywhere, is "the policy of Majuba."[30]

[30] Majuba is a mountain in northern Natal, where the Boers defeated the British in 1881.

VI

CHRISTMAS AND THE AESTHETES

The world is round, so round that the schools of optimism and pessimism have been arguing from the beginning whether it is the right way up. The difficulty does not arise so much from the mere fact that good and evil are mingled in roughly equal proportions; it arises chiefly from the fact that men always differ about what parts are good and what evil. Hence the difficulty which besets "undenominational religions." They profess to include what is beautiful in all creeds, but they appear to many to have collected all that is dull in them. All the colours mixed together in purity ought to make a perfect white. Mixed together on any human paint-box, they make a thing like mud, and a thing very like many new religions. Such a blend is often something much worse than any one creed taken separately, even the creed of the Thugs.[31] The error arises from the difficulty of detecting what is really the good part and what is really the bad part of any given religion. And this pathos falls rather heavily on those persons who have the misfortune to think of some religion or other, that the parts commonly counted good are bad, and the parts commonly counted bad are good.

It is tragic to admire and honestly admire a human group, but to admire it in a photographic negative. It is difficult to congratulate all their whites on being black and all their blacks on their whiteness. This will often happen to us in connection with human religions. Take two institutions which bear witness to the religious energy of the nineteenth century. Take the Salvation Army and the philosophy of Auguste Comte.[32]

The usual verdict of educated people on the Salvation Army is

---

[31] A group of robbers and murderers in India who committed their crimes as sacrifices to the goddess Kali.

[32] Auguste Comte (1798–1857), founder of positivism, which excludes revealed religion. He eventually tried to invest it with religious significance, with its own prayers and rituals.

expressed in some such words as these: "I have no doubt they do a great deal of good, but they do it in a vulgar and profane style; their aims are excellent, but their methods are wrong." To me, unfortunately, the precise reverse of this appears to be the truth. I do not know whether the aims of the Salvation Army are excellent, but I am quite sure their methods are admirable. Their methods are the methods of all intense and hearty religions; they are popular like all religion, military like all religion, public and sensational like all religion. They are not reverent any more than Roman Catholics are reverent, for reverence in the sad and delicate meaning of the term reverence is a thing only possible to infidels. That beautiful twilight you will find in Euripides, in Renan,[33] in Matthew Arnold; but in men who believe you will not find it—you will find only laughter and war. A man cannot pay that kind of reverence to truth solid as marble; they can only be reverent towards a beautiful lie. And the Salvation Army, though their voice has broken out in a mean environment and an ugly shape, are really the old voice of glad and angry faith, hot as the riots of Dionysius, wild as the gargoyles of Catholicism, not to be mistaken for a philosophy. Professor Huxley, in one of his clever phrases, called the Salvation Army "corybantic Christianity."[34] Huxley was the last and noblest of those Stoics who have never understood the Cross. If he had understood Christianity he would have known that there never has been, and never can be, any Christianity that is not corybantic.

And there is this difference between the matter of aims and the matter of methods, that to judge of the aims of a thing like the Salvation Army is very difficult, to judge of their ritual and atmosphere very easy. No one, perhaps, but a sociologist can see whether General Booth's[35] housing scheme is right. But any healthy person can

[33] Joseph Ernest Renan (1823–1892), French writer, anticipated a state in which philosophy and culture would supersede politics and religion. In his best-known book, *La Vie de Jésus* (1863), he regarded Christ as an inspired teacher but a purely human person.

[34] Wild and frenzied, like the behavior of the attendants on the Greek nature goddess Cybele.

[35] General William Booth (1829–1912) was the founder of the Salvation Army.

see that banging brass cymbals together must be right. A page of statistics, a plan of model dwellings, anything which is rational, is always difficult for the lay mind. But the thing which is irrational any one can understand. That is why religion came so early into the world and spread so far, while science came so late into the world and has not spread at all. History unanimously attests the fact that it is only mysticism which stands the smallest chance of being understanded of the people. Common sense has to be kept as an esoteric secret in the dark temple of culture. And so while the philanthropy of the Salvationists and its genuineness may be a reasonable matter for the discussion of the doctors, there can be no doubt about the genuineness of their brass bands, for a brass band is purely spiritual, and seeks only to quicken the internal life. The object of philanthropy is to do good; the object of religion is to be good, if only for a moment, amid a crash of brass.

And the same antithesis exists about another modern religion — I mean the religion of Comte, generally known as Positivism, or the worship of humanity. Such men as Mr. Frederic Harrison,[36] that brilliant and chivalrous philosopher, who still, by his mere personality, speaks for the creed, would tell us that he offers us the philosophy of Comte, but not all Comte's fantastic proposals for pontiffs and ceremonials, the new calendar, the new holidays and saints' days. He does not mean that we should dress ourselves up as priests of humanity or let off fireworks because it is Milton's birthday. To the solid English Comtist all this appears, he confesses, to be a little absurd. To me it appears the only sensible part of Comtism. As a philosophy it is unsatisfactory. It is evidently impossible to worship humanity, just as it is impossible to worship the Savile Club;[37] both are excellent institutions to which we may happen to belong. But we perceive clearly that the Savile Club did not make the stars and does not fill the universe. And it is surely unreasonable to attack the doctrine of the Trinity as a piece of bewildering mysticism, and then to ask men to worship a being who is ninety million

[36] Frederic Harrison (1831–1923) was Comte's translator and most prominent English disciple, president of the English Positivist Committee for twenty-five years.
[37] A London club to which many distinguished writers have belonged.

persons in one God, neither confounding the persons nor dividing the substance.

But if the wisdom of Comte was insufficient, the folly of Comte was wisdom. In an age of dusty modernity, when beauty was thought of as something barbaric and ugliness as something sensible, he alone saw that men must always have the sacredness of mummery. He saw that while the brutes have all the useful things, the things that are truly human are the useless ones. He saw the falsehood of that almost universal notion of to-day, the notion that rites and forms are something artificial, additional, and corrupt. Ritual is really much older than thought; it is much simpler and much wilder than thought. A feeling touching the nature of things does not only make men feel that there are certain proper things to say; it makes them feel that there are certain proper things to do. The more agreeable of these consist of dancing, building temples, and shouting very loud; the less agreeable, of wearing green carnations and burning other philosophers alive. But everywhere the religious dance came before the religious hymn, and man was a ritualist before he could speak. If Comtism had spread the world would have been converted, not by the Comtist philosophy, but by the Comtist calendar. By discouraging what they conceive to be the weakness of their master, the English Positivists have broken the strength of their religion. A man who has faith must be prepared not only to be a martyr, but to be a fool. It is absurd to say that a man is ready to toil and die for his convictions when he is not even ready to wear a wreath round his head for them. I myself, to take a *corpus vile*,[38] am very certain that I would not read the works of Comte through for any consideration whatever. But I can easily imagine myself with the greatest enthusiasm lighting a bonfire on Darwin Day.

That splendid effort failed, and nothing in the style of it has succeeded. There has been no rationalist festival, no rationalist ecstasy. Men are still in black for the death of God. When Christianity was heavily bombarded in the last century upon no point was it more persistently and brilliantly attacked than upon that of its alleged enmity

[38] A worthless body, something so insignificant that it can be experimented upon without concern.

to human joy. Shelley and Swinburne and all their armies have passed again and again over the ground, but they have not altered it. They have not set up a single new trophy or ensign for the world's merriment to rally to. They have not given a name or a new occasion of gaiety. Mr. Swinburne does not hang up his stocking on the eve of the birthday of Victor Hugo. Mr. William Archer[39] does not sing carols descriptive of the infancy of Ibsen outside people's doors in the snow. In the round of our rational and mournful year one festival remains out of all those ancient gaieties that once covered the whole earth. Christmas remains to remind us of those ages, whether Pagan or Christian, when the many acted poetry instead of the few writing it. In all the winter in our woods there is no tree in glow but the holly.

The strange truth about the matter is told in the very word "holiday." A bank holiday means presumably a day which bankers regard as holy. A half-holiday means, I suppose, a day on which a schoolboy is only partially holy. It is hard to see at first sight why so human a thing as leisure and larkiness should always have a religious origin. Rationally there appears no reason why we should not sing and give each other presents in honour of anything—the birth of Michael Angelo or the opening of Euston Station. But it does not work. As a fact, men only become greedily and gloriously material about something spiritualistic. Take away the Nicene Creed and similar things, and you do some strange wrong to the sellers of sausages. Take away the strange beauty of the saints, and what has remained to us is the far stranger ugliness of Wandsworth.[40] Take away the supernatural, and what remains is the unnatural.

And now I have to touch upon a very sad matter. There are in the modern world an admirable class of persons who really make protest on behalf of that *antiqua pulchritudo*[41] of which Augustine spoke,

[39] Mr. William Archer (1856–1924), critic, dramatist and translator of Ibsen's plays into English.

[40] A borough of London south of the Thames.

[41] From St. Augustine's *Confessions*, bk. 10, chap. 27: "*Sero te amavi pulchritudo tam antiqua, et tam nova. . . !*" "Late have I loved thee, O Beauty so ancient and so new; late have I loved thee!"

who do long for the old feasts and formalities of the childhood of the world. William Morris and his followers showed how much brighter were the dark ages than the age of Manchester.[42] Mr. W. B. Yeats frames his steps in prehistoric dances, but no man knows and joins his voice to forgotten choruses that no one but he can hear. Mr. George Moore collects every fragment of Irish paganism that the forgetfulness of the Catholic Church has left or possibly her wisdom preserved. There are innumerable persons with eye-glasses and green garments who pray for the return of the maypole or the Olympian games. But there is about these people a haunting and alarming something which suggests that it is just possible that they do not keep Christmas. It is painful to regard human nature in such a light, but it seems somehow possible that Mr. George Moore does not wave his spoon and shout when the pudding is set alight. It is even possible that Mr. W. B. Yeats never pulls crackers. If so, where is the sense of all their dreams of festive traditions? Here is a solid and ancient festive tradition still plying a roaring trade in the streets, and they think it vulgar. If this is so, let them be very certain of this, that they are the kind of people who in the time of the maypole would have thought the maypole vulgar; who in the time of the Canterbury pilgrimage would have thought the Canterbury pilgrimage vulgar; who in the time of the Olympian games would have thought the Olympian games vulgar. Nor can there be any reasonable doubt that they were vulgar. Let no man deceive himself; if by vulgarity we mean coarseness of speech, rowdiness of behaviour, gossip, horseplay, and some heavy drinking, vulgarity there always was wherever there was joy, wherever there was faith in the gods. Wherever you have belief you will have hilarity, wherever you have hilarity you will have some dangers. And as creed and mythology produce this gross and vigorous life, so in its turn this gross and vigorous life will always produce creed and mythology. If we ever get the English back on to the English land they will become again a religious people, if all goes well, a superstitious people. The absence

[42] After the first application of steam machinery to the spinning of cotton in 1789, Manchester quickly became the world's leading manufacturer of cotton. It developed enormously during the nineteenth century.

from modern life of both the higher and lower forms of faith is largely due to a divorce from nature and the trees and clouds. If we have no more turnip ghosts it is chiefly from the lack of turnips.

VII

OMAR AND THE SACRED VINE

A new morality has burst upon us with some violence in connection with the problem of strong drink; and enthusiasts in the matter range from the man who is violently thrown out at 12:30, to the lady who smashes American bars with an axe. In these discussions it is almost always felt that one very wise and moderate position is to say that wine or such stuff should only be drunk as a medicine. With this I should venture to disagree with a peculiar ferocity. The one genuinely dangerous and immoral way of drinking wine is to drink it as a medicine. And for this reason. If a man drinks wine in order to obtain pleasure, he is trying to obtain something exceptional, something he does not expect every hour of the day, something which, unless he is a little insane, he will not try to get every hour of the day. But if a man drinks wine in order to obtain health, he is trying to get something natural; something, that is, that he ought not to be without; something that he may find it difficult to reconcile himself to being without. The man may not be seduced who has seen the ecstasy of being ecstatic; it is more dazzling to catch a glimpse of the ecstasy of being ordinary. If there were a magic ointment, and we took it to a strong man, and said, "This will enable you to jump off the Monument,"[43] doubtless he would jump off the Monument, but he would not jump off the Monument all day long to the delight of the City. But if we took it to a blind man, saying, "This will enable you to see," he would be under a heavier temptation. It would be hard for him not to rub it on his eyes whenever he heard the hoof of a noble horse or the birds singing at daybreak. It is easy to deny one's self festivity; it is difficult to deny one's self normality. Hence comes the fact which every doctor knows, that it is often perilous to give alcohol to the sick even when they need it. I need hardly say that I do not mean that I think the giving of alcohol to the sick for

[43] Erected by Sir Christopher Wren between 1671 and 1677 to commemorate the Great Fire of London and placed near the spot where the fire broke out.

stimulus is necessarily unjustifiable. But I do mean that giving it to the healthy for fun is the proper use of it, and a great deal more consistent with health.

The sound rule in the matter would appear to be like many other sound rules — a paradox. Drink because you are happy, but never because you are miserable. Never drink when you are wretched without it, or you will be like the grey-faced gin-drinker in the slum; but drink when you would be happy without it, and you will be like the laughing peasant of Italy. Never drink because you need it, for this is rational drinking, and the way to death and hell. But drink because you do not need it, for this is irrational drinking, and the ancient health of the world.

For more than thirty years the shadow and glory of a great Eastern figure has lain upon our English literature. Fitzgerald's translation of Omar Khayyám[44] concentrated into an immortal poignancy all the dark and drifting hedonism of our time. Of the literary splendour of that work it would be merely banal to speak; in few other of the books of men has there been anything so combining the gay pugnacity of an epigram with the vague sadness of a song. But of its philosophical, ethical, and religious influence, which has been almost as great as its brilliancy, I should like to say a word, and that word, I confess, one of uncompromising hostility. There are a great many things which might be said against the spirit of the Rubáiyát, and against its prodigious influence. But one matter of indictment towers ominously above the rest — a genuine disgrace to it, a genuine calamity to us. This is the terrible blow that this great poem has struck against sociability and the joy of life. Some one called Omar "the sad, glad old Persian." Sad he is; glad he is not, in any sense of the word whatever. He has been a worse foe to gladness than the Puritans.

A pensive and graceful Oriental lies under the rose-tree with his wine-pot and his scroll of poems. It may seem strange that any one's thoughts should, at the moment of regarding him, fly back to the dark bedside where the doctor doles out brandy. It may seem stranger

[44] Edward Fitzgerald (1809–1883) published an English poetic version of the Persian *Rubáiyát of Omar Khayyám* in 1859, and it became immensely popular.

still that they should go back to the grey wastrel shaking with gin in Houndsditch.[45] But a great philosophical unity links the three in an evil bond. Omar Khayyám's wine-bibbing is bad, not because it is wine-bibbing. It is bad, and very bad, because it is medical wine-bibbing. It is the drinking of a man who drinks because he is not happy. His is the wine that shuts out the universe, not the wine that reveals it. It is not poetical drinking, which is joyous and instinctive; it is rational drinking, which is as prosaic as an investment, as unsavoury as a dose of camomile. Whole heavens above it, from the point of view of sentiment, though not of style, rises the splendour of some old English drinking-song—

> "Then pass the bowl, my comrades all,
> And let the zider vlow."

For this song was caught up by happy men to express the worth of truly worthy things, of brotherhood and garrulity, and the brief and kindly leisure of the poor. Of course, the great part of the more stolid reproaches directed against the Omarite morality are as false and babyish as such reproaches usually are. One critic, whose work I have read, had the incredible foolishness to call Omar an atheist and a materialist. It is almost impossible for an Oriental to be either; the East understands metaphysics too well for that. Of course, the real objection which a philosophical Christian would bring against the religion of Omar, is not that he gives no place to God, it is that he gives too much place to God. His is that terrible theism which can imagine nothing else but deity, and which denies altogether the outlines of human personality and human will.

> "The ball no question makes of Ayes or Noes,
> But Here or There as strikes the Player goes;
> And He that tossed you down into the field,
> He knows about it all—he knows—he knows."[46]

A Christian thinker, such as Augustine or Dante, would object

---

[45] A street in the City of London whose name suggests the unsavory reputation it once had. It was paved over in 1503.

[46] The quotation is from the *Rubáiyát of Omar Khayyám*, 5th version, ll, 277–80.

to this because it ignores free-will, which is the valour and dignity of the soul. The quarrel of the highest Christianity with this scepticism is not in the least that the scepticism denies the existence of God; it is that it denies the existence of man.

In this cult of the pessimistic pleasure-seeker the Rubáiyát stands first in our time; but it does not stand alone. Many of the most brilliant intellects of our time have urged us to the same self-conscious snatching at a rare delight. Walter Pater[47] said that we were all under sentence of death, and the only course was to enjoy exquisite moments simply for those moments' sake. The same lesson was taught by the very powerful and very desolate philosophy of Oscar Wilde. It is the *carpe diem*[48] religion; but the *carpe diem* religion is not the religion of happy people, but of very unhappy people. Great joy does not gather the rosebuds while it may; its eyes are fixed on the immortal rose which Dante saw.[49] Great joy has in it the sense of immortality; the very splendour of youth is the sense that it has all space to stretch its legs in. In all great comic literature, in "Tristram Shandy" or "Pickwick," there is this sense of space and incorruptibility; we feel the characters are deathless people in an endless tale.

It is true enough, of course, that a pungent happiness comes chiefly in certain passing moments; but it is not true that we should think of them as passing, or enjoy them simply "for those moments' sake." To do this is to rationalize the happiness, and therefore to destroy it. Happiness is a mystery like religion, and should never be rationalized. Suppose a man experiences a really splendid moment of pleasure. I do not mean something connected with a bit of enamel, I mean something with a violent happiness in it—an almost painful happiness. A man may have, for instance, a moment of ecstasy in first love, or a moment of victory in battle. The lover enjoys the moment

[47] In this and the following paragraphs Chesterton is referring to the famous conclusion to Pater's *Studies in the History of the Renaissance* (1873).

[48] Seize the day, enjoy the day.

[49] Mary, often referred to as the "mystical rose", is "the rose in which the Word Divine became incarnate" in *Paradiso* XXIII, ii, 73–74. In Cantos XXX and XXXI, the Church Triumphant, the sacred throng redeemed by Christ's blood, appears as a pure white rose.

but precisely not for the moment's sake. He enjoys it for the woman's sake, or his own sake. The warrior enjoys the moment, but not for the sake of the moment; he enjoys it for the sake of the flag. The cause which the flag stands for may be foolish and fleeting; the love may be calf-love, and last a week. But the patriot thinks of the flag as eternal; the lover thinks of his love as something that cannot end. These moments are filled with eternity; these moments are joyful because they do not seem momentary. Once look at them as moments after Pater's manner, and they become as cold as Pater and his style. Man cannot love mortal things. He can only love immortal things for an instant.

Pater's mistake is revealed in his most famous phrase. He asks us to burn with a hard, gem-like flame. Flames are never hard and never gem-like—they cannot be handled or arranged. So human emotions are never hard and never gem-like; they are always dangerous, like flames, to touch or even to examine. There is only one way in which our passions can become hard and gem-like, and that is by becoming as cold as gems. No blow then has ever been struck at the natural loves and laughter of men so sterilizing as this *carpe diem* of the aesthetes. For any kind of pleasure a totally different spirit is required; a certain shyness, a certain indeterminate hope, a certain boyish expectation. Purity and simplicity are essential to passions— yes, even to evil passions. Even vice demands a sort of virginity.

Omar's (or Fitzgerald's) effect upon the other world we may let go, his hand upon this world has been heavy and paralyzing. The Puritans, as I have said, are far jollier than he. The new ascetics who follow Thoreau or Tolstoy are much livelier company; for, though the surrender of strong drink and such luxuries may strike us as an idle negation, it may leave a man with innumerable natural pleasures, and, above all, with man's natural power of happiness. Thoreau could enjoy the sunrise without a cup of coffee. If Tolstoy cannot admire marriage, at least he is healthy enough to admire mud. Nature can be enjoyed without even the most natural luxuries. A good bush needs no wine. But neither nature nor wine nor anything else can be enjoyed if we have the wrong attitude towards happiness, and Omar (or Fitzgerald) did have the wrong attitude towards happiness. He and those he has influenced do not see that if we are to be truly gay, we must believe that there is some eternal gaity in the nature of things. We cannot enjoy thoroughly even a *pas-de-quatre*[50] at a subscription dance unless we believe that the stars are dancing to the same tune. No one can be really hilarious but the serious man. "Wine," says the Scripture, "maketh glad the heart of man," but only of the man who has a heart. The thing called high spirits is possible only to the spiritual. Ultimately a man cannot rejoice in anything except the nature of things. Ultimately a man can enjoy nothing except religion.

Once in the world's history men did believe that the stars were dancing to the tune of their temples, and they danced as men have never danced since. With this old pagan eudaemonism the sage of the Rubáiyát has quite as little to do as he has with any Christian variety. He is no more a Bacchanal than he is a saint. Dionysius and his church was grounded on a serious *joie-de-vivre* like that of Walt Whitman. Dionysius made wine, not a medicine, but a sacrament. Jesus Christ also made wine, not a medicine, but a sacrament. But Omar makes it, not a sacrament, but a medicine. He feasts because life is not joyful; he revels because he is not glad. "Drink," he says, "for you know not whence you come nor why. Drink, for you know not when you go nor where. Drink, because the stars are cruel and the world as idle as a humming-top. Drink, because there is nothing worth trusting, nothing worth fighting for. Drink, because all things are lapsed in a base equality and an evil peace." So he stands offering us the cup in his hand. And at the high altar of Christianity stands another figure, in whose hand also is the cup of the vine. "Drink," he says, "for the whole world is as red as this wine, with the crimson of the love and wrath of God. Drink, for the trumpets are blowing for battle and this is the stirrup-cup. Drink, for this my blood of the new testament that is shed for you. Drink, for I know of whence you come and why. Drink, for I know of when you go and where."

---

[50] A dance for four people.

VIII

THE MILDNESS OF THE YELLOW PRESS

There is a great deal of protest made from one quarter or another nowadays against the influence of that new journalism which is associated with the names of Sir Alfred Harmsworth[51] and Mr. Pearson.[52] But almost everybody who attacks it attacks on the ground that it is very sensational, very violent and vulgar and startling. I am speaking in no affected contrariety, but in the simplicity of a genuine personal impression, when I say that this journalism offends as being not sensational or violent enough. The real vice is not that it is startling, but that it is quite insupportably tame. The whole object is to keep carefully along a certain level of the expected and the commonplace; it may be low, but it must take care also to be flat. Never by any chance in it is there any of that real plebeian pungency which can be heard from the ordinary cabman in the ordinary street. We have heard of a certain standard of decorum which demands that things should be funny without being vulgar, but the standard of this decorum demands that if things are vulgar they shall be vulgar without being funny. This journalism does not merely fail to exaggerate life — it positively underrates it; and it has to do so because it is intended for the faint and languid recreation of men whom the fierceness of modern life has fatigued. This press is not the yellow press at all; it is the drab press. Sir Alfred Harmsworth must not address to the tired clerk any observation more witty than the tired clerk might be able to address to Sir Alfred Harmsworth. It must not expose anybody (anybody who is powerful, that is), it must not offend anybody, it must not even please anybody, too much. A

[51] Alfred Harmsworth (1865–1922), later Lord Northcliffe, opened a new era in journalism with the launching of a halfpenny newspaper in London, the *Daily Mail*, in 1896. It aimed to present "all the news in the smallest space".

[52] Cyril Arthur Pearson (1866–1921) founded *Pearson's Weekly* in 1890. In 1900, four years after the *Daily Mail* appeared, he launched his own halfpenny paper, the *Daily Express*.

general vague idea that in spite of all this, our yellow press is sensational, arises from such external accidents as large type or lurid headlines. It is quite true that these editors print everything they possibly can in large capital letters. But they do this, not because it is startling, but because it is soothing. To people wholly weary or partly drunk in a dimly lighted train, it is a simplification and a comfort to have things presented in this vast and obvious manner. The editors use this gigantic alphabet in dealing with their readers, for exactly the same reason that parents and governesses use a similar gigantic alphabet in teaching children to spell. The nursery authorities do not use an A as big as a horseshoe in order to make the child jump; on the contrary, they use it to put the child at his ease, to make things smoother and more evident. Of the same character is the dim and quiet dame school which Sir Alfred Harmsworth and Mr. Pearson keep. All their sentiments are spelling-book sentiments—that is to say, they are sentiments with which the pupil is already respectfully familiar. All their wildest posters are leaves torn from a copy-book.

Of real sensational journalism, as it exists in France, in Ireland, and in America, we have no trace in this country. When a journalist in Ireland wishes to create a thrill, he creates a thrill worth talking about. He denounces a leading Irish member for corruption, or he charges the whole police system with a wicked and definite conspiracy. When a French journalist desires a *frisson* there is a *frisson*; he discovers, let us say, that the President of the Republic has murdered three wives. Our yellow journalists invent quite as unscrupulously as this; their moral condition is, as regards careful veracity, about the same. But it is their mental calibre which happens to be such that they can only invent calm and even reassuring things. The fictitious version of the massacre of the envoys of Pekin was mendacious, but it was not interesting, except to those who had private reasons for terror or sorrow. It was not connected with any bold and suggestive view of the Chinese situation. It revealed only a vague idea that nothing could be impressive except a great deal of blood. Real sensationalism, of which I happen to be very fond, may be either moral or immoral. But even when it is most immoral, it requires moral courage. For it is one of the most dangerous things on earth genuinely to surprise anybody. If you make any sentient creature jump, you render it by no means improbable that it will jump on you. But the leaders of this movement have no moral courage or immoral courage; their whole method consists in saying, with large and elaborate emphasis, the things which everybody else says casually, and without remembering what they have said. When they brace themselves up to attack anything, they never reach the point of attacking anything which is large and real, and would resound with the shock. They do not attack the army as men do in France, or the judges as men do in Ireland, or the democracy itself as men did in England a hundred years ago. They attack something like the War Office—something, that is, which everybody attacks and nobody bothers to defend, something which is an old joke in fourth-rate comic papers. Just as a man shows he has a weak voice by straining it to shout, so they show the hopelessly unsensational nature of their minds when they really try to be sensational. With the whole world full of big and dubious institutions, with the whole wickedness of civilization staring them in the face, their idea of being bold and bright is to attack the War Office. They might as well start a campaign against the weather, or form a secret society in order to make jokes about mothers-in-law. Nor is it only from the point of view of particular amateurs of the sensational such as myself, that it is permissible to say, in the words of Cowper's Alexander Selkirk, that "their tameness is shocking to me." The whole modern world is pining for a genuinely sensational journalism. This has been discovered by that very able and honest journalist, Mr. Blatchford, who started his campaign against Christianity, warned on all sides, I believe, that it would ruin his paper, but who continued from an honourable sense of intellectual responsibility. He discovered, however, that while he had undoubtedly shocked his readers, he had also greatly advanced his newspaper. It was bought—first, by all the people who agreed with him and wanted to read it; and secondly, by all the people who disagreed with him, and wanted to write him letters. Those letters were voluminous (I helped, I am glad to say, to swell their volume), and they were generally inserted with a generous fulness. Thus was accidentally discovered (like the steam-engine) the great journalistic maxim — that if an editor can only make people angry enough, they will write half his newspaper for him for nothing.

Some hold that such papers as these are scarcely the proper objects of so serious a consideration; but that can scarcely be maintained from a political or ethical point of view. In this problem of the mildness and tameness of the Harmsworth mind there is mirrored the outlines of a much larger problem which is akin to it.

The Harmsworthian journalist begins with a worship of success and violence, and ends in sheer timidity and mediocrity. But he is not alone in this, nor does he come by this fate merely because he happens personally to be stupid. Every man, however brave, who begins by worshipping violence, must end in mere timidity. Every man, however wise, who begins by worshipping success, must end in mere mediocrity. This strange and paradoxical fate is involved, not in the individual, but in the philosophy, in the point of view. It is not the folly of the man which brings about this necessary fall; it is his wisdom. The worship of success is the only one out of all possible worships of which this is true, that its followers are foredoomed to become slaves and cowards. A man may be a hero for the sake of Mrs. Gallup's ciphers[53] or for the sake of human sacrifice, but not for the sake of success. For obviously a man may choose to fail because he loves Mrs. Gallup or human sacrifice; but he cannot choose to fail because he loves success. When the test of triumph is men's test of everything, they never endure long enough to triumph at all. As long as matters are really hopeful, hope is a mere flattery or platitude; it is only when everything is hopeless that hope begins to be a strength at all. Like all the Christian virtues, it is as unreasonable as it is indispensable.

It was through this fatal paradox in the nature of things that all these modern adventurers come at last to a sort of tedium and acquiescence. They desired strength; and to them to desire strength was to admire strength; to admire strength was simply to admire the

[53] Chesterton is referring to *The bi-lateral cypher of Sir Francis Bacon discovered in his works and deciphered by Mrs. Elizabeth Wells Gallup*, a book published in the United States in 1899.

status quo. They thought that he who wished to be strong ought to respect the strong. They did not realize the obvious verity that he who wishes to be strong must despise the strong. They sought to be everything, to have the whole force of the cosmos behind them, to have an energy that would drive the stars. But they did not realize the two great facts—first, that in the attempt to be everything the first and most difficult step is to be something; second, that the moment a man is something, he is essentially defying everything. The lower animals, say the men of science, fought their way up with a blind selfishness. If this be so, the only real moral of it is that our unselfishness, if it is to triumph, must be equally blind. The mammoth did not put his head on one side and wonder whether mammoths were a little out of date. Mammoths were at least as much up to date as the individual mammoth could make them. The great elk did not say, "Cloven hoofs are very much worn now." He polished his own weapons for his own use. But in the reasoning animal there has arisen a more horrible danger, that he may fail through perceiving his own failure. When modern sociologists talk of the necessity of accommodating one's self to the trend of the time, they forget that the trend of the time at its best consists entirely of people who will not accommodate themselves to anything. At its worst it consists of many millions of frightened creatures all accommodating themselves to a trend that is not there. And that is becoming more and more the situation of modern England. Every man speaks of public opinion, and means by public opinion, public opinion minus his opinion. Every man makes his contribution negative under the erroneous impression that the next man's contribution is positive. Every man surrenders his fancy to a general tone which is itself a surrender. And over all the heartless and fatuous unity spreads this new and wearisome and platitudinous press, incapable of invention, incapable of audacity, capable only of a servility all the more contemptible because it is not even a servility to the strong. But all who begin with force and conquest will end in this.

The chief characteristic of the "New Journalism" is simply that it is bad journalism. It is beyond all comparison the most shapeless, careless, and colourless work done in our day.

I read yesterday a sentence which should be written in letters of

gold and adamant; it is the very motto of the new philosophy of Empire. I found it (as the reader has already eagerly guessed) in *Pearson's
Magazine*, while I was communing (soul to soul) with Mr. C. Arthur
Pearson, whose first and suppressed name I am afraid is Chilperic. It
occurred in an article on the American Presidential Election. This is
the sentence, and every one should read it carefully, and roll it on the
tongue, till all the honey be tasted.

"A little sound common sense often goes further with an audience
of American working-men than much high-flown argument. A
speaker who, as he brought forward his points, hammered nails into
a board, won hundreds of votes for his side at the last Presidential
Election."

I do not wish to soil this perfect thing with comment; the words
of Mercury are harsh after the songs of Apollo. But just think for a
moment of the mind, the strange inscrutable mind, of the man who
wrote that, of the editor who approved it, of the people who are
probably impressed by it, of the incredible American working-man,
of whom, for all I know, it may be true. Think what their notion of
"common sense" must be! It is delightful to realize that you and I
are now able to win thousands of votes should we ever be engaged in
a Presidential Election, by doing something of this kind. For I suppose the nails and the board are not essential to the exhibition of
"common sense;" there may be variations. We may read—

"A little common sense impresses American working-men more
than high-flown argument. A speaker who, as he made his points,
pulled buttons off his waistcoat, won thousands of votes for his
side." Or, "Sound common sense tells better in America than high-
flown argument. Thus Senator Budge, who threw his false teeth in
the air every time he made an epigram, won the solid approval of
American working-men." Or again, "The sound common sense of a
gentleman from Earlswood, who stuck straws in his hair during the
progress of his speech, assured the victory of Mr. Roosevelt."

There are many other elements in this article on which I should
love to linger. But the matter which I wish to point out is that in
that sentence is perfectly revealed the whole truth of what our
Chamberlainites, hustlers, bustlers, Empire-builders, and strong,

silent men, really mean by "common sense." They mean knocking, with deafening noise and dramatic effect, meaningless bits of iron into a useless bit of wood.

A man goes on to an American platform and behaves like a mountebank fool with a board and a hammer; well, I do not blame him; I might even admire him. He may be a dashing and quite decent strategist. He may be a fine romantic actor, like Burke flinging the dagger on the floor.[54] He may even (for all I know) be a sublime mystic, profoundly impressed with the ancient meaning of the divine trade of the Carpenter, and offering to the people a parable in the form of a ceremony. All I wish to indicate is the abyss of mental confusion in which such wild ritualism can be called "sound common sense." And it is in that abyss of mental confusion, and in that alone, that the new Imperialism lives and moves and has its being. The whole glory and greatness of Mr. Chamberlain consists in this: that if a man hits the right nail on the head nobody cares where he hits it to or what it does. They care about the noise of the hammer, not about the silent grip of the nail. Before and throughout the African war, Mr. Chamberlain was always knocking in nails, with ringing decisiveness. But when we ask, "But what have these nails held together? Where is your carpentry? Where are your contented Outlanders? Where is your free South Africa? Where is your British prestige? What have your nails done?" then what answer is there? We must go back (with an affectionate sigh) to our Pearson for the answer to the question of what the nails have done: "The speaker who hammered nails into a board won thousands of votes."

Now the whole of this passage is admirably characteristic of the new journalism which Mr. Pearson represents, the new journalism which has just purchased the *Standard*.[55] To take one instance out of hundreds, the incomparable man with the board and nails is described

[54] Edmund Burke (1729–1796) was a vigorous opponent of the French Revolution. In a debate in the House of Commons on December 28, 1792, after mentioning that an order had been given at Birmingham for 3,000 daggers, he suddenly drew out a dagger and threw it on the floor, saying, "This is what you are to gain by an alliance with France."

[55] A newspaper bought by Pearson in 1904.

in the *Pearson's* article as calling out (as he smote the symbolic nail), "Lie number one. Nailed to the Mast! Nailed to the Mast!" In the whole office there was apparently no compositor or office-boy to point out that we speak of lies being nailed to the counter, and not to the mast. Nobody in the office knew that *Pearson's Magazine* was falling into a stale Irish bull, which must be as old as St. Patrick. This is the real and essential tragedy of the sale of the *Standard*. It is not merely that journalism is victorious over literature. It is that bad journalism is victorious over good journalism.

It is not that one article which we consider costly and beautiful is being ousted by another kind of article which we consider common or unclean. It is that of the same article a worse quality is preferred to a better. If you like popular journalism (as I do), you will know that *Pearson's Magazine* is poor and weak popular journalism. You will know it as certainly as you know bad butter. You will know as certainly that it is poor popular journalism as you know that the *Strand*, in the great days of Sherlock Holmes, was good popular journalism. Mr. Pearson has been a monument of this enormous banality. About everything he says and does there is something infinitely weak-minded. He clamours for home trades and employs foreign ones to print his paper. When this glaring fact is pointed out, he does not say that the thing was an oversight, like a sane man. He cuts it off with scissors, like a child of three. His very cunning is infantile. And like a child of three, he does not cut it quite off. In all human records I doubt if there is such an example of a profound simplicity in deception. This is the sort of intelligence which now sits in the seat of the sane and honourable old Tory journalism. If it were really the triumph of the tropical exuberance of the Yankee press, it would be vulgar, but still tropical. But it is not. We are delivered over to the bramble, and from the meanest of the shrubs comes the fire upon the cedars of Lebanon.

The only question now is how much longer the fiction will endure that journalists of this order represent public opinion. It may be doubted whether any honest and serious Tariff Reformer would for a moment maintain that there was any majority for Tariff Reform in the country comparable to the ludicrous preponderance which money has given it among the great dailies. The only inference is that for purposes of real public opinion the press is now a mere plutocratic oligarchy. Doubtless the public buys the wares of these men, for one reason or another. But there is no more reason to suppose that the public admires their politics than that the public admires the delicate philosophy of Mr. Crosse or the darker and sterner creed of Mr. Blackwell.[56] If these men are merely tradesmen, there is nothing to say except that there are plenty like them in the Battersea Park Road, and many much better. But if they make any sort of attempt to be politicians, we can only point out to them that they are not as yet even good journalists.

[56] The firm of Crosse and Blackwell manufactured (and still does) a wide variety of food products, especially condiments.

IX

THE MOODS OF MR. GEORGE MOORE

Mr. George Moore began his literary career by writing his personal confessions; nor is there any harm in this if he had not continued them for the remainder of his life. He is a man of genuinely forcible mind and of great command over a kind of rhetorical and fugitive conviction which excites and pleases. He is in a perpetual state of temporary honesty. He has admired all the most admirable modern eccentrics until they could stand it no longer. Everything he writes, it is to be fully admitted, has a genuine mental power. His account of his reason for leaving the Roman Catholic Church is possibly the most admirable tribute to that communion which has been written of late years. For the fact of the matter is, that the weakness which has rendered barren the many brilliancies of Mr. Moore is actually that weakness which the Roman Catholic Church is at its best in combating. Mr. Moore hates Catholicism because it breaks up the house of looking-glasses in which he lives. Mr. Moore does not dislike so much being asked to believe in the spiritual existence of miracles or sacraments, but he does fundamentally dislike being asked to believe in the actual existence of other people. Like his master Pater and all the aesthetes, his real quarrel with life is that it is not a dream that can be moulded by the dreamer. It is not the dogma of the reality of the other world that troubles him, but the dogma of the reality of this world.

The truth is that the tradition of Christianity (which is still the only coherent ethic of Europe) rests on two or three paradoxes or mysteries which can easily be impugned in argument and as easily justified in life. One of them, for instance, is the paradox of hope or faith—that the more hopeless is the situation the more hopeful must be the man. Stevenson understood this, and consequently Mr. Moore cannot understand Stevenson. Another is the paradox of charity or chivalry that the weaker a thing is the more it should be respected, that the more indefensible a thing is the more it should appeal to us for a certain kind of defence. Thackeray understood this, and therefore

Mr. Moore does not understand Thackeray. Now, one of these very practical and working mysteries in the Christian tradition, and one which the Roman Catholic Church, as I say, has done her best work in singling out, is the conception of the sinfulness of pride. Pride is a weakness in the character; it dries up laughter, it dries up wonder, it dries up chivalry and energy. The Christian tradition understands this; therefore Mr. Moore does not understand the Christian tradition.

For the truth is much stranger even than it appears in the formal doctrine of the sin of pride. It is not only true that humility is a much wiser and more vigorous thing than pride. It is also true that vanity is a much wiser and more vigorous thing than pride. Vanity is social—it is almost a kind of comradeship; pride is solitary and uncivilized. Vanity is active; it desires the applause of infinite multitudes; pride is passive, desiring only the applause of one person, which it already has. Vanity is humorous, and can enjoy the joke even of itself; pride is dull, and cannot even smile. And the whole of this difference is the difference between Stevenson and Mr. George Moore, who, as he informs us, has "brushed Stevenson aside."[57] I do not know where he has been brushed to, but wherever it is I fancy he is having a good time, because he had the wisdom to be vain, and not proud. Stevenson had a windy vanity; Mr. Moore has a dusty egoism. Hence Stevenson could amuse himself as well as us with his vanity; while the richest effects of Mr. Moore's absurdity are hidden from his eyes.

If we compare this solemn folly with the happy folly with which Stevenson belauds his own books and berates his own critics, we shall not find it difficult to guess why it is that Stevenson at least found a final philosophy of some sort to live by, while Mr. Moore is always walking the world looking for a new one. Stevenson had found that the secret of life lies in laughter and humility. Self is the gorgon. Vanity sees it in the mirror of other men and lives. Pride studies it for itself and is turned to stone.

It is necessary to dwell on this defect in Mr. Moore, because it is

[57] In *Confessions of a Young Man*, Moore criticized Stevenson for wasting his talent on "prettiness of style": "I will state frankly that Mr. R. L. Stevenson never wrote a line that failed to delight me; but he never wrote a book."

really the weakness of work which is not without its strength. Mr. Moore's egoism is not merely a moral weakness, it is a very constant and influential aesthetic weakness as well. We should really be much more interested in Mr. Moore if he were not quite so interested in himself. We feel as if we were being shown through a gallery of really fine pictures, into each of which, by some useless and discordant convention, the artist had represented the same figure in the same attitude. "The Grand Canal with a distant view of Mr. Moore," "Effect of Mr. Moore through a Scotch Mist," "Mr. Moore by Firelight," "Ruins of Mr. Moore by Moonlight," and so on, seems to be the endless series. He would no doubt reply that in such a book as this he intended to reveal himself. But the answer is that in such a book as this he does not succeed. One of the thousand objections to the sin of pride lies precisely in this, that self-consciousness of necessity destroys self-revelation. A man who thinks a great deal about himself will try to be many-sided, attempt a theatrical excellence at all points, will try to be an encyclopaedia of culture, and his own real personality will be lost in that false universalism. Thinking about himself will lead to trying to be the universe; trying to be the universe will lead to ceasing to be anything. If, on the other hand, a man is sensible enough to think only about the universe; he will think about it in his own individual way. He will keep virgin the secret of God; he will see the grass as no other man can see it, and look at a sun that no man has ever known. This fact is very practically brought out in Mr. Moore's "Confessions."[58] In reading them we do not feel the presence of a clean-cut personality like that of Thackeray and Matthew Arnold. We only read a number of quite clever and largely conflicting opinions which might be uttered by any clever person, but which we are called upon to admire specifically, because they are uttered by Mr. Moore. He is the only thread that connects Catholicism and Protestantism, realism and mysticism — he or rather his name. He is profoundly absorbed even in views he no longer holds, and he expects us to be. And he intrudes the capital "I" even where it need not be intruded — even where it weakens the force of a plain statement. Where another man would say, "It is a

[58] *Confessions of a Young Man* (1888).

fine day," Mr. Moore says, "Seen through my temperament, the day appeared fine." Where another man would say, "Milton has obviously a fine style," Mr. Moore would say, "As a stylist Milton had always impressed me." The Nemesis of this self-centred spirit is that of being totally ineffectual. Mr. Moore has started many interesting crusades, but he has abandoned them before his disciples could begin. Even when he is on the side of the truth he is as fickle as the children of falsehood. Even when he has found reality he cannot find rest. One Irish quality he has which no Irishman was ever without—pugnacity; and that is certainly a great virtue, especially in the present age. But he has not the tenacity of conviction which goes with the fighting spirit in a man like Bernard Shaw. His weakness of introspection and selfishness in all their glory cannot prevent him fighting; but they will always prevent him winning.

X

ON SANDALS AND SIMPLICITY

The great misfortune of the modern English is not at all that they are more boastful than other people (they are not); it is that they are boastful about those particular things which nobody can boast of without losing them. A Frenchman can be proud of being bold and logical, and still remain bold and logical. A German can be proud of being reflective and orderly, and still remain reflective and orderly. But an Englishman cannot be proud of being simple and direct, and still remain simple and direct. In the matter of these strange virtues, to know them is to kill them. A man may be conscious of being heroic or conscious of being divine, but he cannot (in spite of all the Anglo-Saxon poets) be conscious of being unconscious.

Now, I do not think that it can be honestly denied that some portion of this impossibility attaches to a class very different in their own opinion, at least, to the school of Anglo-Saxonism. I mean that school of the simple life, commonly associated with Tolstoy.[59] If a perpetual talk about one's own robustness leads to being less robust, it is even more true that a perpetual talking about one's own simplicity leads to being less simple. One great complaint, I think, must stand against the modern upholders of the simple life — the simple life in all its varied forms, from vegetarianism to the honourable consistency of the Doukhobors.[60] This complaint against them stands, that they would make us simple in the unimportant things, but complex in the important things. They would make us simple in the things that do not matter — that is, in diet, in costume, in etiquette, in economic system. But they would make us complex in

[59] Tolstoy underwent a conversion about 1876 to a doctrine of Christian love, nonviolence, and simplicity of life. He expounded this doctrine in a series of books, such as *What I Believe In* (1882), and put it into practice himself, abandoning his earthly goods.

[60] A Russian sect originating in the eighteenth century emphasizing the supreme authority of inner experience and rejecting all ecclesiastical and civil authority.

the things that do matter—in philosophy, in loyalty, in spiritual acceptance, and spiritual rejection. It does not so very much matter whether a man eats a grilled tomato or a plain tomato; it does very much matter whether he eats a plain tomato with a grilled mind. The only kind of simplicity worth preserving is the simplicity of the heart, the simplicity which accepts and enjoys. There may be a reasonable doubt as to what system preserves this; there can surely be no doubt that a system of simplicity destroys it. There is more simplicity in the man who eats caviar on impulse than in the man who eats grape-nuts on principle.

The chief error of these people is to be found in the very phrase to which they are most attached—"plain living and high thinking."[61] These people do not stand in need of, will not be improved by, plain living and high thinking. They stand in need of the contrary. They would be improved by high living and plain thinking. A little high living (I say, having a full sense of responsibility, a little high living) would teach them the force and meaning of the human festivities, of the banquet that has gone on from the beginning of the world. It would teach them the historic fact that the artificial is, if anything, older than the natural. It would teach them that the loving-cup is as old as any hunger. It would teach them that ritualism is older than any religion. And a little plain thinking would teach them how harsh and fanciful are the mass of their own ethics, how very civilized and very complicated must be the brain of the Tolstoyan who really believes it to be evil to love one's country and wicked to strike a blow.

A man approaches, wearing sandals and simple raiment, a raw tomato held firmly in his right hand, and says, "The affections of family and country alike are hindrances to the fuller development of human love;" but the plain thinker will only answer him, with a wonder not untinged with admiration, "What a great deal of trouble you must have taken in order to feel like that." High living will reject the tomato. Plain thinking will equally decisively reject the idea of the invariable sinfulness of war. High living will convince us that

[61] From Wordsworth's sonnet "Written in London, September, 1802".

nothing is more materialistic than to despise a pleasure as purely material. And plain thinking will convince us that nothing is more materialistic than to reserve our horror chiefly for material wounds.

The only simplicity that matters is the simplicity of the heart. If that be gone, it can be brought back by no turnips or cellular clothing; but only by tears and terror and the fires that are not quenched. If that remain, it matters very little if a few Early Victorian armchairs remain along with it. Let us put a complex *entrée* into a simple old gentleman; let us not put a simple *entrée* into a complex old gentleman. So long as human society will leave my spiritual inside alone, I will allow it, with a comparative submission, to work its wild will with my physical interior. I will submit to cigars. I will meekly embrace a bottle of Burgundy. I will humble myself to a hansom cab. If only by this means I may preserve to myself the virginity of the spirit, which enjoys with astonishment and fear. I do not say that these are the only methods of preserving it. I incline to the belief that there are others. But I will have nothing to do with simplicity which lacks the fear, the astonishment, and the joy alike. I will have nothing to do with the devilish vision of a child who is too simple to like toys.

The child is, indeed, in these, and many other matters, the best guide. And in nothing is the child so righteously childlike, in nothing does he exhibit more accurately the sounder order of simplicity, than in the fact that he sees everything with a simple pleasure, even the complex things. The false type of naturalness harps always on the distinction between the natural and the artificial. The higher kind of naturalness ignores that distinction. To the child the tree and the lamp-post are as natural and as artificial as each other; or rather, neither of them are natural but both supernatural. For both are splendid and unexplained. The flower with which God crowns the one, and the flame with which Sam the lamplighter crowns the other, are equally of the gold of fairy-tales. In the middle of the wildest fields the most rustic child is, ten to one, playing at steam-engines. And the only spiritual or philosophical objection to steam-engines is not that men pay for them or work at them, or make them very ugly, or even that men are killed by them; but merely that men do not play at them. The evil is that the childish poetry of clockwork does not remain. The wrong is not that engines are too much admired, but that they are not admired enough. The sin is not that engines are mechanical, but that men are mechanical.

In this matter, then, as in all the other matters treated in this book, our main conclusion is that it is a fundamental point of view, a philosophy or religion which is needed, and not any change in habit or social routine. The things we need most for immediate practical purposes are all abstractions. We need a right view of the human lot, a right view of the human society; and if we were living eagerly and angrily in the enthusiasm of those things, we should, *ipso facto*, be living simply in the genuine and spiritual sense. Desire and danger make every one simple. And to those who talk to us with interfering eloquence about Jaeger[62] and the pores of the skin, and about Plasmon[63] and the coats of the stomach, at them shall only be hurled the words that are hurled at fops and gluttons, "Take no thought what ye shall eat or what ye shall drink, or wherewithal ye shall be clothed. For after all these things do the Gentiles seek. But seek first the kingdom of God and His righteousness, and all these things shall be added unto you." Those amazing words are not only extraordinarily good, practical politics; they are also superlatively good hygiene. The one supreme way of making all those processes go right, the processes of health, and strength, and grace, and beauty, the one and only way of making certain of their accuracy, is to think about something else. If a man is bent on climbing into the seventh heaven, he may be quite easy about the pores of his skin. If he harnesses his waggon to a star, the process will have a most satisfactory effect upon the coats of his stomach. For the thing called "taking thought," the thing for which the best modern word is

[62] Dr. Gustav Jaeger, professor of zoology at Stuttgart, argued in a book translated under the title *Health Culture* that men would be far better off than they were if they dressed in clothes made from animal hair.

[63] The Army and Navy Stores catalogue for 1907 describes Plasmon as "a highly concentrated milk protein food; a soluble, digestible natural albumen, fully replacing meat diet". It came in various forms—Plasmon Tea, Plasmon Cocoa, Plasmon Oats, and so on. A *London Magazine* advertisement of 1913 declares modestly that it is a complete and perfect food, containing all the constituents needed to support life.

"rationalizing," is in its nature, inapplicable to all plain and urgent things. Men take thought and ponder rationalistically, touching remote things—things that only theoretically matter, such as the transit of Venus. But only at their peril can men rationalize about so practical a matter as health.

XI

SCIENCE AND THE SAVAGES

A permanent disadvantage of the study of folk-lore and kindred subjects is that the man of science can hardly be in the nature of things very frequently a man of the world. He is a student of nature; he is scarcely ever a student of human nature. And even where this difficulty is overcome, and he is in some sense a student of human nature, this is only a very faint beginning of the painful progress towards being human. For the study of primitive race and religion stands apart in one important respect from all, or nearly all, the ordinary scientific studies. A man can understand astronomy only by being an astronomer; he can understand entomology only by being an entomologist (or, perhaps, an insect); but he can understand a great deal of anthropology merely by being a man. He is himself the animal which he studies. Hence arises the fact which strikes the eye everywhere in the records of ethnology and folk-lore—the fact that the same frigid and detached spirit which leads to success in the study of astronomy or botany leads to disaster in the study of mythology or human origins. It is necessary to cease to be a man in order to do justice to a microbe; it is not necessary to cease to be a man in order to do justice to men. That same suppression of sympathies, that same waving away of intuitions or guess-work which make a man preternaturally clever in dealing with the stomach of a spider, will make him preternaturally stupid in dealing with the heart of man. He is making himself inhuman in order to understand humanity. An ignorance of the other world is boasted by many men of science; but in this matter their defect arises, not from ignorance of the other world, but from ignorance of this world. For the secrets about which anthropologists concern themselves can be best learnt, not from books or voyages, but from the ordinary commerce of man with man. The secret of why some savage tribe worships monkeys or the moon is not to be found even by travelling among those savages and taking down their answers in a note-book, although the cleverest man may pursue this course. The answer to the riddle is in England; it is in London; nay, it is in his own heart. When a man has discovered why men in Bond Street wear black hats he will at the same moment have discovered why men in Timbuctoo wear red feathers. The mystery in the heart of some savage war-dance should not be studied in books of scientific travel; it should be studied at a subscription ball. If a man desires to find out the origins of religions, let him not go to the Sandwich Islands; let him go to church. If a man wishes to know the origin of human society, to know what society, philosophically speaking, really is, let him not go into the British Museum; let him go into society.

This total misunderstanding of the real nature of ceremonial gives rise to the most awkward and dehumanized versions of the conduct of men in rude lands or ages. The man of science, not realizing that ceremonial is essentially a thing which is done without a reason, has to find a reason for every sort of ceremonial, and, as might be supposed, the reason is generally a very absurd one—absurd because it originates not in the simple mind of the barbarian, but in the sophisticated mind of the professor. The learned man will say, for instance, "The natives of Mumbojumbo Land believe that the dead man can eat, and will require food upon his journey to the other world. This is attested by the fact that they place food in the grave, and that any family not complying with this rite is the object of the anger of the priests and the tribe." To any one acquainted with humanity this way of talking is topsy-turvy. It is like saying, "The English in the twentieth century believed that a dead man could smell. This as attested by the fact that they always covered his grave with lilies, violets, or other flowers. Some priestly and tribal terrors were evidently attached to the neglect of this action, as we have records of several old ladies who were very much disturbed in mind because their wreaths had not arrived in time for the funeral." It may be of course that savages put food with a dead man because they think that a dead man can eat, or weapons with a dead man because they think that a dead man can fight. But personally I do not believe that they think anything of the kind. I believe they put food or weapons on the dead for the same reason that we put flowers, because it is an exceedingly natural and obvious thing to do. We do not understand, it is true, the emotion which makes us think it obvious and natural; but that is because, like all the important emotions of human existence, it is essentially irrational. We do not understand the savage for the same reason that the savage does not understand himself. And the savage does not understand himself for the same reason that we do not understand ourselves either.

The obvious truth is that the moment any matter has passed through the human mind it is finally and for ever spoilt for all purposes of science. It has become a thing incurably mysterious and infinite; this mortal has put on immortality. Even what we call our material desires are spiritual, because they are human. Science can analyse a pork-chop, and say how much of it is phosphorus and how much is protein; but science cannot analyse any man's wish for a pork-chop, and say how much of it is hunger, how much custom, how much nervous fancy, how much a haunting love of the beautiful. The man's desire for the pork-chop remains literally as mystical and ethereal as his desire for heaven. All attempts, therefore, at a science of any human things, at a science of history, a science of folklore, a science of sociology, are by their nature not merely hopeless, but crazy. You can no more be certain in economic history that a man's desire for money was merely a desire for money than you can be certain in hagiology that a saint's desire for God was merely a desire for God. And this kind of vagueness in the primary phenomena of the study is an absolutely final blow to anything in the nature of a science. Men can construct a science with very few instruments, or with very plain instruments; but no one on earth could construct a science with unreliable instruments. A man might work out the whole of mathematics with a handful of pebbles, but not with a handful of clay which was always falling apart into new fragments, and falling together into new combinations. A man might measure heaven and earth with a reed, but not with a growing reed.

As one of the enormous follies of folk-lore, let us take the case of the transmigration of stories, and the alleged unity of their source. Story after story the scientific mythologists have cut out of its place in history, and pinned side by side with similar stories in their museum of fables. The process is industrious, it is fascinating, and the whole of it rests on one of the plainest fallacies in the world. That a story has been told all over the place at some time or other, not only does not prove that it never really happened; it does not even faintly indicate or make slightly more probable that it never happened. That a large number of fishermen have falsely asserted that they have caught a pike two feet long, does not in the least affect the question of whether any one ever really did so. That numberless journalists announce a Franco-German war merely for money is no evidence one way or the other upon the dark question of whether such a war ever occurred. Doubtless in a few hundred years the innumerable Franco-German wars that did not happen will have cleared the scientific mind of any belief in the legendary war of '70 which did. But that will be because if folk-lore students remain at all, their nature will be unchanged; and their services to folk-lore will be still as they are at present, greater than they know. For in truth these men do something far more godlike than studying legends; they create them.

There are two kinds of stories which the scientists say cannot be true, because everybody tells them. The first class consists of the stories which are told everywhere, because they are somewhat odd or clever; there is nothing in the world to prevent their having happened to somebody as an adventure any more than there is anything to prevent their having occurred, as they certainly did occur, to somebody as an idea. But they are not likely to have happened to many people. The second class of their "myths"consist of the stories that are told everywhere for the simple reason that they happen everywhere. Of the first class, for instance, we might take such an example as the story of William Tell, now generally ranked among legends upon the sole ground that it is found in the tales of other peoples. Now, it is obvious that this was told everywhere because whether true or fictitious it is what is called "a good story;" it is odd, exciting, and it has a climax. But to suggest that some such eccentric incident can never have happened in the whole history of archery, or that it did not happen to any particular person of whom it is told, is stark impudence. The idea of shooting at a mark attached to some valuable or beloved person is an idea doubtless that might easily have occurred to any inventive poet. But it is also an idea that might easily occur to any boastful archer. It might be one of the fantastic caprices of some story-teller. It might equally well be one of the fantastic caprices of some tyrant. It might occur first in real life and afterwards occur in legends. Or it might just as well occur first in legends and afterwards occur in real life. If no apple has ever been shot off a boy's head from the beginning of the world, it may be done to-morrow morning, and by somebody who has never heard of William Tell.

This type of tale, indeed, may be pretty fairly paralleled with the ordinary anecdote terminating in a repartee or an Irish bull. Such a retort as the famous "Je ne vois pas la necessité" we have all seen attributed to Talleyrand, to Voltaire, to Henri Quatre, to an anonymous judge, and so on. But this variety does not in any way make it more likely that the thing was never said at all. It is highly likely that it was really said by somebody unknown. It is highly likely that it was really said by Talleyrand. In any case, it is not any more difficult to believe that the *mot* might have occurred to a man in conversation than to a man writing memoirs. It might have occurred to any of the men I have mentioned. But there is this point of distinction about it, that it is not likely to have occurred to all of them. And this is where the first class of so-called myth differs from the second to which I have previously referred. For there is a second class of incident found to be common to the stories of five or six heroes, say to Sigurd,[64] to Hercules, to Rustem,[65] to the Cid,[66] and so on. And the peculiarity of this myth is that not only is it highly reasonable to imagine that it really happened to one hero, but it is highly reasonable to imagine that it really happened to all of them. Such a story, for instance, is that of a great man having his strength swayed or

[64] An English version of the Icelandic saga dealing with Sigurd the Volsung was published by William Morris in 1876.

[65] A great Persian national hero, supposed to have lived and fought—always victoriously—over several centuries. Matthew Arnold's "Sohrab and Rustum" (1853) tells how he unwittingly fought against and killed his own son. (Chesterton's spelling is Rustem. Arnold's is Rustum.)

[66] A Spanish hero who died in 1099 and about whom many legends sprang up. The twelfth-century *Poema del Cid* is an epic account of these.

thwarted by the mysterious weakness of a woman. The anecdotal story, the story of William Tell, is as I have said, popular, because it is peculiar. But this kind of story, the story of Samson and Delilah, of Arthur and Guinevere, is obviously popular because it is not peculiar. It is popular as good, quiet fiction is popular, because it tells the truth about people. If the ruin of Samson by a woman, and the ruin of Hercules by a woman, have a common legendary origin, it is gratifying to know that we can also explain, as a fable, the ruin of Nelson[67] by a woman and the ruin of Parnell[68] by a woman. And, indeed, I have no doubt whatever that, some centuries hence, the students of folk-lore will refuse altogether to believe that Elizabeth Barrett eloped with Robert Browning, and will prove their point up to the hilt by the unquestionable fact that the whole fiction of the period was full of such elopements from end to end.

Possibly the most pathetic of all the delusions of the modern students of primitive belief is the notion they have about the thing they call anthropomorphism. They believe that primitive men attributed phenomena to a god in human form in order to explain them, because his mind in its sullen limitation could not reach any further than his own clownish existence. The thunder was called the voice of a man, the lightning the eyes of a man, because by this explanation they were made more reasonable and comfortable. The final cure for all this kind of philosophy is to walk down a lane at night. Any one who does so will discover very quickly that men pictured something semi-human at the back of all things, not because such a thought was natural, but because it was supernatural; not because it made things more comprehensible, but because it made them a hundred times more incomprehensible and mysterious. For a man walking down a lane at night can see the conspicuous fact that as long as nature keeps to her own course, she has no power with us at all. As long as a tree is a tree, it is a top-heavy monster with a

[67] The reference is to Nelson's involvement with Lady Hamilton.
[68] Charles Stewart Parnell (1846–1891), "the uncrowned king of Ireland", was leader of the Irish Home Rule Party. His political career came to a sudden end in 1890 when he was cited as co-respondent in a divorce case brought by Captain O'Shea.

hundred arms, a thousand tongues, and only one leg. But so long as a tree is a tree, it does not frighten us at all. It begins to be something alien, to be something strange, only when it looks like ourselves. When a tree really looks like a man our knees knock under us. And when the whole universe looks like a man we fall on our faces.

XII

PAGANISM AND MR. LOWES DICKINSON[69]

Of the New Paganism (or neo-Paganism), as it was preached flam-
boyantly by Mr. Swinburne or delicately by Walter Pater, there is
no necessity to take any very grave account, except as a thing which
left behind it incomparable exercises in the English language. The
New Paganism is no longer new, and it never at any time bore the
smallest resemblance to Paganism. The ideas about the ancient civilization which it has left loose in the public mind are certainly extraordinary enough. The term "pagan" is continually used in fiction
and light literature as meaning a man without any religion, whereas
a pagan was generally a man with about half a dozen. The pagans,
according to this notion, were continually crowning themselves
with flowers and dancing about in an irresponsible state, whereas, if
there were two things that the best pagan civilization did honestly
believe in, they were a rather too rigid dignity and a much too rigid
responsibility. Pagans are depicted as above all things inebriate and
lawless, whereas they were above all things reasonable and respectable. They are praised as disobedient when they had only one great
virtue — civic obedience. They are envied and admired as shamelessly
happy when they had only one great sin — despair.

Mr. Lowes Dickinson, the most pregnant and provocative of recent writers on this and similar subjects, is far too solid a man to
have fallen into this old error of the mere anarchy of Paganism. In
order to make hay of that Hellenic enthusiasm which has as its ideal
mere appetite and egotism, it is not necessary to know much philosophy, but merely to know a little Greek. Mr. Lowes Dickinson
knows a great deal of philosophy, and also a great deal of Greek, and
his error, if error he has, is not that of the crude hedonist. But the
contrast which he offers between Christianity and Paganism in the
matter of moral ideals — a contrast which he states very ably in a

[69] Goldsworthy Lowes Dickinson, historian and man of letters (1862–1932) wrote
The Greek View of Life in 1896.

paper called "How long halt ye?" which appeared in the *Independent Review*—does, I think, contain an error of a deeper kind. According to him, the ideal of Paganism was not, indeed, a mere frenzy of lust and liberty and caprice, but was an ideal of full and satisfied humanity. According to him, the ideal of Christianity was the ideal of asceticism. When I say that I think this idea wholly wrong as a matter of philosophy and history, I am not talking for the moment about any ideal Christianity of my own, or even of any primitive Christianity undefiled by after events. I am not, like so many modern Christian idealists, basing my case upon certain things which Christ said. Neither am I, like so many other Christian idealists, basing my case upon certain things that Christ forgot to say. I take historic Christianity with all its sins upon its head; I take it, as I would take Jacobinism, or Mormonism, or any other mixed or unpleasing human product, and I say that the meaning of its action was not to be found in asceticism. I say that its point of departure from Paganism was not asceticism. I say that its point of difference with the modern world was not asceticism. I say that St. Simeon Stylites[70] had not his main inspiration in asceticism. I say that the main Christian impulse cannot be described as asceticism, even in the ascetics.

Let me set about making the matter clear. There is one broad fact about the relations of Christianity and Paganism which is so simple that many will smile at it, but which is so important that all moderns forget it. The primary fact about Christianity and Paganism is that one came after the other. Mr. Lowes Dickinson speaks of them as if they were parallel ideals—even speaks as if Paganism were the newer of the two, and the more fitted for a new age. He suggests that the Pagan ideal will be the ultimate good of man; but if that is so, we must at least ask with more curiosity than he allows for, why it was that man actually found his ultimate good on earth under the stars, and threw it away again. It is this extraordinary enigma to which I propose to attempt an answer.

There is only one thing in the modern world that has been face to face with Paganism; there is only one thing in the modern world

[70] Saint Simeon Stylites (d. 459), an ascetic who spent the last thirty years of his life on top of a 72-foot pillar.

which in that sense knows anything about Paganism: and that is Christianity. That fact is really the weak point in the whole of that hedonistic neo-Paganism of which I have spoken. All that genuinely remains of the ancient hymns or the ancient dances of Europe, all that has honestly come to us from the festivals of Phoebus or Pan, is to be found in the festivals of the Christian Church. If any one wants to hold the end of a chain which really goes back to the heathen mysteries, he had better take hold of a festoon of flowers at Easter or a string of sausages at Christmas. Everything else in the modern world is of Christian origin, even everything that seems most anti-Christian. The French Revolution is of Christian origin. The newspaper is of Christian origin. The anarchists are of Christian origin. Physical science is of Christian origin. The attack on Christianity is of Christian origin. There is one thing, and one thing only, in existence at the present day which can in any sense accurately be said to be of pagan origin, and that is Christianity.

The real difference between Paganism and Christianity is perfectly summed up in the difference between the pagan, or natural, virtues, and those three virtues of Christianity which the Church of Rome calls virtues of grace. The pagan, or rational, virtues are such things as justice and temperance, and Christianity has adopted them. The three mystical virtues which Christianity has not adopted, but invented, are faith, hope, and charity. Now much easy and foolish Christian rhetoric could easily be poured out upon those three words, but I desire to confine myself to the two facts which are evident about them. The first evident fact (in marked contrast to the delusion of the dancing pagan) — the first evident fact, I say, is that the pagan virtues, such as justice and temperance, are the sad virtues, and that the mystical virtues of faith, hope, and charity are the gay and exuberant virtues. And the second evident fact, which is even more evident, is the fact that the pagan virtues are the reasonable virtues, and that the Christian virtues of faith, hope, and charity are in their essence as unreasonable as they can be.

As the word "unreasonable" is open to misunderstanding, the matter may be more accurately put by saying that each one of these Christian or mystical virtues involves a paradox in its own nature, and that this is not true of any of the typically pagan or rationalist virtues. Justice consists in finding out a certain thing due to a certain man and giving it to him. Temperance consists in finding out the proper limit of a particular indulgence and adhering to that. But charity means pardoning what is unpardonable, or it is no virtue at all. Hope means hoping when things are hopeless, or it is no virtue at all. And faith means believing the incredible, or it is no virtue at all.

It is somewhat amusing, indeed, to notice the difference between the fate of these three paradoxes in the fashion of the modern mind. Charity is a fashionable virtue in our time; it is lit up by the gigantic firelight of Dickens. Hope is a fashionable virtue to-day; our attention has been arrested for it by the sudden and silver trumpet of Stevenson. But faith is unfashionable, and it is customary on every side to cast against it the fact that it is a paradox. Everybody mockingly repeats the famous childish definition that faith is "the power of believing that which we know to be untrue." Yet it is not one atom more paradoxical than hope or charity. Charity is the power of defending that which we know to be indefensible. Hope is the power of being cheerful in circumstances which we know to be desperate. It is true that there is a state of hope which belongs to bright prospects and the morning; but that is not the virtue of hope. The virtue of hope exists only in earthquake and eclipse. It is true that there is a thing crudely called charity, which means charity to the deserving poor; but charity to the deserving is not charity at all, but justice. It is the undeserving who require it, and the ideal either does not exist at all, or exists wholly for them. For practical purposes it is at the hopeless moment that we require the hopeful man, and the virtue either does not exist at all, or begins to exist at that moment. Exactly at the instant when hope ceases to be reasonable it begins to be useful.

Now the old pagan world went perfectly straightforward until it discovered that going straightforward is an enormous mistake. It was nobly and beautifully reasonable, and discovered in its death-pang this lasting and valuable truth, a heritage for the ages, that reasonableness will not do. The pagan age was truly an Eden or golden age, in this essential sense, that it is not to be recovered. And it is not to be recovered in this sense again that, while we are certainly jollier than the pagans, and much more right than the pagans, there is not one of us who can, by the utmost stretch of energy, be so sensible as the pagans. That naked innocence of the intellect cannot be recovered by any man after Christianity; and for this excellent reason, that every man after Christianity knows it to be misleading. Let me take an example, the first that occurs to the mind, of this impossible plainness in the pagan point of view. The greatest tribute to Christianity in the modern world is Tennyson's "Ulysses." The poet reads into the story of Ulysses the conception of an incurable desire to wander. But the real Ulysses does not desire to wander at all. He desires to get home. He displays his heroic and unconquerable qualities in resisting the misfortunes which baulk him; but that is all. There is no love of adventure for its own sake; that is a Christian product. There is no love of Penelope for her own sake; that is a Christian product. Everything in that old world would appear to have been clean and obvious. A good man was a good man; a bad man was a bad man. For this reason they had no charity; for charity is a reverent agnosticism towards the complexity of the soul. For this reason they had no such thing as the art of fiction, the novel; for the novel is a creation of the mystical idea of charity. For them a pleasant landscape was pleasant, and an unpleasant landscape unpleasant. Hence they had no idea of romance; for romance consists in thinking a thing more delightful because it is dangerous; it is a Christian idea. In a word, we cannot reconstruct or even imagine the beautiful and astonishing pagan world. It was a world in which common sense was really common.

My general meaning touching the three virtues of which I have spoken will now, I hope, be sufficiently clear. They are all three paradoxical, they are all three practical, and they are all three paradoxical because they are practical. It is the stress of ultimate need, and a terrible knowledge of things as they are, which led men to set up these riddles, and to die for them. Whatever may be the meaning of the contradiction, it is the fact that the only kind of hope that is of any use in a battle is a hope that denies arithmetic. Whatever may be the meaning of the contradiction, it is the fact that the only kind of charity which any weak spirit wants, or which any generous spirit feels, is the charity which forgives the sins that are like scarlet.

Whatever may be the meaning of faith, it must always mean a certainty about something we cannot prove. Thus, for instance, we believe by faith in the existence of other people.

But there is another Christian virtue, a virtue far more obviously and historically connected with Christianity, which will illustrate even better the connection between paradox and practical necessity. This virtue cannot be questioned in its capacity as a historical symbol; certainly Mr. Lowes Dickinson will not question it. It has been the boast of hundreds of the champions of Christianity. It has been the taunt of hundreds of the opponents of Christianity. It is, in essence, the basis of Mr. Lowes Dickinson's whole distinction between Christianity and Paganism. I mean, of course, the virtue of humility. I admit, of course, most readily, that a great deal of false Eastern humility (that is, of strictly ascetic humility) mixed itself with the main stream of European Christianity. We must not forget that when we speak of Christianity we are speaking of a whole continent for about a thousand years. But of this virtue even more than of the other three, I would maintain the general proposition adopted above. Civilization discovered Christian humility for the same urgent reason that it discovered faith and charity—that is, because Christian civilization had to discover it or die.

The great psychological discovery of Paganism, which turned it into Christianity, can be expressed with some accuracy in one phrase. The pagan set out, with admirable sense, to enjoy himself. By the end of his civilization he had discovered that a man cannot enjoy himself and continue to enjoy anything else. Mr. Lowes Dickinson has pointed out in words too excellent to need any further elucidation, the absurd shallowness of those who imagine that the pagan enjoyed himself only in a materialistic sense. Of course, he enjoyed himself, not only intellectually even, he enjoyed himself morally, he enjoyed himself spiritually. But it was himself that he was enjoying; on the face of it, a very natural thing to do. Now, the psychological discovery is merely this, that whereas it had been supposed that the fullest possible enjoyment is to be found by extending our ego to infinity, the truth is that the fullest possible enjoyment is to be found by reducing our ego to zero.

Humility is the thing which is for ever renewing the earth and the stars. It is humility, and not duty, which preserves the stars from wrong, from the unpardonable wrong of casual resignation; it is through humility that the most ancient heavens for us are fresh and strong. The curse that came before history has laid on us all a tendency to be weary of wonders. If we saw the sun for the first time it would be the most fearful and beautiful of meteors. Now that we see it for the hundredth time we call it, in the hideous and blasphemous phrase of Wordsworth, "the light of common day." We are inclined to increase our claims. We are inclined to demand six suns, to demand a blue sun, to demand a green sun. Humility is perpetually putting us back in the primal darkness. There all light is lightning, startling and instantaneous. Until we understand that original dark, in which we have neither sight nor expectation, we can give no hearty and childlike praise to the splendid sensationalism of things. The terms "pessimism" and "optimism," like most modern terms, are unmeaning. But if they can be used in any vague sense as meaning something, we may say that in this great fact pessimism is the very basis of optimism. The man who destroys himself creates the universe. To the humble man, and to the humble man alone, the sun is really a sun; to the humble man, and to the humble man alone, the sea is really a sea. When he looks at all the faces in the street, he does not only realize that men are alive, he realizes with a dramatic pleasure that they are not dead.

I have not spoken of another aspect of the discovery of humility as a psychological necessity, because it is more commonly insisted on, and is in itself more obvious. But it is equally clear that humility is a permanent necessity as a condition of effort and self-examination. It is one of the deadly fallacies of Jingo politics[71] that a nation is stronger for despising other nations. As a matter of fact, the strongest nations are those, like Prussia or Japan, which began from very mean beginnings, but have not been too proud to sit at the feet of the foreigner and learn everything from him. Almost every obvious

[71] Chauvinism or extravagant nationalism, from a song which became popular with supporters of the belligerent British policy toward Russia in a dispute of 1878:

> We don't want to fight, but by Jingo! if we do,
> We've got the ships, we've got the men, and the money too.

and direct victory has been the victory of the plagiarist. This is, indeed, only a very paltry by-product of humility, but it is a product of humility, and, therefore, it is successful. Prussia had no Christian humility in its internal arrangements; hence its internal arrangements were miserable. But it had enough Christian humility slavishly to copy France (even down to Frederick the Great's poetry), and that which it had the humility to copy it had ultimately the honour to conquer. The case of the Japanese is even more obvious; their only Christian and their only beautiful quality is that they have humbled themselves to be exalted. All this aspect of humility, however, as connected with the matter of effort and striving for a standard set above us, I dismiss as having been sufficiently pointed out by almost all idealistic writers.

It may be worth while, however, to point out the interesting disparity in the matter of humility between the modern notion of the strong man and the actual records of strong men. Carlyle objected to the statement that no man could be a hero to his valet. Every sympathy can be extended towards him in the matter if he merely or mainly meant that the phrase was a disparagement of hero-worship. Hero-worship is certainly a generous and human impulse; the hero may be faulty, but the worship can hardly be. It may be that no man would be a hero to his valet. But any man would be a valet to his hero. But in truth both the proverb itself and Carlyle's stricture upon it ignore the most essential matter at issue. The ultimate psychological truth is not that no man is a hero to his valet. The ultimate psychological truth, the foundation of Christianity, is that no man is a hero to himself. Cromwell, according to Carlyle, was a strong man. According to Cromwell, he was a weak one.

The weak point in the whole of Carlyle's case for aristocracy lies, indeed, in his most celebrated phrase. Carlyle said that men were mostly fools. Christianity, with a surer and more reverent realism, says that they are all fools. This doctrine is sometimes called the doctrine of original sin. It may also be described as the doctrine of the equality of men. But the essential point of it is merely this, that whatever primary and far-reaching moral dangers affect any man, affect all men. All men can be criminals, if tempted; all men can be heroes, if inspired. And this doctrine does away altogether with Carlyle's pathetic belief (or any one else's pathetic belief) in "the wise few." There are no wise few. Every aristocracy that has ever existed has behaved, in all essential points, exactly like a small mob. Every oligarchy is merely a knot of men in the street—that is to say, it is very jolly, but not infallible. And no oligarchies in the world's history have ever come off so badly in practical affairs as the very proud oligarchies—the oligarchy of Poland, the oligarchy of Venice. And the armies that have most swiftly and suddenly broken their enemies in pieces have been the religious armies—the Moslem Armies, for instance, or the Puritan Armies. And a religious army may, by its nature, be defined as an army in which every man is taught not to exalt but to abase himself. Many modern Englishmen talk of themselves as the sturdy descendents of their sturdy Puritan fathers. As a fact, they would run away from a cow. If you asked one of their Puritan fathers, if you asked Bunyan, for instance, whether he was sturdy, he would have answered, with tears, that he was as weak as water. And because of this he would have borne tortures. And this virtue of humility, while being practical enough to win battles, will always be paradoxical enough to puzzle pedants. It is at one with the virtue of charity in this respect. Every generous person will admit that the one kind of sin which charity should cover is the sin which is inexcusable. And every generous person will equally agree that the one kind of pride which is wholly damnable is the pride of the man who has something to be proud of. The pride which, proportionally speaking, does not hurt the character, is the pride in things which reflect no credit on the person at all. Thus it does a man no harm to be proud of his country, and comparatively little harm to be proud of his remote ancestors. It does him more harm to be proud of having made money, because in that he has a little more reason for pride. It does him more harm still to be proud of what is nobler than money—intellect. And it does him most harm of all to value himself for the most valuable thing on earth—goodness. The man who is proud of what is really creditable to him is the Pharisee, the man whom Christ Himself could not forbear to strike.

My objection to Mr. Lowes Dickinson and the reassertors of the pagan ideal is, then, this. I accuse them of ignoring definite human discoveries in the moral world, discoveries as definite, though not as material, as the discovery of the circulation of the blood. We cannot go back to an ideal of reason and sanity. For mankind has discovered that reason does not lead to sanity. We cannot go back to an ideal of pride and enjoyment. For mankind has discovered that pride does not lead to enjoyment. I do not know by what extraordinary mental accident modern writers so constantly connect the idea of progress with the idea of independent thinking. Progress is obviously the antithesis of independent thinking. For under independent or individualistic thinking, every man starts at the beginning, and goes, in all probability, just as far as his father before him. But if there really be anything of the nature of progress, it must mean, above all things, the careful study and assumption of the whole of the past. I accuse Mr. Lowes Dickinson and his school of reaction in the only real sense. If he likes, let him ignore these great historic mysteries — the mystery of charity, the mystery of chivalry, the mystery of faith. If he likes, let him ignore the plough or the printing-press. But if we do revive and pursue the pagan ideal of a simple and rational self-completion we shall end — where Paganism ended. I do not mean that we shall end in destruction. I mean that we shall end in Christianity.

XIII

CELTS AND CELTOPHILES

Science in the modern world has many uses; its chief use, however, is to provide long words to cover the errors of the rich. The word "kleptomania" is a vulgar example of what I mean. It is on a par with that strange theory, always advanced when a wealthy or prominent person is in the dock, that exposure is more of a punishment for the rich than for the poor. Of course, the very reverse is the truth. Exposure is more of a punishment for the poor than for the rich. The richer a man is the easier it is for him to be a tramp. The richer a man is the easier it is for him to be popular and generally respected in the Cannibal Islands. But the poorer a man is the more likely it is that he will have to use his past life whenever he wants to get a bed for the night. Honour is a luxury for aristocrats, but it is a necessity for hall-porters. This is a secondary matter, but it is an example of the general proposition I offer — the proposition that an enormous amount of modern ingenuity is expended on finding defences for the indefensible conduct of the powerful. As I have said above, these defences generally exhibit themselves most emphatically in the form of appeals to physical science. And of all the forms in which science, or pseudo-science, has come to the rescue of the rich and stupid, there is none so singular as the singular invention of the theory of races.

When a wealthy nation like the English discovers the perfectly patent fact that it is making a ludicrous mess of the government of a poorer nation like the Irish, it pauses for a moment in consternation, and then begins to talk about Celts and Teutons. As far as I can understand the theory, the Irish are Celts and the English are Teutons. Of course, the Irish are not Celts any more than the English are Teutons. I have not followed the ethnological discussion with much energy, but the last scientific conclusion which I read inclined on the whole to the summary that the English were mainly Celtic and the Irish mainly Teutonic. But no man alive, with even the glimmering of a real scientific sense, would ever dream of applying the terms "Celtic" or "Teutonic" to either of them in any positive or useful sense.

That sort of thing must be left to people who talk about the Anglo-Saxon race, and extend the expression to America. How much of the blood of the Angles and Saxons (whoever they were) there remains in our mixed British, Roman, German, Dane, Norman, and Picard stock is a matter only interesting to wild antiquaries. And how much of the diluted blood can possibly remain in that roaring whirlpool of America into which a cataract of Swedes, Jews, Germans, Irishmen, and Italians is perpetually pouring, is a matter only interesting to lunatics. It would have been wiser for the English governing class to have called upon some other god. All other gods, however weak and warring, at least boast of being constant. But science boasts of being in a flux for ever; boasts of being unstable as water.

And England and the English governing class never did call on this absurd deity of race until it seemed, for an instant, that they had no other god to call on. All the most genuine Englishmen in history would have yawned or laughed in your face if you had begun to talk about Anglo-Saxons. If you had attempted to substitute the ideal of race for the ideal of nationality, I really do not like to think what they would have said. I certainly should not like to have been the officer of Nelson who suddenly discovered his French blood on the eve of Trafalgar. I should not like to have been the Norfolk or Suffolk gentleman who had to expound to Admiral Blake[72] by what demonstrable ties of genealogy he was irrevocably bound to the Dutch. The truth of the whole matter is very simple. Nationality exists, and has nothing in the world to do with race. Nationality is a thing like a church or a secret society; it is a product of the human soul and will; it is a spiritual product. And there are men in the modern world who would think anything and do anything rather than admit that anything could be a spiritual product.

A nation, however, as it confronts the modern world, is a purely

[72] Robert Blake (1599–1657), admiral of the fleet, distinguished himself in the Dutch war which broke out in 1652.

spiritual product. Sometimes it has been born in independence, like Scotland. Sometimes it has been born in dependence, in subjugation, like Ireland. Sometimes it is a large thing cohering out of many smaller things, like Italy. Sometimes it is a small thing breaking away from larger things, like Poland. But in each and every case its quality is purely spiritual, or, if you will, purely psychological. It is a moment when five men become a sixth man. Every one knows it who has ever founded a club. It is a moment when five places become one place. Every one must know it who has ever had to repel an invasion. Mr. Timothy Healy,[73] the most serious intellect in the present House of Commons, summed up nationality to perfection when he simply called it something for which people will die. As he excellently said in reply to Lord Hugh Cecil, "No one, not even the noble lord, would die for the meridian of Greenwich." And that is the great tribute to its purely psychological character. It is idle to ask why Greenwich should not cohere in this spiritual manner while Athens or Sparta did. It is like asking why a man falls in love with one woman and not with another.

Now, of this great spiritual coherence, independent of external circumstances, or of race, or of any obvious physical thing, Ireland is the most remarkable example. Rome conquered nations, but Ireland has conquered races. The Norman has gone there and become Irish, the Scotchman has gone there and become Irish, the Spaniard has gone there and become Irish, even the bitter soldier of Cromwell has gone there and become Irish. Ireland, which did not exist even politically, has been stronger than all the races that existed scientifically. The purest Germanic blood, the purest Norman blood, the purest blood of the passionate Scotch patriot, has not been so attractive as a nation without a flag. Ireland, unrecognized and oppressed, has easily absorbed races, as such trifles are easily absorbed. She has easily disposed of physical science, as such superstitions are easily disposed of. Nationality in its weakness has been stronger than ethnology in its strength. Five triumphant races have been absorbed, have been defeated by a defeated nationality.

This being the true and strange glory of Ireland, it is impossible to

[73] Timothy Healy (1855–1931) Irish politician, advocate of home rule for Ireland, and first Governor-General of the Irish Free State, 1922–1928.

hear without impatience of the attempt so constantly made among her modern sympathizers to talk about Celts and Celticism. Who were the Celts? I defy anybody to say. Who are the Irish? I defy any one to be indifferent, or to pretend not to know. Mr. W. B. Yeats, the great Irish genius who has appeared in our time, shows his own admirable penetration in discarding altogether the argument from a Celtic race. But he does not wholly escape, and his followers hardly ever escape, the general objection to the Celtic argument. The tendency of that argument is to represent the Irish or the Celts as a strange and separate race, as a tribe of eccentrics in the modern world immersed in dim legends and fruitless dreams. Its tendency is to exhibit the Irish as odd, because they see the fairies. Its trend is to make the Irish seem weird and wild because they sing old songs and join in strange dances. But this is quite an error; indeed, it is the opposite of the truth. It is the English who are odd because they do not see the fairies. It is the inhabitants of Kensington who are weird and wild because they do not sing old songs and join in strange dances. In all this the Irish are not in the least strange and separate, are not in the least Celtic, as the word is commonly and popularly used. In all this the Irish are simply an ordinary sensible nation, living the life of any other ordinary and sensible nation which has not been either sodden with smoke or oppressed by money-lenders, or otherwise corrupted with wealth and science. There is nothing Celtic about having legends. It is merely human. The Germans, who are (I suppose) Teutonic, have hundreds of legends, wherever it happens that the Germans are human. There is nothing Celtic about loving poetry; the English loved poetry more, perhaps, than any other people before they came under the shadow of the chimney-pot and the shadow of the chimney-pot hat.[74] It is not Ireland which is mad and mystic; it is Manchester which is mad and mystic, which is incredible, which is a wild exception among human things. Ireland has no need to play the silly game of the science of races; Ireland has no need to pretend to be a tribe of visionaries apart. In the matter of visions, Ireland is more than a nation, it is a model nation.

[74] Top hat, high silk hat.

XIV

ON CERTAIN MODERN WRITERS AND
THE INSTITUTION OF THE FAMILY

The family may fairly be considered, one would think, an ultimate human institution. Every one would admit that it has been the main cell and central unit of almost all societies hitherto, except, indeed, such societies as that of Lacedaemon,[75] which went in for "efficiency," and has, therefore, perished, and left not a trace behind. Christianity, even enormous as was its revolution, did not alter this ancient and savage sanctity; it merely reversed it. It did not deny the trinity of father, mother, and child. It merely read it backwards, making it run child, mother, father. This it called, not the family, but the Holy Family, for many things are made holy by being turned upside down. But some sages of our own decadence have made a serious attack on the family. They have impugned it, as I think wrongly; and its defenders have defended it, and defended it wrongly. The common defence of the family is that, amid the stress and fickleness of life, it is peaceful, pleasant, and at one. But there is another defence of the family which is possible, and to me evident; this defence is that the family is not peaceful and not pleasant and not at one.

It is not fashionable to say much nowadays of the advantages of the small community. We are told that we must go in for large empires and large ideas. There is one advantage, however, in the small state, the city, or the village, which only the wilfully blind can overlook. The man who lives in a small community lives in a much larger world. He knows much more of the fierce varieties and uncompromising divergences of men. The reason is obvious. In a large community we can choose our companions. In a small community our companions are chosen for us. Thus in all extensive and highly civilized societies groups come into existence founded upon what is

[75] Sparta, which produced conquerors and military rulers, never intellectual and cultural leaders.

called sympathy, and shut out the real world more sharply than the gates of a monastery. There is nothing really narrow about the clan; the thing which is really narrow is the clique. The men of the clan live together because they all wear the same tartan or are all descended from the same sacred cow; but in their souls, by the divine luck of things, there will always be more colours than in any tartan. But the men of the clique live together because they have the same kind of soul, and their narrowness is a narrowness of spiritual coherence and contentment, like that which exists in hell. A big society exists in order to form cliques. A big society is a society for the promotion of narrowness. It is a machinery for the purpose of guarding the solitary and sensitive individual from all experience of the bitter and bracing human compromises. It is, in the most literal sense of the words, a society for the prevention of Christian knowledge.

We can see this change, for instance, in the modern transformation of the thing called a club. When London was smaller, and the parts of London more self-contained and parochial, the club was what it still is in villages, the opposite of what it is now in great cities. Then the club was valued as a place where a man could be sociable. Now the club is valued as a place where a man can be unsociable. The more the enlargement and elaboration of our civilization goes on the more the club ceases to be a place where a man can have a noisy argument, and becomes more and more a place where a man can have what is somewhat fantastically called a quiet chop. Its aim is to make a man comfortable, and to make a man comfortable is to make him the opposite of sociable. Sociabilty, like all good things, is full of discomforts, dangers, and renunciations. The club tends to produce the most degraded of all combinations—the luxurious anchorite, the man who combines the self-indulgence of Lucullus[76] with the insane loneliness of St. Simeon Stylites.

If we were to-morrow morning snowed up in the street in which we live, we should step suddenly into a much larger and much wilder world than we have ever known. And it is the whole effort of

[76] A Roman general (circa 157–110 B.C.) who, on retirement, became notorious for his fondness for luxury.

the typically modern person to escape from the street in which he lives. First he invents modern hygiene and goes to Margate.[77] Then he invents modern culture and goes to Florence. Then he invents modern imperialism and goes to Timbuctoo. He goes to the fantastic borders of the earth. He pretends to shoot tigers. He almost rides on a camel. And in all this he is still essentially fleeing from the street in which he was born; and of this flight he is always ready with his own explanation. He says he is fleeing from his street because it is dull; he is lying. He is really fleeing from his street because it is a great deal too exciting. It is exciting because it is exacting; it is exacting because it is alive. He can visit Venice because to him the Venetians are only Venetians; the people in his own street are men. He can stare at the Chinese because for him the Chinese are a passive thing to be stared at; if he stares at the old lady in the next garden, she becomes active. He is forced to flee, in short, from the too stimulating society of his equals — of free men, perverse, personal, deliberately different from himself. The street in Brixton[78] is too glowing and overpowering. He has to soothe and quiet himself among tigers and vultures, camels and crocodiles. These creatures are indeed very different from himself. But they do not put their shape or colour or custom into a decisive intellectual competition with his own. They do not seek to destroy his principles and assert their own; the stranger monsters of the suburban street do seek to do this. The camel does not contort his features into a fine sneer because Mr. Robinson has not got a hump; the cultured gentleman at No. 5 does exhibit a sneer because Robinson has not got a dado. The vulture will not roar with laughter because a man does not fly; but the major at No. 9 will roar with laughter because a man does not smoke. The complaint we commonly have to make of our neighbours is that they will not, as we express it, mind their own business. We do not really mean that they will not mind their own business. If our neighbours did not mind their own business they would be asked abruptly for their rent, and would rapidly cease to be our neighbours. What

---

[77] Going swimming for one's health. Margate is a popular seaside resort on the Thames estuary about seventy-five miles east and slightly south of London.

[78] Part of the borough of Lambeth south of the Thames.

we really mean when we say that they cannot mind their own business is something much deeper. We do not dislike them because they have so little force and fire that they cannot be interested in themselves. We dislike them because they have so much force and fire that they can be interested in us as well. What we dread about our neighbours, in short, is not the narrowness of their horizon, but their superb tendency to broaden it. And all aversions to ordinary humanity have this general character. They are not aversions to its feebleness (as is pretended), but to its energy. The misanthropes pretend that they despise humanity for its weakness. As a matter of fact, they hate it for its strength.

Of course, this shrinking from the brutal vivacity and brutal variety of common men is a perfectly reasonable and excusable thing as long as it does not pretend to any point of superiority. It is when it calls itself aristocracy or aestheticism or a superiority to the bourgeoisie that its inherent weakness has in justice to be pointed out. Fastidiousness is the most pardonable of vices; but it is the most unpardonable of virtues. Nietzsche, who represents most prominently this pretentious claim of the fastidious, has a description somewhere—a very powerful description in the purely literary sense—of the disgust and disdain which consume him at the sight of the common people with their common faces, their common voices, and their common minds. As I have said, this attitude is almost beautiful if we may regard it as pathetic. Nietzsche's aristocracy has about it all the sacredness that belongs to the weak. When he makes us feel that he cannot endure the innumerable faces, the incessant voices, the overpowering omnipresence which belongs to the mob, he will have the sympathy of anybody who has ever been sick on a steamer or tired in a crowded omnibus. Every man has hated mankind when he was less than a man. Every man has had humanity in his eyes like a blinding fog, humanity in his nostrils like a suffocating smell. But when Nietzsche has the incredible lack of humour and lack of imagination to ask us to believe that his aristocracy is an aristocracy of strong muscles or an aristocracy of strong wills, it is necessary to point out the truth. It is an aristocracy of weak nerves.

We make our friends; we make our enemies; but God makes our

next-door neighbour. Hence he comes to us clad in all the careless terrors of nature; he is as strange as the stars, as reckless and indifferent as the rain. He is Man, the most terrible of the beasts. That is why the old religions and the old scriptural language showed so sharp a wisdom when they spoke, not of one's duty towards humanity, but one's duty towards one's neighbour. The duty towards humanity may often take the form of some choice which is personal or even pleasurable. That duty may be a hobby; it may even be a dissipation. We may work in the East End because we are peculiarly fitted to work in the East End, or because we think we are; we may fight for the cause of international peace because we are very fond of fighting. The most monstrous martyrdom, the most repulsive experience, may be the result of choice or a kind of taste. We may be so made as to be particularly fond of lunatics or specially interested in leprosy. We may love negroes because they are black or German Socialists because they are pedantic. But we have to love our neighbour because he is *there* — a much more alarming reason for a much more serious operation. He is the sample of humanity which is actually given us. Precisely because he may be anybody he is everybody. He is a symbol because he is an accident.

Doubtless men flee from small environments into lands that are very deadly. But this is natural enough; for they are not fleeing from death. They are fleeing from life. And this principle applies to ring within ring of the social system of humanity. It is perfectly reasonable that men should seek for some particular variety of the human type, so long as they are seeking for that variety of the human type, and not for mere human variety. It is quite proper that a British diplomatist should seek the society of Japanese generals, if what he wants is Japanese generals. But if what he wants is people different from himself, he had much better stop at home and discuss religion with the housemaid. It is quite reasonable that the village genius should come up to conquer London if what he wants is to conquer London. But if he wants to conquer something fundamentally and symbolically hostile and also very strong, he had much better remain where he is and have a row with the rector. The man in the suburban street is quite right if he goes to Ramsgate[79] for the sake of Ramsgate—a difficult thing to imagine. But if, as he expresses it, he goes to Ramsgate "for a change," then he would have a much more romantic and even melodramatic change if he jumped over the wall into his neighbour's garden. The consequences would be bracing in a sense far beyond the possibilities of Ramsgate hygiene.

Now, exactly as this principle applies to the empire, to the nation within the empire, to the city within the nation, to the street within the city, so it applies to the home within the street. The institution of the family is to be commended for precisely the same reasons that the institution of the nation, or the institution of the city, are in this matter to be commended. It is a good thing for a man to live in a family for the same reason that it is a good thing for a man to be besieged in a city. It is a good thing for a man to live in a family in the same sense that it is a beautiful and delightful thing for a man to be snowed up in a street. They all force him to realize that life is not a thing from outside, but a thing from inside. Above all, they all insist upon the fact that life, if it be a truly stimulating and fascinating life, is a thing which, of its nature, exists in spite of ourselves. The modern writers who have suggested, in a more or less open manner, that the family is a bad institution, have generally confined themselves to suggesting, with much sharpness, bitterness, or pathos, that perhaps the family is not always very congenial. Of course the family is a good institution because it is uncongenial. It is wholesome precisely because it contains so many divergencies and varieties. It is, as the sentimentalists say, like a little kingdom, and, like most other little kingdoms, is generally in a state of something resembling anarchy. It is exactly because our brother George is not interested in our religious difficulties, but is interested in the Trocadero Restaurant, that the family has some of the bracing qualities of the commonwealth. It is precisely because our uncle Henry does not approve of the theatrical ambitions of our sister Sarah that the family is like humanity. The men and women who, for good reasons and

---

[79] A resort on the Strait of Dover four miles south of Margate.

bad, revolt against the family, are, for good reasons and bad, simply revolting against mankind. Aunt Elizabeth is unreasonable, like mankind. Papa is excitable, like mankind. Our youngest brother is mischievous, like mankind. Grandpapa is stupid, like the world; he is old, like the world.

Those who wish, rightly or wrongly, to step out of all this, do definitely wish to step into a narrower world. They are dismayed and terrified by the largeness and variety of the family. Sarah wishes to find a world wholly consisting of private theatricals; George wishes to think the Trocadero a cosmos. I do not say, for a moment, that the flight to this narrower life may not be the right thing for the individual, any more than I say the same thing about flight into a monastery. But I do say that anything is bad and artificial which tends to make these people succumb to the strange delusion that they are stepping into a world which is actually larger and more varied than their own. The best way that a man could test his readiness to encounter the common variety of mankind would be to climb down a chimney into any house at random, and get on as well as possible with the people inside. And that is essentially what each one of us did on the day that he was born.

This is, indeed, the sublime and special romance of the family. It is romantic because it is a toss-up. It is romantic because it is everything that its enemies call it. It is romantic because it is arbitrary. It is romantic because it is there. So long as you have groups of men chosen rationally, you have some special or sectarian atmosphere. It is when you have groups of men chosen irrationally that you have men. The element of adventure begins to exist; for an adventure is, by its nature, a thing that comes to us. It is a thing that chooses us, not a thing that we choose. Falling in love has been often regarded as the supreme adventure, the supreme romantic accident. In so much as there is in it something outside ourselves, something of a sort of merry fatalism, this is very true. Love does take us and transfigure and torture us. It does break our hearts with an unbearable beauty, like the unbearable beauty of music. But in so far as we have certainly something to do with the matter; in so far as we are in some sense prepared to fall in love and in some sense jump into it; in so far as we do to some extent choose and to some extent even judge—in all this falling in love is not truly romantic, is not truly adventurous at all. In this degree the supreme adventure is not falling in love. The supreme adventure is being born. There we do walk suddenly into a splendid and startling trap. There we do see something of which we have not dreamed before. Our father and mother do lie in wait for us and leap out on us, like brigands from a bush. Our uncle is a surprise. Our aunt is, in the beautiful common expression, a bolt from the blue. When we step into the family, by the act of being born, we do step into a world which is incalcuable, into a world which has its own strange laws, into a world which could do without us, into a world that we have not made. In other words, when we step into the family we step into a fairy-tale.

This colour as of a fantastic narrative ought to cling to the family and to our relations with it throughout life. Romance is the deepest thing in life; romance is deeper even than reality. For even if reality could be proved to be misleading, it still could not be proved to be unimportant or unimpressive. Even if the facts are false, they are still very strange. And this strangeness of life, this unexpected and even perverse element of things as they fall out, remains incurably interesting. The circumstances we can regulate may become tame or pessimistic; but the "circumstances over which we have no control" remain god-like to those who, like Mr. Micawber,[80] can call on them and renew their strength. People wonder why the novel is the most popular form of literature; people wonder why it is read more than books of science or books of metaphysics. The reason is very simple; it is merely that the novel is more true than they are. Life may sometimes legitimately appear as a book of science. Life may sometimes appear, and with a much greater legitimacy, as a book of metaphysics. But life is always a novel. Our existence may cease to be a song; it may cease even to be a beautiful lament. Our existence may not be an intelligible justice, or even a recognizable wrong. But our existence is still a story. In the fiery alphabet of every sunset is written, "to be continued in our next." If we have sufficient intellect, we

[80] An improvident but lovable character in Dickens' *David Copperfield*, who eventually becomes a colonial magistrate.

can finish a philosophical and exact deduction, and be certain that we are finishing it right. With the adequate brain-power we could finish any scientific discovery, and be certain that we were finishing it right. But not with the most gigantic intellect could we finish the simplest or silliest story, and be certain that we were finishing it right. That is because a story has behind it, not merely intellect which is partly mechanical, but will, which is in its essence divine. The narrative writer can send his hero to the gallows if he likes in the last chapter but one. He can do it by the same divine caprice whereby he, the author, can go to the gallows himself, and to hell afterwards if he chooses. And the same civilization, the chivalric European civilization which asserted freewill in the thirteenth century, produced the thing called "fiction" in the eighteenth. When Thomas Aquinas asserted the spiritual liberty of man, he created all the bad novels in the circulating libraries.

But in order that life should be a story or romance to us, it is necessary that a great part of it, at any rate, should be settled for us without our permission. If we wish life to be a system, this may be a nuisance; but if we wish it to be a drama, it is an essential. It may often happen, no doubt, that a drama may be written by somebody else which we like very little. But we should like it still less if the author came before the curtain every hour or so, and forced on us the whole trouble of inventing the next act. A man has control over many things in his life; he has control over enough things to be the hero of a novel. But if he had control over everything, there would be so much hero that there would be no novel. And the reason why the lives of the rich are at bottom so tame and uneventful is simply that they can choose the events. They are dull because they are omnipotent. They fail to feel adventures because they can make the adventures. The thing which keeps life romantic and full of fiery possibilities is the existence of these great plain limitations which force all of us to meet the things we do not like or do not expect. It is vain for the supercilious moderns to talk of being in uncongenial surroundings. To be in a romance is to be in uncongenial surroundings. To be born into this earth is to be born into uncongenial surroundings, hence to be born into a romance. Of all these great limitations and frameworks which fashion and create the poetry and variety of life, the family is the most definite and important. Hence it is misunderstood by the moderns, who imagine that romance would exist most perfectly in a complete state of what they call liberty. They think that if a man makes a gesture it would be a startling and romantic matter that the sun should fall from the sky. But the startling and romantic thing about the sun is that it does not fall from the sky. They are seeking under every shape and form a world where there are no limitations — that is, a world where there are no outlines; that is, a world where there are no shapes. There is nothing baser that that infinity. They say they wish to be as strong as the universe, but they really wish the whole universe as weak as themselves.

XV

ON SMART NOVELISTS
AND THE SMART SET

In one sense, at any rate, it is more valuable to read bad literature than good literature. Good literature may tell us the mind of one man; but bad literature may tell us the mind of many men. A good novel tells us the truth about its hero; but a bad novel tells us the truth about its author. It does much more than that, it tells us the truth about its readers; and, oddly enough, it tells us this all the more the more cynical and immoral be the motive of its manufacture. The more dishonest a book is as a book the more honest it is as a public document. A sincere novel exhibits the simplicity of one particular man; an insincere novel exhibits the simplicity of mankind. The pedantic decisions and definable readjustments of man may be found in scrolls and statute books and scriptures; but men's basic assumptions and everlasting energies are to be found in penny dreadfuls and halfpenny novelettes. Thus a man, like many men of real culture in our day, might learn from good literature nothing except the power to appreciate good literature. But from bad literature he might learn to govern empires and look over the map of mankind.

There is one rather interesting example of this state of things in which the weaker literature is really the stronger and the stronger the weaker. It is the case of what may be called, for the sake of an approximate description, the literature of aristocracy; or, if you prefer the description, the literature of snobbishness. Now, if any one wishes to find a really effective and comprehensible and permanent case for aristocracy well and sincerely stated, let him read, not the modern philosophical conservatives, not even Nietzsche, let him read the *Bow Bells Novelettes*.[81] Of the case of Nietzsche I am confessedly more doubtful. Nietzsche and the *Bow Bells Novelettes* have both obviously the same fundamental character; they both worship

---

[81] The name of a periodical that ran from 1879 to 1897.

the tall man with curling moustaches and herculean bodily power, and they both worship him in a manner which is somewhat feminine and hysterical. Even here, however, the *Novelette* easily maintains its philosophical superiority, because it does attribute to the strong man those virtues which do commonly belong to him, such virtues as laziness and kindliness and a rather reckless benevolence, and a great dislike of hurting the weak. Nietzsche, on the other hand, attributes to the strong man that scorn against weakness which only exists among invalids. It is not, however, of the secondary merits of the great German philosopher, but of the primary merits of the *Bow Bells Novelettes*, that it is my present affair to speak. The picture of aristocracy in the popular sentimental novelette seems to me very satisfactory as a permanent political and philosophical guide. It may be inaccurate about details such as the title by which a baronet is addressed or the width of a mountain chasm which a baronet can conveniently leap, but it is not a bad description of the general idea and intention of aristocracy as they exist in human affairs. The essential dream of aristocracy is magnificence and valour; and if the *Family Herald Supplement*[82] sometimes distorts or exaggerates these things, at least, it does not fall short in them. It never errs by making the mountain chasm too narrow or the title of the baronet insufficiently impressive. But above this sane reliable old literature of snobbishness there has arisen in our time another kind of literature of snobbishness which, with its much higher pretensions, seems to me worthy of very much less respect. Incidentally (if that matters), it is much better literature. But it is immeasurably worse philosophy, immeasurably worse ethics and politics, immeasurably worse vital rendering of aristocracy and humanity as they really are. From such books as those of which I wish now to speak we can discover what a clever man can do with the idea of aristocracy. But from the *Family Herald Supplement* literature we can learn what the idea of aristocracy can do with a man who is not clever. And when we know that we know English history.

This new aristocratic fiction must have caught the attention of

[82] The *Family Herald*, "useful information and amusement for the millions", began in 1842 and its *Supplement* in 1877.

everybody who has read the best fiction for the last fifteen years. It is that genuine or alleged literature of the Smart Set which represents that set as distinguished, not only by smart dresses, but by smart sayings. To the bad baronet, to the good baronet, to the romantic and misunderstood baronet who is supposed to be a bad baronet, but is a good baronet, this school has added a conception undreamed of in the former years—the conception of an amusing baronet. The aristocrat is not merely to be taller than mortal men and stronger and handsomer, he is also to be more witty. He is the long man with the short epigram. Many eminent, and deservedly eminent, modern novelists must accept some responsibility for having supported this worst form of snobbishness—an intellectual snobbishness. The talented author of "Dodo"[83] is responsible for having in some sense created the fashion as a fashion. Mr. Hichens, in the "Green Carnation,"[84] reaffirmed the strange idea that young noblemen talk well; though his case had some vague biographical foundation, and in consequence an excuse. Mrs. Craigie[85] is considerably guilty in the matter, although, or rather because, she has combined the aristocratic note with a note of some moral and even religious sincerity. When you are saving a man's soul, even in a novel, it is indecent to mention that he is a gentleman. Nor can blame in this matter be altogether removed from a man of much greater ability, and a man who has proved his possession of the highest of human instinct, the romantic instinct—I mean Mr. Anthony Hope. In a galloping, impossible melodrama like "The Prisoner of Zenda," the blood of kings formed an excellent fantastic thread or theme. But the blood of kings is not a thing that can be taken seriously. And when, for example, Mr. Hope devotes so much serious and sympathetic study to the man called Tristram of Blent, a man who throughout burning boyhood thought of nothing but a silly old estate, we feel even in Mr. Hope the hint of this excessive concern about the oligarchic idea.

[83] A novel published in 1893 by E. F. Benson.

[84] Robert Hichens (1864–1950) satirized the aesthetic movement in this novel, written in 1894.

[85] Pearl Mary Teresa Craigie, American by birth, wrote witty, epigrammatic novels under the pen name John Oliver Hobbes.

It is hard for any ordinary person to feel so much interest in a young man whose whole aim is to own the house of Blent at the time when every other young man is owning the stars.

Mr. Hope, however, is a very mild case, and in him there is not only an element of romance, but also a fine element of irony which warns us against taking all this elegance too seriously. Above all, he shows his sense in not making his noblemen so incredibly equipped with impromptu repartee. This habit of insisting on the wit of the wealthier classes is the last and most servile of all the servilities. It is, as I have said, immeasurably more contemptible than the snobbishness of the novelette which describes the nobleman as smiling like an Apollo or riding a mad elephant. These may be exaggerations of beauty and courage, but beauty and courage are the unconscious ideals of aristocrats, even of stupid aristocrats.

The nobleman of the novelette may not be sketched with any very close or conscientious attention to the daily habits of noblemen. But he is something more important than a reality; he is a practical ideal. The gentleman of fiction may not copy the gentleman of real life; but the gentleman of real life is copying the gentleman of fiction. He may not be particularly good-looking, but he would rather be good-looking than anything else; he may not have ridden on a mad elephant, but he rides a pony as far as possible with an air as if he had. And, upon the whole, the upper class not only especially desire these qualities of beauty and courage, but in some degree, at any rate, especially possess them. Thus there is nothing really mean or sycophantic about the popular literature which makes all its marquises seven feet high. It is snobbish, but it is not servile. Its exaggeration is based on an exuberant and honest admiration; its honest admiration is based upon something which is in some degree, at any rate, really there. The English lower classes do not fear the English upper classes in the least; nobody could. They simply and freely and sentimentally worship them. The strength of the aristocracy is not in the aristocracy at all; it is in the slums. It is not in the House of Lords; it is not in the Civil Service; it is not in the Government offices; it is not even in the huge and disproportionate monopoly of the English land. It is in a certain spirit. It is in the fact that when a navvy wishes

to praise a man, it comes readily to his tongue to say that he has behaved like a gentleman. From a democratic point of view he might
as well say that he had behaved like a viscount. The oligarchic character of the modern English commonwealth does not rest, like many
oligarchies, on the cruelty of the rich to the poor. It does not even
rest on the kindness of the rich to the poor. It rests on the perennial
and unfailing kindness of the poor to the rich.

The snobbishness of bad literature, then, is not servile; but the
snobbishness of good literature is servile. The old-fashioned halfpenny
romance where the duchesses sparkled with diamonds was not servile; but the new romance where they sparkle with epigrams is servile. For in thus attributing a special and startling degree of intellect
and conversational or controversial power to the upper classes, we
are attributing something which is not especially their virtue or even
especially their aim. We are, in the words of Disraeli (who, being a
genius and not a gentleman, has perhaps primarily to answer for the
introduction of this method of flattering the gentry), we are performing the essential function of flattery which is flattering the people for the qualities they have not got. Praise may be gigantic and insane without having any quality of flattery so long as it is praise of
something that is noticeably in existence. A man may say that a giraffe's head strikes the stars, or that a whale fills the German Ocean,
and still be only in a rather excited state about a favourite animal.
But when he begins to congratulate the giraffe on his feathers, and
the whale on the elegance of his legs, we find ourselves confronted
with that social element which we call flattery. The middle and
lower orders of London can sincerely, though not perhaps safely, admire the health and grace of the English aristocracy. And this for the
very simple reason that the aristocrats are, upon the whole, more
healthy and graceful than the poor. But they cannot honestly admire
the wit of the aristocrats. And this for the simple reason that the
aristocrats are not more witty than the poor, but a very great deal
less so. A man does not hear, as in the smart novels, these gems of
verbal felicity dropped between diplomatists at dinner. Where he
really does hear them is between two omnibus conductors in a block
in Holborn. The witty peer whose impromptus fill the books of

Mrs. Craigie or Miss Fowler,[86] would, as a matter of fact, be torn to shreds in the art of conversation by the first boot-black he had the misfortune to fall foul of. The poor are merely sentimental, and very excusably sentimental, if they praise the gentleman for having a ready hand and ready money. But they are strictly slaves and sycophants if they praise him for having a ready tongue. For that they have far more themselves.

The element of oligarchical sentiment in these novels, however, has, I think, another and subtler aspect, an aspect more difficult to understand and more worth understanding. The modern gentleman, particularly the modern English gentleman, has become so central and important in these books, and through them in the whole of our current literature and our current mode of thought, that certain qualities of his, whether original or recent, essential or accidental, have altered the quality of our English comedy. In particular, that stoical ideal, absurdly supposed to be the English ideal, has stiffened and chilled us. It is not the English ideal; but it is to some extent the aristocratic ideal; or it may be only the ideal of aristocracy in its autumn or decay. The gentleman is a Stoic because he is a sort of savage, because he is filled with a great elemental fear that some stranger will speak to him. That is why a third-class carriage is a community, while a first-class carriage is a place of wild hermits. But this matter, which is difficult, I may be permitted to approach in a more circuitous way.

The haunting element of ineffectualness which runs through so much of the witty and epigrammatic fiction fashionable during the last eight or ten years, which runs through such works of a real though varying ingenuity as "Dodo," or "Concerning Isabel Carnaby,"[87] or even "Some Emotions and a Moral,"[88] may be expressed in various ways, but to most of us I think it will ultimately amount to the same thing. This new frivolity is inadequate because there is in it no strong sense of an unuttered joy. The men and women who

---

[86] Ellen Thorneycroft Fowler (Mrs. Felkin, 1860–1929) wrote a number of successful novels between 1898 and 1904.

[87] Published in 1898 by Ellen Thorneycroft Fowler.

[88] Mrs. Craigie's first novel, 1891.

exchange the repartees may not only be hating each other, but hating even themselves. Any one of them might be bankrupt that day, or sentenced to be shot the next. They are joking, not because they are merry, but because they are not; out of the emptiness of the heart the mouth speaketh. Even when they talk pure nonsense it is a careful nonsense—a nonsense of which they are economical, or, to use the perfect expression of Mr. W. S. Gilbert in "Patience," it is such "precious nonsense." Even when they become light-headed they do not become light-hearted. All those who have read anything of the rationalism of the moderns know that their Reason is a sad thing. But even their unreason is sad.

The causes of this incapacity are also not very difficult to indicate. The chief of all, of course, is that miserable fear of being sentimental, which is the meanest of all the modern terrors—meaner even than the terror which produces hygiene. Everywhere the robust and uproarious humour has come from the men who were capable not merely of sentimentalism, but a very silly sentimentalism. There has been no humour so robust or uproarious as that of the sentimentalist Steele or the sentimentalist Sterne or the sentimentalist Dickens. These creatures who wept like women were the creatures who laughed like men. It is true that the humour of Micawber is good literature and that the pathos of little Nell is bad. But the kind of man who had the courage to write so badly in the one case is the kind of man who would have the courage to write so well in the other. The same unconsciousness, the same violent innocence, the same gigantesque scale of action which brought the Napoleon of Comedy his Jena[89] brought him also his Moscow. And herein is especially shown the frigid and feeble limitations of our modern wits. They make violent efforts, they make heroic and almost pathetic efforts, but they cannot really write badly. There are moments when we almost think that they are achieving the effect, but our hope shrivels to nothing the moment we compare their little failures with the enormous imbecilities of Byron or Shakespeare.

For a hearty laugh it is necessary to have touched the heart. I do

[89] Where Napolean inflicted an overwhelming defeat on the Prussians in a battle fought in 1806.

not know why touching the heart should always be connected only
with the idea of touching it to compassion or a sense of distress. The
heart can be touched to joy and triumph; the heart can be touched to
amusement. But all our comedians are tragic comedians. These later
fashionable writers are so pessimistic in bone and marrow that they
never seem able to imagine the heart having any concern with
mirth. When they speak of the heart, they always mean the pangs
and disappointments of the emotional life. When they say that a
man's heart is in the right place, they mean, apparently, that it is in
his boots. Our ethical societies understand fellowship, but they do
not understand good fellowship. Similarly, our wits understand
talk, but not what Dr. Johnson called a good talk. In order to have,
like Dr. Johnson, a good talk, it is emphatically necessary to be, like
Dr. Johnson, a good man — to have friendship and honour and an
abysmal tenderness. Above all, it is necessary to be openly and in-
decently humane, to confess with fulness all the primary pities and
fears of Adam. Johnson was a clear-headed humorous man, and
therefore he did not mind talking seriously about religion. Johnson
was a brave man, one of the bravest that ever walked, and therefore
he did not mind avowing to any one his consuming fear of death.

The idea that there is something English in the repression of one's
feelings is one of those ideas which no Englishman ever heard of until England began to be governed exclusively by Scotchmen, Ameri-
cans, and Jews. At the best, the idea is a generalization from the
Duke of Wellington — who was an Irishman. At the worst, it is a part
of that silly Teutonism which knows as little about England as it does
about anthropology, but which is always talking about Vikings. As
a matter of fact, the Vikings did not repress their feelings in the
least. They cried like babies and kissed each other like girls; in short,
they acted in that respect like Achilles and all strong heroes the
children of the gods. And though the English nationality has probably not much more to do with the Vikings than the French nationality or the Irish nationality, the English have certainly been the children of the Vikings in the matter of tears and kisses. It is not merely
true that all the most typically English men of letters, like Shakespeare and Dickens, Richardson and Thackeray, were sentimentalists.

It is also true that all the most typically English men of action were sentimentalists, if possible, more sentimental. In the great Elizabethan age, when the English nation was finally hammered out, in the great eighteenth century when the British Empire was being built up everywhere, where in all these times, where was this symbolic stoical Englishman who dresses in drab and black and represses his feelings? Were all the Elizabethan palladins and pirates like that? Were any of them like that? Was Grenville concealing his emotions when he broke wine-glasses to pieces with his teeth and bit them till the blood poured down? Was Essex restraining his excitement when he threw his hat into the sea? Did Raleigh think it sensible to answer the Spanish guns only, as Stevenson says, with a flourish of insulting trumpets? Did Sydney ever miss an opportunity of making a theatrical remark in the whole course of his life and death? Were even the Puritans Stoics? The English Puritans repressed a good deal, but even they were too English to repress their feelings. It was by a great miracle of genius assuredly that Carlyle contrived to admire simultaneously two things so irreconcilably opposed as silence and Oliver Cromwell. Cromwell was the very reverse of a strong, silent man. Cromwell was always talking, when he was not crying. Nobody, I suppose, will accuse the author of "Grace Abounding"[90] of being ashamed of his feelings. Milton, indeed, it might be possible to represent as a Stoic; in some sense he was a Stoic, just as he was a prig and a polygamist and several other unpleasant and heathen things. But when we have passed that great and desolate name, which may really be counted an exception, we find the tradition of English emotionalism immediately resumed and unbrokenly continuous. Whatever may have been the moral beauty of the passions of Etheridge and Dorset, Sedley and Buckingham,[91] they cannot be accused of the fault of fastidiously concealing them. Charles the Second was very popular with the English because, like all the jolly English kings, he displayed his passions. William the Dutchman was very unpopular with the English because, not being an Englishman, he did hide his emotions. He was, in fact, precisely the ideal

[90] *Grace Abounding to the Chief of Sinners*, by John Bunyan (1666).
[91] Restoration wits at the court of Charles II.

Englishman of our modern theory; and precisely for that reason all the real Englishmen loathed him like leprosy. With the rise of the great England of the eighteenth century, we find this open and emotional tone still maintained in letters and politics, in arts and in arms. Perhaps the only quality which was possessed in common by the great Fielding and the great Richardson was that neither of them hid their feelings. Swift, indeed, was hard and logical, because Swift was Irish. And when we pass to the soldiers and the rulers, the patriots and the empire-builders of the eighteenth century, we find, as I have said, that they were, if possible, more romantic than the romancers, more poetical than the poets. Chatham, who showed the world all his strength, showed the House of Commons all his weakness. Wolfe walked about the room with a drawn sword calling himself Caesar and Hannibal, and went to death with poetry in his mouth. Clive was a man of the same type as Cromwell or Bunyan, or, for the matter of that, Johnson — that is, he was a strong, sensible man with a kind of running spring of hysteria and melancholy in him. Like Johnson, he was all the more healthy because he was morbid. The tales of all the admirals and adventurers of that England are full of braggadocio, of sentimentality, of splendid affectation. But it is scarcely necessary to multiply examples of the essentially romantic Englishman when one example towers above them all. Mr. Rudyard Kipling has said complacently of the English, "We do not fall on the neck and kiss when we come together." It is true that this ancient and universal custom has vanished with the modern weakening of England. Sydney would have thought nothing of kissing Spenser. But I willingly concede that Mr. Broderick[92] would not be likely to kiss Mr. Arnold-Foster,[93] if that be any proof of the increased manliness and military greatness of England. But the Englishman who does not show his feelings has not altogether given up the power of seeing something English in the great sea-hero of the Napoleonic war. You cannot break the legend of Nelson. And across the sunset

[92] William St. John Broderick (1856–1942) was Secretary of State for War from 1900 to 1903.
[93] Hugh Oakeley Arnold-Foster (1855–1909), was a politician and authority on army and navy affairs.

of that glory is written in flaming letters for ever the great English sentiment, "Kiss me, Hardy."[94]

This ideal of self-repression, then, is, whatever else it is, not English. It is, perhaps, somewhat Oriental, it is slightly Prussian, but in the main it does not come, I think, from any racial or national source. It is, as I have said, in some sense aristocratic; it comes not from a people, but from a class. Even aristocracy, I think, was not quite so stoical in the days when it was really strong. But whether this unemotional ideal be the genuine tradition of the gentleman, or only one of the inventions of the modern gentleman (who may be called the decayed gentleman), it certainly has something to do with the unemotional quality in these society novels. From representing aristocrats as people who suppressed their feelings, it has been an easy step to representing aristocrats as people who had no feelings to suppress. Thus the modern oligarchist has made a virtue for the oligarchy of the hardness as well as the brightness of the diamond. Like a sonneteer addressing his lady in the seventeenth century, he seems to use the word "cold" almost as a eulogium, and the word "heartless" as a kind of compliment. Of course, in people so incurably kind-hearted and babyish as are the English gentry, it would be impossible to create anything that can be called positive cruelty; so in these books they exhibit a sort of negative cruelty. They cannot be cruel in acts, but they can be so in words. All this means one thing, and one thing only. It means that the living and invigorating ideal of England must be looked for in the masses; it must be looked for where Dickens found it — Dickens, among whose glories it was to be a humorist, to be a sentimentalist, to be an optimist, to be a poor man, to be an Englishman, but the greatest of whose glories was that he saw all mankind in its amazing and tropical luxuriance, and did not even notice the aristocracy; Dickens, the greatest of whose glories was that he could not describe a gentleman.

[94] The dying words of Nelson to Vice-Admiral Hardy on the quarter-deck of the *Victory* at Trafalgar in 1805.

XVI

ON MR. MCCABE[95]
AND A DIVINE FRIVOLITY

A critic once remonstrated with me saying, with an air of indignant reasonableness, "If you must make jokes, at least you need not make them on such serious subjects." I replied with a natural simplicity and wonder, "About what other subjects can one make jokes except serious subjects?" It is quite useless to talk about profane jesting. All jesting is in its nature profane, in the sense that it must be the sudden realization that something which thinks itself solemn is not so very solemn after all. If a joke is not a joke about religion or morals, it is a joke about police-magistrates or scientific professors or undergraduates dressed up as Queen Victoria. And people joke about the police-magistrate more than they joke about the Pope, not because the police-magistrate is a more frivolous subject, but, on the contrary, because the police-magistrate is a more serious subject than the Pope. The Bishop of Rome has no jurisdiction in this realm of England; whereas the police-magistrate may bring his solemnity to bear quite suddenly upon us. Men make jokes about old scientific professors, even more than they make them about bishops — not because science is lighter than religion, but because science is always by its nature more solemn and austere than religion. It is not I; it is not even a particular class of journalists or jesters who make jokes about the matters which are of most awful import; it is the whole human race. If there is one thing more than another which any one will admit who has the smallest knowledge of the world, it is that men are always speaking gravely and earnestly and with the utmost possible care about the things that are not important, but always talking frivolously about the things that are. Men talk for hours with

[95] Joseph McCabe (1867–1955), a Roman Catholic priest turned rationalist. After leaving the priesthood in 1896, he began a campaign against Christianity, producing two controversial books in the following year: *Twelve Years in a Monastery* and *Modern Rationalism*.

the faces of a college of cardinals about things like golf, or tobacco, or waistcoats, or party politics. But all the most grave and dreadful things in the world are the oldest jokes in the world— being married; being hanged.

One gentleman, however, Mr. McCabe, has in this matter made to me something that almost amounts to a personal appeal; and as he happens to be a man for whose sincerity and intellectual virtue I have a high respect, I do not feel inclined to let it pass without some attempt to satisfy my critic in the matter. Mr. McCabe devotes a considerable part of the last essay in the collection called "Christianity and Rationalism on Trial" to an objection, not to my thesis, but to my method, and a very friendly and dignified appeal to me to alter it. I am much inclined to defend myself in this matter out of mere respect for Mr. McCabe, and still more so out of mere respect for the truth which is, I think, in danger by his error, not only in this question, but in others. In order that there may be no injustice done in the matter, I will quote Mr. McCabe himself. "But before I follow Mr. Chesterton in some detail, I would make a general observation on his method. He is as serious as I am in his ultimate purpose, and I respect him for that. He knows, as I do, that humanity stands at a solemn parting of the ways. Towards some unknown goal it presses through the ages, impelled by an overmastering desire of happiness. To-day it hesitates, light-heartedly enough, but every serious thinker knows how momentous the decision may be. It is, apparently, deserting the path of religion and entering upon the path of secularism. Will it lose itself in quagmires of sensuality down this new path, and pant and toil through years of civic and industrial anarchy, only to learn it had lost the road, and must return to religion? Or will it find that at last it is leaving the mists and the quagmires behind it; that it is ascending the slope of the hill so long dimly discerned ahead, and making straight for the long-sought Utopia? This is the drama of our time, and every man and every woman should understand it.

"Mr. Chesterton understands it. Further, he gives us credit for understanding it. He has nothing of that paltry meanness or strange density of so many of his colleagues, who put us down as aimless iconoclasts or moral anarchists. He admits that we are waging a thankless war for what we take to be Truth and Progress. He is doing the same. But why, in the name of all that is reasonable, should we, when we are agreed on the momentousness of the issue either way, forthwith desert serious methods of conducting the controversy? Why, when the vital need of our time is to induce men and women to collect their thoughts occasionally, and be men and women — nay, to remember that they are really gods that hold the destinies of humanity on their knees — why should we think that this kaleidoscopic play of phrases is inopportune? The ballets of the Alhambra, [96] and the fireworks of the Crystal Palace, [97] and Mr. Chesterton's *Daily News* articles, have their place in life. But how a serious social student can think of curing the thoughtlessness of our generation by strained paradoxes; of giving people a sane grasp of social problems by literary sleight-of-hand; of settling important questions by a reckless shower of rocket-metaphors and inaccurate 'facts,' and the substitution of imagination for judgment, I cannot see."

I quote this passage with a particular pleasure, because Mr. McCabe certainly cannot put too strongly the degree to which I give him and his school credit for their complete sincerity and responsibility of philosophical attitude. I am quite certain that they mean every word they say. I also mean every word I say. But why is it that Mr. McCabe has some sort of mysterious hestitation about admitting that I mean every word I say; why is it that he is not quite as certain of my mental responsibility as I am of his mental responsibility? If we attempt to answer the question directly and well, we shall, I think, have come to the root of the matter by the shortest cut.

Mr. McCabe thinks that I am not serious but only funny, because Mr. McCabe thinks that funny is the opposite of serious. Funny is the opposite of not funny, and of nothing else. The question of whether a man expresses himself in a grotesque or laughable phraseology, or in a stately and restrained phraseology, is not a question

---

[96] A music hall in Leicester Square built in Moorish style. At the time Chesterton was writing, it had its own resident ballet company.

[97] A glass building constructed in Hyde Park for the Great Exhibition of 1851 and later moved south of the Thames to Sydenham.

of motive or of moral state, it is a question of instinctive language and self-expression. Whether a man chooses to tell the truth in long sentences or short jokes is a problem analogous to whether he chooses to tell the truth in French or German. Whether a man preaches his gospel grotesquely or gravely is merely like the question of whether he preaches it in prose or verse. The question of whether Swift was funny in his irony is quite another sort of question to the question of whether Swift was serious in his pessimism. Surely even Mr. McCabe would not maintain that the more funny "Gulliver" is in its method the less it can be sincere in its object. The truth is, as I have said, that in this sense the two qualities of fun and seriousness have nothing whatever to do with each other, they are no more comparable than black and triangular. Mr. Bernard Shaw is funny and sincere. Mr. George Robey[98] is funny and not sincere. Mr. Mc-Cabe is sincere and not funny. The average Cabinet Minister is not sincere and not funny.

In short, Mr. McCabe is under the influence of a primary fallacy which I have found very common in men of the clerical type. Numbers of clergymen have from time to time reproached me for making jokes about religion; and they have almost always invoked the authority of that very sensible commandment which says, "Thou shalt not take the name of the Lord thy God in vain." Of course, I pointed out that I was not in any conceivable sense taking the name in vain. To take a thing and make a joke out of it is not to take it in vain. It is, on the contrary, to take it and use it for an uncommonly good object. To use a thing in vain means to use it without use. But a joke may be exceedingly useful; it may contain the whole earthly sense, not to mention the whole heavenly sense, of a situation. And those who find in the Bible the commandment can find in the Bible any number of the jokes. In the same book in which God's name is fenced from being taken in vain, God himself overwhelms Job with a torrent of terrible levities. The same book which says that God's name must not be taken vainly, talks easily and carelessly about God laughing and God winking. Evidently it is

---

[98] George Robey (1869–1954), a well-known music hall comedian.

not here that we have to look for genuine examples of what is meant by a vain use of the name. And it is not very difficult to see where we have really to look for it. The people (as I tactfully pointed out to them) who really take the name of the Lord in vain are the clergymen themselves. The thing which is fundamentally and really frivolous is not a careless joke. The thing which is fundamentally and really frivolous is a careless solemnity. If Mr. McCabe really wishes to know what sort of guarantee of reality and solidity is afforded by the mere act of what is called talking seriously, let him spend a happy Sunday in going the round of the pulpits. Or, better still, let him drop in at the House of Commons or the House of Lords. Even Mr. McCabe would admit that these men are solemn — more solemn than I am. And even Mr. McCabe, I think, would admit that these men are frivolous — more frivolous than I am. Why should Mr. McCabe be so eloquent about the danger arising from fantastic and paradoxical writers? Why should he be so ardent in desiring grave and verbose writers? There are not so very many fantastic and paradoxical writers. But there are a gigantic number of grave and verbose writers; and it is by the efforts of the grave and verbose writers that everything that Mr. McCabe detests (and everything that I detest, for that matter) is kept in existence and energy. How can it have come about that a man as intelligent as Mr. McCabe can think that paradox and jesting stop the way? It is solemnity that is stopping the way in every department of modern effort. It is his own favourite "serious methods;" it is his own favourite "momentousness;" it is his own favourite "judgment" which stops the way everywhere. Every man who has ever headed a deputation to a minister knows this. Every man who has ever written a letter to the *Times* knows it. Every rich man who wishes to stop the mouths of the poor talks about "momentousness." Every Cabinet minister who has not got an answer suddenly develops a "judgment." Every sweater who uses vile methods recommends "serious methods." I said a moment ago that sincerity had nothing to do with solemnity, but I confess that I am not so certain that I was right. In the modern world, at any rate, I am not so sure that I was right. In the modern world solemnity is the direct enemy of sincerity. In the modern world sincerity is almost always on one side, and solemnity almost always on the other. The only answer possible to the fierce and glad attack of sincerity is the miserable answer of solemnity. Let Mr. McCabe, or any one else who is much concerned that we should be grave in order to be sincere, simply imagine the scene in some government office in which Mr. Bernard Shaw should head a Socialist deputation to Mr. Austen Chamberlain.[99] On which side would be the solemnity? And on which the sincerity?

I am, indeed, delighted to discover that Mr. McCabe reckons Mr. Shaw along with me in his system of condemnation of frivolity. He said once, I believe, that he always wanted Mr. Shaw to label his paragraphs serious or comic. I do not know which paragraphs of Mr. Shaw are paragraphs to be labelled serious; but surely there can be no doubt that this paragraph of Mr. McCabe's is one to be labelled comic. He also says, in the article I am now discussing, that Mr. Shaw has the reputation of deliberately saying everything which his hearers do not expect him to say. I need not labour the inconclusiveness and weakness of this, because it has already been dealt with in my remarks on Mr. Bernard Shaw. Suffice it to say here that the only serious reason which I can imagine inducing any one person to listen to any other is, that the first person looks to the second person with an ardent faith and a fixed attention, expecting him to say what he does not expect him to say. It may be a paradox, but that is because paradoxes are true. It may not be rational, but that is because rationalism is wrong. But clearly it is quite true that whenever we go to hear a prophet or teacher we may or may not expect wit, we may or may not expect eloquence, but we do expect what we do not expect. We may not expect the true, we may not even expect the wise, but we do expect the unexpected. If we do not expect the unexpected, why do we go there at all? If we expect the expected, why do we not sit at home and expect it by ourselves? If Mr. McCabe means merely this about Mr. Shaw, that he always has some unexpected application of his doctrine to give to those who listen to

[99] Austen Chamberlain (1863–1937), eldest son of Joseph Chamberlain. He spent forty-five years in Parliament and was known as "the last reminiscence of Victorian correctitude".

him, what he says is quite true, and to say it is only to say that Mr. Shaw is an original man. But if he means that Mr. Shaw has ever professed or preached any doctrine but one, and that his own, then what he says is not true. It is not my business to defend Mr. Shaw; as has been seen already, I disagree with him altogether. But I do not mind, on his behalf, offering in this matter a flat defiance to all his ordinary opponents, such as Mr. McCabe. I defy Mr. McCabe, or anybody else, to mention one single instance in which Mr. Shaw has, for the sake of wit or novelty, taken up any position which was not directly deducible from the body of his doctrine as elsewhere expressed. I have been, I am happy to say, a tolerably close student of Mr. Shaw's utterances, and I request Mr. McCabe, if he will not believe that I mean anything else, to believe that I mean this challenge.

All this, however, is a parenthesis. The thing with which I am here immediately concerned is Mr. McCabe's appeal to me not to be so frivolous. Let me return to the actual text of that appeal. There are, of course, a great many things that I might say about it in detail. But I may start with saying that Mr. McCabe is in error in supposing that the danger which I anticipate from the disappearance of religion is the increase of sensuality. On the contrary, I should be inclined to anticipate a decrease in sensuality, because I anticipate a decrease in life. I do not think that under modern Western materialism we should have anarchy. I doubt whether we should have enough individual valour and spirit even to have liberty. It is quite an old-fashioned fallacy to suppose that our objection to scepticism is that it removes the discipline from life. Our objection to scepticism is that it removes the motive power. Materialism is not a thing which destroys mere restraint. Materialism itself is the great restraint. The McCabe school advocates a political liberty, but it denies spiritual liberty. That is, it abolishes the laws which could be broken, and substitutes laws that cannot. And that is the real slavery.

The truth is that the scientific civilization in which Mr. McCabe believes has one rather particular defect; it is perpetually tending to destroy that democracy or power of the ordinary man in which Mr. McCabe also believes. Science means specialism, and specialism means oligarchy. If you once establish the habit of trusting particular men to produce particular results in physics or astronomy, you leave the door open for the equally natural demand that you should trust particular men to do particular things in government and the coercing of men. If you feel it to be reasonable that one beetle should be the only study of one man, and that one man the only student of that one beetle, it is surely a very harmless consequence to go on to say that politics should be the only study of one man, and that one man the only student of politics. As I have pointed out elsewhere in this book, the expert is more aristocratic than the aristocrat, because the aristocrat is only the man who lives well, while the expert is the man who knows better. But if we look at the progress of our scientific civilization we see a gradual increase everywhere of the specialist over the popular function. Once men sang together round a table in chorus; now one man sings alone, for the absurd reason that he can sing better. If scientific civilization goes on (which is most improbable) only one man will laugh, because he can laugh better that the rest.

I do not know that I can express this more shortly than by taking as a text the single sentence of Mr. McCabe, which runs as follows: "The ballets of the Alhambra and the fireworks of the Crystal Palace and Mr. Chesterton's *Daily News* articles have their places in life." I wish that my articles had as noble a place as either of the other two things mentioned. But let us ask ourselves (in a spirit of love, as Mr. Chadband[100] would say), what *are* the ballets of the Alhambra? The ballets of the Alhambra are institutions in which a particular selected row of persons in pink go through an operation known as dancing. Now, in all commonwealths dominated by a religion — in the Christian commonwealths of the Middle Ages and in many rude societies — this habit of dancing was a common habit with everybody, and was not necessarily confined to a professional class. A person could dance without being a dancer; a person could dance without being a specialist; a person could dance without being pink. And, in proportion as Mr. McCabe's scientific civilization advances — that is, in proportion as religious civilization (or real civilization) decays — the

---

[100] A pious hypocrite in Dickens's *Bleak House* (1852–53).

more and more "well trained," the more and more pink, become the people who do dance, and the more and more numerous become the people who don't. Mr. McCabe may recognize an example of what I mean in the gradual discrediting in society of the ancient European waltz or dance with partners, and the substitution of that horrible and degrading oriental interlude which is known as skirt-dancing. That is the whole essence of decadence, the effacement of five people who do a thing for fun by one person who does it for money. Now it follows, therefore, that when Mr. McCabe says that the ballets of the Alhambra and my articles "have their place in life," it ought to be pointed out to him that he is doing his best to create a world in which dancing, properly speaking, will have no place in life at all. He is, indeed, trying to create a world in which there will be no life for dancing to have a place in. The very fact that Mr. McCabe thinks of dancing as a thing belonging to some hired women at the Alhambra is an illustration of the same principle by which he is able to think of religion as a thing belonging to some hired men in white neckties. Both these things are things which should not be done for us, but by us. If Mr. McCabe were really religious he would be happy. If he were really happy he would dance.

Briefly, we may put the matter in this way. The main point of modern life is not that the Alhambra ballet has its place in life. The main point, the main enormous tragedy of modern life, is that Mr. McCabe has not his place in the Alhambra ballet. The joy of changing and graceful posture, the joy of suiting the swing of music to the swing of limbs, the joy of whirling drapery, the joy of standing on one leg, — all these should belong by rights to Mr. McCabe and to me; in short, to the ordinary healthy citizen. Probably we should not consent to go through these evolutions. But that is because we are miserable moderns and rationalists. We do not merely love ourselves more than we love duty; we actually love ourselves more than we love joy.

When, therefore, Mr. McCabe says that he gives the Alhambra dances (and my articles) their place in life, I think we are justified in pointing out that by the very nature of the case of his philosophy and of his favourite civilization he gives them a very inadequate place. For (if I may pursue the too flattering parallel) Mr. McCabe thinks of the Alhambra and of my articles as two very odd and absurd things, which some special people do (probably for money) in order to amuse him. But if he had ever felt himself the ancient, sublime, elemental, human instinct to dance, he would have discovered that dancing is not a frivolous thing at all, but a very serious thing. He would have discovered that it is the one grave and chaste and decent method of expressing a certain class of emotions. And similarly, if he had ever had, as Mr. Shaw and I have had, the impulse to what he calls paradox, he would have discovered that paradox again is not a frivolous thing, but a very serious thing. He would have found that paradox simply means a certain defiant joy which belongs to belief. I should regard any civilization which was without a universal habit of uproarious dancing as being, from the full human point of view, a defective civilization. And I should regard any mind which had not got the habit in one form or another of uproarious thinking as being, from the full human point of view, a defective mind. It is vain for Mr. McCabe to say that a ballet is a part of him. He should be part of a ballet, or else he is only part of a man. It is in vain for him to say that he is "not quarrelling with the importation of humour into the controversy." He ought himself to be importing humour into every controversy; for unless a man is in part a humorist, he is only in part a man. To sum up the whole matter very simply, if Mr. McCabe asks me why I import frivolity into a discussion of the nature of man, I answer, because frivolity is a part of the nature of man. If he asks me why I introduce what he calls paradoxes into a philosophical problem, I answer, because all philosophical problems tend to become paradoxical. If he objects to my treating of life riotously, I reply that life is a riot. And I say that the Universe as I see it, at any rate, is very much more like the fireworks at the Crystal Palace than it is like his own philosophy. About the whole cosmos there is a tense and secret festivity—like preparations for Guy Fawkes' day. Eternity is the eve of something. I never look up at the stars without feeling that they are the fires of a schoolboy's rocket, fixed in their everlasting fall.

XVII

ON THE WIT OF WHISTLER

That capable and ingenious writer, Mr. Arthur Symons,[101] has included in a book of essays recently published, I believe, an apologia for "London Nights," in which he says that morality should be wholly subordinated to art in criticism, and he uses the somewhat singular argument that art or the worship of beauty is the same in all ages, while morality differs in every period and in every respect. He appears to defy his critics or his readers to mention any permanent feature or quality in ethics. This is surely a very curious example of that extravagant bias against morality which makes so many ultramodern aesthetes as morbid and fanatical as any Eastern hermit. Unquestionably it is a very common phrase of modern intellectualism to say that the morality of one age can be entirely different to the morality of another. And like a great many other phrases of modern intellectualism, it means literally nothing at all. If the two moralities are entirely different, why do you call them both moralities? It is as if a man said, "Camels in various places are totally diverse; some have six legs, some have none, some have scales, some have feathers, some have horns, some have wings, some are green, some are triangular. There is no point which they have in common." The ordinary man of sense would reply, "Then what makes you call them all camels? What do you mean by a camel? How do you know a camel when you see one?" Of course, there is a permanent substance of morality, as much as there is a permanent substance of art; to say that is only to say that morality is morality, and that art is art. An ideal art critic would, no doubt, see the enduring beauty under every school; equally an ideal moralist would see the enduring ethic under every code. But practically some of the best Englishmen that ever lived could see nothing but filth and idolatry in the starry piety of the Brahmin. And it is equally true that practically the greatest

[101] Arthur Symons, poet and critic (1865–1945), published *London Nights*, a volume of poetry, in 1896.

group of artists that the world has ever seen, the giants of the Renaissance, could see nothing but barbarism in the ethereal energy of Gothic.

This bias against morality among the modern aesthetes is a thing very much paraded. And yet it is not really a bias against morality; it is a bias against other people's morality. It is generally founded on a very definite moral preference for a certain sort of life, pagan, plausible, humane. The modern aesthete, wishing us to believe that he values beauty more than conduct, reads Mallarmé, and drinks absinthe in a tavern. But this is not only his favourite kind of beauty; it is also his favourite kind of conduct. If he really wished us to believe that he cared for beauty only, he ought to go to nothing but Wesleyan school treats, and paint the sunlight in the hair of the Wesleyan babies. He ought to read nothing but very eloquent theological sermons by old-fashioned Presbyterian divines. Here the lack of all possible moral sympathy would prove that his interest was purely verbal or pictorial, as it is; in all the books he reads and writes he clings to the skirts of his own morality and his own immorality. The champion of *l'art pour l'art* is always denouncing Ruskin for his moralizing. If he were really a champion of *l'art pour l'art*, he would be always insisting on Ruskin for his style.

The doctrine of the distinction between art and morality owes a great part of its success to art and morality being hopelessly mixed up in the persons and performances of its greatest exponents. Of this lucky contradiction the very incarnation was Whistler. No man ever preached the impersonality of art so well; no man ever preached the impersonality of art so personally. For him pictures had nothing to do with the problems of character; but for all his fiercest admirers his character was, as a matter of fact, far more interesting than his pictures. He gloried in standing as an artist apart from right and wrong. But he succeeded by talking from morning till night about his rights and about his wrongs. His talents were many, his virtues, it must be confessed, not many, beyond that kindness to tried friends, on which many of his biographers insist, but which surely is a quality of all sane men, of pirates and pickpockets; beyond this, his outstanding virtues limit themselves chiefly to two admirable ones—courage and an abstract love of good work. Yet I fancy he won at last more by those two virtues than by all his talents. A man must be something of a moralist if he is to preach, even if he is to preach unmorality. Professor Walter Raleigh, in his "In Memoriam: James McNeill Whistler," insists, truly enough, on the strong streak of an eccentric honesty in matters strictly pictorial, which ran through his complex and slightly confused character. "He would destroy any of his works rather than leave a careless or inexpressive touch within the limits of the frame. He would begin again a hundred times over rather than attempt by patching to make his work seem better than it was."

No one will blame Professor Raleigh, who had to read a sort of funeral oration over Whistler at the opening of the Memorial Exhibition, if, finding himself in that position, he confined himself mostly to the merits and the stronger qualities of his subject. We should naturally go to some other type of composition for a proper consideration of the weaknesses of Whistler. But these must never be omitted from our view of him. Indeed, the truth is that it was not so much a question of the weaknesses of Whistler as of the intrinsic and primary weakness of Whistler. He was one of those people who live up to their emotional incomes, who are always taut and tingling with vanity. Hence he had no strength to spare; hence he had no kindness, no geniality; for geniality is almost definable as strength to spare. He had no god-like carelessness; he never forgot himself; his whole life was, to use his own expression, an arrangement. He went in for "the art of living" — a miserable trick. In a word, he was a great artist; but emphatically not a great man. In this connection I must differ strongly with Professor Raleigh upon what is, from a superficial literary point of view, one of his most effective points. He compares Whistler's laughter to the laughter of another man who was a great man as well as a great artist. "His attitude to the public was exactly the attitude taken up by Robert Browning, who suffered as long a period of neglect and mistake, in those lines of 'The Ring and the Book' —

> "'Well, British Public, ye who like me not,
> (God love you!) and will have your proper laugh
> At the dark question; laugh it! I'd laugh first.'"

"Mr. Whistler," adds Professor Raleigh, "always laughed first."

The truth is, I believe, that Whistler never laughed at all. There was no laughter in his nature; because there was no thoughtlessness and self-abandonment, no humility. I cannot understand anybody reading "The Gentle Art of Making Enemies" and thinking that there is any laughter in the wit. His wit is a torture to him. He twists himself into arabesques of verbal felicity; he is full of a fierce carefulness; he is inspired with the complete seriousness of sincere malice. He hurts himself to hurt his opponent. Browning did laugh, because Browning did not care; Browning did not care, because Browning was a great man. And when Browning said in brackets to the simple, sensible people who did not like his books, "God love you!" he was not sneering in the least. He was laughing—that is to say, he meant exactly what he said.

There are three distinct classes of great satirists who are also great men—that is to say, three classes of men who can laugh at something without losing their souls. The satirist of the first type is the man who, first of all, enjoys himself, and then enjoys his enemies. In this sense he loves his enemy, and by a kind of exaggeration of Christianity he loves his enemy the more the more he becomes an enemy. He has a sort of overwhelming and aggressive happiness in his assertion of anger; his curse is as human as a benediction. Of this type of satire the great example is Rabelais. This is the first typical example of satire, the satire which is voluble, which is violent, which is indecent, but which is not malicious. The satire of Whistler was not this. He was never in any of his controversies simply happy; the proof of it is that he never talked absolute nonsense. There is a second type of mind which produces satire with the quality of greatness. That is embodied in the satirist whose passions are released and let go by some intolerable sense of wrong. He is maddened by the sense of men being maddened; his tongue becomes an unruly member, and testifies against all mankind. Such a man was Swift, in whom the *saeva indignatio* was a bitterness to others, because it was a bitterness to himself. Such a satirist Whistler was not. He did not laugh because he was happy, like Rabelais. But neither did he laugh because he was unhappy, like Swift.

The third type of great satire is that in which the satirist is enabled to rise superior to his victim in the only serious sense which superiority can bear, in that of pitying the sinner and respecting the man even while he satirises both. Such an achievement can be found in a thing like Pope's "Atticus,"[102] a poem in which the satirist feels that he is satirising the weaknesses which belong specially to literary genius. Consequently he takes a pleasure in pointing out his enemy's strength before he points out his weakness. That is, perhaps, the highest and most honourable form of satire. That is not the satire of Whistler. He is not full of a great sorrow for the wrong done to human nature; for him the wrong is altogether done to himself.

He was not a great personality, because he thought so much about himself. And the case is stronger even than that. He was sometimes not even a great artist, because he thought so much about art. Any man with a vital knowledge of the human psychology ought to have the most profound suspicion of anybody who claims to be an artist, and talks a great deal about art. Art is a right and human thing, like walking or saying one's prayers; but the moment it begins to be talked about very solemnly, a man may be fairly certain that the thing has come into a congestion and a kind of difficulty.

The artistic temperament is a disease that afflicts amateurs. It is a disease which arises from men not having sufficient power of expression to utter and get rid of the element of art in their being. It is healthful to every sane man to utter the art within him; it is essential to every sane man to get rid of the art within him at all costs. Artists of a large and wholesome vitality get rid of their art easily, as they breathe easily, or perspire easily. But in artists of less force, the thing becomes a pressure, and produces a definite pain, which is called the artistic temperament. Thus, very great artists are able to be ordinary men — men like Shakespeare or Browning. There are many real tragedies of the artistic temperament, tragedies of vanity or violence or fear. But the great tragedy of the artistic temperament is that it cannot produce any art.

Whistler could produce art; and in so far he was a great man. But he could not forget art; and in so far he was only a man with the

[102] Not a poem but a satiric portrait of Addison in Pope's "Epistle to Dr. Arbuthnot", lines 194–214.

artistic temperament. There can be no stronger manifestation of the man who is a really great artist than the fact that he can dismiss the subject of art; that he can, upon due occasion, wish art at the bottom of the sea. Similarly, we should always be much more inclined to trust a solicitor who did not talk about conveyancing over the nuts and wine. What we really desire of any man conducting any business is that the full force of an ordinary man should be put into that particular study. We do not desire that the full force of that study should be put into an ordinary man. We do not in the least wish that our particular law-suit should pour its energy into our barrister's games with his children, or rides on his bicycle, or meditations on the morning star. But we do, as a matter of fact, desire that his games with his children, and his rides on his bicycle, and his meditations on the morning star should pour something of their energy into our law-suit. We do desire that if he has gained any especial lung development from the bicycle, or any bright and pleasing metaphors from the morning star, that they should be placed at our disposal in that particular forensic controversy. In a word, we are very glad that he is an ordinary man, since that may help him to be an exceptional lawyer.

Whistler never ceased to be an artist. As Mr. Max Beerbohm[103] pointed out in one of his extraordinarily sensible and sincere critiques, Whistler really regarded Whistler as his greatest work of art. The white lock, the single eye-glass, the remarkable hat — these were much dearer to him than any nocturnes or arrangements that he ever threw off. He could throw off the nocturnes; for some mysterious reason he could not throw off the hat. He never threw off from himself that disproportionate accumulation of aestheticism which is the burden of the amateur.

It need hardly be said that this is the real explanation of the thing which has puzzled so many dilettante critics, the problem of the extreme ordinariness of the behaviour of so many great geniuses in history. Their behaviour was so ordinary that it was not recorded; hence it was so ordinary that it seemed mysterious. Hence people say

[103] The reference is to "Whistler's Writing", first published in 1903, the year of Whistler's death, and republished in *Yet Again* (1909).

that Bacon wrote Shakespeare. The modern artistic temperament cannot understand how a man who could write such lyrics as Shakespeare wrote, could be as keen as Shakespeare was on business transactions in a little town in Warwickshire. The explanation is simple enough; it is that Shakespeare had a real lyrical impulse, wrote a real lyric, and so got rid of the impulse and went about his business. Being an artist did not prevent him from being an ordinary man, any more than being a sleeper at night or being a diner at dinner prevented him from being an ordinary man.

All very great teachers and leaders have had this habit of assuming their point of view to be one which was human and casual, one which would readily appeal to every passing man. If a man is genuinely superior to his fellows the first thing that he believes in is the equality of man. We can see this, for instance, in that strange and innocent rationality with which Christ addressed any motley crowd that happened to stand about Him. "What man of you having a hundred sheep, and losing one, would not leave the ninety and nine in the wilderness, and go after that which was lost?" Or, again, "What man of you if his son ask for bread will he give him a stone, or if he ask for a fish will he give him a serpent?" This plainness, this almost prosaic camaraderie, is the note of all very great minds.

To very great minds the things on which men agree are so immeasurably more important than the things on which they differ, that the latter, for all practical purposes, disappear. They have too much in them of an ancient laughter even to endure to discuss the difference between the hats of two men who were both born of a woman, or between the subtly varied cultures of two men who have both to die. The first-rate great man is equal with other men, like Shakespeare. The second-rate great man is on his knees to other men, like Whitman. The third-rate great man is superior to other men, like Whistler.

XVIII

THE FALLACY OF THE YOUNG NATION

To say that a man is an idealist is merely to say that he is a man; but, nevertheless, it might be possible to effect some valid distinction between one kind of idealist and another. One possible distinction, for instance, could be effected by saying that humanity is divided into conscious idealists and unconscious idealists. In a similar way, humanity is divided into conscious ritualists and unconscious ritualists. The curious thing is, in that example as in others, that it is the conscious ritualism which is comparatively simple, the unconscious ritual which is really heavy and complicated. The ritual which is comparatively rude and straightforward is the ritual which people call "ritualistic." It consists of plain things like bread and wine and fire, and men falling on their faces. But the ritual which is really complex, and many coloured, and elaborate, and needlessly formal, is the ritual which people enact without knowing it. It consists not of plain things like wine and fire, but of really peculiar, and local, and exceptional, and ingenious things — things like door-mats, and door-knockers, and electric bells, and silk hats, and white ties, and shiny cards, and confetti. The truth is that the modern man scarcely ever gets back to very old and simple things except when he is performing some religious mummery. The modern man can hardly get away from ritual except by entering a ritualistic church. In the case of these old and mystical formalities we can at least say that the ritual is not mere ritual; that the symbols employed are in most cases symbols which belong to a primary human poetry. The most ferocious opponent of the Christian ceremonials must admit that if Catholicism had not instituted the bread and wine, somebody else would most probably have done so. Any one with a poetical instinct will admit that to the ordinary human instinct bread symbolizes something which cannot very easily be symbolized otherwise; that wine, to the ordinary human instinct, symbolizes something which cannot very easily by symbolized otherwise. But white ties in the

174

evening are ritual, and nothing else but ritual. No one would pretend that white ties in the evening are primary and poetical. Nobody would maintain that the ordinary human instinct would in any age or country tend to symbolize the idea of evening by a white necktie. Rather, the ordinary human instinct would, I imagine, tend to symbolize evening by cravats with some of the colours of the sunset, not white neckties, but tawny or crimson neckties — neckties of purple or olive, or some darkened gold. Mr. J. A. Kensit,[104] for example, is under the impression that he is not a ritualist. But the daily life of Mr. J. A. Kensit, like that of any ordinary modern man, is, as a matter of fact, one continual and compressed catalogue of mystical mummery and flummery. To take one instance out of an inevitable hundred: I imagine that Mr. Kensit takes off his hat to a lady; and what can be more solemn and absurd, considered in the abstract, than symbolizing the existence of the other sex by taking off a portion of your clothing and waving it in the air? This, I repeat, is not a natural and primitive symbol, like fire or food. A man might just as well have to take off his waistcoat to a lady; and if a man, by the social ritual of his civilization, had to take off his waistcoat to a lady, every chivalrous and sensible man would take off his waistcoat to a lady. In short, Mr. Kensit, and those who agree with him, may think, and quite sincerely think, that men give too much incense and ceremonial to their adoration of the other world. But nobody thinks that he can give too much incense and ceremonial to the adoration of this world.

All men, then, are ritualists, but are either conscious or unconscious ritualists. The conscious ritualists are generally satisfied with a few very simple and elementary signs; the unconscious ritualists are not satisfied with anything short of the whole of human life, being almost insanely ritualistic. The first is called a ritualist because he invents and remembers one rite; the other is called an anti-ritualist because he obeys and forgets a thousand. And a somewhat similar distinction to this which I have drawn with some unavoidable length, between the conscious ritualist and the unconscious ritualist,

[104] John Kensit (1853–1902) was a fanatical Protestant agitator and opponent of ritualism and Romanizing tendencies in the Anglican Church. He began an organized antiritualistic campaign in London in 1898.

exists between the conscious idealist and the unconscious idealist. It is idle to inveigh against cynics and materialists — there are no cynics, there are no materialists. Every man is idealistic; only it so often happens that he has the wrong ideal. Every man is incurably sentimental; but, unfortunately, it is so often a false sentiment. When we talk, for instance, of some unscrupulous commercial figure, and say that he would do anything for money, we use quite an inaccurate expression, and we slander him very much. He would not do anything for money. He would do some things for money; he would sell his soul for money, for instance; and, as Mirabeau[105] humorously said, he would be quite wise "to take money for muck." He would oppress humanity for money; but then it happens that humanity and the soul are not things that he believes in; they are not his ideals. But he has his own dim and delicate ideals; and he would not violate these for money. He would not drink out of the soup-tureen, for money. He would not wear his coat-tails in front, for money. He would not spread a report that he had softening of the brain, for money. In the actual practice of life we find, in the matter of ideals, exactly what we have already found in the matter of ritual. We find that while there is a perfectly genuine danger of fanaticism from the men who have unworldly ideals, the permanent and urgent danger of fanaticism is from the men who have worldly ideals.

People who say that an ideal is a dangerous thing, that it deludes and intoxicates, are perfectly right. But the ideal which intoxicates most is the least idealistic kind of ideal. The ideal which intoxicates least is the very ideal ideal; that sobers us suddenly, as all heights and precipices and great distances do. Granted that it is a great evil to mistake a cloud for a cape; still, the cloud which can be most easily mistaken for a cape, is the cloud that is nearest the earth. Similarly, we may grant that it may be dangerous to mistake an ideal for something practical. But we shall still point out that, in this respect, the most dangerous ideal of all is the ideal which looks a little practical. It is difficult to attain a high ideal; consequently, it is almost impossible to persuade ourselves that we have attained it. But it is easy

---

[105] Honore Gabriel Riquetti, Comte de Mirabeau (1749–1791), was one of the leaders of the French Revolution.

to attain a low ideal; consequently, it is easier still to persuade ourselves that we have attained it when we have done nothing of the
kind. To take a random example. It might be called a high ambition
to wish to be an archangel; the man who entertained such an ideal
would very possibly exhibit asceticism, or even frenzy, but not, I
think, delusion. He would not think he was an archangel, and go
about flapping his hands under the impression that they were wings.
But suppose that a sane man had a low ideal; suppose he wished to
be a gentleman. Any one who knows the world knows that in nine
weeks he would have persuaded himself that he was a gentleman;
and this being manifestly not the case, the result will be very real and
practical dislocations and calamities in social life. It is not the wild
ideals which wreck the practical world; it is the tame ideals.

The matter may, perhaps, be illustrated by a parallel from our
modern politics. When men tell us that the old Liberal politicians of
the type of Gladstone cared only for ideals, of course, they are talking nonsense—they cared for a great many other things, including
votes. And when men tell us that modern politicians of the type of
Mr. Chamberlain or, in another way, Lord Rosebery, care only for
votes or for material interest, then again they are talking nonsense—
these men care for ideals like all other men. But the real distinction
which may be drawn is this, that to the older politician the ideal was
an ideal, and nothing else. To the new politician his dream is not only
a good dream, it is a reality. The old politician would have said, "It
would be a good thing if there were a Republican Federation dominating the world." But the modern politician does not say, "It
would be a good thing if there were a British Imperialism dominating the world." He says, "It is a good thing that there is a British
Imperialism dominating the world;" whereas clearly there is nothing of the kind. The old Liberal would say, "There ought to be a
good Irish government in Ireland." But the ordinary modern Unionist does not say, "There ought to be a good English government in
Ireland." He says, "There is a good English government in Ireland;"
which is absurd. In short, the modern politicians seem to think that
a man becomes practical merely by making assertions entirely about
practical things. Apparently, a delusion does not matter as long as

it is a materialistic delusion. Instinctively most of us feel that, as a practical matter, even the contrary is true. I certainly would much rather share my apartments with a gentleman who thought he was God than with a gentleman who thought he was a grasshopper. To be continually haunted by practical images and practical problems, to be constantly thinking of things as actual, as urgent, as in process of completion — these things do not prove a man to be practical; these things, indeed, are among the most ordinary signs of a lunatic. That our modern statesmen are materialistic is nothing against their being also morbid. Seeing angels in a vision may make a man a supernaturalist to excess. But merely seeing snakes in *delirium tremens* does not make him a naturalist.

And when we come actually to examine the main stock notions of our modern practical politicians, we find that those main stock notions are mainly delusions. A great many instances might be given of the fact. We might take, for example, the case of that strange class of notions which underlie the word "union," and all the eulogies heaped upon it. Of course, union is no more a good thing in itself than separation is a good thing in itself. To have a party in favour of union and a party in favour of separation, is as absurd as to have a party in favour of going upstairs and a party in favour of going downstairs. The question is not whether we go up or down stairs, but where we are going to, and what we are going for? Union is strength; union is also weakness. It is a good thing to harness two horses to a cart; but it is not a good thing to try and turn two hansom cabs into one four-wheeler. Turning ten nations into one empire may happen to be as feasible as turning ten shillings into one half-sovereign. Also it may happen to be as preposterous as turning ten terriers into a mastiff. The question in all cases is not a question of union or absence of union, but of identity or absence of identity. Owing to certain historical and moral causes, two nations may be so united as upon the whole to help each other. Thus England and Scotland pass their time in paying each other compliments; but their energies and atmospheres run distinct and parallel, and consequently do not clash. Scotland continues to be educated and Calvinistic; England continues to be uneducated and happy. But owing to certain other moral and certain other political causes, two nations may be so united as only to hamper each other; their lines do clash and do not run parallel. Thus, for instance, England and Ireland are so united that the Irish can sometimes rule England, but can never rule Ireland. The educational systems, including the last Education Act, are here, as in the case of Scotland, a very good test of the matter. The overwhelming majority of Irishmen believe in a strict Catholicism; the overwhelming majority of Englishmen believe in a vague Protestantism. The Irish party in the Parliament of Union is just large enough to prevent the English education being indefinitely Protestant, and just small enough to prevent the Irish education being definitely Catholic. Here we have a state of things which no man in his senses would ever dream of wishing to continue if he had not been bewitched by the sentimentalism of the mere word "union."

This example of union, however, is not the example which I propose to take of the ingrained futility and deception underlying all the assumptions of the modern practical politician. I wish to speak especially of another and much more general delusion. It pervades the minds and speeches of all the practical men of all parties; and it is a childish blunder built upon a single false metaphor. I refer to the universal modern talk about young nations and new nations; about America being young, about New Zealand being new. The whole thing is a trick of words. America is not young, New Zealand is not new. It is a very discussable question whether they are not both much older than England or Ireland.

Of course we may use the metaphor of youth about America or the colonies, if we use it strictly as implying only a recent origin. But if we use it (as we do use it) as implying vigour, or vivacity, or crudity, or inexperience, or hope, or a long life before them, or any of the romantic attributes of youth, then it is surely as clear as daylight that we are duped by a stale figure of speech. We can easily see the matter clearly by applying it to any other institution parallel to the institution of an independent nationality. If the club called "The Milk and Soda League" (let us say) was set up yesterday, as I have no doubt it was, then, of course, "The Milk and Soda League" is a young club in the sense that it was set up yesterday, but in no other sense. It may consist entirely of moribund old gentlemen. It may be moribund itself. We may call it a young club, in the light of the fact that it was founded yesterday. We may also call it a very old club in the light of the fact that it will most probably go bankrupt to-morrow. All this appears very obvious when we put it in this form. Any one who adopted the young-community delusion with regard to a bank or a butcher's shop would be sent to an asylum. But the whole modern political notion that America and the colonies must be very vigorous because they are very new, rests upon no better foundation. That America was founded long after England does not make it even in the faintest degree more probable that America will not perish a long time before England. That England existed before her colonies does not make it any the less likely that she will exist after her colonies. And when we look at the actual history of the world, we find that great European nations almost invariably have survived the vitality of their colonies. When we look at the actual history of the world, we find that if there is a thing that is born old and dies young, it is a colony. The Greek colonies went to pieces long before the Greek civilization. The Spanish colonies have gone to pieces long before the nation of Spain—nor does there seem to be any reason to doubt the possibility or even the probability of the conclusion that the colonial civilization, which owes its origin to England, will be much briefer and much less vigorous than the civilization of England itself. The English nation will still be going the way of all European nations when the Anglo-Saxon race has gone the way of all fads. Now, of course, the interesting question is, have we, in the case of America and the colonies, any real evidence of a moral and intellectual youth as opposed to the indisputable triviality of a merely chronological youth? Consciously or unconsciously, we know that we have no such evidence, and consciously or unconsciously, therefore, we proceed to make it up. Of this pure and placid invention, a good example, for instance, can be found in a recent poem of Mr. Rudyard Kipling's. Speaking of the English people and the South African War, Mr. Kipling says that "we fawned on the younger nations for the men that could shoot and ride." Some people considered this sentence insulting. All that I am concerned with at present is the evident fact that it is not true. The colonies provided very useful volunteer troops, but they did not provide the best troops, nor achieve the most successful exploits. The best work in the war on the English side was done, as might have been expected, by the best English regiments. The men who could shoot and ride were not the enthusiastic corn merchants from Melbourne, any more than they were the enthusiastic clerks from Cheapside. The men who could shoot and ride were the men who had been taught to shoot and ride in the discipline of the standing army of a great European power. Of course, the colonials are as brave and athletic as any other average white men. Of course, they acquitted themselves with reasonable credit. All I have here to indicate is that, for the purposes of this theory of the new nation, it is necessary to maintain that the colonial forces were more useful or more heroic than the gunners at Colenso or the Fighting Fifth.[106] And of this contention there is not, and never has been, one stick or straw of evidence.

A similar attempt is made, and with even less success, to represent the literature of the colonies as something fresh and vigorous and important. The imperialist magazines are constantly springing upon us some genius from Queensland or Canada, through whom we are expected to smell the odours of the bush or the prairie. As a matter of fact, any one who is even slightly interested in literature as such (and I, for one, confess that I am only slightly interested in literature as such), will freely admit that the stories of these geniuses smell of nothing but printer's ink, and that not of first-rate quality. By a great effort of Imperial imagination the generous English people reads into these works a force and a novelty. But the force and the novelty are not in the new writers; the force and the novelty are in the ancient heart of the English. Anybody who studies them impartially will know that the first-rate writers of the colonies are not

[106] Chesterton refers to two episodes of heroic but futile courage during General Buller's unsuccessful attempt to force a crossing of the Tugela River at Colenso on December 15, 1899. When he moved his artillery within a thousand yards of the river, Colonel Long took them far ahead of the infantry battalions that were supposed to screen them and brought them under the fire of a thousand Boer rifles. Major-General Fitzroy Hart marched his Fifth or Irish Brigade into a loop of the river and similarly brought them under devastating fire from three sides.

even particularly novel in their note and atmosphere, are not only not producing a new kind of good literature, but are not even in any particular sense producing a new kind of bad literature. The first-rate writers of the new countries are really almost exactly like the second-rate writers of the old countries. Of course they do feel the mystery of the wilderness, the mystery of the bush, for all simple and honest men feel this in Melbourne, or Margate, or South St. Pancras.[107] But when they write most sincerely and most successfully, it is not with a background of the mystery of the bush, but with a background, expressed or assumed, of our own romantic cockney civilization. What really moves their souls with a kindly terror is not the mystery of the wilderness, but the Mystery of a Hansom Cab.

Of course there are some exceptions to this generalization. The one really arresting exception is Olive Schreiner, and she is quite as certainly an exception that proves the rule. Olive Schreiner is a fierce, brilliant, and realistic novelist; but she is all this precisely because she is not English at all. Her tribal kinship is with the country of Teniers[108] and Maarten Maartens[109] — that is, with a country of realists. Her literary kinship is with the pessimistic fiction of the continent; with the novelists whose very pity is cruel. Olive Schreiner is the one English colonial who is not conventional, for the simple reason that South Africa is the one English colony which is not English, and probably never will be. And, of course, there are individual exceptions in a minor way. I remember in particular some Australian tales by Mr. McIlwain[110] which were really able and effective, and which, for that reason, I suppose, are not presented to the public with blasts of a trumpet. But my general contention, if put before any one with a love of letters, will not be disputed if it is understood.

[107] St. Pancras is a borough in central London.

[108] Either David Teniers the Elder (1582–1649) or David Teniers the Younger (1610–1694), both Flemish painters.

[109] The pseudonym of Jozue Marius Willem van der Poorten Schwartz (1858–1915), the Dutch author of a detective story, *The Black Box Murder* (1890), written in English, as well as of other stories and novels.

[110] Herbert C. McIlwaine, who wrote *Dinkinbar: A Romance of an Australian Stockrider* (1898), *The White Stone: A Story of a Boy from the Bush* (1900), etc. Chesterton may have been thinking of his collection of stories *The Undersong* (1903).

It is not the truth that the colonial civilization as a whole is giving us, or shows any signs of giving us, a literature which will startle and renovate our own. It may be a very good thing for us to have an affectionate illusion in the matter; that is quite another affair. The colonies may have given England a new emotion; I only say that they have not given the world a new book.

Touching these English colonies, I do not wish to be misunderstood. I do not say of them or of America that they have not a future, or that they will not be great nations. I merely deny the whole established modern expression about them. I deny that they are "destined" to a future. I deny that they are "destined" to be great nations. I deny (of course) that any human thing is destined to be anything. All the absurd physical metaphors, such as youth and age, living and dying, are, when applied to nations, but pseudo-scientific attempts to conceal from men the awful liberty of their lonely souls.

In the case of America, indeed, a warning to this effect is instant and essential. America, of course, like every other human thing, can in a spiritual sense live or die as much as it chooses. But at the present moment the matter which America has very seriously to consider is not how near it is to its birth and beginning, but how near it may be to its end. It is only a verbal question whether the American civilization is young; it may become a very practical and urgent question whether it is dying. When once we have cast aside, as we inevitably have after a moment's thought, the fanciful physical metaphor involved in the word "youth," what serious evidence have we that America is a fresh force and not a stale one? It has a great many people, like China; it has a great deal of money, like defeated Carthage or dying Venice. It is full of bustle and excitability, like Athens after its ruin, and all the Greek cities in their decline. It is fond of new things; but the old are always fond of new things. Young men read chronicles, but old men read newspapers. It admires strength and good looks; it admires a big and barbaric beauty in its women, for instance; but so did Rome when the Goth was at the gates. All these are things quite compatible with fundamental tedium and decay. There are three main shapes or symbols in which a nation can show itself essentially glad and great—by the heroic in government, by the heroic in arms, and by the heroic in art. Beyond government, which is, as it were, the very shape and body of a nation, the most significant thing about any citizen is his artistic attitude towards a holiday and his moral attitude towards a fight — that is, his way of accepting life and his way of accepting death.

Subjected to these eternal tests, America does not appear by any means as particularly fresh or untouched. She appears with all the weakness and weariness of modern England or of any other Western power. In her politics she has broken up exactly as England has broken up, into a bewildering opportunism and insincerity. In this matter of war and the national attitude towards war, her resemblance to England is even more manifest and melancholy. It may be said with rough accuracy that there are three stages in the life of a strong people. First, it is a small power, and fights small powers. Then it is a great power, and fights great powers. Then it is a great power, and fights small powers, but pretends that they are great powers, in order to rekindle the ashes of its ancient emotion and vanity. After that, the next step is to become a small power itself. England exhibited this symptom of decadence very badly in the war with the Transvaal; but America exhibited it worse in the war with Spain. There was exhibited more sharply and absurdly than anywhere else the ironic contrast between the very careless choice of a strong line and the very careful choice of a weak enemy. America added to all her other late Roman or Byzantine elements the element of the Caracallan triumph,[111] the triumph over nobody.

But when we come to the last test of nationality, the test of art and letters, the case is almost terrible. The English colonies have produced no great artists; and that fact may prove that they are still full of silent possibilities and reserve force. But America has produced great artists. And that fact most certainly proves that she is full of a fine futility and the end of all things. Whatever the American men of genius are, they are not young gods making a young world. Is the art of Whistler a brave, barbaric art, happy and headlong? Does Mr. Henry James infect us with the spirit of a schoolboy? No; the colonies

[111] Caracalla (b. 188, Emperor of Rome 211–217) came to the throne by murder, and his reign was described as "a series of cruelties and extortions".

have not spoken, and they are safe. Their silence may be the silence of the unborn. But out of America has come a sweet and startling cry, as unmistakable as the cry of a dying man.

XIX

SLUM NOVELISTS AND THE SLUMS

Odd ideas are entertained in our time about the real nature of the doctrine of human fraternity. The real doctrine is something which we do not, with all our modern humanitarianism, very clearly understand, much less very closely practise. There is nothing, for instance, particularly undemocratic about kicking your butler downstairs. It may be wrong, but it is not unfraternal. In a certain sense, the blow or kick may be considered as a confession of equality: you are meeting your butler body to body; you are almost according him the privilege of the duel. There is nothing undemocratic, though there may be something unreasonable, in expecting a great deal from the butler, and being filled with a kind of frenzy of surprise when he falls short of the divine stature. The thing which is really undemocratic and unfraternal is not to expect the butler to be more or less divine. The thing which is really undemocratic and unfraternal is to say, as so many modern humanitarians say, "Of course one must make allowances for those on a lower plane." All things considered, indeed, it may be said, without undue exaggeration, that the really undemocratic and unfraternal thing is the common practice of not kicking the butler downstairs.

It is only because such a vast section of the modern world is out of sympathy with the serious democratic sentiment that this statement will seem to many to be lacking in seriousness. Democracy is not philanthropy; it is not even altruism or social reform. Democracy is not founded on pity for the common man; democracy is founded on reverence for the common man, or, if you will, even on fear of him. It does not champion man because man is so miserable, but because man is so sublime. It does not object so much to the ordinary man being a slave as to his not being a king, for its dream is always the dream of the first Roman republic, a nation of kings.

Next to a genuine republic, the most democratic thing in the world is a hereditary despotism. I mean a despotism in which there is absolutely no trace whatever of any nonsense about intellect or special fitness for the post. Rational despotism — that is, selective despotism — is always a curse to mankind, because with that you have the ordinary man misunderstood and misgoverned by some prig who has no brotherly respect for him at all. But irrational despotism is always democratic, because it is the ordinary man enthroned. The worst form of slavery is that which is called Caesarism, or the choice of some bold or brilliant man as despot because he is suitable. For that means that men choose a representative, not because he represents them, but because he does not. Men trust an ordinary man like George III. or William IV. because they are themselves ordinary men and understand him. Men trust an ordinary man because they trust themselves. But men trust a great man because they do not trust themselves. And hence the worship of great men always appears in times of weakness and cowardice; we never hear of great men until the time when all other men are small.

Hereditary despotism is, then, in essence and sentiment democratic because it chooses from mankind at random. If it does not declare that every man may rule, it declares the next most democratic thing; it declares that any man may rule. Hereditary aristocracy is a far worse and more dangerous thing, because the numbers and multiplicity of an aristocracy make it sometimes possible for it to figure as an aristocracy of intellect. Some of its members will presumably have brains, and thus they, at any rate, will be an intellectual aristocracy within the social one. They will rule the aristocracy by virtue of their intellect, and they will rule the country by virtue of their aristocracy. Thus a double falsity will be set up, and millions of the images of God, who, fortunately for their wives and families, are neither gentlemen nor clever men, will be represented by a man like Mr. Balfour[112] or Mr. Wyndham,[113] because he is too gentlemanly to be called merely clever, and just too clever to be called merely a gentleman. But even an hereditary aristocracy may exhibit,

[112] Arthur Balfour (1848–1930) was a Conservative politician and Prime Minister from 1902 to 1905.

[113] George Wyndham (1863–1913), also a Conservative politician, was Chief Secretary for Ireland from 1900 to 1905.

by a sort of accident, from time to time some of the basically democratic quality which belongs to a hereditary despotism. It is amusing to think how much conservative ingenuity has been wasted in the defence of the House of Lords by men who were desperately endeavouring to prove that the House of Lords consisted of clever men. There is one really good defence of the House of Lords, though admirers of the peerage are strangely coy about using it; and that is, that the House of Lords, in its full and proper strength, consists of stupid men. It really would be a plausible defence of that otherwise indefensible body to point out that the clever men in the Commons, who owed their power to cleverness, ought in the last resort to be checked by the average man in the Lords, who owed their power to accident. Of course, there would be many answers to such a contention, as, for instance, that the House of Lords is largely no longer a House of Lords, but a House of tradesmen and financiers, or that the bulk of the commonplace nobility do not vote, and so leave the chamber to the prigs and the specialists and the mad old gentlemen with hobbies. But on some occasions the House of Lords, even under all these disadvantages, is in some sense representative. When all the peers flocked together to vote against Mr. Gladstone's second Home Rule Bill, for instance, those who said that the peers represented the English people, were perfectly right. All those dear old men who happened to be born peers were at that moment, and upon that question, the precise counterpart of all the dear old men who happened to be born paupers or middle-class gentlemen. That mob of peers did really represent the English people — that is to say, it was honest, ignorant, vaguely excited, almost unanimous, and obviously wrong. Of course, rational democracy is better as an expression of the public will than the haphazard hereditary method. While we are about having any kind of democracy, let it be rational democracy. But if we are to have any kind of oligarchy, let it be irrational oligarchy. Then at least we shall be ruled by men.

But the thing which is really required for the proper working of democracy is not merely the democratic system, or even the democratic philosophy, but the democratic emotion. The democratic emotion, like most elementary and indispensable things, is a thing difficult to describe at any time. But it is peculiarly difficult to describe it in our enlightened age, for the simple reason that it is peculiarly difficult to find it. It is a certain instinctive attitude which feels the things in which all men agree to be unspeakably important, and all the things in which they differ (such as mere brains) to be almost unspeakably unimportant. The nearest approach to it in our ordinary life would be the promptitude with which we should consider mere humanity in any circumstance of shock or death. We should say, after a somewhat disturbing discovery, "There is a dead man under the sofa." We should not be likely to say, "There is a dead man of considerable personal refinement under the sofa." We should say, "A woman has fallen into the water." We should not say, "A highly educated woman has fallen into the water." Nobody would say, "There are the remains of a clear thinker in your back garden." Nobody would say, "Unless you hurry up and stop him, a man with a very fine ear for music will have jumped off that cliff." But this emotion, which all of us have in connection with such things as birth and death, is to some people native and constant at all ordinary times and in all ordinary places. It was native to St. Francis of Assisi. It was native to Walt Whitman. In this strange and splendid degree it cannot be expected, perhaps, to pervade a whole commonwealth or a whole civilization; but one commonwealth may have it much more than another commonwealth, one civilization much more than another civilization. No community, perhaps, ever had it so much as the early Franciscans. No community, perhaps, ever had it so little as ours.

Everything in our age has, when carefully examined, this fundamentally undemocratic quality. In religion and morals we should admit, in the abstract, that the sins of the educated classes were as great as, or perhaps greater than, the sins of the poor and ignorant. But in practice the great difference between the mediaeval ethics and ours is that ours concentrate attention on the sins which are the sins of the ignorant, and practically deny that the sins which are the sins of the educated are sins at all. We are always talking about the sin of intemperate drinking, because it is quite obvious that the poor have it more than the rich. But we are always denying that there is any

such thing as the sin of pride, because it would be quite obvious that
the rich have it more than the poor. We are always ready to make a
saint or prophet of the educated man who goes into cottages to give
a little kindly advice to the uneducated. But the mediaeval idea of a
saint or prophet was something quite different. The mediaeval saint
or prophet was an uneducated man who walked into grand houses
to give a little kindly advice to the educated. The old tyrants had
enough insolence to despoil the poor, but they had not enough insolence to preach to them. It was the gentleman who oppressed the
slums; but it was the slums that admonished the gentleman. And
just as we are undemocratic in faith and morals, so we are, by the
very nature of our attitude in such matters, undemocratic in the tone
of our practical politics. It is a sufficient proof that we are not an
essentially democratic state that we are always wondering what we
shall do with the poor. If we were democrats, we should be wondering what the poor will do with us. With us the governing class is
always saying to itself, "What laws shall we make?" In a purely
democratic state it would be always saying, "What laws can we
obey?" A purely democratic state perhaps there has never been. But
even the feudal ages were in practice thus far democratic, that every
feudal potentate knew that any laws which he made would in all
probability return upon himself. His feathers might be cut off for
breaking a sumptuary law. His head might be cut off for high
treason. But the modern laws are almost always laws made to affect
the governed class, but not the governing. We have public-house
licensing laws, but not sumptuary laws. That is to say, we have laws
against the festivity and hospitality of the poor, but no laws against
the festivity and hospitality of the rich. We have laws against
blasphemy—that is, against a kind of coarse and offensive speaking
in which nobody but a rough and obscure man would be likely to
indulge. But we have no laws against heresy—that is, against the intellectual poisoning of the whole people, in which only a prosperous
and prominent man would be likely to be successful. The evil of
aristocracy is not that it necessarily leads to the infliction of bad
things or the suffering of sad ones; the evil of aristocracy is that it
places everything in the hands of a class of people who can always

inflict what they can never suffer. Whether what they inflict is, in their intention, good or bad, they become equally frivolous. The case against the governing class of modern England is not in the least that it is selfish; if you like, you may call the English oligarchs too fantastically unselfish. The case against them simply is that when they legislate for all men, they always omit themselves.

We are undemocratic, then, in our religion, as is proved by our efforts to "raise" the poor. We are undemocratic in our government, as is proved by our innocent attempt to govern them well. But above all we are undemocratic in our literature, as is proved by the torrent of novels about the poor and serious studies of the poor which pour from our publishers every month. And the more "modern" the book is the more certain it is to be devoid of democratic sentiment.

A poor man is a man who has not got much money. This may seem a simple and unnecessary description, but in the face of a great mass of modern fact and fiction, it seems very necessary indeed; most of our realists and sociologists talk about a poor man as if he were an octopus or an alligator. There is no more need to study the psychology of poverty than to study the psychology of bad temper, or the psychology of vanity, or the psychology of animal spirits. A man ought to know something of the emotions of an insulted man, not by being insulted, but simply by being a man. And he ought to know something of the emotions of a poor man, not by being poor, but simply by being a man. Therefore, in any writer who is describing poverty, my first objection to him will be that he has studied his subject. A democrat would have imagined it.

A great many hard things have been said about religious slumming and political or social slumming, but surely the most despicable of all is artistic slumming. The religious teacher is at least supposed to be interested in the costermonger because he is a man; the politician is in some dim and perverted sense interested in the costermonger because he is a citizen; it is only the wretched writer who is interested in the costermonger merely because he is a costermonger. Nevertheless, so long as he is merely seeking impressions, or in other words copy, his trade, though dull, is honest. But when he endeavours to represent that he is describing the spiritual core of a costermonger, his dim vices and his delicate virtues, then we must object that his claim is preposterous; we must remind him that he is a journalist and nothing else. He has far less psychological authority even than the foolish missionary. For he is in the literal and derivative sense a journalist, while the missionary is an eternalist. The missionary at least pretends to have a version of the man's lot for all time; the journalist only pretends to have a version of it from day to day. The missionary comes to tell the poor man that he is in the same condition with all men. The journalist comes to tell other people how different the poor man is from everybody else.

If the modern novels about the slums, such as novels of Mr. Arthur Morrison,[114] or the exceedingly able novels of Mr. Somerset Maugham,[115] are intended to be sensational, I can only say that that is a noble and reasonble object, and that they attain it. A sensation, a shock to the imagination, like the contact with cold water, is always a good and exhilarating thing; and, undoubtedly, men will always seek this sensation (among other forms) in the form of the study of the strange antics of remote or alien peoples. In the twelfth century men obtained this sensation by reading about dog-headed men in Africa. In the twentieth century they obtained it by reading about pig-headed Boers in Africa. The men of the twentieth century were certainly, it must be admitted, somewhat the more credulous of the two. For it is not recorded of the men in the twelfth century that they organized a sanguinary crusade solely for the purpose of altering the singular formation of the heads of the Africans. But it may be, and it may even legitimately be, that since all these monsters have faded from the popular mythology, it is necessary to have in our fiction the image of the horrible and hairy East-ender, merely to keep alive in us a fearful and childlike wonder at external peculiarities. But the Middle Ages (with a great deal more common sense

---

[114] Arthur Morrison (1863–1945), an author best known for stories of the London slums, such as *Tales of Mean Streets* (1864) and *A Child of the Jago* (1896).

[115] Maugham's best-known novels were to come later than 1905, but he had employed his experiences as a medical student as background for a naturalistic novel, *Liza of Lambeth*, in 1897.

than it would now be fashionable to admit) regarded natural history at bottom rather as a kind of joke; they regarded the soul as very important. Hence, while they had a natural history of dog-headed men, they did not profess to have a psychology of dog-headed men. They did not profess to mirror the mind of a dog-headed man, to share his tenderest secrets, or mount with his most celestial musings. They did not write novels about the semi-canine creature, attributing to him all the oldest morbidities and all the newest fads. It is permissible to present men as monsters if we wish to make the reader jump; and to make anybody jump is always a Christian act. But it is not permissible to present men as regarding themselves as monsters, or as making themselves jump. To summarize, our slum fiction is quite defensible as aesthetic fiction; it is not defensible as spiritual fact.

One enormous obstacle stands in the way of its actuality. The men who write it, and the men who read it, are men of the middle classes or the upper classes; at least, of those who are loosely termed the educated classes. Hence, the fact that it is the life as the refined man sees it proves that it cannot be the life as the unrefined man lives it. Rich men write stories about poor men, and describe them as speaking with a coarse, or heavy, or husky enunciation. But if poor men wrote novels about you or me they would describe us as speaking with some absurd shrill and affected voice, such as we only hear from a duchess in a three-act farce. The slum novelist gains his whole effect by the fact that some detail is strange to the reader; but that detail by the nature of the case cannot be strange in itself. It cannot be strange to the soul which he is professing to study. The slum novelist gains his effects by describing the same grey mist as draping the dingy factory and the dingy tavern. But to the man he is supposed to be studying there must be exactly the same difference between the factory and the tavern that there is to a middle-class man between a late night at the office and a supper at Pagani's. The slum novelist is content with pointing out that to the eye of his particular class a pickaxe looks dirty and a pewter pot looks dirty. But the man he is supposed to be studying sees the difference between them exactly as a clerk sees the difference between a ledger and an *edition de luxe*.

The chiaroscuro of the life is inevitably lost; for to us the high lights and the shadows are a light grey. But the high lights and the shadows are not a light grey in that life any more than in any other. The kind of man who could really express the pleasures of the poor would be also the kind of man who could share them. In short, these books are not a record of the psychology of poverty. They are a record of the psychology of wealth and culture when brought in contact with poverty. They are not a description of the state of the slums. They are only a very dark and dreadful description of the state of the slummers.

One might give innumerable examples of the essentially unsympathetic and unpopular quality of these realistic writers. But perhaps the simplest and most obvious example with which we could conclude is the mere fact that these writers are realistic. The poor have many other vices, but, at least, they are never realistic. The poor are melodramatic and romantic in grain; the poor all believe in high moral platitudes and copy-book maxims; probably this is the ultimate meaning of the great saying, "Blessed are the poor." Blessed are the poor, for they are always making life, or trying to make life like an Adelphi play.[116] Some innocent educationalists and philanthropists (for even philanthropists can be innocent) have expressed a grave astonishment that the masses prefer shilling shockers to scientific treatises and melodramas to problem plays. The reason is very simple. The realistic story is certainly more artistic than the melodramatic story. If what you desire is deft handling, delicate proportions, a unity of artistic atmosphere, the realistic story has a full advantage over the melodrama. In everything that is light and bright and ornamental the realistic story has a full advantage over the melodrama. But, at least, the melodrama has one indisputable advantage over the realistic story. The melodrama is much more like life. It is much more like man, and especially the poor man. It is very banal and very inartistic when a poor woman at the Adelphi says, "Do you think I will sell my own child?" But poor women in the Battersea High Road do say, "Do you think I will sell my own child?" They

---

[116] The Adelphi Theatre, in the Strand, was famous for its melodramas.

say it on every available occasion; you can hear a sort of murmur or babble of it all the way down the street. It is very stale and weak dramatic art (if that is all) when the workman confronts his master and says, "I'm a man." But a workman does say "I'm a man" two or three times a day. In fact, it is tedious, possibly, to hear poor men being melodramatic behind the footlights; but that is because one can always hear them being melodramatic in the street outside. In short, melodrama, if it is dull, is dull because it is too accurate. Somewhat the same problem exists in the case of stories about schoolboys. Mr. Kipling's "Stalky and Co." is much more amusing (if you are talking about amusement) than the late Dean Farrar's "Eric; or, Little by Little."[117] But "Eric" is immeasurably more like real school-life. For real school-life, real boyhood, is full of the things of which Eric is full — priggishness, a crude piety, a silly sin, a weak but continual attempt at the heroic, in a word, melodrama. And if we wish to lay a firm basis for any efforts to help the poor, we must not become realistic and see them from the outside. We must become melodramatic, and see them from the inside. The novelist must not take out his notebook and say, "I am an expert." No; he must imitate the workman in the Adelphi play. He must slap himself on the chest and say, "I am a man."

[117] Frederic William Farrar (1831–1903), clergyman and eventually Dean of Canterbury, wrote this novel of schoolboy life in 1858.

XX

CONCLUDING REMARKS ON
THE IMPORTANCE OF ORTHODOXY

Whether the human mind can advance or not, is a question too little discussed, for nothing can be more dangerous than to found our social philosophy on any theory which is debatable but has not been debated. But if we assume, for the sake of argument, that there has been in the past, or will be in the future, such a thing as a growth or improvement of the human mind itself, there still remains a very sharp objection to be raised against the modern version of that improvement. The vice of the modern notion of mental progress is that it is always something concerned with the breaking of bonds, the effacing of boundaries, the casting away of dogmas. But if there be such a thing as mental growth, it must mean the growth into more and more definite convictions, into more and more dogmas. The human brain is a machine for coming to conclusions; if it cannot come to conclusions it is rusty. When we hear of a man too clever to believe, we are hearing of something having almost the character of a contradiction in terms. It is like hearing of a nail that was too good to hold down a carpet; or a bolt that was too strong to keep a door shut. Man can hardly be defined, after the fashion of Carlyle, as an animal who makes tools; ants and beavers and many other animals make tools, in the sense that they make an apparatus. Man can be defined as an animal that makes dogmas. As he piles doctrine on doctrine and conclusion on conclusion in the formation of some tremendous scheme of philosophy and religion, he is, in the only legitimate sense of which the expression is capable, becoming more and more human. When he drops one doctrine after another in a refined scepticism, when he declines to tie himself to a system, when he says that he has outgrown definitions, when he says that he disbelieves in finality, when, in his own imagination, he sits as God, holding no form of creed but contemplating all, then he is by that very process sinking slowly backwards into the vagueness of the vagrant animals and the unconsciousness of the grass. Trees have no dogmas. Turnips are singularly broad-minded.

If then, I repeat, there is to be mental advance, it must be mental advance in the construction of a definite philosophy of life. And that philosophy of life must be right and the other philosophies wrong. Now of all, or nearly all, the able modern writers whom I have briefly studied in this book, this is especially and pleasingly true, that they do each of them have a constructive and affirmative view, and that they do take it seriously and ask us to take it seriously. There is nothing merely sceptically progressive about Mr. Rudyard Kipling. There is nothing in the least broad-minded about Mr. Bernard Shaw. The paganism of Mr. Lowes Dickinson is more grave than any Christianity. Even the opportunism of Mr. H. G. Wells is more dogmatic than the idealism of anybody else. Somebody complained, I think, to Matthew Arnold that he was getting as dogmatic as Carlyle. He replied, "That may be true; but you overlook an obvious difference. I am dogmatic and right, and Carlyle is dogmatic and wrong." The strong humour of the remark ought not to disguise from us its everlasting seriousness and common sense; no man ought to write at all, or even to speak at all, unless he thinks that he is in truth and the other man in error. In similar style, I hold that I am dogmatic and right, while Mr. Shaw is dogmatic and wrong. But my main point, at present, is to notice that the chief among these writers I have discussed do most sanely and courageously offer themselves as dogmatists, as founders of a system. It may be true that the thing in Mr. Shaw most interesting to me, is the fact that Mr. Shaw is wrong. But it is equally true that the thing in Mr. Shaw most interesting to himself, is the fact that Mr. Shaw is right. Mr. Shaw may have none with him but himself; but it is not for himself he cares. It is for the vast and universal church, of which he is the only member.

The two typical men of genius whom I have mentioned here, and with whose names I have begun this book, are very symbolic, if only because they have shown that the fiercest dogmatists can make the best artists. In the *fin de siècle* atmosphere every one was crying out that literature should be free from all causes and all ethical creeds.

Art was to produce only exquisite workmanship, and it was especially the note of those days to demand brilliant plays and brilliant short stories. And when they got them, they got them from a couple of moralists. The best short stories were written by a man trying to preach Imperialism. The best plays were written by a man trying to preach Socialism. All the art of all the artists looked tiny and tedious beside the art which was a by-product of propaganda.

The reason, indeed, is very simple. A man cannot be wise enough to be a great artist without being wise enough to wish to be a philosopher. A man cannot have the energy to produce good art without having the energy to wish to pass beyond it. A small artist is content with art; a great artist is content with nothing except everything. So we find that when real forces, good or bad, like Kipling and G. B. S., enter our arena, they bring with them not only startling and arresting art, but very startling and arresting dogmas. And they care even more, and desire us to care even more, about their startling and arresting dogmas than about their startling and arresting art. Mr. Shaw is a good dramatist, but what he desires more than anything else to be is a good politician. Mr. Rudyard Kipling is by divine caprice and natural genius an unconventional poet; but what he desires more than anything else to be is a conventional poet. He desires to be the poet of his people, bone of their bone, and flesh of their flesh, understanding their origins, celebrating their destiny. He desires to be Poet Laureate, a most sensible and honourable and public-spirited desire. Having been given by the gods originality—that is, disagreement with others—he desires divinely to agree with them. But the most striking instance of all, more striking, I think, even than either of these, is the instance of Mr. H. G. Wells. He began in a sort of insane infancy of pure art. He began by making a new heaven and a new earth, with the same irresponsible instinct by which men buy a new necktie or button-hole. He began by trifling with the stars and systems in order to make ephemeral anecdotes; he killed the universe for a joke. He has since become more and more serious, and has become, as men inevitably do when they become more and more serious, more and more parochial. He was frivolous about the twilight of the gods; but he is serious about the

London omnibus. He was careless in "The Time Machine," for that dealt only with the destiny of all things; but he is careful, and even cautious, in "Mankind in the Making," for that deals with the day after to-morrow. He began with the end of the world, and that was easy. Now he has gone on to the beginning of the world, and that is difficult. But the main result of all this is the same as in the other cases. The men who have really been the bold artists, the realistic artists, the uncompromising artists, are the men who have turned out, after all, to be writing "with a purpose." Suppose that any cool and cynical art-critic, any art-critic fully impressed with the conviction that artists were greatest when they were most purely artistic, suppose that a man who professed ably a humane aestheticism, as did Mr. Max Beerbohm, or a cruel aestheticism, as did Mr. W. E. Henley, had cast his eye over the whole fictional literature which was recent in the year 1895, and had been asked to select the three most vigorous and promising and original artists and artistic works, he would, I think, most certainly have said that for a fine artistic audacity, for a real artistic delicacy, or for a whiff of true novelty in art, the things that stood first were "Soldiers Three," by a Mr. Rudyard Kipling; "Arms and the Man," by a Mr. Bernard Shaw; and "The Time Machine," by a man called Wells. And all these men have shown themselves ingrainedly didactic. You may express the matter if you will by saying that if we want doctrines we go to the great artists. But it is clear from the psychology of the matter that this is not the true statement; the true statement is that when we want any art tolerably brisk and bold we have to go to the doctrinaires.

In concluding this book, therefore, I would ask, first and foremost, that men such as these of whom I have spoken should not be insulted by being taken for artists. No man has any right whatever merely to enjoy the work of Mr. Bernard Shaw; he might as well enjoy the invasion of his country by the French. Mr. Shaw writes either to convince or to enrage us. No man has any business to be a Kiplingite without being a politician, and an Imperialist politician. If a man is first with us, it should be because of what is first with him. If a man convinces us at all, it should be by his convictions. If we hate a poem of Kipling's from political passion, we are hating it for the same reason that the poet loved it; if we dislike him because of his opinions, we are disliking him for the best of all possible reasons. If a man comes into Hyde Park to preach it is permissible to hoot him; but it is discourteous to applaud him as a performing bear. And an artist is only a performing bear compared with the meanest man who fancies he has anything to say.

There is, indeed, one class of modern writers and thinkers who cannot altogether be overlooked in this question, though there is no space here for a lengthy account of them, which, indeed, to confess the truth, would consist chiefly of abuse. I mean those who get over all these abysses and reconcile all these wars by talking about "aspects of truth," by saying that the art of Kipling represents one aspect of the truth, and the art of William Watson[118] another; the art of Mr. Bernard Shaw one aspect of the truth, and the art of Mr. Cunningham Grahame[119] another; the art of Mr. H. G. Wells one aspect, and the art of Mr. Coventry Patmore[120] (say) another. I will only say here that this seems to me an evasion which has not even had the sense to disguise itself ingeniously in words. If we talk of a certain thing being an aspect of truth, it is evident that we claim to know what is truth; just as, if we talk of the hind leg of a dog, we claim to know what is a dog. Unfortunately, the philosopher who talks about aspects of truth generally also asks, "What is truth?" Frequently even he denies the existence of truth, or says it is inconceivable by the human intelligence. How, then, can he recognize its aspects? I should not like to be an artist who brought an architectural sketch to a builder, saying, "This is the south aspect of Sea-View Cottage. Sea-View Cottage, of course, does not exist." I should not even like very much to have to explain, under such circumstances, that Sea-View Cottage might exist, but was unthinkable by the

[118] William Watson (1850–1935) gained sufficient eminence through his poetry to be knighted and to be considered an obvious choice for the post of poet laureate in 1896. It went to Alfred Austin instead, largely because of Watson's opposition to the Boer War.

[119] R. B. Cunninghame Grahame (1852–1936) wrote many books based on his adventures in remote parts of the world.

[120] Coventry Patmore (1823–1896) wrote poems chiefly on married love and on religious themes.

human mind. Nor should I like any better to be the bungling and absurd metaphysician who professed to be able to see everywhere the aspects of a truth that is not there. Of course, it is perfectly obvious that there are truths in Kipling, that there are truths in Shaw or Wells. But the degree to which we can perceive them depends strictly upon how far we have a definite conception inside us of what is truth. It is ludicrous to suppose that the more sceptical we are the more we see good in everything. It is clear that the more we are certain what good is, the more we shall see good in everything.

I plead, then, that we should agree or disagree with these men. I plead that we should agree with them at least in having an abstract belief. But I know that there are current in the modern world many vague objections to having an abstract belief, and I feel that we shall not get any further until we have dealt with some of them. The first objection is easily stated.

A common hesitation in our day touching the use of extreme convictions is a sort of notion that extreme convictions, specially upon cosmic matters, have been responsible in the past for the thing which is called bigotry. But a very small amount of direct experience will dissipate this view. In real life the people who are most bigoted are the people who have no convictions at all. The economists of the Manchester school who disagree with Socialism take Socialism seriously. It is the young man in Bond Street, who does not know what socialism means, much less whether he agrees with it, who is quite certain that these socialist fellows are making a fuss about nothing. The man who understands the Calvinist philosophy enough to agree with it must understand the Catholic philosophy in order to disagree with it. It is the vague modern who is not at all certain what is right who is most certain that Dante was wrong. The serious opponent of the Latin Church in history, even in the act of showing that it produced great infamies, must know that it produced great saints. It is the hard-headed stockbroker, who knows no history and believes no religion, who is, nevertheless, perfectly convinced that all these priests are knaves. The Salvationist at the Marble Arch may be bigoted, but he is not too bigoted to yearn from a common human kinship after the dandy on church parade. But the dandy on church parade is so bigoted that he does not in the least yearn after the Salvationist at the Marble Arch. Bigotry may be roughly defined as the anger of men who have no opinions. It is the resistance offered to definite ideas by that vague bulk of people whose ideas are indefinite to excess. Bigotry may be called the appalling frenzy of the indifferent. This frenzy of the indifferent is in truth a terrible thing; it has made all monstrous and widely pervading persecutions. In this degree it was not the people who cared who ever persecuted; the people who cared were not sufficiently numerous. It was the people who did not care who filled the world with fire and oppression. It was the hands of the indifferent that lit the faggots; it was the hands of the indifferent that turned the rack. There have come some persecutions out of the pain of a passionate certainty; but this produced, not bigotry, but fanaticism — a very different and a somewhat admirable thing. Bigotry in the main has always been the pervading omnipotence of those who do not care crushing out those who care in darkness and blood.

There are people, however, who dig somewhat deeper than this into the possible evils of dogma. It is felt by many that strong philosophical conviction, while it does not (as they perceive) produce that sluggish and fundamentally frivolous condition which we call bigotry, does produce a certain concentration, exaggeration, and moral impatience, which we may agree to call fanaticism. They say, in brief, that ideas are dangerous things. In politics, for example, it is commonly urged against a man like Mr. Balfour, or against a man like Mr. John Morley,[121] that a wealth of ideas is dangerous. The true doctrine on this point, again, is surely not very difficult to state. Ideas are dangerous, but the man to whom they are least dangerous is the man of ideas. He is acquainted with ideas, and moves among them like a lion-tamer. Ideas are dangerous, but the man to whom they are most dangerous is the man of no ideas. The man of no ideas will find the first idea fly to his head like wine to the head of a teetotaller. It is a common error, I think, among the Radical idealists of my own party and period to suggest that financiers and

[121] John Morley (1838–1923), a Liberal statesman and man of letters, who wrote biographies of a number of literary and political figures, especially Gladstone.

business men are a danger to the empire because they are so sordid or so materialistic. The truth is that financiers and business men are a danger to the empire because they can be sentimental about any sentiment, and idealistic about any ideal, any ideal that they find lying about. Just as a boy who has not known much of women is apt too easily to take a woman for *the* woman, so these practical men, unaccustomed to causes, are always inclined to think that if a thing is proved to be an ideal it is proved to be the ideal. Many, for example, avowedly followed Cecil Rhodes because he had a vision. They might as well have followed him because he had a nose; a man without some kind of dream of perfection is quite as much of a monstrosity as a noseless man. People say of such a figure, in almost feverish whispers, "He knows his own mind," which is exactly like saying in equally feverish whispers, "He blows his own nose." Human nature simply cannot subsist without a hope and aim of some kind; as the sanity of the Old Testament truly said, where there is no vision the people perisheth. But it is precisely because an ideal is necessary to man that the man without ideals is in permanent danger of fanaticism. There is nothing which is so likely to leave a man open to the sudden and irresistible inroad of an unbalanced vision as the cultivation of business habits. All of us know angular business men who think that the earth is flat, or that Mr. Kruger[122] was at the head of a great military despotism, or that men are graminivorous, or that Bacon wrote Shakespeare. Religious and philosophical beliefs are, indeed, as dangerous as fire, and nothing can take from them that beauty of danger. But there is only one way of really guarding ourselves against the excessive danger of them, and that is to be steeped in philosophy and soaked in religion.

Briefly, then, we dismiss the two opposite dangers of bigotry and fanaticism, bigotry which is a too great vagueness and fanaticism which is a too great concentration. We say that the cure for the bigot is belief; we say that the cure for the idealist is ideas. To know the best theories of existence and to choose the best from them (that

[122] Paul Kruger (1825–1904), South African political leader, four times president of the Transvaal Republic, strongly resisted Cecil Rhodes's plan for a unified South Africa.

is, to the best of our own strong conviction) appears to us the proper way to be neither bigot nor fanatic, but something more firm than a bigot and more terrible than a fanatic, a man with a definite opinion. But that definite opinion must in this view begin with the basic matters of human thought, and these must not be dismissed as irrelevant, as religion, for instance, is too often in our days dismissed as irrelevant. Even if we think religion insoluble, we cannot think it irrelevant. Even if we ourselves have no view of the ultimate verities, we must feel that wherever such a view exists in a man it must be more important than anything else in him. The instant that the thing ceases to be the unknowable, it becomes the indispensible.

There can be no doubt, I think, that the idea does exist in our time that there is something narrow or irrelevant or even mean about attacking a man's religion, or arguing from it in matters of politics or ethics. There can be quite as little doubt that such an accusation of narrowness is itself almost grotesquely narrow. To take an example from comparatively current events: we all know that it was not uncommon for a man to be considered a scarecrow of bigotry and obscurantism because he distrusted the Japanese, or lamented the rise of the Japanese, on the ground that the Japanese were Pagans. Nobody would think that there was anything antiquated or fanatical about distrusting a people because of some difference between them and us in practice or political machinery. Nobody would think it bigoted to say of a people, "I distrust their influence because they are Protectionists." No one would think it narrow to say, "I lament their rise because they are Socialists, or Manchester Individualists, or strong believers in militarism and conscription." A difference of opinion about the nature of Parliaments matters very much; but a difference of opinion about the nature of sin does not matter at all. A difference of opinion about the object of taxation matters very much; but a difference of opinion about the object of human existence does not matter at all. We have a right to distrust a man who is in a different kind of municipality; but we have no right to mistrust a man who is in a different kind of cosmos. This sort of enlightenment is surely about the most unenlightened that it is possible to imagine. To recur to the phrase which I employed earlier, this is tantamount to saying that everything is important with the exception of everything. Religion is exactly the thing which cannot be left out — because it includes everything. The most absent-minded person cannot well pack his Gladstone-bag and leave out the bag. We have a general view of existence, whether we like it or not; it alters, or, to speak more accurately, it creates and involves everything we say or do, whether we like it or not. If we regard the Cosmos as a dream, we regard the Fiscal Question as a dream. If we regard the Cosmos as a joke, we regard St. Paul's Cathedral as a joke. If everything is bad, then we must believe (if it be possible) that beer is bad; if everything be good, we are forced to the rather fantastic conclusion that scientific philanthropy is good. Every man in the street must hold a metaphysical system, and hold it firmly. The utmost possibility is that he may have held it so firmly and so long as to have forgotten all about its existence.

This latter situation is certainly possible; in fact, it is the situation of the whole modern world. The modern world is filled with men who hold dogmas so strongly that they do not even know that they are dogmas. It may be said even that the modern world, as a corporate body, holds certain dogmas so strongly that it does not know that they are dogmas. It may be thought "dogmatic," for instance, in some circles accounted progressive, to assume the perfection or improvement of man in another world. But it is not thought "dogmatic" to assume the perfection or improvement of man in this world; though that idea of progress is quite as unproved as the idea of immortality, and from a rationalistic point of view quite as improbable. Progress happens to be one of our dogmas, and a dogma means a thing which is not thought dogmatic. Or, again, we see nothing "dogmatic" in the inspiring, but certainly most startling, theory of physical science, that we should collect facts for the sake of facts, even though they seem as useless as sticks and straws. This is a great and suggestive idea, and its utility may, if you will, be proving itself, but its utility is, in the abstract, quite as disputable as the utility of that calling on oracles or consulting shrines which is also said to prove itself. Thus, because we are not in a civilization which believes strongly in oracles or sacred places, we see the full frenzy of those who killed themselves to find the sepulchre of Christ. But being in a civilization which does believe in this dogma of fact for facts' sake, we do not see the full frenzy of those who kill themselves to find the North Pole. I am not speaking of a tenable ultimate utility which is true both of the Crusades and the polar explorations. I mean merely that we do see the superficial and aesthetic singularity, the startling quality, about the idea of men crossing a continent with armies to conquer the place where a man died. But we do not see the aesthetic singularity and startling quality of men dying in agonies to find a place where no man can live—a place only interesting because it is supposed to be the meeting-place of some lines that do not exist.

Let us, then, go upon a long journey and enter on a dreadful search. Let us, at least, dig and seek till we have discovered our own opinions. The dogmas we really hold are far more fantastic, and, perhaps, far more beautiful than we think. In the course of these essays I fear that I have spoken from time to time of rationalists and rationalism, and that in a disparaging sense. Being full of that kindliness which should come at the end of everything, even of a book, I apologize to the rationalists even for calling them rationalists. There are no rationalists. We all believe fairy-tales, and live in them. Some, with a sumptuous literary turn, believe in the existence of the lady clothed with the sun. Some, with a more rustic, elvish instinct, like Mr. McCabe, believe merely in the impossible sun itself. Some hold the undemonstrable dogma of the existence of God; some the equally undemonstrable dogma of the existence of the man next door.

Truths turn into dogmas the instant that they are disputed. Thus every man who utters a doubt defines a religion. And the scepticism of our time does not really destroy the beliefs, rather it creates them; gives them their limits and their plain and defiant shape. We who are Liberals once held Liberalism lightly as a truism. Now it has been disputed, and we hold it fiercely as a faith. We who believe in patriotism once thought patriotism to be reasonable, and thought little more about it. Now we know it to be unreasonable, and know it to be right. We who are Christians never knew the great philosophic common sense which inheres in that mystery until the anti-Christian writers pointed it out to us. The great march of mental destruction will go on. Everything will be denied. Everything will become a creed. It is a reasonable position to deny the stones in the street; it will be a religious dogma to assert them. It is a rational thesis that we are all in a dream; it will be a mystical sanity to say that we are all awake. Fires will be kindled to testify that two and two make four. Swords will be drawn to prove that leaves are green in summer. We shall be left defending, not only the incredible virtues and sanities of human life, but something more incredible still, this huge impossible universe which stares us in the face. We shall fight for visible prodigies as if they were invisible. We shall look on the impossible grass and the skies with a strange courage. We shall be of those who have seen and yet have believed.

ORTHODOXY

1908

I

INTRODUCTION IN DEFENCE
OF EVERYTHING ELSE

The only possible excuse for this book is that it is an answer to a challenge. Even a bad shot is dignified when he accepts a duel. When some time ago I published a series of hasty but sincere papers, under the name of "Heretics," several critics for whose intellect I have a warm respect (I may mention specially Mr. G. S. Street) said that it was all very well for me to tell everybody to affirm his cosmic theory, but that I had carefully avoided supporting my precepts with example. "I will begin to worry about my philosophy," said Mr. Street, "when Mr. Chesterton has given us his."[1] It was perhaps an incautious suggestion to make to a person only too ready to write books upon the feeblest provocation. But after all, though Mr. Street has inspired and created this book, he need not read it. If he does read it, he will find that in its pages I have attempted in a vague and personal way, in a set of mental pictures rather than in a series of deductions, to state the philosophy in which I have come to believe. I will not call it my philosophy; for I did not make it. God and humanity made it; and it made me.

I have often had a fancy for writing a romance about an English yachtsman who slightly miscalculated his course and discovered England under the impression that it was a new island in the South Seas. I always find, however, that I am either too busy or too lazy to write this fine work, so I may as well give it away for the purposes of philosophical illustration. There will probably be a general impression that the man who landed (armed to the teeth and talking by signs) to plant the British flag on that barbaric temple which turned out to be the Pavilion at Brighton,[2] felt rather a fool. I am not here

[1] This comment appeared in a review in the *Outlook* for June 17, 1905. Street's exact words were, "I shall not begin to worry about my philosophy of life until Mr. Chesterton discloses his."

[2] Built by the Prince of Wales (later George IV.) in 1784 as a summer residence and transformed by John Nash into an oriental palace.

concerned to deny that he looked a fool. But if you imagine that he felt a fool, or at any rate that the sense of folly was his sole or his dominant emotion, then you have not studied with sufficient delicacy the rich romantic nature of the hero of this tale. His mistake was really a most enviable mistake; and he knew it, if he was the man I take him for. What could be more delightful than to have in the same few minutes all the fascinating terrors of going abroad combined with all the humane security of coming home again? What could be better than to have all the fun of discovering South Africa without the disgusting necessity of landing there? What could be more glorious than to brace one's self up to discover New South Wales and then realize, with a gush of happy tears, that it was really old South Wales. This at least seems to me the main problem for philosophers, and is in a manner the main problem of this book. How can we contrive to be at once astonished at the world and yet at home in it? How can this queer cosmic town, with its many-legged citizens, with its monstrous and ancient lamps, how can this world give us at once the fascination of a strange town and the comfort and honour of being our own town?

To show that a faith or a philosophy is true from every standpoint would be too big an undertaking even for a much bigger book than this; it is necessary to follow one path of argument; and this is the path that I here propose to follow. I wish to set forth my faith as particularly answering this double spiritual need, the need for that mixture of the familiar and the unfamiliar which Christendom has rightly named romance. For the very word "romance" has in it the mystery and ancient meaning of Rome. Any one setting out to dispute anything ought always to begin by saying what he does not dispute. Beyond stating what he proposes to prove he should always state what he does not propose to prove. The thing I do not propose to prove, the thing I propose to take as common ground between myself and any average reader, is this desirability of an active and imaginative life, picturesque and full of a poetical curiosity, a life such as western man at any rate always seems to have desired. If a man says that extinction is better than existence or blank existence better than variety and adventure, then he is not one of the ordinary people to whom I am talking. If a man prefers nothing I can give him nothing. But nearly all people I have ever met in this western society in which I live would agree to the general proposition that we need this life of practical romance; the combination of something that is strange with something that is secure. We need so to view the world as to combine an idea of wonder and an idea of welcome. We need to be happy in this wonderland without once being merely comfortable. It is *this* achievement of my creed that I shall chiefly pursue in these pages.

But I have a peculiar reason for mentioning the man in a yacht, who discovered England. For I am that man in a yacht. I discovered England. I do not see how this book can avoid being egotistical; and I do not quite see (to tell the truth) how it can avoid being dull. Dulness will, however, free me from the charge which I most lament; the charge of being flippant. Mere light sophistry is the thing that I happen to despise most of all things, and it is perhaps a wholesome fact that this is the thing of which I am generally accused. I know nothing so contemptible as a mere paradox; a mere ingenious defence of the indefensible. If it were true (as has been said) that Mr. Bernard Shaw lived upon paradox, then he ought to be a mere common millionaire; for a man of his mental activity could invent a sophistry every six minutes. It is as easy as lying; because it is lying. The truth is, of course, that Mr. Shaw is cruelly hampered by the fact that he cannot tell any lie unless he thinks it is the truth. I find myself under the same intolerable bondage. I never in my life said anything merely because I thought it funny; though of course, I have had ordinary human vainglory, and may have thought it funny because I had said it. It is one thing to describe an interview with a gorgon or a griffin, a creature who does not exist. It is another thing to discover that the rhinoceros does exist and then take pleasure in the fact that he looks as if he didn't. One searches for truth, but it may be that one pursues instinctively the more extraordinary truths. And I offer this book with the heartiest sentiments to all the jolly people who hate what I write, and regard it (very justly, for all I know) as a piece of poor clowning or a single tiresome joke.

For if this book is a joke it is a joke against me. I am the man who with the utmost daring discovered what had been discovered before. If there is an element of farce in what follows, the farce is at my own expense; for this book explains how I fancied I was the first to set foot in Brighton and then found I was the last. It recounts my elephantine adventures in pursuit of the obvious. No one can think my case more ludicrous than I think it myself; no reader can accuse me here of trying to make a fool of him: I am the fool of this story, and no rebel shall hurl me from my throne. I freely confess all the idiotic ambitions of the end of the nineteenth century. I did, like all other solemn little boys, try to be in advance of the age. Like them I tried to be some ten minutes in advance of the truth. And I found that I was eighteen hundred years behind it. I did strain my voice with a painfully juvenile exaggeration in uttering my truths. And I was punished in the fittest and funniest way, for I have kept my truths: but I have discovered, not that they were not truths, but simply that they were not mine. When I fancied that I stood alone I was really in the ridiculous position of being backed up by all Christendom. It may be, Heaven forgive me, that I did try to be original; but I only succeeded in inventing all by myself an inferior copy of the existing traditions of civilized religion. The man from the yacht thought he was the first to find England; I thought I was the first to find Europe. I did try to found a heresy of my own; and when I had put the last touches to it, I discovered that it was orthodoxy.

It may be that somebody will be entertained by the account of this happy fiasco. It might amuse a friend or an enemy to read how I gradually learnt from the truth of some stray legend or from the falsehood of some dominant philosophy, things that I might have learnt from my catechism—if I had ever learnt it. There may or may not be some entertainment in reading how I found at last in an anarchist club or a Babylonian temple what I might have found in the nearest parish church. If any one is entertained by learning how the flowers of the field or the phrases in an omnibus, the accidents of politics or the pains of youth came together in a certain order to produce a certain conviction of Christian orthodoxy, he may possibly read this book. But there is in everything a reasonable division of labour. I have written the book, and nothing on earth would induce me to read it.

I add one purely pedantic note which comes, as a note naturally should, at the beginning of the book. These essays are concerned only to discuss the actual fact that the central Christian theology (sufficiently summarized in the Apostles' Creed) is the best root of energy and sound ethics. They are not intended to discuss the very fascinating but quite different question of what is the present seat of authority for the proclamation of that creed. When the word "orthodoxy" is used here it means the Apostles' Creed, as understood by everybody calling himself Christian until a very short time ago and the general historic conduct of those who held such a creed. I have been forced by mere space to confine myself to what I have got from this creed; I do not touch the matter much disputed among modern Christians, of where we ourselves got it. This is not an ecclesiastical treatise but a sort of slovenly autobiography. But if any one wants my opinions about the actual nature of the authority, Mr. G. S. Street has only to throw me another challenge, and I will write him another book.

II

THE MANIAC

Thoroughly worldly people never understand even the world; they rely altogether on a few cynical maxims which are not true. Once I remember walking with a prosperous publisher, who made a remark which I had often heard before; it is, indeed, almost a motto of the modern world. Yet I had heard it once too often, and I saw suddenly that there was nothing in it. The publisher said of somebody, "That man will get on; he believes in himself." And I remember that as I lifted my head to listen, my eye caught an omnibus on which was written "Hanwell."[3] I said to him, "Shall I tell you where the men are who believe most in themselves? For I can tell you. I know of men who believe in themselves more colossally than Napoleon or Caesar. I know where flames the fixed star of certainty and success. I can guide you to the thrones of the Supermen. The men who really believe in themselves are all in lunatic asylums." He said mildly that there were a good many men after all who believed in themselves and who were not in lunatic asylums. "Yes, there are," I retorted, "and you of all men ought to know them. That drunken poet from whom you would not take a dreary tragedy, he believed in himself. That elderly minister with an epic from whom you were hiding in a back room, he believed in himself. If you consulted your business experience instead of your ugly individualistic philosophy, you would know that believing in himself is one of the commonest signs of a rotter. Actors who can't act believe in themselves; and debtors who won't pay. It would be much truer to say that a man will certainly fail, because he believes in himself. Complete self-confidence is not merely a sin; complete self-confidence is a weakness. Believing utterly in one's self is a hysterical and superstitious belief like believing in Joanna Southcote:[4] the man who has it has 'Hanwell' written on his

[3] The location of an asylum to the west of London.

[4] An English religious visionary (1750–1814) whose "revelations" attracted many followers.

face as plain as it is written on that omnibus." And to all this my friend the publisher made this very deep and effective reply, "Well, if a man is not to believe in himself, in what is he to believe?" After a long pause I replied, "I will go home and write a book in answer to that question." This is the book that I have written in answer to it.

But I think this book may well start where our argument started—in the neighbourhood of the mad-house. Modern masters of science are much impressed with the need of beginning all inquiry with a fact. The ancient masters of religion were quite equally impressed with that necessity. They began with the fact of sin—a fact as practical as potatoes. Whether or no man could be washed in miraculous waters, there was no doubt at any rate that he wanted washing. But certain religious leaders in London, not mere materialists, have begun in our day not to deny the highly disputable water, but to deny the indisputable dirt. Certain new theologians dispute original sin, which is the only part of Christian theology which can really be proved. Some followers of the Reverend R. J. Campbell,[5] in their almost too fastidious spirituality, admit divine sinlessness, which they cannot see even in their dreams. But they essentially deny human sin, which they can see in the street. The strongest saints and the strongest sceptics alike took positive evil as the starting-point of their argument. If it be true (as it certainly is) that a man can feel exquisite happiness in skinning a cat, then the religious philosopher can only draw one of two deductions. He must either deny the existence of God, as all atheists do; or he must deny the present union between God and man, as all Christians do. The new theologians seem to think it a highly rationalistic solution to deny the cat.

In this remarkable situation it is plainly not now possible (with any hope of a universal appeal) to start, as our fathers did, with the fact of sin. This very fact which was to them (and is to me) as plain as a pikestaff, is the very fact that has been specially diluted or denied. But though moderns deny the existence of sin, I do not think that they have yet denied the existence of a lunatic asylum. We all agree

[5] Rev. R. J. Campbell (1867–1956) was pastor of the City Temple in London at this time. He was in the van of the "modernizers" of Christianity, and his book *New Theology* (1907) had attracted considerable attention.

still that there is a collapse of the intellect as unmistakable as a falling house. Men deny hell, but not, as yet, Hanwell. For the purpose of our primary argument the one may very well stand where the other stood. I mean that as all thoughts and theories were once judged by whether they tended to make a man lose his soul, so for our present purpose all modern thoughts and theories may be judged by whether they tend to make a man lose his wits.

It is true that some speak lightly and loosely of insanity as in itself attractive. But a moment's thought will show that if disease is beautiful, it is generally some one else's disease. A blind man may be picturesque; but it requires two eyes to see the picture. And similarly even the wildest poetry of insanity can only be enjoyed by the sane. To the insane man his insanity is quite prosaic, because it is quite true. A man who thinks himself a chicken is to himself as ordinary as a chicken. A man who thinks he is a bit of glass is to himself as dull as a bit of glass. It is the homogeneity of his mind which makes him dull, and which makes him mad. It is only because we see the irony of his idea that we think him even amusing; it is only because he does not see the irony of his idea that he is put in Hanwell at all. In short, oddities only strike ordinary people. Oddities do not strike odd people. This is why ordinary people have a much more exciting time; while odd people are always complaining of the dulness of life. This is also why the new novels die so quickly, and why the old fairy tales endure for ever. The old fairy tale makes the hero a normal human boy; it is his adventures that are startling; they startle him because he is normal. But in the modern psychological novel the hero is abnormal; the centre is not central. Hence the fiercest adventures fail to affect him adequately, and the book is monotonous. You can make a story out of a hero among dragons; but not out of a dragon among dragons. The fairy tale discusses what a sane man will do in a mad world. The sober realistic novel of to-day discusses what an essential lunatic will do in a dull world.

Let us begin, then, with the mad-house; from this evil and fantastic inn let us set forth on our intellectual journey. Now, if we are to glance at the philosophy of sanity, the first thing to do in the matter is to blot out one big and common mistake. There is a notion adrift everywhere that imagination, especially mystical imagination, is dangerous to man's mental balance. Poets are commonly spoken of as psychologically unreliable; and generally there is a vague association between wreathing laurels in your hair and sticking straws in it. Facts and history utterly contradict this view. Most of the very great poets have been not only sane, but extremely business-like; and if Shakespeare ever really held horses, it was because he was much the safest man to hold them. Imagination does not breed insanity. Exactly what does breed insanity is reason. Poets do not go mad; but chess-players do. Mathematicians go mad, and cashiers; but creative artists very seldom. I am not, as will be seen, in any sense attacking logic: I only say that this danger does lie in logic, not in imagination. Artistic paternity is as wholesome as physical paternity. Moreover, it is worthy of remark that when a poet really was morbid it was commonly because he had some weak spot of rationality on his brain. Poe, for instance, really was morbid; not because he was poetical, but because he was specially analytical. Even chess was too poetical for him; he disliked chess because it was full of knights and castles, like a poem. He avowedly preferred the black discs of draughts, because they were more like the mere black dots on a diagram. Perhaps the strongest case of all is this: that only one great English poet went mad, Cowper.[6] And he was definitely driven mad by logic, by the ugly and alien logic of predestination. Poetry was not the disease, but the medicine; poetry partly kept him in health. He could sometimes forget the red and thirsty hell to which his hideous necessitarianism dragged him among the wide waters and the white flat lilies of the Ouse. He was damned by John Calvin; he was almost saved by John Gilpin. Everywhere we see that men do not go mad by dreaming. Critics are much madder than poets. Homer is complete and calm enough; it is his critics who tear him into extravagant tatters. Shakespeare is quite himself; it is only some of his critics who have discovered that he was somebody else. And though St. John

[6] During periodic fits of insanity, William Cowper (1731–1800) sometimes thought that he was damned for committing the unforgivable sin. "The Diverting History of John Gilpin" is a humorous poem by Cowper about a linen draper who borrows a horse that runs away with him.

the Evangelist saw many strange monsters in his vision, he saw no creature so wild as one of his own commentators. The general fact is simple. Poetry is sane because it floats easily in an infinite sea; reason seeks to cross the infinite sea, and so make it finite. The result is mental exhaustion, like the physical exhaustion of Mr. Holbein.[7] To accept everything is an exercise, to understand everything a strain. The poet only desires exaltation and expansion, a world to stretch himself in. The poet only asks to get his head into the heavens. It is the logician who seeks to get the heavens into his head. And it is his head that splits.

It is a small matter, but not irrelevant, that this striking mistake is commonly supported by a striking misquotation. We have all heard people cite the celebrated line of Dryden as "Great genius is to madness near allied." But Dryden did not say that great genius was to madness near allied. Dryden was a great genius himself, and knew better. It would have been hard to find a man more romantic than he, or more sensible. What Dryden said was this, "Great wits are oft to madness near allied"; and that is true. It is the pure promptitude of the intellect that is in peril of a breakdown. Also people might remember of what sort of man Dryden was talking. He was not talking of any unworldly visionary like Vaughan or George Herbert.[8] He was talking of a cynical man of the world, a sceptic, a diplomatist, a great practical politician. Such men are indeed to madness near allied. Their incessant calculation of their own brains and other people's brains is a dangerous trade. It is always perilous to the mind to reckon up the mind. A flippant person has asked why we say, "As mad as a hatter." A more flippant person might answer that a hatter is mad because he has to measure the human head.

And if great reasoners are often maniacal, it is equally true that maniacs are commonly great reasoners. When I was engaged in a controversy with the *Clarion* on the matter of free will, that able

[7] Presumably Hans Holbein the Younger (1497–1543), known for the meticulous finish of his portraits.

[8] Henry Vaughan (1622–1695) and George Herbert (1593–1633) both wrote religious poetry.

writer Mr. R. B. Suthers[9] said that free will was lunacy, because it meant causeless actions, and the actions of a lunatic would be causeless. I do not dwell here upon the disastrous lapse in determinist logic. Obviously if any actions, even a lunatic's, can be causeless, determinism is done for. If the chain of causation can be broken for a madman, it can be broken for a man. But my purpose is to point out something more practical. It was natural, perhaps, that a modern Marxian Socialist should not know anything about free will. But it was certainly remarkable that a modern Marxian Socialist should not know anything about lunatics. Mr. Suthers evidently did not know anything about lunatics. The last thing that can be said of a lunatic is that his actions are causeless. If any human acts may loosely be called causeless, they are the minor acts of a healthy man; whistling as he walks; slashing the grass with a stick; kicking his heels or rubbing his hands. It is the happy man who does the useless things; the sick man is not strong enough to be idle. It is exactly such careless and causeless actions that the madman could never understand; for the madman (like the determinist) generally sees too much cause in everything. The madman would read a conspiratorial significance into those empty activities. He would think that the lopping of the grass was an attack on private property. He would think that the kicking of the heels was a signal to an accomplice. If the madman could for an instant become careless, he would become sane. Every one who has had the misfortune to talk with people in the heart or on the edge of mental disorder, knows that their most sinister quality is a horrible clarity of detail; a connecting of one thing with another in a map more elaborate than a maze. If you argue with a madman, it is extremely probable that you will get the worst of it; for in many ways his mind moves all the quicker for not being delayed by the things that go with good judgment. He is not hampered by a sense of humour or by charity, or by the dumb certainties of experience. He is the more logical for losing certain sane affections. Indeed, the common phrase for insanity is in

[9] An editor of the *Clarion* and a supporter of Robert Blatchford in his controversy with Chesterton.

this respect a misleading one. The madman is not the man who has
lost his reason. The madman is the man who has lost everything except his reason.

The madman's explanation of a thing is always complete, and
often in a purely rational sense satisfactory. Or, to speak more strictly,
the insane explanation, if not conclusive, is at least unanswerable;
this may be observed specially in the two or three commonest kinds
of madness. If a man says (for instance) that men have a conspiracy
against him, you cannot dispute it except by saying that all the men
deny that they are conspirators; which is exactly what conspirators
would do. His explanation covers the facts as much as yours. Or if a
man says that he is the rightful King of England, it is no complete
answer to say that the existing authorities call him mad; for if he
were King of England that might be the wisest thing for the existing authorities to do. Or if a man says that he is Jesus Christ, it is
no answer to tell him that the world denies his divinity; for the
world denied Christ's.

Nevertheless he is wrong. But if we attempt to trace his error in
exact terms, we shall not find it quite so easy as we had supposed.
Perhaps the nearest we can get to expressing it is to say this: that his
mind moves in a perfect but narrow circle. A small circle is quite as
infinite as a large circle; but, though it is quite as infinite, it is not so
large. In the same way the insane explanation is quite as complete as
the sane one, but it is not so large. A bullet is quite as round as the
world, but it is not the world. There is such a thing as a narrow
universality; there is such a thing as a small and cramped eternity;
you may see it in many modern religions. Now, speaking quite ex-
ternally and empirically, we may say that the strongest and most unmistakable *mark* of madness is this combination between a logical
completeness and a spiritual contraction. The lunatic's theory explains a large number of things, but it does not explain them in a
large way. I mean that if you or I were dealing with a mind that was
growing morbid, we should be chiefly concerned not so much to
give it arguments as to give it air, to convince it that there was
something cleaner and cooler outside the suffocation of a single
argument. Suppose, for instance, it were the first case that I took as

typical; suppose it were the case of a man who accused everybody of conspiring against him. If we could express our deepest feelings of protest and appeal against this obsession, I suppose we should say something like this: "Oh, I admit that you have your case and have it by heart, and that many things do fit into other things as you say. I admit that your explanation explains a great deal; but what a great deal it leaves out! Are there no other stories in the world except yours; and are all men busy with your business? Suppose we grant the details; perhaps when the man in the street did not seem to see you it was only his cunning; perhaps when the policeman asked you your name it was only because he knew it already. But how much happier you would be if you only knew that these people cared nothing about you! How much larger your life would be if your self could become smaller in it; if you could really look at other men with common curiosity and pleasure; if you could see them walking as they are in their sunny selfishness and their virile indifference! You would begin to be interested in them, because they were not interested in you. You would break out of this tiny and tawdry theatre in which your own little plot is always being played, and you would find yourself under a freer sky, in a street full of splendid strangers." Or suppose it were the second case of madness, that of a man who claims the crown, your impulse would be to answer, "All right! Perhaps you know that you are the King of England; but why do you care? Make one magnificent effort and you will be a human being and look down on all the kings of the earth." Or it might be the third case, of the madman who called himself Christ. If we said what we felt, we should say, "So you are the Creator and Redeemer of the world: but what a small world it must be! What a little heaven you must inhabit, with angels no bigger than butterflies! How sad it must be to be God; and an inadequate God! Is there really no life fuller and no love more marvellous than yours; and is it really in your small and painful pity that all flesh must put its faith? How much happier you would be, how much more of you there would be, if the hammer of a higher God could smash your small cosmos, scattering the stars like spangles, and leave you in the open, free like other men to look up as well as down!"

And it must be remembered that the most purely practical science does take this view of mental evil; it does not seek to argue with it like a heresy but simply to snap it like a spell. Neither modern science nor ancient religion believes in complete free thought. Theology rebukes certain thoughts by calling them blasphemous. Science rebukes certain thoughts by calling them morbid. For example, some religious societies discouraged men more or less from thinking about sex. The new scientific society definitely discourages men from thinking about death; it is a fact, but it is considered a morbid fact. And in dealing with those whose morbidity has a touch of mania, modern science cares far less for pure logic than a dancing Dervish. In these cases it is not enough that the unhappy man should desire truth; he must desire health. Nothing can save him but a blind hunger for normality, like that of a beast. A man cannot think himself out of mental evil; for it is actually the organ of thought that has become diseased, ungovernable, and, as it were, independent. He can only be saved by will or faith. The moment his mere reason moves, it moves in the old circular rut; he will go round and round his logical circle, just as a man in a third-class carriage on the Inner Circle[10] will go round and round the Inner Circle unless he performs the voluntary, vigorous, and mystical act of getting out at Gower Street. Decision is the whole business here; a door must be shut for ever. Every remedy is a desperate remedy. Every cure is a miraculous cure. Curing a madman is not arguing with a philosopher; it is casting out a devil. And however quietly doctors and psychologists may go to work in the matter, their attitude is profoundly intolerant — as intolerant as Bloody Mary.[11] Their attitude is really this: that the man must stop thinking, if he is to go on living. Their counsel is one of intellectual amputation. If thy *head* offend thee, cut it off; for it is better, not merely to enter the Kingdom of Heaven as a child, but to enter it as an imbecile, rather than with your whole intellect to be cast into hell — or into Hanwell.

Such is the madman of experience; he is commonly a reasoner,

[10] A circular route on the London Underground.

[11] Mary Tudor, Queen of England from 1553–1558, who resorted to religious persecution in an attempt to restore Catholicism.

frequently a successful reasoner. Doubtless he could be vanquished in mere reason, and the case against him put logically. But it can be put much more precisely in more general and even aesthetic terms. He is in the clean and well-lit prison of one idea: he is sharpened to one painful point. He is without healthy hesitation and healthy complexity. Now, as I explain in the introduction, I have determined in these early chapters to give not so much a diagram of a doctrine as some pictures of a point of view. And I have described at length my vision of the maniac for this reason: that just as I am affected by the maniac, so I am affected by most modern thinkers. That unmistakable mood or note that I hear from Hanwell, I hear also from half the chairs of science and seats of learning to-day; and most of the mad doctors are mad doctors in more senses than one. They all have exactly that combination we have noted: the combination of an expansive and exhaustive reason with a contracted common sense. They are universal only in the sense that they take one thin explanation and carry it very far. But a pattern can stretch for ever and still be a small pattern. They see a chess-board white on black, and if the universe is paved with it, it is still white on black. Like the lunatic, they cannot alter their standpoint; they cannot make a mental effort and suddenly see it black on white.

Take first the more obvious case of materialism. As an explanation of the world, materialism has a sort of insane simplicity. It has just the quality of the madman's argument; we have at once the sense of it covering everything and the sense of it leaving everything out. Contemplate some able and sincere materialist, as, for instance, Mr. McCabe,[12] and you will have exactly this unique sensation. He understands everything, and everything does not seem worth understanding. His cosmos may be complete in every rivet and cog-wheel, but still his cosmos is smaller than our world. Somehow his scheme, like the lucid scheme of the madman, seems unconscious of the alien energies and the large indifference of the earth; it is not thinking of the real things of the earth, of fighting peoples or proud mothers, or first love or fear upon the sea. The earth is so very large, and the

[12] A freethinker and opponent of Chesterton in the *Clarion* controversy. See chapter 16 of *Heretics*.

cosmos is so very small. The cosmos is about the smallest hole that a man can hide his head in.

It must be understood that I am not now discussing the relation of these creeds to truth; but, for the present, solely their relation to health. Later in the argument I hope to attack the question of objective verity; here I speak only of a phenomenon of psychology. I do not for the present attempt to prove to Haeckel[13] that materialism is untrue, any more than I attempted to prove to the man who thought he was Christ that he was labouring under an error. I merely remark here on the fact that both cases have the same kind of completeness and the same kind of incompleteness. You can explain a man's detention at Hanwell by an indifferent public by saying that it is the crucifixion of a god of whom the world is not worthy. The explanation does explain. Similarly you may explain the order in the universe by saying that all things, even the souls of men, are leaves inevitably unfolding on an utterly unconscious tree—the blind destiny of matter. The explanation does explain, though not, of course, so completely as the madman's. But the point here is that the normal human mind not only objects to both, but feels to both the same objection. Its approximate statement is that if the man in Hanwell is the real God, he is not much of a god. And, similarly, if the cosmos of the materialist is the real cosmos, it is not much of a cosmos. The thing has shrunk. The deity is less divine than many men; and (according to Haeckel) the whole of life is something much more grey, narrow, and trivial than many separate aspects of it. The parts seem greater than the whole.

For we must remember that the materialist philosophy (whether true or not) is certainly much more limiting than any religion. In one sense, of course, all intelligent ideas are narrow. They cannot be broader than themselves. A Christian is only restricted in the same sense that an atheist is restricted. He cannot think Christianity false and continue to be a Christian; and the atheist cannot think atheism false and continue to be an atheist. But as it happens, there is a very

---

[13] Ernst Haeckel (1834–1919), a German biologist, monistic philosopher and evolutionary theorist who believed that he had proved that there was no immortal soul, free will or personal God.

special sense in which materialism has more restrictions than spiritualism. Mr. McCabe thinks me a slave because I am not allowed to believe in determinism. I think Mr. McCabe a slave because he is not allowed to believe in fairies. But if we examine the two vetoes we shall see that his is really much more of a pure veto than mine. The Christian is quite free to believe that there is a considerable amount of settled order and inevitable development in the universe. But the materialist is not allowed to admit into his spotless machine the slightest speck of spiritualism or miracle. Poor Mr. McCabe is not allowed to retain even the tiniest imp, though it might be hiding in a pimpernel. The Christian admits that the universe is manifold and even miscellaneous, just as a sane man knows that he is complex. The sane man knows that he has a touch of the beast, a touch of the devil, a touch of the saint, a touch of the citizen. Nay, the really sane man knows that he has a touch of the madman. But the materialist's world is quite simple and solid, just as the madman is quite sure he is sane. The materialist is sure that history has been simply and solely a chain of causation, just as the interesting person before mentioned is quite sure that he is simply and solely a chicken. Materialists and madmen never have doubts.

Spiritual doctrines do not actually limit the mind as do materialistic denials. Even if I believe in immortality I need not think about it. But if I disbelieve in immortality I must not think about it. In the first case the road is open and I can go as far as I like; in the second the road is shut. But the case is even stronger, and the parallel with madness is yet more strange. For it was our case against the exhaustive and logical theory of the lunatic that, right or wrong, it gradually destroyed his humanity. Now it is the charge against the main deductions of the materialist that, right or wrong, they gradually destroy his humanity; I do not mean only kindness, I mean hope, courage, poetry, initiative, all that is human. For instance, when materialism leads men to complete fatalism (as it generally does), it is quite idle to pretend that it is in any sense a liberating force. It is absurd to say that you are especially advancing freedom when you only use free thought to destroy free will. The determinists come to bind, not to loose. They may well call their law the "chain" of causation. It is the worst chain that ever fettered a human being. You may use the language of liberty, if you like, about materialistic teaching, but it is obvious that this is just as inapplicable to it as a whole as the same language when applied to a man locked up in a mad-house. You may say, if you like, that the man is free to think himself a poached egg. But it is surely a more massive and important fact that if he is a poached egg he is not free to eat, drink, sleep, walk, or smoke a cigarette. Similarly you may say, if you like, that the bold determinist speculator is free to disbelieve in the reality of the will. But it is a much more massive and important fact that he is not free to raise, to curse, to thank, to justify, to urge, to punish, to resist temptations, to incite mobs, to make New Year resolutions, to pardon sinners, to rebuke tyrants, or even to say "thank you" for the mustard.

In passing from this subject I may note that there is a queer fallacy to the effect that materialistic fatalism is in some way favourable to mercy, to the abolition of cruel punishments or punishments of any kind. This is startlingly the reverse of the truth. It is quite tenable that the doctrine of necessity makes no difference at all; that it leaves the flogger flogging and the kind friend exhorting as before. But obviously if it stops either of them it stops the kind exhortation. That the sins are inevitable does not prevent punishment; if it prevents anything it prevents persuasion. Determinism is quite as likely to lead to cruelty as it is certain to lead to cowardice. Determinism is not inconsistent with the cruel treatment of criminals. What it is (perhaps) inconsistent with is the generous treatment of criminals; with any appeal to their better feelings or encouragement in their moral struggle. The determinist does not believe in appealing to the will, but he does believe in changing the environment. He must not say to the sinner, "Go and sin no more," because the sinner cannot help it. But he can put him in boiling oil; for boiling oil is an environment. Considered as a figure, therefore, the materialist has the fantastic outline of the figure of the madman. Both take up a position at once unanswerable and intolerable.

Of course it is not only of the materialist that all this is true. The same would apply to the other extreme of speculative logic. There is a sceptic far more terrible than he who believes that everything began in matter. It is possible to meet the sceptic who believes that everything began in himself. He doubts not the existence of angels or devils, but the existence of men and cows. For him his own friends are a mythology made up by himself. He created his own father and his own mother. This horrible fancy has in it something decidedly attractive to the somewhat mystical egoism of our day. That publisher who thought that men would get on if they believed in themselves, those seekers after the Superman who are always looking for him in the looking-glass, those writers who talk about impressing their personalities instead of creating life for the world, all these people have really only an inch between them and this awful emptiness. Then when this kindly world all round the man has been blackened out like a lie; when friends fade into ghosts, and the foundations of the world fail; then when the man, believing in nothing and in no man, is alone in his own nightmare, then the great individualistic motto shall be written over him in avenging irony. The stars will be only dots in the blackness of his own brain; his mother's face will be only a sketch from his own insane pencil on the walls of his cell. But over his cell shall be written, with dreadful truth, "He believes in himself."

All that concerns us here, however, is to note that this panegoistic extreme of thought exhibits the same paradox as the other extreme of materialism. It is equally complete in theory and equally crippling in practice. For the sake of simplicity, it is easier to state the notion by saying that a man can believe that he is always in a dream. Now, obviously there can be no positive proof given to him that he is not in a dream, for the simple reason that no proof can be offered that might not be offered in a dream. But if the man began to burn down London and say that his housekeeper would soon call him to breakfast, we should take him and put him with other logicians in a place which has often been alluded to in the course of this chapter. The man who cannot believe his senses, and the man who cannot believe anything else, are both insane, but their insanity is proved not by any error in their argument, but by the manifest mistake of their whole lives. They have both locked themselves up in two boxes,

painted inside with the sun and stars; they are both unable to get
out, the one into the health and happiness of heaven, the other even
into the health and happiness of the earth. Their position is quite
reasonable; nay, in a sense it is infinitely reasonable, just as a three-
penny bit is infinitely circular. But there is such a thing as a mean infinity, a base and slavish eternity. It is amusing to notice that many
of the moderns, whether sceptics or mystics, have taken as their sign
a certain eastern symbol, which is the very symbol of this ultimate
nullity. When they wish to represent eternity, they represent it by a
serpent with his tail in his mouth. There is a startling sarcasm in the
image of that very unsatisfactory meal. The eternity of the material
fatalists, the eternity of the eastern pessimists, the eternity of the
supercilious theosophists and higher scientists of to-day is, indeed,
very well presented by a serpent eating his tail, a degraded animal
who destroys even himself.

This chapter is purely practical and is concerned with what actually
is the chief mark and element of insanity; we may say in summary
that it is reason used without root, reason in the void. The man who
begins to think without the proper first principles goes mad; he
begins to think at the wrong end. And for the rest of these pages we
have to try and discover what is the right end. But we may ask in
conclusion, if this be what drives men mad, what is it that keeps
them sane? By the end of this book I hope to give a definite, some
will think a far too definite, answer. But for the moment it is possible in the same solely practical manner to give a general answer
touching what in actual human history keeps men sane. Mysticism
keeps men sane. As long as you have mystery you have health; when
you destroy mystery you create morbidity. The ordinary man has
always been sane because the ordinary man has always been a mystic.
He has permitted the twilight. He has always had one foot in earth
and the other in fairyland. He has always left himself free to doubt
his gods; but (unlike the agnostic of to-day) free also to believe in
them. He has always cared more for truth than for consistency. If he
saw two truths that seemed to contradict each other, he would take
the two truths and the contradiction along with them. His spiritual
sight is stereoscopic, like his physical sight: he sees two different

pictures at once and yet sees all the better for that. Thus he has always believed that there was such a thing as fate, but such a thing as free will also. Thus he believed that children were indeed the kingdom of heaven, but nevertheless ought to be obedient to the kingdom of earth. He admired youth because it was young and age because it was not. It is exactly this balance of apparent contradictions that has been the whole buoyancy of the healthy man. The whole secret of mysticism is this: that man can understand everything by the help of what he does not understand. The morbid logician seeks to make everything lucid, and succeeds in making everything mysterious. The mystic allows one thing to be mysterious, and everything else becomes lucid. The determinist makes the theory of causation quite clear, and then finds that he cannot say "if you please" to the housemaid. The Christian permits free will to remain a sacred mystery; but because of this his relations with the housemaid become of a sparkling and crystal clearness. He puts the seed of dogma in a central darkness; but it branches forth in all directions with abounding natural health. As we have taken the circle as the symbol of reason and madness, we may very well take the cross as the symbol at once of mystery and of health. Buddhism is centripetal, but Christianity is centrifugal: it breaks out. For the circle is perfect and infinite in its nature; but it is fixed for ever in its size; it can never be larger or smaller. But the cross, though it has at its heart a collision and a contradiction, can extend its four arms for ever without altering its shape. Because it has a paradox in its centre it can grow without changing. The circle returns upon itself and is bound. The cross opens its arms to the four winds; it is a signpost for free travellers.

Symbols alone are of even a cloudy value in speaking of this deep matter; and another symbol from physical nature will express sufficiently well the real place of mysticism before mankind. The one created thing which we cannot look at is the one thing in the light of which we look at everything. Like the sun at noonday, mysticism explains everything else by the blaze of its own victorious invisibility. Detached intellectualism is (in the exact sense of a popular phrase) all moonshine; for it is light without heat, and it is secondary light, reflected from a dead world. But the Greeks were right

when they made Apollo the god both of imagination and of sanity;
for he was both the patron of poetry and the patron of healing. Of
necessary dogmas and a special creed I shall speak later. But that tran-
scendentalism by which all men live has primarily much the position
of the sun in the sky. We are conscious of it as of a kind of splendid
confusion; it is something both shining and shapeless, at once a blaze
and a blur. But the circle of the moon is as clear and unmistakable, as
recurrent and inevitable, as the circle of Euclid on a blackboard. For
the moon is utterly reasonable; and the moon is the mother of lunatics
and has given to them all her name.

III

THE SUICIDE OF THOUGHT

The phrases of the street are not only forcible but subtle: for a figure of speech can often get into a crack too small for a definition. Phrases like "put out" or "off colour" might have been coined by Mr. Henry James in an agony of verbal precision. And there is no more subtle truth than that of the everyday phrase about a man having "his heart in the right place." It involves the idea of normal proportion; not only does a certain function exist, but it is rightly related to other functions. Indeed, the negation of this phrase would describe with peculiar accuracy the somewhat morbid mercy and perverse tenderness of the most representative moderns. If, for instance, I had to describe with fairness the character of Mr. Bernard Shaw, I could not express myself more exactly than by saying that he has a heroically large and generous heart; but not a heart in the right place. And this is so of the typical society of our time.

The modern world is not evil; in some ways the modern world is far too good. It is full of wild and wasted virtues. When a religious scheme is shattered (as Christianity was shattered at the Reformation), it is not merely the vices that are let loose. The vices are, indeed, let loose, and they wander and do damage. But the virtues are let loose also; and the virtues wander more wildly, and the virtues do more terrible damage. The modern world is full of the old Christian virtues gone mad. The virtues have gone mad because they have been isolated from each other and are wandering alone. Thus some scientists care for truth; and their truth is pitiless. Thus some humanitarians only care for pity; and their pity (I am sorry to say) is often untruthful. For example, Mr. Blatchford[14] attacks Christianity because he is mad on one Christian virtue: the merely mystical and almost irrational virtue of charity. He has a strange idea that he will make it easier to forgive sins by saying that there are no sins to

---

[14] Robert Blatchford (1851–1943), editor of the *Clarion*, with whom Chesterton carried on a controversy over Christianity from 1903 to 1904.

forgive. Mr. Blatchford is not only an early Christian, he is the only early Christian who ought really to have been eaten by lions. For in his case the pagan accusation is really true: his mercy would mean mere anarchy. He really is the enemy of the human race—because he is so human. As the other extreme, we may take the acrid realist, who has deliberately killed in himself all human pleasure in happy tales or in the healing of the heart. Torquemada[15] tortured people physically for the sake of moral truth. Zola[16] tortured people morally for the sake of physical truth. But in Torquemada's time there was at least a system that could to some extent make righteousness and peace kiss each other. Now they do not even bow. But a much stronger case than these two of truth and pity can be found in the remarkable case of the dislocation of humility.

It is only with one aspect of humility that we are here concerned. Humility was largely meant as a restraint upon the arrogance and infinity of the appetite of man. He was always outstripping his mercies with his own newly invented needs. His very power of enjoyment destroyed half his joys. By asking for pleasure, he lost the chief pleasure; for the chief pleasure is surprise. Hence it became evident that if a man would make his world large, he must be always making himself small. Even the haughty visions, the tall cities, and the toppling pinnacles are the creations of humility. Giants that tread down forests like grass are the creations of humility. Towers that vanish upwards above the loneliest star are the creations of humility. For towers are not tall unless we look up at them; and giants are not giants unless they are larger than we. All this gigantesque imagination, which is, perhaps, the mightiest of the pleasures of man, is at bottom entirely humble. It is impossible without humility to enjoy anything—even pride.

But what we suffer from to-day is humility in the wrong place. Modesty has moved from the organ of ambition. Modesty has settled upon the organ of conviction; where it was never meant to be. A

---

[15] Spanish inquisitor (1420–1498) who carried out harsh measures in the suppression of heresy.

[16] Emile Zola (1804–1902), a French novelist who saw people as products of their environment.

man was meant to be doubtful about himself, but undoubting about the truth; this has been exactly reversed. Nowadays the part of a man that a man does assert is exactly the part he ought not to assert — himself. The part he doubts is exactly the part he ought not to doubt — the Divine Reason. Huxley preached a humility content to learn from Nature. But the new sceptic is so humble that he doubts if he can even learn. Thus we should be wrong if we had said hastily that there is no humility typical of our time. The truth is that there is a real humility typical of our time; but it so happens that it is practically a more poisonous humility than the wildest prostrations of the ascetic. The old humility was a spur that prevented a man from stopping; not a nail in his boot that prevented him from going on. For the old humility made a man doubtful about his efforts, which might make him work harder. But the new humility makes a man doubtful about his aims, which will make him stop working altogether.

At any street corner we may meet a man who utters the frantic and blasphemous statement that he may be wrong. Every day one comes across somebody who says that of course his view may not be the right one. Of course his view must be the right one, or it is not his view. We are on the road to producing a race of men too mentally modest to believe in the multiplication table. We are in danger of seeing philosophers who doubt the law of gravity as being a mere fancy of their own. Scoffers of old time were too proud to be convinced; but these are too humble to be convinced. The meek do inherit the earth; but the modern sceptics are too meek even to claim their inheritance. It is exactly this intellectual helplessness which is our second problem.

The last chapter has been concerned only with a fact of observation: that what peril of morbidity there is for man comes rather from his reason than his imagination. It was not meant to attack the authority of reason; rather it is the ultimate purpose to defend it. For it needs defence. The whole modern world is at war with reason; and the tower already reels.

The sages, it is often said, can see no answer to the riddle of religion. But the trouble with our sages is not that they cannot see the answer; it is that they cannot even see the riddle. They are like

children so stupid as to notice nothing paradoxical in the playful assertion that a door is not a door. The modern latitudinarians speak, for
instance, about authority in religion not only as if there were no reason in it, but as if there had never been any reason for it. Apart from
seeing its philosophical basis, they cannot even see its historical cause.
Religious authority has often, doubtless, been oppressive or unreasonable; just as every legal system (and especially our present one) has
been callous and full of a cruel apathy. It is rational to attack the police; nay, it is glorious. But the modern critics of religious authority
are like men who should attack the police without ever having heard
of burglars. For there is a great and possible peril to the human mind:
a peril as practical as burglary. Against it religious authority was
reared, rightly or wrongly, as a barrier. And against it something certainly must be reared as a barrier, if our race is to avoid ruin.

That peril is that the human intellect is free to destroy itself. Just
as one generation could prevent the very existence of the next generation, by all entering a monastery or jumping into the sea, so one set
of thinkers can in some degree prevent further thinking by teaching
the next generation that there is no validity in any human thought.
It is idle to talk always of the alternative of reason and faith. Reason
is itself a matter of faith. It is an act of faith to assert that our
thoughts have any relation to reality at all. If you are merely a sceptic, you must sooner or later ask yourself the question, "Why should
anything go right; even observation and deduction? Why should not
good logic be as misleading as bad logic? They are both movements in
the brain of a bewildered ape?" The young sceptic says, "I have a right
to think for myself." But the old sceptic, the complete sceptic, says, "I
have no right to think for myself. I have no right to think at all."

There is a thought that stops thought. That is the only thought
that ought to be stopped. That is the ultimate evil against which all
religious authority was aimed. It only appears at the end of decadent
ages like our own: and already Mr. H. G. Wells has raised its ruinous banner; he has written a delicate piece of scepticism called
"Doubts of the Instrument."[17] In this he questions the brain itself,

[17] Wells read a paper entitled "Scepticism of the Instrument" before the Oxford
Philosophical Society in 1903.

and endeavours to remove all reality from all his own assertions, past, present, and to come. But it was against this remote ruin that all the military systems in religion were originally ranked and ruled. The creeds and the crusades, the hierarchies and the horrible persecutions were not organized, as is ignorantly said, for the suppression of reason. They were organized for the difficult defence of reason. Man, by a blind instinct, knew that if once things were wildly questioned, reason could be questioned first. The authority of priests to absolve, the authority of popes to define the authority, even of inquisitors to terrify: these were all only dark defences erected round one central authority, more undemonstrable, more supernatural than all — the authority of a man to think. We know now that this is so; we have no excuse for not knowing it. For we can hear scepticism crashing through the old ring of authorities, and at the same moment we can see reason swaying upon her throne. In so far as religion is gone, reason is going. For they are both of the same primary and authoritative kind. They are both methods of proof which cannot themselves be proved. And in the act of destroying the idea of Divine authority we have largely destroyed the idea of that human authority by which we do a long-division sum. With a long and sustained tug we have attempted to pull the mitre off pontifical man; and his head has come off with it.

Lest this should be called loose assertion, it is perhaps desirable, though dull, to run rapidly through the chief modern fashions of thought which have this effect of stopping thought itself. Materialism and the view of everything as a personal illusion have some such effect; for if the mind is mechanical, thought cannot be very exciting, and if the cosmos is unreal, there is nothing to think about. But in these cases the effect is indirect and doubtful. In some cases it is direct and clear; notably in the case of what is generally called evolution.

Evolution is a good example of that modern intelligence which, if it destroys anything, destroys itself. Evolution is either an innocent scientific description of how certain earthly things came about; or, if it is anything more than this, it is an attack upon thought itself. If evolution destroys anything, it does not destroy religion but rationalism. If evolution simply means that a positive thing called an ape turned very slowly into a positive thing called a man, then it is stingless for the most orthodox; for a personal God might just as well do things slowly as quickly, especially if, like the Christian God, he were outside time. But if it means anything more, it means that there is no such thing as an ape to change, and no such thing as a man for him to change into. It means that there is no such thing as a thing. At best, there is only one thing, and that is a flux of everything and anything. This is an attack not upon the faith, but upon the mind; you cannot think if there are no things to think about. You cannot think if you are not separate from the subject of thought. Descartes said, "I think; therefore I am." The philosophic evolutionist reverses and negatives the epigram. He says, "I am not; therefore I cannot think."

Then there is the opposite attack on thought: that urged by Mr. H. G. Wells when he insists that every separate thing is "unique," and there are no categories at all. This also is merely destructive. Thinking means connecting things, and stops if they cannot be connected. It need hardly be said that this scepticism forbidding thought necessarily forbids speech; a man cannot open his mouth without contradicting it. Thus when Mr. Wells says (as he did somewhere), "All chairs are quite different," he utters not merely a misstatement, but a contradiction in terms. If all chairs were quite different, you could not call them "all chairs."

Akin to these is the false theory of progress, which maintains that we alter the test instead of trying to pass the test. We often hear it said, for instance, "What is right in one age is wrong in another." This is quite reasonable, if it means that there is a fixed aim, and that certain methods attain at certain times and not at other times. If women, say, desire to be elegant, it may be that they are improved at one time by growing fatter and at another time by growing thinner. But you cannot say that they are improved by ceasing to wish to be elegant and beginning to wish to be oblong. If the standard changes, how can there be improvement, which implies a standard? Nietzsche started a nonsensical idea that men had once sought as good what we now call evil; if it were so, we could not talk of surpassing or even falling short of them. How can you overtake Jones if you walk in the other direction? You cannot discuss whether one people has succeeded more in being miserable than another succeeded in being happy. It would be like discussing whether Milton was more puritanical than a pig is fat.

It is true that a man (a silly man) might make change itself his object or ideal. But as an ideal, change itself becomes unchangeable. If the change-worshipper wishes to estimate his own progress, he must be sternly loyal to the ideal of change; he must not begin to flirt gaily with the ideal of monotony. Progress itself cannot progress. It is worth remark, in passing, that when Tennyson, in a wild and rather weak manner, welcomed the idea of infinite alteration in society, he instinctively took a metaphor which suggests an imprisoned tedium. He wrote —

> Let the great world spin for ever down the ringing
> grooves of change.

He thought of change itself as an unchangeable groove; and so it is. Change is about the narrowest and hardest groove that a man can get into.

The main point here, however, is that this idea of a fundamental alteration in the standard is one of the things that make thought about the past or future simply impossible. The theory of a complete change of standards in human history does not merely deprive us of the pleasure of honouring our fathers; it deprives us even of the more modern and aristocratic pleasure of despising them.

This bald summary of the thought-destroying forces of our time would not be complete without some reference to pragmatism; for though I have here used and should everywhere defend the pragmatist method as a preliminary guide to truth, there is an extreme application of it which involves the absence of all truth whatever. My meaning can be put shortly thus. I agree with the pragmatists that apparent objective truth is not the whole matter; that there is an authoritative need to believe the things that are necessary to the human mind. But I say that one of those necessities precisely is a belief in objective truth. The pragmatist tells a man to think what he must think and never mind the Absolute. But precisely one of the things that he must think is the Absolute. This philosophy, indeed, is a kind of verbal paradox. Pragmatism is a matter of human needs; and one of the first of human needs is to be something more than a pragmatist. Extreme pragmatism is just as inhuman as the determinism it so powerfully attacks. The determinist (who, to do him justice, does not pretend to be a human being) makes nonsense of the human sense of actual choice. The pragmatist, who professes to be specially human, makes nonsense of the human sense of actual fact.

To sum up our contention so far, we may say that the most characteristic current philosophies have not only a touch of mania, but a touch of suicidal mania. The mere questioner has knocked his head against the limits of human thought; and cracked it. This is what makes so futile the warnings of the orthodox and the boasts of the advanced about the dangerous boyhood of free thought. What we are looking at is not the boyhood of free thought; it is the old age and ultimate dissolution of free thought. It is vain for bishops and pious bigwigs to discuss what dreadful things will happen if wild scepticism runs its course. It has run its course. It is vain for eloquent atheists to talk of the great truths that will be revealed if once we see free thought begin. We have seen it end. It has no more questions to ask; it has questioned itself. You cannot call up any wilder vision than a city in which men ask themselves if they have any selves. You cannot fancy a more sceptical world than that in which men doubt if there is a world. It might certainly have reached its bankruptcy more quickly and cleanly if it had not been feebly hampered by the application of indefensible laws of blasphemy or by the absurd pretence that modern England is Christian. But it would have reached the bankruptcy anyhow. Militant atheists are still unjustly persecuted; but rather because they are an old minority than because they are a new one. Free thought has exhausted its own freedom. It is weary of its own success. If any eager freethinker now hails philosophic freedom as the dawn, he is only like the man in Mark Twain who came out wrapped in blankets to see the sun rise and was just in time to see it set. If any frightened curate still says that it will be awful if the darkness of free thought should spread, we can only answer him in the high and powerful words of Mr. Belloc,

"Do not, I beseech you, be troubled about the increase of forces already in dissolution. You have mistaken the hour of the night: it is already morning." We have no more questions left to ask. We have looked for questions in the darkest corners and on the wildest peaks. We have found all the questions that can be found. It is time we gave up looking for questions and began looking for answers.

But one more word must be added. At the beginning of this preliminary negative sketch I said that our mental ruin has been wrought by wild reason, not by wild imagination. A man does not go mad because he makes a statue a mile high, but he may go mad by thinking it out in square inches. Now, one school of thinkers has seen this and jumped at it as a way of renewing the pagan health of the world. They see that reason destroys; but Will, they say, creates. The ultimate authority, they say, is in will, not in reason. The supreme point is not why a man demands a thing, but the fact that he does demand it. I have no space to trace or expound this philosophy of Will. It came, I suppose, through Nietzsche, who preached something that is called egoism. That, indeed, was simple-minded enough; for Nietzsche denied egoism simply by preaching it. To preach anything is to give it away. First, the egoist calls life a war without mercy, and then he takes the greatest possible trouble to drill his enemies in war. To preach egoism is to practise altruism. But however it began, the view is common enough in current literature. The main defence of these thinkers is that they are not thinkers; they are makers. They say that choice is itself the divine thing. Thus Mr. Bernard Shaw has attacked the old idea that men's acts are to be judged by the standard of the desire of happiness. He says that a man does not act for his happiness, but from his will. He does not say, "Jam will make me happy," but "I want jam." And in all this others follow him with yet greater enthusiasm. Mr. John Davidson, a remarkable poet, is so passionately excited about it that he is obliged to write prose. He publishes a short play with several long prefaces. This is natural enough in Mr. Shaw, for all his plays are prefaces: Mr. Shaw is (I suspect) the only man on earth who has never written any poetry. But that Mr. Davidson (who can write excellent poetry) should write instead laborious metaphysics in defence of this doctrine of will, does show that the doctrine of will has taken hold of men. Even Mr. H. G. Wells has half spoken in its language; saying that one should test acts not like a thinker, but like an artist, saying, "I *feel* this curve is right," or "that line *shall* go thus." They are all excited; and well they may be. For by this doctrine of the divine authority of will, they think they can break out of the doomed fortress of rationalism. They think they can escape.

But they cannot escape. This pure praise of volition ends in the same break up and blank as the mere pursuit of logic. Exactly as complete free thought involves the doubting of thought itself, so the acceptation of mere "willing" really paralyzes the will. Mr. Bernard Shaw has not perceived the real difference between the old utilitarian test of pleasure[18] (clumsy, of course, and easily misstated) and that which he propounds. The real difference between the test of happiness and the test of will is simply that the test of happiness is a test and the other isn't. You can discuss whether a man's act in jumping over a cliff was directed towards happiness; you cannot discuss whether it was derived from will. Of course it was. You can praise an action by saying that it is calculated to bring pleasure or pain to discover truth or to save the soul. But you cannot praise an action because it shows will; for to say that is merely to say that it is an action. By this praise of will you cannot really choose one course as better than another. And yet choosing one course as better than another is the very definition of the will you are praising.

The worship of will is the negation of will. To admire mere choice is to refuse to choose. If Mr. Bernard Shaw comes up to me and says, "Will something," that is tantamount to saying, "I do not mind what you will," and that is tantamount to saying, "I have no will in the matter." You cannot admire will in general, because the essence of will is that it is particular. A brilliant anarchist like Mr. John Davidson feels an irritation against ordinary morality, and therefore he invokes will—will to anything. He only wants humanity to want something. But humanity does want something. It wants ordinary

---

[18] Jeremy Bentham (1748–1832), in his *Introduction to the Principles of Morals and Legislation* (1789), claimed that pleasure, or the principle of greatest happiness, was the only measure of right and wrong.

morality. He rebels against the law and tells us to will something or anything. But we have willed something. We have willed the law against which he rebels.

All the will-worshippers, from Nietzsche to Mr. Davidson, are really quite empty of volition. They cannot will, they can hardly wish. And if any one wants a proof of this, it can be found quite easily. It can be found in this fact: that they always talk of will as something that expands and breaks out. But it is quite the opposite. Every act of will is an act of self-limitation. To desire action is to desire limitation. In that sense every act is an act of self-sacrifice. When you choose anything, you reject everything else. That objection, which men of this school used to make to the act of marriage, is really an objection to every act. Every act is an irrevocable selection and exclusion. Just as when you marry one woman you give up all the others, so when you take one course of action you give up all the other courses. If you become King of England, you give up the post of Beadle in Brompton. If you go to Rome, you sacrifice a rich suggestive life in Wimbledon. It is the existence of this negative or limiting side of will that makes most of the talk of the anarchic will-worshippers little better than nonsense. For instance, Mr. John Davidson tells us to have nothing to do with "Thou shalt not"; but it is surely obvious that "Thou shalt not" is only one of the necessary corollaries of "I will." "I will go to the Lord Mayor's Show, and thou shalt not stop me." Anarchism adjures us to be bold creative artists, and care for no laws or limits. But it is impossible to be an artist and not care for laws or limits. Art is limitation; the essence of every picture is the frame. If you draw a giraffe, you must draw him with a long neck. If, in your bold creative way, you hold yourself free to draw a giraffe with a short neck, you will really find that you are not free to draw a giraffe. The moment you step into the world of facts, you step into a world of limits. You can free things from alien or accidental laws, but not from the laws of their own nature. You may, if you like, free a tiger from his bars; but do not free him from his stripes. Do not free a camel of the burden of his hump: you may be freeing him from being a camel. Do not go about as a demagogue, encouraging triangles to break out of the prison of their three sides. If a triangle breaks out of its three sides, its life comes to a lamentable end. Somebody wrote a work called "The Loves of the Triangles"; I never read it, but I am sure that if triangles ever were loved, they were loved for being triangular. This is certainly the case with all artistic creation, which is in some ways the most decisive example of pure will. The artist loves his limitations: they constitute the *thing* he is doing. The painter is glad that the canvas is flat. The sculptor is glad that the clay is colourless.

In case the point is not clear, an historic example may illustrate it. The French Revolution was really an heroic and decisive thing, because the Jacobins willed something definite and limited. They desired the freedoms of democracy, but also all the vetoes of democracy. They wished to have votes and *not* to have titles. Republicanism had an ascetic side in Franklin or Robespierre as well as an expansive side in Danton or Wilkes.[19] Therefore they have created something with a solid substance and shape, the square social equality and peasant wealth of France. But since then the revolutionary or speculative mind of Europe has been weakened by shrinking from any proposal because of the limits of that proposal. Liberalism has been degraded into liberality. Men have tried to turn "revolutionise" from a transitive to an intransitive verb. The Jacobin could tell you not only the system he would rebel against, but (what was more important) the system he would *not* rebel against, the system he would trust. But the new rebel is a sceptic, and will not entirely trust anything. He has no loyalty; therefore he can never be really a revolutionist. And the fact that he doubts everything really gets in his way when he wants to denounce anything. For all denunciation implies a moral doctrine of some kind; and the modern revolutionist doubts not only the institution he denounces, but the doctrine by which he denounces it. Thus he writes one book complaining that imperial oppression insults the purity of women, and then he writes another book (about the sex problem) in which he insults it himself. He curses the Sultan because Christian girls lose their virginity, and

[19] John Wilkes (1727–1797), political agitator and champion of the rights of the individual. He was several times elected to the House of Commons and repeatedly prevented from taking his seat.

then curses Mrs. Grundy[20] because they keep it. As a politician, he will cry out that war is a waste of life, and then, as a philosopher, that all life is waste of time. A Russian pessimist will denounce a policeman for killing a peasant, and then prove by the highest philosophical principles that the peasant ought to have killed himself. A man denounces marriage as a lie, and then denounces aristocratic profligates for treating it as a lie. He calls a flag a bauble, and then blames the oppressors of Poland or Ireland because they take away that bauble. The man of this school goes first to a political meeting, where he complains that savages are treated as if they were beasts; then he takes his hat and umbrella and goes on to a scientific meeting, where he proves that they practically are beasts. In short, the modern revolutionist, being an infinite sceptic, is always engaged in undermining his own mines. In his book on politics he attacks men for trampling on morality; in his book on ethics he attacks morality for trampling on men. Therefore the modern man in revolt has become practically useless for all purposes of revolt. By rebelling against everything he has lost his right to rebel against anything.

It may be added that the same blank and bankruptcy can be observed in all fierce and terrible types of literature, especially in satire. Satire may be mad and anarchic, but it presupposes an admitted superiority in certain things over others; it presupposes a standard. When little boys in the street laugh at the fatness of some distinguished journalist, they are unconsciously assuming a standard of Greek sculpture. They are appealing to the marble Apollo. And the curious disappearance of satire from our literature is an instance of the fierce things fading for want of any principle to be fierce about. Nietzsche had some natural talent for sarcasm: he could sneer, though he could not laugh; but there is always something bodiless and without weight in his satire, simply because it has not any mass of common morality behind it. He is himself more preposterous than anything he denounces. But, indeed, Nietzsche will stand very well as the type of the whole of this failure of abstract violence. The softening of the

[20] The name of a character referred to in Thomas Morton's play *Speed the Plough* (1798) by other characters asking, "What will Mrs. Grundy say?" Hence, she became a byword for prudery and respectability.

brain which ultimately overtook him was not a physical accident. If Nietzsche had not ended in imbecility, Nietzscheism would end in imbecility. Thinking in isolation and with pride ends in being an idiot. Every man who will not have softening of the heart must at last have softening of the brain.

This last attempt to evade intellectualism ends in intellectualism, and therefore in death. The sortie has failed. The wild worship of lawlessness and the materialist worship of law end in the same void. Nietzsche scales staggering mountains, but he turns up ultimately in Tibet. He sits down beside Tolstoy in the land of nothing and Nirvâna. They are both helpless—one because he must not grasp anything, and the other because he must not let go of anything. The Tolstoyan's will is frozen by a Buddhist instinct that all special actions are evil. But the Nietzscheite's will is quite equally frozen by his view that all special actions are good; for if all special actions are good, none of them are special. They stand at the cross-roads, and one hates all the roads and the other likes all the roads. The result is—well, some things are not hard to calculate. They stand at the cross-roads.

Here I end (thank God) the first and dullest business of this book—the rough review of recent thought. After this I begin to sketch a view of life which may not interest my reader, but which, at any rate, interests me. In front of me, as I close this page, is a pile of modern books that I have been turning over for the purpose—a pile of ingenuity, a pile of futility. By the accident of my present detachment, I can see the inevitable smash of the philosophies of Schopenhauer and Tolstoy, Nietzsche and Shaw, as clearly as an inevitable railway smash could be seen from a balloon. They are all on the road to the emptiness of the asylum. For madness may be defined as using mental activity so as to reach mental helplessness; and they have nearly reached it. He who thinks he is made of glass, thinks to the destruction of thought; for glass cannot think. So he who wills to reject nothing, wills the destruction of will; for will is not only the choice of something, but the rejection of almost everything. And as I turn and tumble over the clever, wonderful, tiresome, and useless modern books, the title of one of them rivets my eye. It is called

"Jeanne d'Arc," by Anatole France.[21] I have only glanced at it, but a glance was enough to remind me of Renan's "Vie de Jésus."[22] It has the same strange method of the reverent sceptic. It discredits supernatural stories that have some foundation, simply by telling natural stories that have no foundation. Because we cannot believe in what a saint did, we are to pretend that we know exactly what he felt. But I do not mention either book in order to criticise it, but because the accidental combination of the names called up two startling images of sanity which blasted all the books before me. Joan of Arc was not stuck at the cross-roads, either by rejecting all the paths like Tolstoy, or by accepting them all like Nietzsche. She chose a path, and went down it like a thunderbolt. Yet Joan, when I came to think of her, had in her all that was true either in Tolstoy or Nietzsche, all that was even tolerable in either of them. I thought of all that is noble in Tolstoy, the pleasure in plain things, especially in plain pity, the actualities of the earth, the reverence for the poor, the dignity of the bowed back. Joan of Arc had all that and with this great addition, that she endured poverty as well as admiring it; whereas Tolstoy is only a typical aristocrat trying to find out its secret. And then I thought of all that was brave and proud and pathetic in poor Nietzsche, and his mutiny against the emptiness and timidity of our time. I thought of his cry for the ecstatic equilibrium of danger, his hunger for the rush of great horses, his cry to arms. Well, Joan of Arc had all that, and again with this difference, that she did not praise fighting, but fought. We *know* that she was not afraid of an army, while Nietzsche, for all we know, was afraid of a cow. Tolstoy only praised the peasant; she was the peasant. Nietzsche only praised the warrior; she was the warrior. She beat them both at their own antagonistic ideals; she was more gentle than the one, more violent than the other. Yet she was a perfectly practical person who

[21] Jacques Anatole Thibault, who used "Anatole France" as a pseudonym, wrote a life of Joan of Arc in 1908 in which he viewed her as perpetually under hallucination and a tool of the clergy.

[22] A former seminarian who became bitterly anticlerical, Joseph Ernest Renan (1823–1892) wrote a life of Christ in which he treated Him as an inspired teacher but a merely human person.

did something, while they are wild speculators who do nothing. It was impossible that the thought should not cross my mind that she and her faith had perhaps some secret of moral unity and utility that has been lost. And with that thought came a larger one, and the colossal figure of her Master had also crossed the theatre of my thoughts. The same modern difficulty which darkened the subject-matter of Anatole France also darkened that of Ernest Renan. Renan also divided his hero's pity from his hero's pugnacity. Renan even represented the righteous anger at Jerusalem as a mere nervous breakdown after the idyllic expectations of Galilee. As if there were any inconsistency between having a love for humanity and having a hatred for inhumanity! Altruists, with thin, weak voices, denounce Christ as an egoist. Egoists (with even thinner and weaker voices) denounce Him as an altruist. In our present atmosphere such cavils are comprehensible enough. The love of a hero is more terrible than the hatred of a tyrant. The hatred of a hero is more generous than the love of a philanthropist. There is a huge and heroic sanity of which moderns can only collect the fragments. There is a giant of whom we see only the lopped arms and legs walking about. They have torn the soul of Christ into silly strips, labelled egoism and altruism, and they are equally puzzled by His insane magnificence and His insane meekness. They have parted His garments among them, and for His vesture they have cast lots; though the coat was without seam woven from the top throughout.

IV

THE ETHICS OF ELFLAND

When the business man rebukes the idealism of his office-boy, it is commonly in some such speech as this: "Ah, yes, when one is young, one has these ideals in the abstract and these castles in the air; but in middle age they all break up like clouds, and one comes down to a belief in practical politics, to using the machinery one has and getting on with the world as it is." Thus, at least, venerable and philanthropic old men now in their honoured graves used to talk to me when I was a boy. But since then I have grown up and have discovered that these philanthropic old men were telling lies. What has really happened is exactly the opposite of what they said would happen. They said that I should lose my ideals and begin to believe in the methods of practical politicians. Now, I have not lost my ideals in the least; my faith in fundamentals is exactly what it always was. What I have lost is my old childlike faith in practical politics. I am still as much concerned as ever about the Battle of Armageddon; but I am not so much concerned about the General Election. As a babe I leapt up on my mother's knee at the mere mention of it. No; the vision is always solid and reliable. The vision is always a fact. It is the reality that is often a fraud. As much as I ever did, more than I ever did, I believe in Liberalism. But there was a rosy time of innocence when I believed in Liberals.

I take this instance of one of the enduring faiths because, having now to trace the roots of my personal speculation, this may be counted, I think, as the only positive bias. I was brought up a Liberal, and have always believed in democracy, in the elementary liberal doctrine of a self-governing humanity. If any one finds the phrase vague or threadbare, I can only pause for a moment to explain that the principle of democracy, as I mean it, can be stated in two propositions. The first is this: that the things common to all men are more important than the things peculiar to any men. Ordinary things are more valuable than extraordinary things; nay, they are more extraordinary. Man is something more awful than men; something more strange. The sense of the miracle of humanity itself should be always more vivid to us than any marvels of power, intellect, art, or civilization. The mere man on two legs, as such, should be felt as something more heartbreaking than any music and more startling than any caricature. Death is more tragic even than death by starvation. Having a nose is more comic even than having a Norman nose.

This is the first principle of democracy: that the essential things in men are the things they hold in common, not the things they hold separately. And the second principle is merely this: that the political instinct or desire is one of these things which they hold in common. Falling in love is more poetical than dropping into poetry. The democratic contention is that government (helping to rule the tribe) is a thing like falling in love, and not a thing like dropping into poetry. It is not something analogous to playing the church organ, painting on vellum, discovering the North Pole (that insidious habit), looping the loop, being Astronomer Royal, and so on. For these things we do not wish a man to do at all unless he does them well. It is, on the contrary, a thing analogous to writing one's own love-letters or blowing one's own nose. These things we want a man to do for himself, even if he does them badly. I am not here arguing the truth of any of these conceptions; I know that some moderns are asking to have their wives chosen by scientists, and they may soon be asking, for all I know, to have their noses blown by nurses. I merely say that mankind does recognize these universal human functions, and that democracy classes government among them. In short, the democratic faith is this: that the most terribly important things must be left to ordinary men themselves—the mating of the sexes, the rearing of the young, the laws of the state. This is democracy; and in this I have always believed.

But there is one thing that I have never from my youth up been able to understand. I have never been able to understand where people got the idea that democracy was in some way opposed to tradition. It is obvious that tradition is only democracy extended through time. It is trusting to a consensus of common human voices rather than to some isolated or arbitrary record. The man who quotes some German historian against the tradition of the Catholic Church, for instance, is strictly appealing to aristocracy. He is appealing to the superiority of one expert against the awful authority of a mob. It is quite easy to see why a legend is treated, and ought to be treated, more respectfully than a book of history. The legend is generally made by the majority of people in the village, who are sane. The book is generally written by the one man in the village who is mad. Those who urge against tradition that men in the past were ignorant may go and urge it at the Carlton Club,[23] along with the statement that voters in the slums are ignorant. It will not do for us. If we attach great importance to the opinion of ordinary men in great unanimity when we are dealing with daily matters, there is no reason why we should disregard it when we are dealing with history or fable. Tradition may be defined as an extension of the franchise. Tradition means giving votes to the most obscure of all classes, our ancestors. It is the democracy of the dead. Tradition refuses to submit to the small and arrogant oligarchy of those who merely happen to be walking about. All democrats object to men being disqualified by the accident of birth; tradition objects to their being disqualified by the accident of death. Democracy tells us not to neglect a good man's opinion, even if he is our groom; tradition asks us not to neglect a good man's opinion, even if he is our father. I, at any rate, cannot separate the two ideas of democracy and tradition; it seems evident to me that they are the same idea. We will have the dead at our councils. The ancient Greeks voted by stones; these shall vote by tombstones. It is all quite regular and official, for most tombstones, like most ballot papers, are marked with a cross.

I have first to say, therefore, that if I have had a bias, it was always a bias in favour of democracy, and therefore of tradition. Before we come to any theoretic or logical beginnings I am content to allow for that personal equation; I have always been more inclined to believe the ruck of hard-working people than to believe that special and troublesome literary class to which I belong. I prefer even the fancies

---

[23] A Conservative political club in Pall Mall, London.

and prejudices of the people who see life from the inside to the clearest demonstrations of the people who see life from the outside. I would always trust the old wives' fables against the old maids' facts. As long as wit is mother wit it can be as wild as it pleases.

Now, I have to put together a general position, and I pretend to no training in such things. I propose to do it, therefore, by writing down one after another the three or four fundamental ideas which I have found for myself, pretty much in the way that I found them. Then I shall roughly synthesise them, summing up my personal philosophy or natural religion; then I shall describe my startling discovery that the whole thing had been discovered before. It had been discovered by Christianity. But of these profound persuasions which I have to recount in order, the earliest was concerned with this element of popular tradition. And without the foregoing explanation touching tradition and democracy I could hardly make my mental experience clear. As it is, I do not know whether I can make it clear, but I now propose to try.

My first and last philosophy, that which I believe in with unbroken certainty, I learnt in the nursery. I generally learnt it from a nurse; that is, from the solemn and star-appointed priestess at once of democracy and tradition. The things I believed most then, the things I believe most now, are the things called fairy tales. They seem to me to be the entirely reasonable things. They are not fantasies: compared with them other things are fantastic. Compared with them religion and rationalism are both abnormal, though religion is abnormally right and rationalism abnormally wrong. Fairyland is nothing but the sunny country of common sense. It is not earth that judges heaven, but heaven that judges earth; so for me at least it was not earth that criticised elfland, but elfland that criticised the earth. I knew the magic beanstalk before I had tasted beans; I was sure of the Man in the Moon before I was certain of the moon. This was at one with all popular tradition. Modern minor poets are naturalists, and talk about the bush or the brook; but the singers of the old epics and fables were supernaturalists, and talked about the gods of brook and bush. That is what the moderns mean when they say that the ancients did not "appreciate Nature," because they said that Nature was divine. Old nurses do not tell children about the grass, but about the fairies that dance on the grass; and the old Greeks could not see the trees for the dryads.

But I deal here with what ethic and philosophy come from being fed on fairy tales. If I were describing them in detail I could note many noble and healthy principles that arise from them. There is the chivalrous lesson of "Jack the Giant Killer"; that giants should be killed because they are gigantic. It is a manly mutiny against pride as such. For the rebel is older than all the kingdoms, and the Jacobin has more tradition than the Jacobite.[24] There is the lesson of "Cinderella," which is the same as that of the Magnificat — *exaltavit humiles*. There is the great lesson of "Beauty and the Beast"; that a thing must be loved *before* it is loveable. There is the terrible allegory of the "Sleeping Beauty," which tells how the human creature was blessed with all birthday gifts, yet cursed with death; and how death also may perhaps be softened to a sleep. But I am not concerned with any of the separate statutes of elfland, but with the whole spirit of its law, which I learnt before I could speak, and shall retain when I cannot write. I am concerned with a certain way of looking at life, which was created in me by the fairy tales, but has since been meekly ratified by the mere facts.

It might be stated this way. There are certain sequences or developments (cases of one thing following another), which are, in the true sense of the word, reasonable. They are, in the true sense of the word, necessary. Such are mathematical and merely logical sequences. We in fairyland (who are the most reasonable of all creatures) admit that reason and that necessity. For instance, if the Ugly Sisters are older than Cinderella, it is (in an iron and awful sense) *necessary* that Cinderella is younger than the Ugly Sisters. There is no getting out of it. Haeckel may talk as much fatalism about that fact as he pleases: it really must be. If Jack is the son of a miller, a miller is the father of Jack. Cold reason decrees it from her awful throne: and we in fairyland submit. If the three brothers all

---

[24] The first one signifies a political group in the French Revolution, the second a Scottish supporter of the House of Stuart following the Revolution of 1688, when the last Stuart monarch, James II, was deposed.

ride horses, there are six animals and eighteen legs involved: that is true rationalism, and fairyland is full of it. But as I put my head over the hedge of the elves and began to take notice of the natural world, I observed an extraordinary thing. I observed that learned men in spectacles were talking of the actual things that happened—dawn and death and so on—as if *they* were rational and inevitable. They talked as if the fact that trees bear fruit were just as *necessary* as the fact that two and one trees make three. But it is not. There is an enormous difference by the test of fairyland; which is the test of the imagination. You cannot *imagine* two and one not making three. But you can easily imagine trees not growing fruit; you can imagine them growing golden candlesticks or tigers hanging on by the tail. These men in spectacles spoke much of a man named Newton, who was hit by an apple, and who discovered a law. But they could not be got to see the distinction between a true law, a law of reason, and the mere fact of apples falling. If the apple hit Newton's nose, Newton's nose hit the apple. That is a true necessity: because we cannot conceive the one occurring without the other. But we can quite well conceive the apple not falling on his nose; we can fancy it flying ardently through the air to hit some other nose, of which it had a more definite dislike. We have always in our fairy tales kept this sharp distinction between the science of mental relations, in which there really are laws, and the science of physical facts, in which there are no laws, but only weird repetitions. We believe in bodily miracles, but not in mental impossibilities. We believe that a Beanstalk climbed up to heaven; but that does not at all confuse our convictions on the philosophical question of how many beans make five.

Here is the peculiar perfection of tone and truth in the nursery tales. The man of science says, "Cut the stalk, and the apple will fall"; but he says it calmly, as if the one idea really led up to the other. The witch in the fairy tale says, "Blow the horn, and the ogre's castle will fall"; but she does not say it as if it were something in which the effect obviously arose out of the cause. Doubtless she has given the advice to many champions, and has seen many castles fall, but she does not lose either her wonder or her reason. She does not muddle her head until it imagines a necessary mental connection between a horn and a falling tower. But the scientific men do muddle their heads, until they imagine a necessary mental connection between an apple leaving the tree and an apple reaching the ground. They do really talk as if they had found not only a set of marvellous facts, but a truth connecting those facts. They do talk as if the connection of two strange things physically connected them philosophically. They feel that because one incomprehensible thing constantly follows another incomprehensible thing the two together somehow make up a comprehensible thing. Two black riddles make a white answer.

In fairyland we avoid the word "law"; but in the land of science they are singularly fond of it. Thus they will call some interesting conjecture about how forgotten folks pronounced the alphabet, Grimm's Law. But Grimm's Law is far less intellectual than Grimm's Fairy Tales. The tales are, at any rate, certainly tales; while the law is not a law. A law implies that we know the nature of the generalisation and enactment; not merely that we have noticed some of the effects. If there is a law that pick-pockets shall go to prison, it implies that there is an imaginable mental connection between the idea of prison and the idea of picking pockets. And we know what the idea is. We can say why we take liberty from a man who takes liberties. But we cannot say why an egg can turn into a chicken any more than we can say why a bear could turn into a fairy prince. As *ideas*, the egg and the chicken are further off from each other than the bear and the prince; for no egg in itself suggests a chicken, whereas some princes do suggest bears. Granted, then, that certain transformations do happen, it is essential that we should regard them in the philosophic manner of fairy tales, not in the unphilosophic manner of science and the "Laws of Nature." When we are asked why eggs turn to birds or fruits fall in autumn, we must answer exactly as the fairy godmother would answer if Cinderella asked her why mice turned to horses or her clothes fell from her at twelve o'clock. We must answer that it is *magic*. It is not a "law," for we do not understand its general formula. It is not a necessity, for though we can count on it happening practically, we have no right to say that it must always happen. It is no argument for unalterable law (as Huxley fancied) that we count on the ordinary course of things. We do not count on it; we bet on it. We risk the remote possibility of a miracle as we do that of a poisoned pancake or a world-destroying comet. We leave it out of account, not because it is a miracle, and therefore an impossibility, but because it is a miracle, and therefore an exception. All the terms used in the science books, "law," "necessity," "order," "tendency," and so on, are really unintellectual, because they assume an inner synthesis, which we do not possess. The only words that ever satisfied me as describing Nature are the terms used in the fairy books, "charm," "spell," "enchantment." They express the arbitrariness of the fact and its mystery. A tree grows fruit because it is a *magic* tree. Water runs downhill because it is bewitched. The sun shines because it is bewitched.

I deny altogether that this is fantastic or even mystical. We may have some mysticism later on; but this fairy-tale language about things is simply rational and agnostic. It is the only way I can express in words my clear and definite perception that one thing is quite distinct from another; that there is no logical connection between flying and laying eggs. It is the man who talks about "a law" that he has never seen who is the mystic. Nay, the ordinary scientific man is strictly a sentimentalist. He is a sentimentalist in this essential sense, that he is soaked and swept away by mere associations. He has so often seen birds fly and lay eggs that he feels as if there must be some dreamy, tender connection between the two ideas, whereas there is none. A forlorn lover might be unable to dissociate the moon from lost love; so the materialist is unable to dissociate the moon from the tide. In both cases there is no connection, except that one has seen them together. A sentimentalist might shed tears at the smell of apple-blossom, because, by a dark association of his own, it reminded him of his boyhood. So the materialist professor (though he conceals his tears) is yet a sentimentalist, because, by a dark association of his own, apple-blossoms remind him of apples. But the cool rationalist from fairyland does not see why, in the abstract, the apple tree should not grow crimson tulips; it sometimes does in his country.

This elementary wonder, however, is not a mere fancy derived from the fairy tales; on the contrary, all the fire of the fairy tales is derived from this. Just as we all like love tales because there is an instinct of sex, we all like astonishing tales because they touch the nerve of the ancient instinct of astonishment. This is proved by the fact that when we are very young children we do not need fairy tales: we only need tales. Mere life is interesting enough. A child of seven is excited by being told that Tommy opened a door and saw a dragon. But a child of three is excited by being told that Tommy opened a door. Boys like romantic tales; but babies like realistic tales—because they find them romantic. In fact, a baby is about the only person, I should think, to whom a modern realistic novel could be read without boring him. This proves that even nursery tales only echo an almost pre-natal leap of interest and amazement. These tales say that apples were golden only to refresh the forgotten moment when we found that they were green. They make rivers run with wine only to make us remember, for one wild moment, that they run with water. I have said that this is wholly reasonable and even agnostic. And, indeed, on this point I am all for the higher agnosticism; its better name is Ignorance. We have all read in scientific books, and, indeed, in all romances, the story of the man who has forgotten his name. This man walks about the streets and can see and appreciate everything; only he cannot remember who he is. Well, every man is that man in the story. Every man has forgotten who he is. One may understand the cosmos, but never the ego; the self is more distant than any star. Thou shalt love the Lord thy God; but thou shalt not know thyself. We are all under the same mental calamity; we have all forgotten our names. We have all forgotten what we really are. All that we call common sense and rationality and practicality and positivism only means that for certain dead levels of our life we forget that we have forgotten. All that we call spirit and art and ecstacy only means that for one awful instant we remember that we forget.

But though (like the man without memory in the novel) we walk the streets with a sort of half-witted admiration, still it is admiration. It is admiration in English and not only admiration in Latin. The wonder has a positive element of praise. This is the next milestone to be definitely marked on our road through fairyland. I shall speak in the next chapter about optimists and pessimists in their intellectual aspect, so far as they have one. Here I am only trying to describe the enormous emotions which cannot be described. And the strongest emotion was that life was as precious as it was puzzling. It was an ecstacy because it was an adventure; it was an adventure because it was an opportunity. The goodness of the fairy tale was not affected by the fact that there might be more dragons than princesses; it was good to be in a fairy tale. The test of all happiness is gratitude; and I felt grateful, though I hardly knew to whom. Children are grateful when Santa Claus puts in their stockings gifts of toys or sweets. Could I not be grateful to Santa Claus when he put in my stockings the gift of two miraculous legs? We thank people for birthday presents of cigars and slippers. Can I thank no one for the birthday present of birth?

There were, then, these two first feelings, indefensible and indisputable. The world was a shock, but it was not merely shocking; existence was a surprise, but it was a pleasant surprise. In fact, all my first views were exactly uttered in a riddle that stuck in my brain from boyhood. The question was, "What did the first frog say?" And the answer was, "Lord, how you made me jump!" That says succinctly all that I am saying. God made the frog jump; but the frog prefers jumping. But when these things are settled there enters the second great principle of the fairy philosophy.

Any one can see it who will simply read "Grimm's Fairy Tales" or the fine collections of Mr. Andrew Lang.[25] For the pleasure of pedantry I will call it the Doctrine of Conditional Joy. Touchstone talked of much virtue in an "if"; according to elfin ethics all virtue is in an "if." The note of the fairy utterance always is, "You may live in a palace of gold and sapphire, *if* you do not say the word 'cow'"; or "You may live happily with the King's daughter, *if* you do not show her an onion." The vision always hangs upon a veto. All the dizzy and colossal things conceded depend upon one small thing withheld. All the wild and whirling things that are let loose depend upon one thing that is forbidden. Mr. W. B. Yeats, in his exquisite and piercing elfin poetry, describes the elves as lawless; they plunge in innocent anarchy on the unbridled horses of the air—

[25] Andrew Lang (1844–1912), a Scottish man of letters who compiled several collections of fairy stories, each named after a different color.

Ride on the crest of the dishevelled tide,[26]
And dance upon the mountains like a flame.

It is a dreadful thing to say that Mr. W. B. Yeats does not understand fairyland. But I do say it. He is an ironical Irishman, full of intellectual reactions. He is not stupid enough to understand fairyland. Fairies prefer people of the yokel type like myself; people who gape and grin and do as they are told. Mr. Yeats reads into elfland all the righteous insurrection of his own race. But the lawlessness of Ireland is a Christian lawlessness, founded on reason and justice. The Fenian[27] is rebelling against something he understands only too well; but the true citizen of fairyland is obeying something he does not understand at all. In the fairy tale an incomprehensible happiness rests upon an incomprehensible condition. A box is opened, and all evils fly out. A word is forgotten, and cities perish. A lamp is lit, and love flies away. A flower is plucked, and human lives are forfeited. An apple is eaten, and the hope of God is gone.

This is the tone of fairy tales, and it is certainly not lawlessness or even liberty, though men under a mean modern tyranny may think it liberty by comparison. People out of Portland Gaol might think Fleet Street free; but closer study will prove that both fairies and journalists are the slaves of duty. Fairy godmothers seem at least as strict as other godmothers. Cinderella received a coach out of Wonderland and a coachman out of nowhere, but she received a command — which might have come out of Brixton — that she should be back by twelve. Also, she had a glass slipper; and it cannot be a coincidence that glass is so common a substance in folk-lore. This princess lives in a glass castle, that princess on a glass hill; this one sees all things in a mirror; they may all live in glass houses if they will not throw stones. For this thin glitter of glass everywhere is the expression of the fact that the happiness is bright but brittle, like the substance most easily smashed by a housemaid or a cat. And this fairy-tale sentiment also sank into me and became my sentiment towards the whole world. I felt and feel that life itself is as bright as the diamond,

[26] A good example of Chesterton's casual approach to quotations. The line in Yeat's play *The Land of Heart's Desire* actually begins "Run on the top . . . ."

[27] Member of a secret revolutionary society formed in Ireland and the United States in the mid-nineteenth century to achieve Irish independence from Great Britain.

but as brittle as the window-pane; and when the heavens were compared to the terrible crystal I can remember a shudder. I was afraid that God would drop the cosmos with a crash.

Remember, however, that to be breakable is not the same as to be perishable. Strike a glass, and it will not endure an instant; simply do not strike it, and it will endure a thousand years. Such, it seemed, was the joy of man, either in elfland or on earth; the happiness depended on *not doing something* which you could at any moment do and which, very often, it was not obvious why you should not do. Now, the point here is that to *me* this did not seem unjust. If the miller's third son said to the fairy, "Explain why I must not stand on my head in the fairy palace," the other might fairly reply, "Well, if it comes to that, explain the fairy palace." If Cinderella says, "How is it that I must leave the ball at twelve?" her godmother might answer, "How is it that you are going there till twelve?" If I leave a man in my will ten talking elephants and a hundred winged horses, he cannot complain if the conditions partake of the slight eccentricity of the gift. He must not look a winged horse in the mouth. And it seemed to me that existence was itself so very eccentric a legacy that I could not complain of not understanding the limitations of the vision when I did not understand the vision they limited. The frame was no stranger than the picture. The veto might well be as wild as the vision; it might be as startling as the sun, as elusive as the waters, as fantastic and terrible as the towering trees.

For this reason (we may call it the fairy godmother philosophy) I never could join the young men of my time in feeling what they called the general sentiment of *revolt*. I should have resisted, let us hope, any rules that were evil, and with these and their definition I shall deal in another chapter. But I did not feel disposed to resist any rule merely because it was mysterious. Estates are sometimes held by foolish forms, the breaking of a stick or the payment of a peppercorn: I was willing to hold the huge estate of earth and heaven by any such feudal fantasy. It could not well be wilder than the fact that I was allowed to hold it at all. At this stage I give only one ethical instance to show my meaning. I could never mix in the common murmur of that rising generation against monogamy, because no restriction on sex seemed so odd and unexpected as sex itself. To be allowed, like Endymion,[28] to make love to the moon and then to complain that Jupiter kept his own moons in a harem seemed to me (bred on fairy tales like Endymion's) a vulgar anti-climax. Keeping to one woman is a small price for so much as seeing one woman. To complain that I could only be married once was like complaining that I had only been born once. It was incommensurate with the terrible excitement of which one was talking. It showed, not an exaggerated sensibility to sex, but a curious insensibility to it. A man is a fool who complains that he cannot enter Eden by five gates at once. Polygamy is a lack of the realization of sex; it is like a man plucking five pears in mere absence of mind. The aesthetes touched the last insane limits of language in their eulogy on lovely things. The thistledown made them weep; a burnished beetle brought them to their knees. Yet their emotion never impressed me for an instant, for this reason, that it never occurred to them to pay for their pleasure in any sort of symbolic sacrifice. Men (I felt) might fast forty days for the sake of hearing a blackbird sing. Men might go through fire to find a cowslip. Yet these lovers of beauty could not even keep sober for the blackbird. They would not go through common Christian marriage by way of recompense to the cowslip. Surely one might pay for extraordinary joy in ordinary morals. Oscar Wilde said that sunsets were not valued because we could not pay for sunsets. But Oscar Wilde was wrong; we can pay for sunsets. We can pay for them by not being Oscar Wilde.

Well, I left the fairy tales lying on the floor of the nursery, and I have not found any books so sensible since. I left the nurse guardian of tradition and democracy, and I have not found any modern type so sanely radical or so sanely conservative. But the matter for important comment was here: that when I first went out into the mental atmosphere of the modern world, I found that the modern world was positively opposed on two points to my nurse and to the nursery tales. It has taken me a long time to find out that the modern world is wrong and my nurse was right. The really curious

[28] A shepherd prince, the most handsome of men, with whom the moon goddess fell in love.

thing was this: that modern thought contradicted this basic creed of my boyhood on its two most essential doctrines. I have explained that the fairy tales founded in me two convictions; first, that this world is a wild and startling place, which might have been quite different, but which is quite delightful; second, that before this wildness and delight one may well be modest and submit to the queerest limitations of so queer a kindness. But I found the whole modern world running like a high tide against both my tendernesses; and the shock of that collision created two sudden and spontaneous sentiments, which I have had ever since and which, crude as they were, have since hardened into convictions.

First, I found the whole modern world talking scientific fatalism; saying that everything is as it must always have been, being unfolded without fault from the beginning. The leaf on the tree is green because it could never have been anything else. Now, the fairy-tale philosopher is glad that the leaf is green precisely because it might have been scarlet. He feels as if it had turned green an instant before he looked at it. He is pleased that snow is white on the strictly reasonable ground that it might have been black. Every colour has in it a bold quality as of choice; the red of garden roses is not only decisive but dramatic, like suddenly spilt blood. He feels that something has been *done*. But the great determinists of the nineteenth century were strongly against this native feeling that something had happened an instant before. In fact, according to them, nothing ever really had happened since the beginning of the world. Nothing ever had happened since existence had happened; and even about the date of that they were not very sure.

The modern world as I found it was solid for modern Calvinism, for the necessity of things being as they are. But when I came to ask them I found they had really no proof of this unavoidable repetition in things except the fact that the things were repeated. Now, the mere repetition made the things to me rather more weird than more rational. It was as if, having seen a curiously shaped nose in the street and dismissed it as an accident, I had then seen six other noses of the same astonishing shape. I should have fancied for a moment that it must be some local secret society. So one elephant having a trunk was odd; but all elephants having trunks looked like a plot. I speak here only of an emotion, and of an emotion at once stubborn and subtle. But the repetition in Nature seemed sometimes to be an excited repetition, like that of an angry schoolmaster saying the same thing over and over again. The grass seemed signalling to me with all its fingers at once; the crowded stars seemed bent upon being understood. The sun would make me see him if he rose a thousand times. The recurrences of the universe rose to the maddening rhythm of an incantation, and I began to see an idea.

All the towering materialism which dominates the modern mind rests ultimately upon one assumption; a false assumption. It is supposed that if a thing goes on repeating itself it is probably dead; a piece of clockwork. People feel that if the universe was personal it would vary; if the sun were alive it would dance. This is a fallacy even in relation to known fact. For the variation in human affairs is generally brought into them, not by life, but by death; by the dying down or breaking off of their strength or desire. A man varies his movements because of some slight element of failure or fatigue. He gets into an omnibus because he is tired of walking; or he walks because he is tired of sitting still. But if his life and joy were so gigantic that he never tired of going to Islington, he might go to Islington as regularly as the Thames goes to Sheerness. The very speed and ecstacy of his life would have the stillness of death. The sun rises every morning. I do not rise every morning; but the variation is due not to my activity, but to my inaction. Now, to put the matter in a popular phrase, it might be true that the sun rises regularly because he never gets tired of rising. His routine might be due, not to a lifelessness, but to a rush of life. The thing I mean can be seen, for instance, in children, when they find some game or joke that they specially enjoy. A child kicks his legs rhythmically through excess, not absence, of life. Because children have abounding vitality, because they are in spirit fierce and free, therefore they want things repeated and unchanged. They always say, "Do it again"; and the grown-up person does it again until he is nearly dead. For grown-up people are not strong enough to exult in monotony. But perhaps God is strong enough to exult in monotony. It is possible that God says every morning, "Do it again" to the sun; and every evening, "Do it again" to the moon. It may not be automatic necessity that makes all daisies alike; it may be that God makes every daisy separately, but has never got tired of making them. It may be that He has the eternal appetite of infancy; for we have sinned and grown old, and our Father is younger than we. The repetition in Nature may not be a mere recurrence; it may be a theatrical *encore*. Heaven may *encore* the bird who laid an egg. If the human being conceives and brings forth a human child instead of bringing forth a fish, or a bat, or a griffin, the reason may not be that we are fixed in an animal fate without life or purpose. It may be that our little tragedy has touched the gods, that they admire it from their starry galleries, and that at the end of every human drama man is called again and again before the curtain. Repetition may go on for millions of years, by mere choice, and at any instant it may stop. Man may stand on the earth generation after generation, and yet each birth be his positively last appearance.

This was my first conviction; made by the shock of my childish emotions meeting the modern creed in mid-career. I had always vaguely felt facts to be miracles in the sense that they are wonderful: now I began to think them miracles in the stricter sense that they were *wilful*. I mean that they were, or might be, repeated exercises of some will. In short, I had always believed that the world involved magic: now I thought that perhaps it involved a magician. And this pointed a profound emotion always present and sub-conscious; that this world of ours has some purpose; and if there is a purpose, there is a person. I had always felt life first as a story: and if there is a story there is a story-teller.

But modern thought also hit my second human tradition. It went against the fairy feeling about strict limits and conditions. The one thing it loved to talk about was expansion and largeness. Herbert Spencer[29] would have been greatly annoyed if any one had called him an imperialist, and therefore it is highly regrettable that nobody did. But he was an imperialist of the lowest type. He popularized this contemptible notion that the size of the solar system ought to overawe the spiritual dogma of man. Why should a man surrender his

[29] Herbert Spencer (1820–1903), an evolutionary philosopher.

dignity to the solar system any more than to a whale? If mere size proves that man is not the image of God, then a whale may be the image of God; a somewhat formless image; what one might call an impressionist portrait. It is quite futile to argue that man is small compared to the cosmos; for man was always small compared to the nearest tree. But Herbert Spencer, in his headlong imperialism, would insist that we had in some way been conquered and annexed by the astronomical universe. He spoke about men and their ideals exactly as the most insolent Unionist[30] talks about the Irish and their ideals. He turned mankind into a small nationality. And his evil influence can be seen even in the most spirited and honourable of later scientific authors; notably in the early romances of Mr. H. G. Wells. Many moralists have in an exaggerated way represented the earth as wicked. But Mr. Wells and his school made the heavens wicked. We should lift up our eyes to the stars from whence would come our ruin.

But the expansion of which I speak was much more evil than all this. I have remarked that the materialist, like the madman, is in prison; in the prison of one thought. These people seemed to think it singularly inspiring to keep on saying that the prison was very large. The size of this scientific universe gave one no novelty, no relief. The cosmos went on for ever, but not in its wildest constellation could there be anything really interesting; anything, for instance, such as forgiveness or free will. The grandeur or infinity of the secret of its cosmos added nothing to it. It was like telling a prisoner in Reading gaol that he would be glad to hear that the gaol now covered half the county. The warder would have nothing to show the man except more and more long corridors of stone lit by ghastly lights and empty of all that is human. So these expanders of the universe had nothing to show us except more and more infinite corridors of space lit by ghastly suns and empty of all that is divine.

In fairyland there had been a real law; a law that could be broken, for the definition of a law is something that can be broken. But the machinery of this cosmic prison was something that could not be broken; for we ourselves were only a part of its machinery. We were

[30] A member of the political party that advocated maintenance of the parliamentary union between Great Britain and Ireland, in opposition to Irish home rule.

either unable to do things or we were destined to do them. The idea of the mystical condition quite disappeared; one can neither have the firmness of keeping laws nor the fun of breaking them. The largeness of this universe had nothing of that freshness and airy outbreak which we have praised in the universe of the poet. This modern universe is literally an empire; that is, it was vast, but it is not free. One went into larger and larger windowless rooms, rooms big with Babylonian perspective; but one never found the smallest window or a whisper of outer air.

Their infernal parallels seemed to expand with distance; but for me all good things come to a point, swords for instance. So finding the boast of the big cosmos so unsatisfactory to my emotions I began to argue about it a little; and I soon found that the whole attitude was even shallower than could have been expected. According to these people the cosmos was one thing since it had one unbroken rule. Only (they would say) while it is one thing it is also the only thing there is. Why, then, should one worry particularly to call it large? There is nothing to compare it with. It would be just as sensible to call it small. A man may say, "I like this vast cosmos, with its throng of stars and its crowd of varied creatures." But if it comes to that why should not a man say, "I like this cosy little cosmos, with its decent number of stars and as neat a provision of live stock as I wish to see"? One is as good as the other; they are both mere sentiments. It is mere sentiment to rejoice that the sun is larger than the earth; it is quite as sane a sentiment to rejoice that the sun is no larger than it is. A man chooses to have an emotion about the largeness of the world: why should he not choose to have an emotion about its smallness?

It happened that I had that emotion. When one is fond of anything one addresses it by diminutives, even if it is an elephant or a life-guardsman. The reason is, that anything, however huge, that can be conceived of as complete, can be conceived of as small. If military moustaches did not suggest a sword or tusks a tail, then the object would be vast because it would be immeasurable. But the moment you can imagine a guardsman you can imagine a small guardsman. The moment you really see an elephant you can call it "Tiny." If you can make a statue of a thing you can make a statuette of it. These people professed that the universe was one coherent thing; but they were not fond of the universe. But I was frightfully fond of the universe and wanted to address it by a diminutive. I often did so; and it never seemed to mind. Actually and in truth I did feel that these dim dogmas of vitality were better expressed by calling the world small than by calling it large. For about infinity there was a sort of carelessness which was the reverse of the fierce and pious care which I felt touching the pricelessness and the peril of life. They showed only a dreary waste; but I felt a sort of sacred thrift. For economy is far more romantic than extravagance. To them stars were an unending income of halfpence; but I felt about the golden sun and the silver moon as a schoolboy feels if he has one sovereign and one shilling.

These subconscious convictions are best hit off by the colour and tone of certain tales. Thus I have said that stories of magic alone can express my sense that life is not only a pleasure but a kind of eccentric privilege. I may express this other feeling of cosmic cosiness by allusion to another book always read in boyhood, "Robinson Crusoe," which I read about this time, and which owes its eternal vivacity to the fact that it celebrates the poetry of limits, nay, even the wild romance of prudence. Crusoe is a man on a small rock with a few comforts just snatched from the sea: the best thing in the book is simply the list of things saved from the wreck. The greatest of poems is an inventory. Every kitchen tool becomes ideal because Crusoe might have dropped it in the sea. It is a good exercise, in empty or ugly hours of the day, to look at anything, the coal-scuttle or the bookcase, and think how happy one could be to have brought it out of the sinking ship on to the solitary island. But it is a better exercise still to remember how all things have had this hair-breadth escape: everything has been saved from a wreck. Every man has had one horrible adventure: as a hidden untimely birth he had not been, as infants that never see the light. Men spoke much in my boyhood of restricted or ruined men of genius: and it was common to say that many a man was a Great Might-Have-Been. To me it is a more solid and startling fact that any man in the street is a Great Might-Not-Have-Been.

But I really felt (the fancy may seem foolish) as if all the order and number of things were the romantic remnant of Crusoe's ship. That there are two sexes and one sun, was like the fact that there were two guns and one axe. It was poignantly urgent that none should be lost; but somehow, it was rather fun that none could be added. The trees and the planets seemed like things saved from the wreck: and when I saw the Matterhorn I was glad that it had not been overlooked in the confusion. I felt economical about the stars as if they were sapphires (they are called so in Milton's Eden): I hoarded the hills. For the universe is a single jewel, and while it is a natural cant to talk of a jewel as peerless and priceless, of this jewel it is literally true. This cosmos is indeed without peer and without price: for there cannot be another one.

Thus ends, in unavoidable inadequacy, the attempt to utter the unutterable things. These are my ultimate attitudes towards life; the soils for the seeds of doctrine. These in some dark way I thought before I could write, and felt before I could think: that we may proceed more easily afterwards, I will roughly recapitulate them now. I felt in my bones; first, that this world does not explain itself. It may be a miracle with a supernatural explanation; it may be a conjuring trick, with a natural explanation. But the explanation of the conjuring trick, if it is to satisfy me, will have to be better than the natural explanations I have heard. The thing is magic, true or false. Second, I came to feel as if magic must have a meaning, and meaning must have some one to mean it. There was something personal in the world, as in a work of art; whatever it meant it meant violently. Third, I thought this purpose beautiful in its old design, in spite of its defects, such as dragons. Fourth, that the proper form of thanks to it is some form of humility and restraint: we should thank God for beer and Burgundy by not drinking too much of them. We owed, also, an obedience to whatever made us. And last, and strangest, there had come into my mind a vague and vast impression that in some way all good was a remnant to be stored and held sacred out of some primordial ruin. Man had saved his good as Crusoe saved his goods: he had saved them from a wreck. All this I felt and the age gave me no encouragement to feel it. And all this time I had not even thought of Christian theology.

V

THE FLAG OF THE WORLD

When I was a boy there were two curious men running about who were called the optimist and the pessimist. I constantly used the words myself, but I cheerfully confess that I never had any very special idea of what they meant. The only thing which might be considered evident was that they could not mean what they said; for the ordinary verbal explanation was that the optimist thought this world as good as it could be, while the pessimist thought it as bad as it could be. Both these statements being obviously raving nonsense, one had to cast about for other explanations. An optimist could not mean a man who thought everything right and nothing wrong. For that is meaningless; it is like calling everthing right and nothing left. Upon the whole, I came to the conclusion that the optimist thought everything good except the pessimist, and that the pessimist thought everything bad, except himself. It would be unfair to omit altogether from the list the mysterious but suggestive definition said to have been given by a little girl, "An optimist is a man who looks after your eyes, and a pessimist is a man who looks after your feet." I am not sure that this is not the best definition of all. There is even a sort of allegorical truth in it. For there might, perhaps, be a profitable distinction drawn between that more dreary thinker who thinks merely of our contact with the earth from moment to moment, and that happier thinker who considers rather our primary power of vision and of choice of road.

But this is a deep mistake in this alternative of the optimist and the pessimist. The assumption of it is that a man criticises this world as if he were house-hunting, as if he were being shown over a new suite of apartments. If a man came to this world from some other world in full possession of his powers he might discuss whether the advantage of midsummer woods made up for the disadvantage of mad dogs, just as a man looking for lodgings might balance the presence of a telephone against the absence of a sea view. But no man is in that position. A man belongs to this world before he begins to ask if it is nice to belong to it. He has fought for the flag, and often won heroic victories for the flag long before he has ever enlisted. To put shortly what seems the essential matter, he has a loyalty long before he has any admiration.

In the last chapter it has been said that the primary feeling that this world is strange and yet attractive is best expressed in fairy tales. The reader may, if he likes, put down the next stage to that bellicose and even jingo literature which commonly comes next in the history of a boy. We all owe much sound morality to the penny dreadfuls. Whatever the reason, it seemed and still seems to me that our attitude towards life can be better expressed in terms of a kind of military loyalty than in terms of criticism and approval. My acceptance of the universe is not optimism, it is more like patriotism. It is a matter of primary loyalty. The world is not a lodging-house at Brighton, which we are to leave because it is miserable. It is the fortress of our family, with the flag flying on the turret, and the more miserable it is the less we should leave it. The point is not that this world is too sad to love or too glad not to love; the point is that when you do love a thing, its gladness is a reason for loving it, and its sadness a reason for loving it more. All optimistic thoughts about England and all pessimistic thoughts about her are alike reasons for the English patriot. Similarly, optimism and pessimism are alike arguments for the cosmic patriot.

Let us suppose we are confronted with a desperate thing—say Pimlico. If we think what is really best for Pimlico we shall find the thread of thought leads to the throne or the mystic and the arbitrary. It is not enough for a man to disapprove of Pimlico: in that case he will merely cut his throat or move to Chelsea.[31] Nor, certainly, is it enough for a man to approve of Pimlico: for then it will remain Pimlico, which would be awful. The only way out of it seems to be for somebody to love Pimlico: to love it with a transcendental tie and without any earthly reason. If there arose a man who loved Pimlico, then Pimlico would rise into ivory towers and golden

[31] A borough of London west of Westminster and fronting on the Thames.

pinnacles; Pimlico would attire herself as a woman does when she is loved. For decoration is not given to hide horrible things: but to decorate things already adorable. A mother does not give her child a blue bow because he is so ugly without it. A lover does not give a girl a necklace to hide her neck. If men loved Pimlico as mothers love children, arbitrarily, because it is *theirs*, Pimlico in a year or two might be fairer than Florence. Some readers will say that this is a mere fantasy. I answer that this is the actual history of mankind. This, as a fact, is how cities did grow great. Go back to the darkest roots of civilization and you will find them knotted round some sacred stone or encircling some sacred well. People first paid honour to a spot and afterwards gained glory for it. Men did not love Rome because she was great. She was great because they had loved her.

The eighteenth-century theories of the social contract have been exposed to much clumsy criticism in our time; in so far as they meant that there is at the back of all historic government an idea of content and co-operation, they were demonstrably right. But they really were wrong in so far as they suggested that men had ever aimed at order or ethics directly by a conscious exchange of interests. Morality did not begin by one man saying to another, "I will not hit you if you do not hit me"; there is no trace of such a transaction. There *is* a trace of both men having said, "We must not hit each other in the holy place." They gained their morality by guarding their religion. They did not cultivate courage. They fought for the shrine, and found they had become courageous. They did not cultivate cleanliness. They purified themselves for the altar, and found that they were clean. The history of the Jews is the only early document known to most Englishmen, and the facts can be judged sufficiently from that. The Ten Commandments which have been found substantially common to mankind were merely military commands; a code of regimental orders, issued to protect a certain ark across a certain desert. Anarchy was evil because it endangered the sanctity. And only when they made a holy day for God did they find they had made a holiday for men.

If it be granted that this primary devotion to a place or thing is a source of creative energy, we can pass on to a very peculiar fact. Let us reiterate for an instant that the only right optimism is a sort of universal patriotism. What is the matter with the pessimist? I think it can be stated by saying that he is the cosmic anti-patriot. And what is the matter with the anti-patriot? I think it can be stated, without undue bitterness, by saying that he is the candid friend. And what is the matter with the candid friend? There we strike the rock of real life and immutable human nature.

I venture to say that what is bad in the candid friend is simply that he is not candid. He is keeping something back — his own gloomy pleasure in saying unpleasant things. He has a secret desire to hurt, not merely to help. This is certainly, I think, what makes a certain sort of anti-patriot irritating to healthy citizens. I do not speak (of course) of the anti-patriotism which only irritates feverish stock-brokers and gushing actresses; that is only patriotism speaking plainly. A man who says that no patriot should attack the Boer War until it is over is not worth answering intelligently; he is saying that no good son should warn his mother off a cliff until she has fallen over it. But there is an anti-patriot who honestly angers honest men, and the explanation of him is, I think, what I have suggested: he is the uncandid candid friend; the man who says, "I am sorry to say we are ruined," and is not sorry at all. And he may be said, without rhetoric, to be a traitor; for he is using that ugly knowledge which was allowed him to strengthen the army, to discourage people from joining it. Because he is allowed to be pessimistic as a military adviser he is being pessimistic as a recruiting sergeant. Just in the same way the pessimist (who is the cosmic anti-patriot) uses the freedom that life allows to her counsellors to lure away the people from her flag. Granted that he states only facts, it is still essential to know what are his emotions, what is his motive. It may be that twelve hundred men in Tottenham are down with smallpox; but we want to know whether this is stated by some great philosopher who wants to curse the gods, or only by some common clergyman who wants to help the men.

The evil of the pessimist is, then, not that he chastises gods and men, but that he does not love what he chastises — he has not this primary and supernatural loyalty to things. What is the evil of the man commonly called an optimist? Obviously, it is felt that the optimist, wishing to defend the honour of this world, will defend the indefensible. He is the jingo of the universe; he will say, "My cosmos, right or wrong." He will be less inclined to the reform of things; more inclined to a sort of front-bench official answer to all attacks, soothing every one with assurances. He will not wash the world, but whitewash the world. All this (which is true of a type of optimist) leads us to the one really interesting point of psychology, which could not be explained without it.

We say there must be a primal loyalty to life: the only question is, shall it be a natural or a supernatural loyalty? If you like to put it so, shall it be a reasonable or an unreasonable loyalty? Now, the extraordinary thing is that the bad optimism (the whitewashing, the weak defence of everything) comes in with the reasonable optimism. Rational optimism leads to stagnation: it is irrational optimism that leads to reform. Let me explain by using once more the parallel of patriotism. The man who is most likely to ruin the place he loves is exactly the man who loves it with a reason. The man who will improve the place is the man who loves it without a reason. If a man loves some feature of Pimlico (which seems unlikely), he may find himself defending that feature against Pimlico itself. But if he simply loves Pimlico itself, he may lay it waste and turn it into the New Jerusalem. I do not deny that reform may be excessive; I only say that it is the mystic patriot who reforms. Mere jingo self-contentment is commonest among those who have some pedantic reason for their patriotism. The worst jingoes do not love England, but a theory of England. If we love England for being an empire, we may overrate the success with which we rule the Hindoos. But if we love it only for being a nation, we can face all events: for it would be a nation even if the Hindoos ruled us. Thus also only those will permit their patriotism to falsify history whose patriotism depends on history. A man who loves England for being English will not mind how she arose. But a man who loves England for being Anglo-Saxon may go against all facts for his fancy. He may end (like Carlyle and

Freeman[32]) by maintaining that the Norman Conquest was a Saxon Conquest. He may end in utter unreason—because he has a reason. A man who loves France for being military will palliate the army of 1870. But a man who loves France for being France will improve the army of 1870. This is exactly what the French have done, and France is a good instance of the working paradox. Nowhere else is patriotism more purely abstract and arbitrary; and nowhere else is reform more drastic and sweeping. The more transcendental is your patriotism, the more practical are your politics.

Perhaps the most everyday instance of this point is in the case of women; and their strange and strong loyalty. Some stupid people started the idea that because women obviously back up their own people through everything, therefore women are blind and do not see anything. They can hardly have known any women. The same women who are ready to defend their men through thick and thin are (in their personal intercourse with the man) almost morbidly lucid about the thinness of his excuses or the thickness of his head. A man's friend likes him but leaves him as he is: his wife loves him and is always trying to turn him into somebody else. Women who are utter mystics in their creed are utter cynics in their criticism. Thackeray expressed this well when he made Pendennis' mother, who worshipped her son as a god, yet assume that he would go wrong as a man. She underrated his virtue, though she overrated his value. The devotee is entirely free to criticise; the fanatic can safely be a sceptic. Love is not blind; that is the last thing that it is. Love is bound; and the more it is bound the less it is blind.

This at least had come to be my position about all that was called optimism, pessimism, and improvement. Before any cosmic act of reform we must have a cosmic oath of allegiance. A man must be interested in life, then he could be disinterested in his views of it. "My son give me thy heart"; the heart must be fixed on the right thing: the moment we have a fixed heart we have a free hand. I must pause to anticipate an obvious criticism. It will be said that a rational person

[32] Edward Augustus Freeman (1823–1892), Regius Professor of History at Oxford, who maintained in his *History of the Norman Conquest* (1867–1879) that the Conquest produced no fundamental change in the character of the English population.

accepts the world as mixed of good and evil with a decent satisfaction and a decent endurance. But this is exactly the attitude which I maintain to be defective. It is, I know, very common in this age; it was perfectly put in those quiet lines of Matthew Arnold which are more piercingly blasphemous than the shrieks of Schopenhauer—

> *Enough we live:—and if a life,*
> *With large results so little rife,*
> *Though bearable, seem hardly worth*
> *This pomp of worlds, this pain of birth.*

I know this feeling fills our epoch, and I think it freezes our epoch. For our Titanic purposes of faith and revolution, what we need is not the cold acceptance of the world as a compromise, but some way in which we can heartily hate and heartily love it. We do not want joy and anger to neutralize each other and produce a surly contentment; we want a fiercer delight and a fiercer discontent. We have to feel the universe at once as an ogre's castle, to be stormed, and yet as our own cottage, to which we can return at evening.

No one doubts that an ordinary man can get on with this world: but we demand not strength enough to get on with it, but strength enough to get it on. Can he hate it enough to change it, and yet love it enough to think it worth changing? Can he look up at its colossal good without once feeling acquiescence? Can he look up at its colossal evil without once feeling despair? Can he, in short, be at once not only a pessimist and an optimist, but a fanatical pessimist and a fanatical optimist? Is he enough of a pagan to die for the world, and enough of a Christian to die to it? In this combination, I maintain, it is the rational optimist who fails, the irrational optimist who succeeds. He is ready to smash the whole universe for the sake of itself.

I put these things not in their mature logical sequence, but as they came: and this view was cleared and sharpened by an accident of the time. Under the lengthening shadow of Ibsen, an argument arose whether it was not a very nice thing to murder one's self. Grave moderns told us that we must not even say "poor fellow," of a man who had blown his brains out, since he was an enviable person, and had only blown them out because of their exceptional excellence.

Mr. William Archer[33] even suggested that in the golden age there would be penny-in-the-slot machines, by which a man could kill himself for a penny. In all this I found myself utterly hostile to many who called themselves liberal and humane. Not only is suicide a sin, it is the sin. It is the ultimate and absolute evil, the refusal to take an interest in existence; the refusal to take the oath of loyalty to life. The man who kills a man, kills a man. The man who kills himself, kills all men; as far as he is concerned he wipes out the world. His act is worse (symbolically considered) than any rape or dynamite outrage. For it destroys all buildings: it insults all women. The thief is satisfied with diamonds; but the suicide is not: that is his crime. He cannot be bribed, even by the blazing stones of the Celestial City. The thief compliments the things he steals, if not the owner of them. But the suicide insults everything on earth by not stealing it. He defiles every flower by refusing to live for its sake. There is not a tiny creature in the cosmos at whom his death is not a sneer. When a man hangs himself on a tree, the leaves might fall off in anger and the birds fly away in fury: for each has received a personal affront. Of course there may be pathetic emotional excuses for the act. There often are for rape, and there almost always are for dynamite. But if it comes to clear ideas and the intelligent meaning of things, then there is much more rational and philosophic truth in the burial at the crossroads and the stake driven through the body, than in Mr. Archer's suicidal automatic machines. There is a meaning in burying the suicide apart. The man's crime is different from other crimes—for it makes even crimes impossible.

About the same time I read a solemn flippancy by some freethinker: he said that a suicide was only the same as a martyr. The open fallacy of this helped to clear the question. Obviously a suicide is the opposite of a martyr. A martyr is a man who cares so much for something outside him, that he forgets his own personal life. A suicide is a man who cares so little for anything outside him, that he wants to see the last of everything. One wants something to begin: the other wants everything to end. In other words, the martyr is noble, exactly

[33] William Archer (1856–1924), translator and editor of Ibsen's plays, and a strong anticleric.

because (however he renounces the world or execrates all humanity) he confesses this ultimate link with life; he sets his heart outside himself: he dies that something may live. The suicide is ignoble because he has not this link with being: he is a mere destroyer; spiritually, he destroys the universe. And then I remembered the stake and the cross-roads, and the queer fact that Christianity had shown this weird harshness to the suicide. For Christianity had shown a wild encouragement of the martyr. Historic Christianity was accused, not entirely without reason, of carrying martyrdom and asceticism to a point, desolate and pessimistic. The early Christian martyrs talked of death with a horrible happiness. They blasphemed the beautiful duties of the body: they smelt the grave afar off like a field of flowers. All this has seemed to many the very poetry of pessimism. Yet there is the stake at the cross-roads to show what Christianity thought of the pessimist.

This was the first of the long train of enigmas with which Christianity entered the discussion. And there went with it a peculiarity of which I shall have to speak more markedly, as a note of all Christian notions, but which distinctly began in this one. The Christian attitude to the martyr and the suicide was not what is so often affirmed in modern morals. It was not a matter of degree. It was not that a line must be drawn somewhere, and that the self-slayer in exaltation fell within the line, the self-slayer in sadness just beyond it. The Christian feeling evidently was not merely that the suicide was carrying martyrdom too far. The Christian feeling was furiously for one and furiously against the other: these two things that looked so much alike were at opposite ends of heaven and hell. One man flung away his life; he was so good that his dry bones could heal cities in pestilence. Another man flung away life; he was so bad that his bones would pollute his brethren's. I am not saying this fierceness was right; but why was it so fierce?

Here it was that I first found that my wandering feet were in some beaten track. Christianity had also felt this opposition of the martyr to the suicide: had it perhaps felt it for the same reason? Had Christianity felt what I felt, but could not (and cannot) express—this need for a first loyalty to things, and then for a ruinous reform of things?

Then I remembered that it was actually the charge against Christianity that it combined these two things which I was wildly trying to combine. Christianity was accused, at one and the same time, of being too optimistic about the universe and of being too pessimistic about the world. The coincidence made me suddenly stand still.

An imbecile habit has arisen in modern controversy of saying that such and such a creed can be held in one age but cannot be held in another. Some dogma, we are told, was credible in the twelfth century, but is not credible in the twentieth. You might as well say that a certain philosophy can be believed on Mondays, but cannot be believed on Tuesdays. You might as well say of a view of the cosmos that it was suitable to half-past three, but not suitable to half-past four. What a man can believe depends upon his philosophy, not upon the clock or the century. If a man believes in unalterable natural law, he cannot believe in any miracle in any age. If a man believes in a will behind law, he can believe in any miracle in any age. Suppose, for the sake of argument, we are concerned with a case of thaumaturgic healing. A materialist of the twelfth century could not believe it any more than a materialist of the twentieth century. But a Christian Scientist of the twentieth century can believe it as much as a Christian of the twelfth century. It is simply a matter of a man's theory of things. Therefore in dealing with any historical answer, the point is not whether it was given in our time, but whether it was given in answer to our question. And the more I thought about when and how Christianity had come into the world, the more I felt that it had actually come to answer this question.

It is commonly the loose and latitudinarian Christians who pay quite indefensible compliments to Christianity. They talk as if there had never been any piety or pity until Christianity came, a point on which any mediaeval would have been eager to correct them. They represent that the remarkable thing about Christianity was that it was the first to preach simplicity or self-restraint, or inwardness and sincerity. They will think me very narrow (whatever that means) if I say that the remarkable thing about Christianity was that it was the first to preach Christianity. Its peculiarity was that it was peculiar, and simplicity and sincerity are not peculiar, but obvious ideals for all mankind. Christianity was the answer to a riddle, not the last truism uttered after a long talk. Only the other day I saw in an excellent weekly paper of Puritan tone this remark, that Christianity when stripped of its armour of dogma (as who should speak of a man stripped of his armour of bones), turned out to be nothing but the Quaker doctrine of the Inner Light. Now, if I were to say that Christianity came into the world specially to destroy the doctrine of the Inner Light, that would be an exaggeration. But it would be very much nearer to the truth. The last Stoics, like Marcus Aurelius, were exactly the people who did believe in the Inner Light. Their dignity, their weariness, their sad external care for others, their incurable internal care for themselves, were all due to the Inner Light, and existed only by that dismal illumination. Notice that Marcus Aurelius insists, as such introspective moralists always do, upon small things done or undone; it is because he has not hate or love enough to make a moral revolution. He gets up early in the morning, just as our own aristocrats living the Simple Life get up early in the morning; because such altruism is much easier than stopping the games of the amphitheatre or giving the English people back their land. Marcus Aurelius is the most intolerable of human types. He is an unselfish egoist. An unselfish egoist is a man who has pride without the excuse of passion. Of all conceivable forms of enlightenment the worst is what these people call the Inner Light. Of all horrible religions the most horrible is the worship of the god within. Any one who knows any body knows how it would work; any one who knows any one from the Higher Thought Centre knows how it does work. That Jones shall worship the god within him turns out ultimately to mean that Jones shall worship Jones. Let Jones worship the sun or moon, anything rather than the Inner Light; let Jones worship cats or crocodiles, if he can find any in his street, but not the god within. Christianity came into the world firstly in order to assert with violence that a man had not only to look inwards, but to look outwards, to behold with astonishment and enthusiasm a divine company and a divine captain. The only fun of being a Christian was that a man was not left alone with the Inner Light, but definitely recognized an outer light, fair as the sun, clear as the moon, terrible as an army with banners.

All the same, it will be as well if Jones does not worship the sun and moon. If he does, there is a tendency for him to imitate them; to say, that because the sun burns insects alive, he may burn insects alive. He thinks that because the sun gives people sun-stroke, he may give his neighbour measles. He thinks that because the moon is said to drive men mad, he may drive his wife mad. This ugly side of mere external optimism had also shown itself in the ancient world. About the time when the Stoic idealism had begun to show the weaknesses of pessimism, the old nature worship of the ancients had begun to show the enormous weaknesses of optimism. Nature worship is natural enough while the society is young, or, in other words, Pantheism is all right as long as it is the worship of Pan. But Nature has another side which experience and sin are not slow in finding out, and it is no flippancy to say of the god Pan that he soon showed the cloven hoof. The only objection to Natural Religion is that somehow it always becomes unnatural. A man loves Nature in the morning for her innocence and amiability, and at nightfall, if he is loving her still, it is for her darkness and her cruelty. He washes at dawn in clear water as did the Wise Man of the Stoics, yet, somehow at the dark end of the day, he is bathing in hot bull's blood, as did Julian the Apostate. The mere pursuit of health always leads to something unhealthy. Physical nature must not be made the direct object of obedience; it must be enjoyed, not worshipped. Stars and mountains must not be taken seriously. If they are, we end where the pagan nature worship ended. Because the earth is kind, we can imitate all her cruelties. Because sexuality is sane, we can all go mad about sexuality. Mere optimism had reached its insane and appropriate termination. The theory that everything was good had become an orgy of everything that was bad.

On the other side our idealist pessimists were represented by the old remnant of the Stoics. Marcus Aurelius and his friends had really given up the idea of any god in the universe and looked only to the god within. They had no hope of any virtue in nature, and hardly any hope of any virtue in society. They had not enough interest in the outer world really to wreck or revolutionise it. They did not love the city enough to set fire to it. Thus the ancient world was exactly in our own desolate dilemma. The only people who really enjoyed this world were busy breaking it up; and the virtuous people did not care enough about them to knock them down. In this dilemma (the same as ours) Christianity suddenly stepped in and offered a singular answer, which the world eventually accepted as *the* answer. It was the answer then, and I think it is the answer now.

This answer was like the slash of a sword; it sundered; it did not in any sense sentimentally unite. Briefly, it divided God from the cosmos. That transcendence and distinctness of the deity which some Christians now want to remove from Christianity, was really the only reason why any one wanted to be a Christian. It was the whole point of the Christian answer to the unhappy pessimist and the still more unhappy optimist. As I am here only concerned with their particular problem, I shall indicate only briefly this great metaphysical suggestion. All descriptions of the creating or sustaining principle in things must be metaphorical, because they must be verbal. Thus the pantheist is forced to speak of God *in* all things as if he were in a box. Thus the evolutionist has, in his very name, the idea of being unrolled like a carpet. All terms, religious and irreligious, are open to this charge. The only question is whether all terms are useless, or whether one can, with such a phrase, cover a distinct *idea* about the origin of things. I think one can, and so evidently does the evolutionist, or he would not talk about evolution. And the root phrase for all Christian theism was this, that God was a creator, as an artist is a creator. A poet is so separate from his poem that he himself speaks of it as a little thing he has "thrown off." Even in giving it forth he has flung it away. This principle that all creation and procreation is a breaking off is at least as consistent through the cosmos as the evolutionary principle that all growth is a branching out. A woman loses a child even in having a child. All creation is separation. Birth is as solemn a parting as death.

It was the prime philosophic principle of Christianity that this divorce in the divine act of making (such as severs the poet from the poem or the mother from the new-born child) was the true description of the act whereby the absolute energy made the world. According to most philosophers, God in making the world enslaved it.

According to Christianity, in making it, He set it free. God had written, not so much a poem, but rather a play; a play he had planned
as perfect, but which had necessarily been left to human actors and
stage-managers, who had since made a great mess of it. I will discuss
the truth of this theorem later. Here I have only to point out with
what a startling smoothness it passed the dilemma we have discussed
in this chapter. In this way at least one could be both happy and indignant without degrading one's self to be either a pessimist or an
optimist. On this system one could fight all the forces of existence
without deserting the flag of existence. One could be at peace with
the universe and yet be at war with the world. St. George could still
fight the dragon, however big the monster bulked in the cosmos,
though he were bigger than the mighty cities or bigger than the
everlasting hills. If he were as big as the world he could yet be killed
in the name of the world. St. George had not to consider any obvious odds or proportions in the scale of things, but only the original
secret of their design. He can shake his sword at the dragon, even if
it is everything; even if the empty heavens over his head are only the
huge arch of its open jaws.

And then followed an experience impossible to describe. It was as
if I had been blundering about since my birth with two huge and
unmanageable machines, of different shapes and without apparent
connection—the world and the Christian tradition. I had found this
hole in the world: the fact that one must somehow find a way of loving the world without trusting it; somehow one must love the
world without being worldly. I found this projecting feature of
Christian theology, like a sort of hard spike, the dogmatic insistence
that God was personal, and had made a world separate from Himself. The spike of dogma fitted exactly into the hole in the world—it
had evidently been meant to go there—and then the strange thing
began to happen. When once these two parts of the two machines
had come together, one after another, all the other parts fitted and
fell in with an eerie exactitude. I could hear bolt after bolt over all
the machinery falling into its place with a kind of click of relief.
Having got one part right, all the other parts were repeating that
rectitude, as clock after clock strikes noon. Instinct after instinct was

answered by doctrine after doctrine. Or, to vary the metaphor, I was like one who had advanced into a hostile country to take one high fortress. And when that fort had fallen the whole country surrendered and turned solid behind me. The whole land was lit up, as it were, back to the first fields of my childhood. All those blind fancies of boyhood which in the fourth chapter I have tried in vain to trace on the darkness, became suddenly transparent and sane. I was right when I felt that roses were red by some sort of choice: it was the divine choice. I was right when I felt that I would almost rather say that grass was the wrong colour than say it must by necessity have been that colour: it might verily have been any other. My sense that happiness hung on the crazy thread of a condition did mean something when all was said: it meant the whole doctrine of the Fall. Even those dim and shapeless monsters of notions which I have not been able to describe, much less defend, stepped quietly into their places like colossal caryatides of the creed. The fancy that the cosmos was not vast and void, but small and cosy, had a fulfilled significance now, for anything that is a work of art must be small in the sight of the artist; to God the stars might be only small and dear, like diamonds. And my haunting instinct that somehow good was not merely a tool to be used, but a relic to be guarded, like the goods from Crusoe's ship—even that had been the wild whisper of something originally wise, for, according to Christianity, we were indeed the survivors of a wreck, the crew of a golden ship that had gone down before the beginning of the world.

But the important matter was this, that it entirely reversed the reason for optimism. And the instant the reversal was made it felt like the abrupt ease when a bone is put back in the socket. I had often called myself an optimist, to avoid the too evident blasphemy of pessimism. But all the optimism of the age had been false and disheartening for this reason, that it had always been trying to prove that we fit in to the world. The Christian optimism is based on the fact that we do *not* fit in to the world. I had tried to be happy by telling myself that man is an animal, like any other which sought its meat from God. But now I really was happy, for I had learnt that man is a monstrosity. I had been right in feeling all things as odd, for

I myself was at once worse and better than all things. The optimist's pleasure was prosaic, for it dwelt on the naturalness of everything; the Christian pleasure was poetic, for it dwelt on the unnaturalness of everything in the light of the supernatural. The modern philosopher had told me again and again that I was in the right place, and I had still felt depressed even in acquiescence. But I had heard that I was in the *wrong* place, and my soul sang for joy, like a bird in spring. The knowledge found out and illuminated forgotten chambers in the dark house of infancy. I knew now why grass had always seemed to me as queer as the green beard of a giant, and why I could feel homesick at home.

VI

THE PARADOXES OF CHRISTIANITY

The real trouble with this world of ours is not that it is an unreasonable world, nor even that it is a reasonable one. The commonest kind of trouble is that it is nearly reasonable, but not quite. Life is not an illogicality; yet it is a trap for logicians. It looks just a little more mathematical and regular than it is; its exactitude is obvious, but its inexactitude is hidden; its wildness lies in wait. I give one coarse instance of what I mean. Suppose some mathematical creature from the moon were to reckon up the human body; he would at once see that the essential thing about it was that it was duplicate. A man is two men, he on the right exactly resembling him on the left. Having noted that there was an arm on the right and one on the left, a leg on the right and one on the left, he might go further and still find on each side the same number of fingers, the same number of toes, twin eyes, twin ears, twin nostrils and even twin lobes of the brain. At last he would take it as a law; and then, where he found a heart on one side, would deduce that there was another heart on the other. And just then, where he most felt he was right, he would be wrong.

It is this silent swerving from accuracy by an inch that is the uncanny element in everything. It seems a sort of secret treason in the universe. An apple or an orange is round enough to get itself called round, and yet is not round after all. The earth itself is shaped like an orange in order to lure some simple astronomer into calling it a globe. A blade of grass is called after the blade of a sword, because it comes to a point; but it doesn't. Everywhere in things there is this element of the quiet and incalculable. It escapes the rationalists, but it never escapes till the last moment. From the grand curve of our earth it could easily be inferred that every inch of it was thus curved. It would seem rational that as a man has a brain on both sides, he should have a heart on both sides. Yet scientific men are still organizing expeditions to find the North Pole, because they are so fond of flat country. Scientific men are also still organizing expeditions to find a man's heart; and when they try to find it, they generally get on the wrong side of him.

Now, actual insight or inspiration is best tested by whether it guesses these hidden malformations or surprises. If our mathematician from the moon saw the two arms and the two ears, he might deduce the two shoulder-blades and the two halves of the brain. But if he guessed that the man's heart was in the right place, then I should call him something more than a mathematician. Now, this is exactly the claim which I have since come to propound for Christianity. Not merely that it deduces logical truths, but that when it suddenly becomes illogical, it has found, so to speak, an illogical truth. It not only goes right about things, but it goes wrong (if one may say so) exactly where the things go wrong. Its plan suits the secret irregularities, and expects the unexpected. It is simple about the simple truth; but it is stubborn about the subtle truth. It will admit that a man has two hands, it will not admit (though all the Modernists wail to it) the obvious deduction that he has two hearts. It is my only purpose in this chapter to point this out; to show that whenever we feel there is something odd in Christian theology, we shall generally find that there is something odd in the truth.

I have alluded to an unmeaning phrase to the effect that such and such a creed cannot be believed in our age. Of course, anything can be believed in any age. But, oddly enough, there really is a sense in which a creed, if it is believed at all, can be believed more fixedly in a complex society than in a simple one. If a man finds Christianity true in Birmingham, he has actually clearer reasons for faith than if he had found it true in Mercia.[34] For the more complicated seems the coincidence, the less it can be a coincidence. If snowflakes fell in the shape, say, of the heart of Midlothian, it might be an accident. But if snowflakes fell in the exact shape of the maze at Hampton Court, I think one might call it a miracle. It is exactly as of such a miracle that I have since come to feel of the philosophy of Christianity. The complication of our modern world proves the truth of the creed

---

[34] Anglo-Saxon kingdom in the Midlands founded in the sixth century.

more perfectly than any of the plain problems of the ages of faith. It was in Notting Hill and Battersea that I began to see that Christianity was true. This is why the faith has that elaboration of doctrines and details which so much distresses those who admire Christianity without believing in it. When once one believes in a creed, one is proud of its complexity, as scientists are proud of the complexity of science. It shows how rich it is in discoveries. If it is right at all, it is a compliment to say that it's elaborately right. A stick might fit a hole or a stone a hollow by accident. But a key and a lock are both complex. And if a key fits a lock, you know it is the right key.

But this involved accuracy of the thing makes it very difficult to do what I now have to do, to describe this accumulation of truth. It is very hard for a man to defend anything of which he is entirely convinced. It is comparatively easy when he is only partially convinced. He is partially convinced because he has found this or that proof of the thing, and he can expound it. But a man is not really convinced of a philosophic theory when he finds that something proves it. He is only really convinced when he finds that everything proves it. And the more converging reasons he finds pointing to this conviction, the more bewildered he is if asked suddenly to sum them up. Thus, if one asked an ordinary intelligent man, on the spur of the moment, "Why do you prefer civilization to savagery?" he would look wildly round at object after object, and would only be able to answer vaguely, "Why, there is that bookcase . . . and the coals in the coal-scuttle . . . and pianos . . . and policemen." The whole case for civilization is that the case for it is complex. It has done so many things. But that very multiplicity of proof which ought to make reply overwhelming makes reply impossible.

There is, therefore, about all complete conviction a kind of huge helplessness. The belief is so big that it takes a long time to get it into action. And this hesitation chiefly arises, oddly enough, from an indifference about where one should begin. All roads lead to Rome; which is one reason why many people never get there. In the case of this defence of the Christian conviction I confess that I would as soon begin the argument with one thing as another; I would begin it with a turnip or a taximeter cab. But if I am to be at all careful

about making my meaning clear, it will, I think, be wiser to continue the current arguments of the last chapter, which was concerned
to urge the first of these mystical coincidences, or rather ratifica-
tions. All I had hitherto heard of Christian theology had alienated
me from it. I was a pagan at the age of twelve, and a complete agnostic by the age of sixteen; and I cannot understand any one passing
the age of seventeen without having asked himself so simple a question. I did, indeed, retain a cloudy reverence for a cosmic deity and a
great historical interest in the Founder of Christianity. But I certainly regarded Him as a man; though perhaps I thought that, even
in that point, He had an advantage over some of His modern critics.
I read the scientific and sceptical literature of my time — all of it, at
least, that I could find written in English and lying about; and I read
nothing else; I mean I read nothing else on any other note of philosophy. The penny dreadfuls which I also read were indeed in a healthy
and heroic tradition of Christianity; but I did not know this at the
time. I never read a line of Christian apologetics. I read as little as I
can of them now. It was Huxley and Herbert Spencer and Bradlaugh[35] who brought me back to orthodox theology. They sowed in
my mind my first wild doubts of doubt. Our grandmothers were
quite right when they said that Tom Paine[36] and the freethinkers
unsettled the mind. They do. They unsettled mine horribly. The rationalist made me question whether reason was of any use whatever;
and when I had finished Herbert Spencer I had got as far as doubting
(for the first time) whether evolution had occurred at all. As I laid
down the last of Colonel Ingersoll's[37] atheistic lectures the dreadful
thought broke across my mind, "Almost thou persuadest me to be a
Christian." I was in a desperate way.

This odd effect of the great agnostics in arousing doubts deeper
than their own might be illustrated in many ways. I take only one.

[35] Charles Bradlaugh (1833–1891), Victorian freethinker.

[36] Tom Paine (1737–1809), eighteenth-century advocate of free thought and
revolution, involved in both the American and French Revolutions, and author of
The Rights of Man (1791–1792).

[37] Robert Ingersoll (1833–1899) American lawyer and noted agnostic.

As I read and re-read all the non-Christian or anti-Christian accounts of the faith, from Huxley to Bradlaugh, a slow and awful impression grew gradually but graphically upon my mind—the impression that Christianity must be a most extraordinary thing. For not only (as I understood) had Christianity the most flaming vices, but it had apparently a mystical talent for combining vices which seemed inconsistent with each other. It was attacked on all sides and for all contradictory reasons. No sooner had one rationalist demonstrated that it was too far to the east than another demonstrated with equal clearness that it was much too far to the west. No sooner had my indignation died down at its angular and aggressive squareness than I was called up again to notice and condemn its enervating and sensual roundness. In case any reader has not come across the thing I mean, I will give such instances as I remember at random of this self-contradiction in the sceptical attack. I give four or five of them; there are fifty more.

Thus, for instance, I was much moved by the eloquent attack on Christianity as a thing of inhuman gloom; for I thought (and still think) sincere pessimism the unpardonable sin. Insincere pessimism is a social accomplishment, rather agreeable than otherwise; and fortunately nearly all pessimism is insincere. But if Christianity was, as these people said, a thing purely pessimistic and opposed to life, then I was quite prepared to blow up St. Paul's Cathedral. But the extraordinary thing is this. They did prove to me in Chapter I. (to my complete satisfaction) that Christianity was too pessimistic; and then, in Chapter II., they began to prove to me that it was a great deal too optimistic. One accusation against Christianity was that it prevented men, by morbid tears and terrors, from seeking joy and liberty in the bosom of Nature. But another accusation was that it comforted men with a fictitious providence, and put them in a pink-and-white nursery. One great agnostic asked why Nature was not beautiful enough, and why it was hard to be free. Another great agnostic objected that Christian optimism, "the garment of make-believe woven by pious hands," hid from us the fact that Nature was ugly, and that it was impossible to be free. One rationalist had hardly done calling Christianity a nightmare before another began to call it a fool's paradise. This puzzled me; the charges seemed inconsistent. Christianity could not at once be the black mask on a white world, and also the white mask on a black world. The state of the Christian could not be at once so comfortable that he was a coward to cling to it, and so uncomfortable that he was a fool to stand it. If it falsified human vision it must falsify it one way or another; it could not wear both green and rose-coloured spectacles. I rolled on my tongue with a terrible joy, as did all young men of that time, the taunts which Swinburne hurled at the dreariness of the creed—

> *Thou hast conquered, O pale Galilaean, the world has*
> *grown gray with Thy breath.*

But when I read the same poet's accounts of paganism (as in "Atalanta"), I gathered that the world was, if possible, more gray before the Galilaean breathed on it than afterwards. The poet maintained, indeed, in the abstract, that life itself was pitch dark. And yet, somehow, Christianity had darkened it. The very man who denounced Christianity for pessimism was himself a pessimist. I thought there must be something wrong. And it did for one wild moment cross my mind that, perhaps, those might not be the very best judges of the relation of religion to happiness who, by their own account, had neither one nor the other.

It must be understood that I did not conclude hastily that the accusations were false or the accusers fools. I simply deduced that Christianity must be something even weirder and wickeder than they made out. A thing might have these two opposite vices; but it must be a rather queer thing if it did. A man might be too fat in one place and too thin in another; but he would be an odd shape. At this point my thoughts were only of the odd shape of the Christian religion; I did not allege any odd shape in the rationalistic mind.

Here is another case of the same kind. I felt that a strong case against Christianity lay in the charge that there is something timid, monkish, and unmanly about all that is called "Christian," especially in its attitude towards resistance and fighting. The great sceptics of the nineteenth century were largely virile. Bradlaugh in an expansive way, Huxley, in a reticent way, were decidedly men. In comparison, it did seem tenable that there was something weak and over patient about Christian counsels. The Gospel paradox about the other cheek, the fact that priests never fought, a hundred things made plausible the accusation that Christianity was an attempt to make a man too like a sheep. I read it and believed it, and if I had read nothing different, I should have gone on believing it. But I read something very different. I turned the next page in my agnostic manual, and my brain turned upside down. Now I found that I was to hate Christianity not for fighting too little, but for fighting too much. Christianity, it seemed, was the mother of wars. Christianity had deluged the world with blood. I had got thoroughly angry with the Christian, because he never was angry. And now I was told to be angry with him because his anger had been the most huge and horrible thing in human history; because his anger had soaked the earth and smoked to the sun. The very people who reproached Christianity with the meekness and non-resistance of the monasteries were the very people who reproached it also with the violence and valour of the Crusades. It was the fault of poor old Christianity (somehow or other) both that Edward the Confessor did not fight and that Richard Coeur de Leon did. The Quakers (we were told) were the only characteristic Christians; and yet the massacres of Cromwell and Alva[38] were characteristic Christian crimes. What could it all mean? What was this Christianity which always forbade war and always produced wars? What could be the nature of the thing which one could abuse first because it would not fight, and second because it was always fighting? In what world of riddles was born this monstrous murder and this monstrous meekness? The shape of Christianity grew a queerer shape every instant.

I take a third case; the strangest of all, because it involves the one real objection to the faith. The one real objection to the Christian religion is simply that it is one religion. The world is a big place, full of very different kinds of people. Christianity (it may reasonably be said) is one thing confined to one kind of people; it began in

[38] Duke of Alva (1508–1582), who advocated and carried out a stern policy toward the rebels against Spain in the Netherlands. He is supposed to have been responsible for the execution of eighteen thousand persons.

Palestine, it has practically stopped with Europe. I was duly impressed with this argument in my youth, and I was much drawn towards the doctrine often preached in Ethical Societies—I mean the doctrine that there is one great unconscious church of all humanity founded on the omnipresence of the human conscience. Creeds, it was said, divided men; but at least morals united them. The soul might seek the strangest and most remote lands and ages and still find essential ethical common sense. It might find Confucius under Eastern trees, and he would be writing "Thou shalt not steal." It might decipher the darkest hieroglyphic on the most primeval desert, and the meaning when deciphered would be "Little boys should tell the truth." I believed this doctrine of the brotherhood of all men in the possession of a moral sense, and I believe it still—with other things. And I was thoroughly annoyed with Christianity for suggesting (as I supposed) that whole ages and empires of men had utterly escaped this light of justice and reason. But then I found an astonishing thing. I found that the very people who said that mankind was one church from Plato to Emerson were the very people who said that morality had changed altogether, and that what was right in one age was wrong in another. If I asked, say, for an altar, I was told that we needed none, for men our brothers gave us clear oracles and one creed in their universal customs and ideals. But if I mildly pointed out that one of men's universal customs was to have an altar, then my agnostic teachers turned clean round and told me that men had always been in darkness and the superstitions of savages. I found it was their daily taunt against Christianity that it was the light of one people and had left all others to die in the dark. But I also found that it was their special boast for themselves that science and progress were the discovery of one people, and that all other peoples had died in the dark. Their chief insult to Christianity was actually their chief compliment to themselves, and there seemed to be a strange unfairness about all their relative insistence on the two things. When considering some pagan or agnostic, we were to remember that all men had one religion; when considering some mystic or spiritualist, we were only to consider what absurd religions some men had. We could trust the ethics of Epictetus, because ethics had never changed. We must not trust the ethics of Bossuet,[39] because ethics had changed. They changed in two hundred years, but not in two thousand.

This began to be alarming. It looked not so much as if Christianity was bad enough to include any vices, but rather as if any stick was good enough to beat Christianity with. What again could this astonishing thing be like which people were so anxious to contradict, that in doing so they did not mind contradicting themselves? I saw the same thing on every side. I can give no further space to this discussion of it in detail; but lest any one supposes that I have unfairly selected three accidental cases I will run briefly through a few others. Thus, certain sceptics wrote that the great crime of Christianity had been its attack on the family; it had dragged women to the loneliness and contemplation of the cloister, away from their homes and their children. But, then, other sceptics (slightly more advanced) said that the great crime of Christianity was forcing the family and marriage upon us; that it doomed women to the drudgery of their homes and children, and forbade them loneliness and contemplation. The charge was actually reversed. Or, again, certain phrases in the Epistles or the marriage service, were said by the anti-Christians to show contempt for woman's intellect. But I found that the anti-Christians themselves had a contempt for woman's intellect; for it was their great sneer at the Church on the Continent that "only women" went to it. Or again, Christianity was reproached with its naked and hungry habits; with its sackcloth and dried peas. But the next minute Christianity was being reproached with its pomp and its ritualism; its shrines of porphyry and its robes of gold. It was abused for being too plain and for being too coloured. Again Christianity had always been accused of restraining sexuality too much, when Bradlaugh the Malthusian discovered that it restrained it too little. It is often accused in the same breath of prim respectability and of religious extravagance. Between the covers of the same atheistic pamphlet I have found the faith rebuked for its disunion, "One thinks one thing, and one another," and rebuked also for its union, "It is difference of opinion that prevents the world from going to the

[39] Jacques Bénigne Bossuet (1627–1704), French bishop and moralist, and one of the greatest French orators.

dogs." In the same conversation a freethinker, a friend of mine, blamed Christianity for despising Jews, and then despised it himself for being Jewish.

I wished to be quite fair then, and I wish to be quite fair now; and I did not conclude that the attack on Christianity was all wrong. I only concluded that if Christianity was wrong, it was very wrong indeed. Such hostile horrors might be combined in one thing, but that thing must be very strange and solitary. There are men who are misers, and also spendthrifts; but they are rare. There are men sensual and also ascetic; but they are rare. But if this mass of mad contradictions really existed, quakerish and bloodthirsty, too gorgeous and too thread-bare, austere, yet pandering preposterously to the lust of the eye, the enemy of women and their foolish refuge, a solemn pessimist and a silly optimist, if this evil existed then there was in this evil something quite supreme and unique. For I found in my rationalist teachers no explanation of such exceptional corruption. Christianity (theoretically speaking) was in their eyes only one of the ordinary myths and errors of mortals. *They* gave me no key to this twisted and unnatural badness. Such a paradox of evil rose to the stature of the supernatural. It was, indeed, almost as supernatural as the infallibility of the Pope. An historic institution, which never went right, is really quite as much of a miracle as an institution that cannot go wrong. The only explanation which immediately occurred to my mind was that Christianity did not come from heaven, but from hell. Really, if Jesus of Nazareth was not Christ, He must have been Antichrist.

And then in a quiet hour a strange thought struck me like a still thunderbolt. There had suddenly come into my mind another explanation. Suppose we heard an unknown man spoken of by many men. Suppose we were puzzled to hear that some men said he was too tall and some too short; some objected to his fatness, some lamented his leanness; some thought him too dark, and some too fair. One explanation (as has been already admitted) would be that he might be an odd shape. But there is another explanation. He might be the right shape. Outrageously tall men might feel him to be short. Very short men might feel him to be tall. Old bucks who are growing stout might consider him insufficiently filled out; old beaux who were growing thin might feel that he expanded beyond the narrow lines of elegance. Perhaps Swedes (who have pale hair like tow) called him a dark man, while negroes considered him distinctly blonde. Perhaps (in short) this extraordinary thing is really the ordinary thing; at least the normal thing, the centre. Perhaps, after all, it is Christianity that is sane and all its critics that are mad — in various ways. I tested this idea by asking myself whether there was about any of the accusers anything morbid that might explain the accusation. I was startled to find that this key fitted a lock. For instance, it was certainly odd that the modern world charged Christianity at once with bodily austerity and with artistic pomp. But then it was also odd, very odd, that the modern world itself combined extreme bodily luxury with an exteme absence of artistic pomp. The modern man thought Becket's robes too rich and his meals too poor. But then the modern man was really exceptional in history; no man before ever ate such elaborate dinners in such ugly clothes. The modern man found the church too simple exactly where modern life is too complex; he found the church too gorgeous exactly where modern life is too dingy. The man who disliked the plain fasts and feasts was mad on *entrées*. The man who disliked vestments wore a pair of preposterous trousers. And surely if there was any insanity involved in the matter at all it was in the trousers, not in the simply falling robe. If there was any insanity at all, it was in the extravagant *entrées*, not in the bread and wine.

I went over all the cases, and I found the key fitted so far. The fact that Swinburne was irritated at the unhappiness of Christians and yet more irritated at their happiness was easily explained. It was no longer a complication of diseases in Christianity, but a complication of diseases in Swinburne. The restraints of Christians saddened him simply because he was more hedonist than a healthy man should be. The faith of Christians angered him because he was more pessimist than a healthy man should be. In the same way the Malthusians by instinct attacked Christianity; not because there is anything especially anti-Malthusian about Christianity, but because there is something a little anti-human about Malthusianism.

Nevertheless it could not, I felt, be quite true that Christianity was merely sensible and stood in the middle. There was really an element in it of emphasis and even frenzy which had justified the secularists in their superficial criticism. It might be wise, I began more and more to think that it was wise, but it was not merely worldly wise; it was not merely temperate and respectable. Its fierce crusaders and meek saints might balance each other; still, the crusaders were very fierce and the saints were very meek, meek beyond all decency. Now, it was just at this point of the speculation that I remembered my thoughts about the martyr and the suicide. In that matter there had been this combination between two almost insane positions which yet somehow amounted to sanity. This was just such another contradiction; and this I had already found to be true. This was exactly one of the paradoxes in which sceptics found the creed wrong; and in this I had found it right. Madly as Christians might love the martyr or hate the suicide, they never felt these passions more madly than I had felt them long before I dreamed of Christianity. Then the most difficult and interesting part of the mental process opened, and I began to trace this idea darkly through all the enormous thoughts of our theology. The idea was that which I had outlined touching the optimist and the pessimist; that we want not an amalgam or compromise, but both things at the top of their energy; love and wrath both burning. Here I shall only trace it in relation to ethics. But I need not remind the reader that the idea of this combination is indeed central in orthodox theology. For orthodox theology has specially insisted that Christ was not a being apart from God and man, like an elf, nor yet a being half human and half not, like a centaur, but both things at once and both things thoroughly, very man and very God. Now let me trace this notion as I found it.

All sane men can see that sanity is some kind of equilibrium; that one may be mad and eat too much, or mad and eat too little. Some moderns have indeed appeared with vague versions of progress and evolution which seeks to destroy the μέσον or balance of Aristotle. They seem to suggest that we are meant to starve progressively, or to go on eating larger and larger breakfasts every morning for ever. But the great truism of the μέσον remains for all thinking men, and these people have not upset any balance except their own. But granted that we have all to keep a balance, the real interest comes in with the question of how that balance can be kept. That was the problem which Paganism tried to solve: that was the problem which I think Christianity solved and solved in a very strange way.

Paganism declared that virtue was in a balance; Christianity declared it was in a conflict: the collision of two passions apparently opposite. Of course they were not really inconsistent; but they were such that it was hard to hold simultaneously. Let us follow for a moment the clue of the martyr and the suicide; and take the case of courage. No quality has ever so much addled the brains and tangled the definitions of merely rational sages. Courage is almost a contradiction in terms. It means a strong desire to live taking the form of a readiness to die. "He that will lose his life, the same shall save it," is not a piece of mysticism for saints and heroes. It is a piece of everyday advice for sailors or mountaineers. It might be printed in an Alpine guide or a drill book. This paradox is the whole principle of courage; even of quite earthly or quite brutal courage. A man cut off by the sea may save his life if he will risk it on the precipice. He can only get away from death by continually stepping within an inch of it. A soldier surrounded by enemies, if he is to cut his way out, needs to combine a strong desire for living with a strange carelessness about dying. He must not merely cling to life, for then he will be a coward, and will not escape. He must not merely wait for death, for then he will be a suicide, and will not escape. He must seek his life in a spirit of furious indifference to it; he must desire life like water and yet drink death like wine. No philosopher, I fancy, has ever expressed this romantic riddle with adequate lucidity, and I certainly have not done so. But Christianity has done more: it has marked the limits of it in the awful graves of the suicide and the hero, showing the distance between him who dies for the sake of living and him who dies for the sake of dying. And it has held up ever since above the European lances the banner of the mystery of chivalry: the Christian courage, which is a disdain of death; not the Chinese courage, which is a disdain of life.

And now I began to find that this duplex passion was the Christian key to ethics everywhere. Everywhere the creed made a moderation out of the still crash of two impetuous emotions. Take, for instance, the matter of modesty, of the balance between mere pride and mere prostration. The average pagan, like the average agnostic, would merely say that he was content with himself, but not insolently self-satisfied, that there were many better and many worse, that his deserts were limited, but he would see that he got them. In short, he would walk with his head in the air; but not necessarily with his nose in the air. This is a manly and rational position, but it is open to the objection we noted against the compromise between optimism and pessimism—the "resignation" of Matthew Arnold. Being a mixture of two things, it is a dilution of two things; neither is present in its full strength or contributes its full colour. This proper pride does not lift the heart like the tongue of trumpets; you cannot go clad in crimson and gold for this. On the other hand, this mild rationalist modesty does not cleanse the soul with fire and make it clear like crystal; it does not (like a strict and searching humility) make a man as a little child, who can sit at the feet of the grass. It does not make him look up and see marvels; for Alice must grow small if she is to be Alice in Wonderland. Thus it loses both the poetry of being proud and the poetry of being humble. Christianity sought by this same strange expedient to save both of them.

It separated the two ideas and then exaggerated them both. In one way Man was to be haughtier than he had ever been before; in another way he was to be humbler than he had ever been before. In so far as I am Man I am the chief of creatures. In so far as I am *a* man I am the chief of sinners. All humility that had meant pessimism, that had meant man taking a vague or mean view of his whole destiny—all that was to go. We were to hear no more the wail of Ecclesiastes that humanity had no pre-eminence over the brute, or the awful cry of Homer that man was only the saddest of all the beasts of the field. Man was a statue of God walking about the garden. Man had pre-eminence over all the brutes; man was only sad because he was not a beast, but a broken god. The Greek had spoken of men creeping on the earth, as if clinging to it. Now Man was to tread on the earth as if to subdue it. Christianity thus held a thought of the dignity of man that could only be expressed in crowns rayed like the sun and fans of peacock plumage. Yet at the same time it could hold a thought about the abject smallness of man that could only be expressed in fasting and fantastic submission, in the gray ashes of St. Dominic and the white snows of St. Bernard. When one came to think of *one's self*, there was vista and void enough for any amount of bleak abnegation and bitter truth. There the realistic gentleman could let himself go — as long as he let himself go at himself. There was an open playground for the happy pessimist. Let him say anything against himself short of blaspheming the original aim of his being; let him call himself a fool and even a damned fool (though that is Calvinistic); but he must not say that fools are not worth saving. He must not say that a man, *quâ* man, can be valueless. Here, again in short, Christianity got over the difficulty of combining furious opposites, by keeping them both, and keeping them both furious. The Church was positive on both points. One can hardly think too little of one's self. One can hardly think too much of one's soul.

Take another case: the complicated question of charity, which some highly uncharitable idealists seem to think quite easy. Charity is a paradox, like modesty and courage. Stated baldly, charity certainly means one of two things — pardoning unpardonable acts, or loving unlovable people. But if we ask ourselves (as we did in the case of pride) what a sensible pagan would feel about such a subject, we shall probably be beginning at the bottom of it. A sensible pagan would say that there were some people one could forgive, and some one couldn't: a slave who stole wine could be laughed at; a slave who betrayed his benefactor could be killed, and cursed even after he was killed. In so far as the act was pardonable, the man was pardonable. That again is rational, and even refreshing; but it is a dilution. It leaves no place for a pure horror of injustice, such as that which is a great beauty in the innocent. And it leaves no place for a mere tenderness for men as men, such as is the whole fascination of the charitable. Christianity came in here as before. It came in startlingly with a sword, and clove one thing from another. It divided the crime from the criminal. The criminal we must forgive unto seventy times seven. The crime we must not forgive at all. It was not enough that slaves who stole wine inspired partly anger and partly kindness. We must be much more angry with theft than before, and yet much kinder to thieves than before. There was room for wrath and love to run wild. And the more I considered Christianity, the more I found that while it had established a rule and order, the chief aim of that order was to give room for good things to run wild.

Mental and emotional liberty are not so simple as they look. Really they require almost as careful a balance of laws and conditions as do social and political liberty. The ordinary aesthetic anarchist who sets out to feel everything freely gets knotted at last in a paradox that prevents him feeling at all. He breaks away from home limits to follow poetry. But in ceasing to feel home limits he has ceased to feel the "Odyssey." He is free from national prejudices and outside patriotism. But being outside patriotism he is outside "Henry V." Such a literary man is simply outside all literature: he is more of a prisoner than any bigot. For if there is a wall between you and the world, it makes little difference whether you describe yourself as locked in or as locked out. What we want is not the universality that is outside all normal sentiments; we want the universality that is inside all normal sentiments. It is all the difference between being free from them, as a man is free from a prison, and being free of them as a man is free of a city. I am free from Windsor Castle (that is, I am not forcibly detained there), but I am by no means free of that building. How can man be approximately free of fine emotions, able to swing them in a clear space without breakage or wrong? *This* was the achievement of this Christian paradox of the parallel passions. Granted the primary dogma of the war between divine and diabolic, the revolt and ruin of the world, their optimism and pessimism, as pure poetry, could be loosened like cataracts.

St. Francis, in praising all good, could be a more shouting optimist than Walt Whitman. St. Jerome, in denouncing all evil, could paint the world blacker than Schopenhauer. Both passions were free because both were kept in their place. The optimist could pour out all the praise he liked on the gay music of the march, the golden trumpets, and the purple banners going into battle. But he must not call the fight needless. The pessimist might draw as darkly as he chose the sickening marches or the sanguine wounds. But he must not call the fight hopeless. So it was with all the other moral problems, with pride, with protest, and with compassion. By defining its main doctrine, the Church not only kept seemingly inconsistent things side by side, but, what was more, allowed them to break out in a sort of artistic violence otherwise possible only to anarchists. Meekness grew more dramatic than madness. Historic Christianity rose into a high and strange *coup de théatre* of morality — things that are to virtue what the crimes of Nero are to vice. The spirits of indignation and of charity took terrible and attractive forms, ranging from that monkish fierceness that scourged like a dog the first and greatest of the Plantagenets,[40] to the sublime pity of St. Catherine,[41] who, in the official shambles, kissed the bloody head of the criminal. Poetry could be acted as well as composed. This heroic and monumental manner in ethics has entirely vanished with supernatural religion. They, being humble, could parade themselves: but we are too proud to be prominent. Our ethical teachers write reasonably for prison reform; but we are not likely to see Mr. Cadbury,[42] or any eminent philanthropist, go into Reading Gaol and embrace the strangled corpse before it is cast into the quicklime. Our ethical teachers write mildly against the power of millionaires; but we are not likely to see Mr. Rockefeller, or any modern tyrant, publicly whipped in Westminster Abbey.

Thus, the double charges of the secularists, though throwing nothing but darkness and confusion on themselves, throw a real light on the faith. It *is* true that the historic Church has at once emphasised celibacy and emphasised the family; has at once (if one may put it so) been fiercely for having children and fiercely for not having children. It has kept them side by side like two strong colours, red

[40] Refers to the public penance done by Henry II (1154–1189), King of England, after the murder of Thomas à Becket.

[41] Chesterton is referring to an episode in the life of St. Catherine of Siena (1347–1380). She comforted a Perugian knight, Nicholas di Toldo, in prison, accompanied him to the scaffold and received his severed head in her hands.

[42] George Cadbury (1839–1922), cocoa manufacturer, philanthropist, Liberal and proprietor of the *Daily News*, to which Chesterton was a regular contributor.

and white, like the red and white upon the shield of St. George. It has always had a healthy hatred of pink. It hates that combination of two colours which is the feeble expedient of the philosophers. It hates that evolution of black into white which is tantamount to a dirty gray. In fact, the whole theory of the Church on virginity might be symbolized in the statement that white is a colour: not merely the absence of a colour. All that I am urging here can be expressed by saying that Christianity sought in most of these cases to keep two colours coexistent but pure. It is not a mixture like russet or purple; it is rather like a shot silk, for a shot silk is always at right angles, and is in the pattern of the cross.

So it is also, of course, with the contradictory charges of the anti-Christians about submission and slaughter. It *is* true that the Church told some men to fight and others not to fight; and it *is* true that those who fought were like thunderbolts and those who did not fight were like statues. All this simply means that the Church preferred to use its Supermen and to use its Tolstoyans. There must be *some* good in the life of battle, for so many good men have enjoyed being soldiers. There must be *some* good in the idea of non-resistance, for so many good men seem to enjoy being Quakers. All that the Church did (so far as that goes) was to prevent either of these good things from ousting the other. They existed side by side. The Tolstoyans, having all the scruples of monks, simply became monks. The Quakers became a club instead of becoming a sect. Monks said all that Tolstoy says; they poured out lucid lamentations about the cruelty of battles and the vanity of revenge. But the Tolstoyans are not quite right enough to run the whole world; and in the ages of faith they were not allowed to run it. The world did not lose the last charge of Sir James Douglas[43] or the banner of Joan the Maid. And sometimes this pure gentleness and this pure fierceness met and justified their juncture; the paradox of all the prophets was fulfilled, and, in the soul of St. Louis, the lion lay down with

---

[43] Sir James Douglas (1286?–1330), a Scot who invaded England in 1319 and plundered many towns. After the conclusion of peace with Edward III, he set out on a pilgrimage to the Holy Land but was killed on the way, fighting against the Moors in Andalusia.

the lamb. But remember that this text is too lightly interpreted. It is constantly assured, especially in our Tolstoyan tendencies, that when the lion lies down with the lamb the lion becomes lamb-like. But that is brutal annexation and imperialism on the part of the lamb. That is simply the lamb absorbing the lion instead of the lion eating the lamb. The real problem is — Can the lion lie down with the lamb and still retain his royal ferocity? *That* is the problem the Church attempted; *that* is the miracle she achieved.

This is what I have called guessing the hidden eccentricities of life. This is knowing that a man's heart is to the left and not in the middle. This is knowing not only that the earth is round, but knowing exactly where it is flat. Christian doctrine detected the oddities of life. It not only discovered the law, but it foresaw the exceptions. Those underrate Christianity who say that it discovered mercy; any one might discover mercy. In fact every one did. But to discover a plan for being merciful and also severe — *that* was to anticipate a strange need of human nature. For no one wants to be forgiven for a big sin as if it were a little one. Any one might say that we should be neither quite miserable nor quite happy. But to find out how far one *may* be quite miserable without making it impossible to be quite happy — that was a discovery in psychology. Any one might say, "Neither swagger nor grovel"; and it would have been a limit. But to say, "Here you can swagger and there you can grovel" — that was an emancipation.

This was the big fact about Christian ethics; the discovery of the new balance. Paganism had been like a pillar of marble, upright because proportioned with symmetry. Christianity was like a huge and ragged and romantic rock, which, though it sways on its pedestal at a touch, yet, because its exaggerated excrescences exactly balance each other, is enthroned there for a thousand years. In a Gothic cathedral the columns were all different, but they were all necessary. Every support seemed an accidental and fantastic support; every buttress was a flying buttress. So in Christendom apparent accidents balanced. Becket wore a hair shirt under his gold and crimson, and there is much to be said for the combination; for Becket got the benefit of the hair shirt while the people in the street got the benefit of the crimson and gold. It is at least better than the manner of the modern millionaire, who has the black and the drab outwardly for others, and the gold next his heart. But the balance was not always in one man's body as in Becket's; the balance was often distributed over the whole body of Christendom. Because a man prayed and fasted on the Northern snows, flowers could be flung at his festival in the Southern cities; and because fanatics drank water on the sands of Syria, men could still drink cider in the orchards of England. This is what makes Christendom at once so much more perplexing and so much more interesting than the Pagan empire; just as Amiens Cathedral is not better but more interesting than the Parthenon. If any one wants a modern proof of all this, let him consider the curious fact that, under Christianity, Europe (while remaining a unity) has broken up into individual nations. Patriotism is a perfect example of this deliberate balancing of one emphasis against another emphasis. The instinct of the Pagan empire would have said, "You shall all be Roman citizens, and grow alike; let the German grow less slow and reverent; the Frenchman less experimental and swift." But the instinct of Christian Europe says, "Let the German remain slow and reverent, that the Frenchman may the more safely be swift and experimental. We will make an equipoise out of these excesses. The absurdity called Germany shall correct the insanity called France."

Last and most important, it is exactly this which explains what is so inexplicable to all the modern critics of the history of Christianity. I mean the monstrous wars about small points of theology, the earthquakes of emotion about a gesture or a word. It was only a matter of an inch; but an inch is everything when you are balancing. The Church could not afford to swerve a hair's breadth on some things if she was to continue her great and daring experiment of the irregular equilibrium. Once let one idea become less powerful and some other idea would become too powerful. It was no flock of sheep the Christian shepherd was leading, but a herd of bulls and tigers, of terrible ideals and devouring doctrines, each one of them strong enough to turn to a false religion and lay waste the world. Remember that the Church went in specifically for dangerous ideas; she was a lion tamer. The idea of birth through a Holy Spirit, of the death of a divine being, of the forgiveness of sins, or the fulfilment of prophecies, are ideas which, any one can see, need but a touch to turn them into something blasphemous or ferocious. The smallest link was let drop by the artificers of the Mediterranean, and the lion of ancestral pessimism burst his chain in the forgotten forests of the north. Of these theological equalisations I have to speak afterwards. Here it is enough to notice that if some small mistake were made in doctrine, huge blunders might be made in human happiness. A sentence phrased wrong about the nature of symbolism would have broken all the best statues in Europe. A slip in the definitions might stop all the dances; might wither all the Christmas trees or break all the Easter eggs. Doctrines had to be defined within strict limits, even in order that man might enjoy general human liberties. The Church had to be careful, if only that the world might be careless.

This is the thrilling romance of Orthodoxy. People have fallen into a foolish habit of speaking of orthodoxy as something heavy, humdrum, and safe. There never was anything so perilous or so exciting as orthodoxy. It was sanity: and to be sane is more dramatic than to be mad. It was the equilibrium of a man behind madly rushing horses, seeming to stoop this way and to sway that, yet in every attitude having the grace of statuary and the accuracy of arithmetic. The Church in its early days went fierce and fast with any warhorse; yet it is utterly unhistoric to say that she merely went mad along one idea, like a vulgar fanaticism. She swerved to left and right, so exactly as to avoid enormous obstacles. She left on one hand the huge bulk of Arianism, buttressed by all the worldly powers to make Christianity too worldly. The next instant she was swerving to avoid an orientalism, which would have made it too unworldly. The orthodox Church never took the tame course or accepted the conventions; the orthodox Church was never respectable. It would have been easier to have accepted the earthly power of the Arians. It would have been easy, in the Calvinistic seventeenth century, to fall into the bottomless pit of predestination. It is easy to be a madman: it is easy to be a heretic. It is always easy to let the age have its head; the difficult thing is to keep one's own. It is always easy to be a modernist; as it is easy to be a snob. To have fallen into any of those open traps of error and exaggeration which fashion after fashion and sect after sect set along the historic path of Christendom — that would indeed have been simple. It is always simple to fall; there are an infinity of angles at which one falls, only one at which one stands. To have fallen into any one of the fads from Gnosticism to Christian Science would indeed have been obvious and tame. But to have avoided them all has been one whirling adventure; and in my vision the heavenly chariot flies thundering through the ages, the dull heresies sprawling and prostrate, the wild truth reeling but erect.

VII

THE ETERNAL REVOLUTION

The following propositions have been urged: First, that some faith in our life is required even to improve it; second, that some dissatisfaction with things as they are is necessary even in order to be satisfied; third, that to have this necessary content and necessary discontent it is not sufficient to have the obvious equilibrium of the Stoic. For mere resignation has neither the gigantic levity of pleasure nor the superb intolerance of pain. There is a vital objection to the advice merely to grin and bear it. The objection is that if you merely bear it, you do not grin. Greek heroes do not grin: but gargoyles do—because they are Christian. And when a Christian is pleased, he is (in the most exact sense) frightfully pleased; his pleasure is frightful. Christ prophesied the whole of Gothic architecture in that hour when nervous and respectable people (such people as now object to barrel organs) objected to the shouting of the gutter-snipes of Jerusalem. He said, "If these were silent, the very stones would cry out." Under the impulse of His spirit arose like a clamorous chorus the façades of the mediaeval cathedrals, thronged with shouting faces and open mouths. The prophecy has fulfilled itself: the very stones cry out.

If these things be conceded, though only for argument, we may take up where we left it the thread of the thought of the natural man, called by the Scotch (with regrettable familiarity), "The Old Man." We can ask the next question so obviously in front of us. Some satisfaction is needed even to make things better. But what do we mean by making things better? Most modern talk on this matter is a mere argument in a circle—that circle which we have already made the symbol of madness and of mere rationalism. Evolution is only good if it produces good; good is only good if it helps evolution. The elephant stands on the tortoise, and the tortoise on the elephant.

Obviously, it will not do to take our ideal from the principle in nature; for the simple reason that (except for some human or divine theory), there is no principle in nature. For instance, the cheap anti-democrat of to-day will tell you solemnly that there is no equality in nature. He is right, but he does not see the logical addendum. There is no equality in nature; also there is no inequality in nature. Inequality, as much as equality, implies a standard of value. To read aristocracy into the anarchy of animals is just as sentimental as to read democracy into it. Both aristocracy and democracy are human ideals: the one saying that all men are valuable, the other that some men are more valuable. But nature does not say that cats are more valuable than mice; nature makes no remark on the subject. She does not even say that the cat is enviable or the mouse pitiable. We think the cat superior because we have (or most of us have) a particular philosophy to the effect that life is better than death. But if the mouse were a German pessimist mouse, he might not think that the cat had beaten him at all. He might think he had beaten the cat by getting to the grave first. Or he might feel that he had actually inflicted frightful punishment on the cat by keeping him alive. Just as a microbe might feel proud of spreading a pestilence, so the pessimistic mouse might exult to think that he was renewing in the cat the torture of conscious existence. It all depends on the philosophy of the mouse. You cannot even say that there is victory or superiority in nature unless you have some doctrine about what things are superior. You cannot even say that the cat scores unless there is a system of scoring. You cannot even say that the cat gets the best of it unless there is some best to be got.

We cannot, then, get the ideal itself from nature, and as we follow here the first and natural speculation, we will leave out (for the present) the idea of getting it from God. We must have our own vision. But the attempts of most moderns to express it are highly vague.

Some fall back simply on the clock: they talk as if mere passage through time brought some superiority; so that even a man of the first mental calibre carelessly uses the phrase that human morality is never up to date. How can anything be up to date?—a date has no character. How can one say that Christmas celebrations are not suitable to the twenty-fifth of a month? What the writer meant, of course, was that the majority is behind his favourite minority—or in front of it. Other vague modern people take refuge in material metaphors; in fact, this is the chief mark of vague modern people. Not daring to define their doctrine of what is good, they use physical figures of speech without stint or shame, and, what is worst of all, seem to think these cheap analogies are exquisitely spiritual and superior to the old morality. Thus they think it intellectual to talk about things being "high." It is at least the reverse of intellectual; it is a mere phrase from a steeple or a weathercock. "Tommy was a good boy" is a pure philosophical statement, worthy of Plato or Aquinas. "Tommy lived the higher life" is a gross metaphor from a ten-foot rule.

This, incidentally, is almost the whole weakness of Nietzsche, whom some are representing as a bold and strong thinker. No one will deny that he was a poetical and suggestive thinker; but he was quite the reverse of strong. He was not at all bold. He never put his own meaning before himself in bald abstract words: as did Aristotle and Calvin, and even Karl Marx, the hard, fearless men of thought. Nietzsche always escaped a question by a physical metaphor, like a cheery minor poet. He said, "beyond good and evil," because he had not the courage to say, "more good than good and evil," or, "more evil than good and evil." Had he faced his thought without metaphors, he would have seen that it was nonsense. So, when he describes his hero, he does not dare to say, "the purer man," or "the happier man," or "the sadder man," for all these are ideas; and ideas are alarming. He says "the upper man," or "over man," a physical metaphor from acrobats or alpine climbers. Nietzsche is truly a very timid thinker. He does not really know in the least what sort of man he wants evolution to produce. And if he does not know, certainly the ordinary evolutionists, who talk about things being "higher," do not know either.

Then again, some people fall back on sheer submission and sitting still. Nature is going to do something some day; nobody knows what, and nobody knows when. We have no reason for acting, and no reason for not acting. If anything happens it is right: if anything is prevented it was wrong. Again, some people try to anticipate nature by doing something, by doing anything. Because we may possibly grow wings they cut off their legs. Yet nature may be trying to make them centipedes for all they know.

Lastly, there is a fourth class of people who take whatever it is that they happen to want, and say that that is the ultimate aim of evolution. And these are the only sensible people. This is the only really healthy way with the word evolution, to work for what you want, and to call *that* evolution. The only intelligible sense that progress or advance can have among men, is that we have a definite vision, and that we wish to make the whole world like that vision. If you like to put it so, the essence of the doctrine is that what we have around us is the mere method and preparation for something that we have to create. This is not a world, but rather the material for a world. God has given us not so much the colours of a picture as the colours of a palette. But he has also given us a subject, a model, a fixed vision. We must be clear about what we want to paint. This adds a further principle to our previous list of principles. We have said we must be fond of this world, even in order to change it. We now add that we must be fond of another world (real or imaginary) in order to have something to change it to.

We need not debate about the mere words evolution or progress: personally I prefer to call it reform. For reform implies form. It implies that we are trying to shape the world in a particular image; to make it something that we see already in our minds. Evolution is a metaphor from mere automatic unrolling. Progress is a metaphor from merely walking along a road—very likely the wrong road. But reform is a metaphor for reasonable and determined men: it means that we see a certain thing out of shape and we mean to put it into shape. And we know what shape.

Now here comes in the whole collapse and huge blunder of our age. We have mixed up two different things, two opposite things. Progress should mean that we are always changing the world to suit the vision. Progress does mean (just now) that we are always changing the vision. It should mean that we are slow but sure in bringing justice and mercy among men: it does mean that we are very swift in doubting the desirability of justice and mercy: a wild page from any Prussian sophist makes men doubt it. Progress should mean that we are always walking towards the New Jerusalem. It does mean that the New Jerusalem is always walking away from us. We are not altering the real to suit the ideal. We are altering the ideal: it is easier.

Silly examples are always simpler; let us suppose a man wanted a particular kind of world; say, a blue world. He would have no cause to complain of the slightness or swiftness of his task; he might toil for a long time at the transformation; he could work away (in every sense) until all was blue. He could have heroic adventures; the putting of the last touches to a blue tiger. He could have fairy dreams; the dawn of a blue moon. But if he worked hard, that high-minded reformer would certainly (from his own point of view) leave the world better and bluer than he found it. If he altered a blade of grass to his favourite colour every day, he would get on slowly. But if he altered his favourite colour every day, he would not get on at all. If, after reading a fresh philosopher, he started to paint everything red or yellow, his work would be thrown away: there would be nothing to show except a few blue tigers walking about, specimens of his early bad manner. This is exactly the position of the average modern thinker. It will be said that this is avowedly a preposterous example. But it is literally the fact of recent history. The great and grave changes in our political civilization all belonged to the early nineteenth century, not to the later. They belonged to the black and white epoch when men believed fixedly in Toryism, in Protestantism, in Calvinism, in Reform, and not unfrequently in Revolution. And whatever each man believed in he hammered at steadily, without scepticism: and there was a time when the Established Church might have fallen, and the House of Lords nearly fell. It was because Radicals were wise enough to be constant and consistent; it was because Radicals were wise enough to be Conservative. But in the existing atmosphere there is not enough time and tradition in Radicalism to pull anything down. There is a great deal of truth in Lord Hugh Cecil's[44] suggestion (made in a fine speech) that the era of change is over, and that ours is an era of conservation and repose. But probably it would pain Lord Hugh Cecil if he realized (what is certainly the case) that ours is only an age of conservation because it is an age of complete unbelief. Let beliefs fade fast and frequently, if you wish institutions to remain the same. The more the life of the mind is unhinged, the more the machinery of matter will be left to

[44] Lord Hugh Cecil (1869–1956), a prominent Conservative politician and High Churchman.

itself. The net result of all our political suggestions, Collectivism, Tolstoyanism, Neo-Feudalism, Communism, Anarchy, Scientific Bureaucracy—the plain fruit of all of them is that the Monarchy and the House of Lords will remain. The net result of all the new religions will be that the Church of England will not (for heaven knows how long) be disestablished. It was Karl Marx, Nietzsche, Tolstoy, Cunninghame Graham,[45] Bernard Shaw and Auberon Herbert,[46] who between them, with bowed gigantic backs, bore up the throne of the Archbishop of Canterbury.

We may say broadly that free thought is the best of all the safe-guards against freedom. Managed in a modern style the emancipation of the slave's mind is the best way of preventing the emancipation of the slave. Teach him to worry about whether he wants to be free, and he will not free himself. Again, it may be said that this instance is remote or extreme. But, again, it is exactly true of the men in the streets around us. It is true that the negro slave, being a debased barbarian, will probaby have either a human affection of loyalty, or a human affection for liberty. But the man we see every day—the worker in Mr. Gradgrind's[47] factory, the little clerk in Mr. Gradgrind's office—he is too mentally worried to believe in freedom. He is kept quiet with revolutionary literature. He is calmed and kept in his place by a constant succession of wild philosophies. He is a Marxian one day, a Nietzscheite the next day, a Superman (probably) the next day; and a slave every day. The only thing that remains after all the philosophies is the factory. The only man who gains by all the philosophies is Gradgrind. It would be worth his while to keep his commercial helotry supplied with sceptical literature. And now I come to think of it, of course, Gradgrind is famous for giving libraries. He shows his sense. All modern books are on his side. As long as the vision of heaven is always changing, the vision

[45] R. B. Cunninghame Graham (1852–1936), Scottish author, traveller, romantic adventurer and Socialist.

[46] Auberon Herbert (1838–1906), political philosopher and author, avid secularist and agnostic.

[47] In Dicken's *Hard Times* (1854), a materialistic and practical man, an uninspired seeker after facts.

of earth will be exactly the same. No ideal will remain long enough to be realised, or even partly realised. The modern young man will never change his environment; for he will always change his mind.

This, therefore, is our first requirement about the ideal towards which progress is directed; it must be fixed. Whistler used to make many rapid studies of a sitter; it did not matter if he tore up twenty portraits. But it would matter if he looked up twenty times, and each time saw a new person sitting placidly for his portrait. So it does not matter (comparatively speaking) how often humanity fails to imitate its ideal; for then all its old failures are fruitful. But it does frightfully matter how often humanity changes its ideal; for then all its old failures are fruitless. The question therefore becomes this: How can we keep the artist discontented with his pictures while preventing him from being vitally discontented with his art? How can we make a man always dissatisfied with his work, yet always satisfied with working? How can we make sure that the portrait painter will throw the portrait out of window instead of taking the natural and more human course of throwing the sitter out of window?

A strict rule is not only necessary for ruling; it is also necessary for rebelling. This fixed and familiar ideal is necessary to any sort of revolution. Man will sometimes act slowly upon new ideas; but he will only act swiftly upon old ideas. If I am merely to float or fade or evolve, it may be towards something anarchic; but if I am to riot, it must be for something respectable. This is the whole weakness of certain schools of progress and moral evolution. They suggest that there has been a slow movement towards morality, with an imperceptible ethical change in every year or at every instant. There is only one great disadvantage in this theory. It talks of a slow movement towards justice; but it does not permit a swift movement. A man is not allowed to leap up and declare a certain state of things to be intrinsically intolerable. To make the matter clear, it is better to take a specific example. Certain of the idealistic vegetarians, such as Mr. Salt, say that the time has now come for eating no meat; by implication they assume that at one time it was right to eat meat, and they suggest (in words that could be quoted) that some day it may be wrong to eat milk and eggs. I do not discuss here the question of what is justice to animals. I only say that whatever is justice ought, under given conditions, to be prompt justice. If an animal is wronged, we ought to be able to rush to his rescue. But how can we rush if we are, perhaps, in advance of our time? How can we rush to catch a train which may not arrive for a few centuries? How can I denounce a man for skinning cats, if he is only now what I may possibly become in drinking a glass of milk? A splendid and insane Russian sect ran about taking all the cattle out of all the carts. How can I pluck up courage to take the horse out of my hansom-cab, when I do not know whether my evolutionary watch is only a little fast or the cabman's a little slow? Suppose I say to a sweater, "Slavery suited one stage of evolution." And suppose he answers, "And sweating suits this stage of evolution." How can I answer if there is no eternal test? If sweaters can be behind the current morality, why should not philanthropists be in front of it? What on earth is the current morality, except in its literal sense—the morality that is always running away?

Thus we may say that a permanent ideal is as necessary to the innovator as to the conservative; it is necessary whether we wish the king's orders to be promptly executed or whether we only wish the king to be promptly executed. The guillotine has many sins, but to do it justice there is nothing evolutionary about it. The favourite evolutionary argument finds its best answer in the axe. The Evolutionist says, "Where do you draw the line?" the Revolutionist answers, "I draw it *here*: exactly between your head and body." There must at any given moment be an abstract right and wrong if any blow is to be struck; there must be something eternal if there is to be anything sudden. Therefore for all intelligible human purposes, for altering things or for keeping things as they are, for founding a system for ever, as in China, or for altering it every month as in the early French Revolution, it is equally necessary that the vision should be a fixed vision. This is our first requirement.

When I had written this down, I felt once again the presence of something else in the discussion: as a man hears a church bell above the sound of the street. Something seemed to be saying, "My ideal at least is fixed; for it was fixed before the foundations of the world.

My vision of perfection assuredly cannot be altered; for it is called Eden. You may alter the place to which you are going; but you cannot alter the place from which you have come. To the orthodox there must always be a case for revolution; for in the hearts of men God has been put under the feet of Satan. In the upper world hell once rebelled against heaven. But in this world heaven is rebelling against hell. For the orthodox there can always be a revolution; for a revolution is a restoration. At any instant you may strike a blow for the perfection which no man has seen since Adam. No unchanging custom, no changing evolution can make the original good any thing but good. Man may have had concubines as long as cows have had horns: still they are not a part of him if they are sinful. Men may have been under oppression ever since fish were under water; still they ought not to be, if oppression is sinful. The chain may seem as natural to the slave, or the paint to the harlot, as does the plume to the bird or the burrow to the fox; still they are not, if they are sinful. I lift my prehistoric legend to defy all your history. Your vision is not merely a fixture: it is a fact." I paused to note the new coincidence of Christianity: but I passed on.

I passed on to the next necessity of any ideal of progress. Some people (as we have said) seem to believe in an automatic and impersonal progress in the nature of things. But it is clear that no political activity can be encouraged by saying that progress is natural and inevitable; that is not a reason for being active, but rather a reason for being lazy. If we are bound to improve, we need not trouble to improve. The pure doctrine of progress is the best of all reasons for not being a progressive. But it is to none of these obvious comments that I wish primarily to call attention.

The only arresting point is this: that if we suppose improvement to be natural, it must be fairly simple. The world might conceivably be working towards one consummation, but hardly towards any particular arrangement of many qualities. To take our original simile: Nature by herself may be growing more blue; that is, a process so simple that it might be impersonal. But Nature cannot be making a careful picture made of many picked colours, unless Nature is personal. If the end of the world were mere darkness or mere light it might come as slowly and inevitably as dusk or dawn. But if the end of the world is to be a piece of elaborate and artistic chiaroscuro, then there must be design in it, either human or divine. The world, through mere time, might grow black like an old picture, or white like an old coat; but if it is turned into a particular piece of black and white art—then there is an artist.

If the distinction be not evident, I give an ordinary instance. We constantly hear a particularly cosmic creed from the modern humanitarians; I use the word humanitarian in the ordinary sense, as meaning one who upholds the claims of all creatures against those of humanity. They suggest that through the ages we have been growing more and more humane, that is to say, that one after another, groups or sections of beings, slaves, children, women, cows, or what not, have been gradually admitted to mercy or to justice. They say that we once thought it right to eat men (we didn't); but I am not here concerned with their history, which is highly unhistorical. As a fact, anthropophagy is certainly a decadent thing, not a primitive one. It is much more likely that modern men will eat human flesh out of affectation than that primitive man ever ate it out of ignorance. I am here only following the outlines of their argument, which consists in maintaining that man has been progressively more lenient, first to citizens, then to slaves, then to animals, and then (presumably) to plants. I think it wrong to sit on a man. Soon, I shall think it wrong to sit on a horse. Eventually (I suppose) I shall think it wrong to sit on a chair. That is the drive of the argument. And for this argument it can be said that it is possible to talk of it in terms of evolution or inevitable progress. A perpetual tendency to touch fewer and fewer things might—one feels, be a mere brute unconscious tendency, like that of a species to produce fewer and fewer children. This drift may be really evolutionary, because it is stupid.

Darwinism can be used to back up two mad moralities, but it cannot be used to back up a single sane one. The kinship and competition of all living creatures can be used as a reason for being insanely cruel or insanely sentimental; but not for a healthy love of animals. On the evolutionary basis you may be inhumane, or you may be absurdly humane; but you cannot be human. That you and a tiger are one may be a reason for being tender to a tiger. Or it may be a reason for being as cruel as the tiger. It is one way to train the tiger to imitate you, it is a shorter way to imitate the tiger. But in neither case does evolution tell you how to treat a tiger reasonably, that is, to admire his stripes while avoiding his claws.

If you want to treat a tiger reasonably, you must go back to the garden of Eden. For the obstinate reminder continued to recur: only the supernatural has taken a sane view of Nature. The essence of all pantheism, evolutionism, and modern cosmic religion is really in this proposition: that Nature is our mother. Unfortunately, if you regard Nature as a mother, you discover that she is a step-mother. The main point of Christianity was this: that Nature is not our mother: Nature is our sister. We can be proud of her beauty, since we have the same father; but she has no authority over us; we have to admire, but not to imitate. This gives to the typically Christian pleasure in this earth a strange touch of lightness that is almost frivolity. Nature was a solemn mother to the worshippers of Isis and Cybele.[48] Nature was a solemn mother to Wordsworth or to Emerson. But Nature is not solemn to Francis of Assisi or to George Herbert. To St. Francis, Nature is a sister, and even a younger sister: a little, dancing sister, to be laughed at as well as loved.

This, however, is hardly our main point at present; I have admitted it only in order to show how constantly, and as it were accidentally, the key would fit the smallest doors. Our main point is here, that if there be a mere trend of impersonal improvement in Nature, it must presumably be a simple trend towards some simple triumph. One can imagine that some automatic tendency in biology might work for giving us longer and longer noses. But the question is, do we want to have longer and longer noses? I fancy not; I believe that we most of us want to say to our noses, "thus far, and no farther; and here shall thy proud point be stayed": we require a nose of such length as may ensure an interesting face. But we cannot imagine a mere biological trend towards producing interesting faces; because an interesting face is one particular arrangement of eyes,

[48] Nature goddesses, one worshipped in Egypt and the other in Asia, especially Phrygia.

nose, and mouth, in a most complex relation to each other. Proportion cannot be a drift: it is either an accident or a design. So with the ideal of human morality and its relation to the humanitarians and the anti-humanitarians. It is conceivable that we are going more and more to keep our hands off things: not to drive horses; not to pick flowers. We may eventually be bound not to disturb a man's mind even by argument; not to disturb the sleep of birds even by coughing. The ultimate apotheosis would appear to be that of a man sitting quite still, nor daring to stir for fear of disturbing a fly, nor to eat for fear of incommoding a microbe. To so crude a consummation as that we might perhaps unconsciously drift. But do we want so crude a consummation? Similarly, we might unconsciously evolve along the opposite or Nietzschean line of development — superman crushing superman in one tower of tyrants until the universe is smashed up for fun. But do we want the universe smashed up for fun? Is it not quite clear that what we really hope for is one particular management and proposition of these two things; a certain amount of restraint and respect, a certain amount of energy and mastery? If our life is ever really as beautiful as a fairy-tale, we shall have to remember that all the beauty of a fairy-tale lies in this: that the prince has a wonder which just stops short of being fear. If he is afraid of the giant, there is an end of him; but also if he is not astonished at the giant, there is an end of the fairy-tale. The whole point depends upon his being at once humble enough to wonder, and haughty enough to defy. So our attitude to the giant of the world must not merely be increasing delicacy or increasing contempt: it must be one particular proportion of the two — which is exactly right. We must have in us enough reverence for all things outside us to make us tread fearfully on the grass. We must also have enough disdain for all things outside us, to make us, on due occasion, spit at the stars. Yet these two things (if we are to be good or happy) must be combined, not in any combination, but in one particular combination. The perfect happiness of men on the earth (if it ever comes) will not be a flat and solid thing, like the satisfaction of animals. It will be an exact and perilous balance; like that of a desperate romance. Man must have just enough faith in himself to have adventures, and just enough doubt of himself to enjoy them.

This, then, is our second requirement for the ideal of progress. First, it must be fixed; second, it must be composite. It must not (if it is to satisfy our souls) be the mere victory of some one thing swallowing up everything else, love or pride or peace or adventure; it must be a definite picture composed of these elements in their best proportion and relation. I am not concerned at this moment to deny that some such good culmination may be, by the constitution of things, reserved for the human race. I only point out that if this composite happiness is fixed for us it must be fixed by some mind; for only a mind can place the exact proportions of a composite happiness. If the beatification of the world is a mere work of nature, then it must be as simple as the freezing of the world, or the burning up of the world. But if the beatification of the world is not a work of nature but a work of art, then it involves an artist. And here again my contemplation was cloven by the ancient voice which said, "I could have told you all this a long time ago. If there is any certain progress it can only be my kind of progress, the progress towards a complete city of virtues and dominations where righteousness and peace contrive to kiss each other. An impersonal force might be leading you to a wilderness of perfect flatness or a peak of perfect height. But only a personal God can possibly be leading you (if, indeed, you are being led) to a city with just streets and architectural proportions, a city in which each of you can contribute exactly the right amount of your own colour to the many coloured coat of Joseph."

Twice again, therefore, Christianity had come in with the exact answer that I required. I had said, "The ideal must be fixed," and the Church had answered, "Mine is literally fixed, for it existed before anything else." I said secondly, "It must be artistically combined, like a picture"; and the Church answered, "Mine is quite literally a picture, for I know who painted it." Then I went on to the third thing, which, as it seemed to me, was needed for an Utopia or goal of progress. And of all the three it is infinitely the hardest to express. Perhaps it might be put thus: that we need watchfulness even in Utopia, lest we fall from Utopia as we fell from Eden.

We have remarked that one reason offered for being a progressive is that things naturally tend to grow better. But the only real reason for being a progressive is that things naturally tend to grow worse. The corruption in things is not only the best argument for being progressive; it is also the only argument against being conservative. The conservative theory would really be quite sweeping and unanswerable if it were not for this one fact. But all conservatism is based upon the idea that if you leave things alone you leave them as they are. But you do not. If you leave a thing alone you leave it to a torrent of change. If you leave a white post alone it will soon be a black post. If you particularly want it to be white you must be always painting it again; that is, you must be always having a revolution. Briefly, if you want the old white post you must have a new white post. But this which is true even of inanimate things is in a quite special and terrible sense true of all human things. An almost unnatural vigilance is really required of the citizen because of the horrible rapidity with which human institutions grow old. It is the custom in passing romance and journalism to talk of men suffering under old tyrannies. But, as a fact, men have almost always suffered under new tyrannies; under tyrannies that had been public liberties hardly twenty years before. Thus England went mad with joy over the patriotic monarchy of Elizabeth; and then (almost immediately afterwards) went mad with rage in the trap of the tyranny of Charles the First. So, again, in France the monarchy became intolerable, not just after it had been tolerated, but just after it had been adored. The son of Louis the well-beloved was Louis the guillotined. So in the same way in England in the nineteenth century the Radical manufacturer was entirely trusted as a mere tribune of the people, until suddenly we heard the cry of the Socialist that he was a tyrant eating the people like bread. So again, we have almost up to the last instant trusted the newspapers as organs of public opinion. Just recently some of us have seen (not slowly, but with a start) that they are obviously nothing of the kind. They are, by the nature of the case, the hobbies of a few rich men. We have not any need to rebel against antiquity; we have to rebel against novelty. It is the new rulers, the capitalist or the editor, who really hold up the modern world. There is no fear that a modern king will attempt to override the constitution; it is more likely that he will ignore the constitution and work behind its back; he will take no advantage of his kingly power; it is more likely that he will take advantage of his kingly powerlessness, of the fact that he is free from criticism and publicity. For the king is the most private person of our time. It will not be necessary for any one to fight again against the proposal of a censorship of the press. We do not need a censorship of the press. We have a censorship by the press.

This startling swiftness with which popular systems turn oppressive is the third fact for which we shall ask our perfect theory of progress to allow. It must always be on the look out for every privilege being abused, for every working right becoming a wrong. In this matter I am entirely on the side of the revolutionists. They are really right to be always suspecting human institutions; they are right not to put their trust in princes nor in any child of man. The chieftain chosen to be the friend of the people becomes the enemy of the people; the newspaper started to tell the truth now exists to prevent the truth being told. Here, I say, I felt that I was really at last on the side of the revolutionary. And then I caught my breath again: for I remembered that I was once again on the side of the orthodox.

Christianity spoke again and said: "I have always maintained that men were naturally backsliders; that human virtue tended of its own nature to rust or to rot; I have always said that human beings as such go wrong, especially happy human beings, especially proud and prosperous human beings. This eternal revolution, this suspicion sustained through centuries, you (being a vague modern) call the doctrine of progress. If you were a philosopher you would call it, as I do, the doctrine of original sin. You may call it the cosmic advance as much as you like; I call it what it is—the Fall."

I have spoken of orthodoxy coming in like a sword; here I confess it came in like a battle-axe. For really (when I came to think of it) Christianity is the only thing left that has any real right to question the power of the well-nurtured or the well-bred. I have listened often enough to Socialists, or even to democrats, saying that the physical conditions of the poor must of necessity make them mentally and morally degraded. I have listened to scientific men (and there are still scientific men not opposed to democracy) saying that if we give the poor healthier conditions vice and wrong will disappear. I have listened to them with a horrible attention, with a hideous fascination. For it was like watching a man energetically sawing from the tree the branch he is sitting on. If these happy democrats could prove their case, they would strike democracy dead. If the poor are thus utterly demoralized, it may or may not be practical to raise them. But it is certainly quite practical to disfranchise them. If the man with a bad bedroom cannot give a good vote, then the first and swiftest deduction is that he shall give no vote. The governing class may not unreasonably say: "It may take us some time to reform his bedroom. But if he is the brute you say, it will take him very little time to ruin our country. Therefore we will take your hint and not give him the chance." It fills me with horrible amusement to observe the way in which the earnest Socialist industriously lays the foundation of all aristocracy, expatiating blandly upon the evident unfitness of the poor to rule. It is like listening to somebody at an evening party apologising for entering without evening dress, and explaining that he had recently been intoxicated, had a personal habit of taking off his clothes in the street, and had, moreover, only just changed from prison uniform. At any moment, one feels, the host might say that really, if it was as bad as that, he need not come in at all. So it is when the ordinary Socialist, with a beaming face, proves that the poor, after their smashing experiences, cannot be really trustworthy. At any moment the rich may say, "Very well, then, we won't trust them," and bang the door in his face. On the basis of Mr. Blatchford's view of heredity and environment, the case for the aristocracy is quite overwhelming. If clean homes and clean air make clean souls, why not give the power (for the present at any rate) to those who undoubtedly have the clean air? If better conditions will make the poor more fit to govern themselves, why should not better conditions already make the rich more fit to govern them? On the ordinary environment argument the matter is fairly manifest. The comfortable class must be merely our vanguard in Utopia.

Is there any answer to the proposition that those who have had the best opportunities will probably be our best guides? Is there any answer to the argument that those who have breathed clean air had better decide for those who have breathed foul? As far as I know, there is only one answer, and that answer is Christianity. Only the Christian Church can offer any rational objection to a complete confidence in the rich. For she has maintained from the beginning that the danger was not in man's environment, but in man. Further, she has maintained that if we come to talk of a dangerous environment, the most dangerous environment of all is the commodious environment. I know that the most modern manufacture has been really occupied in trying to produce an abnormally large needle. I know that the most recent biologists have been chiefly anxious to discover a very small camel. But if we diminish the camel to his smallest, or open the eye of the needle to its largest — if, in short, we assume the words of Christ to have meant the very least that they could mean, His words must at the very least mean this — that rich men are not very likely to be morally trustworthy. Christianity even when watered down is hot enough to boil all modern society to rags. The mere minimum of the Church would be a deadly ultimatum to the world. For the whole modern world is absolutely based on the assumption, not that the rich are necessary (which is tenable), but that the rich are trustworthy, which (for a Christian) is not tenable. You will hear everlastingly, in all discussions about newspapers, companies, aristocracies, or party politics, this argument that the rich man cannot be bribed. The fact is, of course, that the rich man is bribed; he has been bribed already. That is why he is a rich man. The whole case for Christianity is that a man who is dependent upon the luxuries of this life is a corrupt man, spiritually corrupt, politically corrupt, financially corrupt. There is one thing that Christ and all the Christian saints have said with a sort of savage monotony. They have said simply that to be rich is to be in peculiar danger of moral wreck. It is not demonstrably un-Christian to kill the rich as violators of definable justice. It is not demonstrably un-Christian to crown the rich as convenient rulers of society. It is not certainly un-Christian to rebel against the rich or to submit to the rich. But it is quite certainly un-Christian to trust the rich, to regard the rich as more morally safe than the poor. A Christian may consistently say, "I respect that man's rank, although he takes bribes." But a Christian cannot say, as all modern men are saying at lunch and breakfast, "a man of that rank would not take bribes." For it is a part of Christian dogma that any man in any rank may take bribes. It is a part of Christian dogma; it also happens by a curious coincidence that it is a part of obvious human history. When people say that a man "in that position" would be incorruptible, there is no need to bring Christianity into the discussion. Was Lord Bacon a bootblack? Was the Duke of Marlborough[49] a crossing sweeper? In the best Utopia, I must be prepared for the moral fall of any man in any position at any moment; especially for my fall from my position at this moment.

Much vague and sentimental journalism has been poured out to the effect that Christianity is akin to democracy, and most of it is scarcely strong or clear enough to refute the fact that the two things have often quarrelled. The real ground upon which Christianity and democracy are one is very much deeper. The one specially and peculiarly un-Christian idea is the idea of Carlyle—the idea that the man should rule who feels that he can rule. Whatever else is Christian, this is heathen. If our faith comments on government at all, its comment must be this—that the man should rule who does *not* think that he can rule. Carlyle's hero may say, "I will be king"; but the Christian saint must say "Nolo episcopari."[50] If the great paradox of Christianity means anything, it means this—that we must take the crown in our hands, and go hunting in dry places and dark corners of the earth until we find the one man who feels himself unfit to wear it. Carlyle was quite wrong; we have not got to crown the exceptional man who knows he can rule. Rather we must crown the much more exceptional man who knows he can't.

Now, this is one of the two or three vital defences of working democracy. The mere machinery of voting is not democracy, though at present it is not easy to effect any simpler democratic method. But even the machinery of voting is profoundly Christian in this practical sense—that it is an attempt to get at the opinion of those who would be too modest to offer it. It is a mystical adventure; it is

[49] Francis Bacon, Lord Verulam (1561-1626) was tried for bribery before the House of Lords in 1621, fined, and imprisoned. The first Duke of Marlborough (1650-1722) was accused of malversation in 1711 and dismissed from all his offices.

[50] I do not wish to be bishop.

specially trusting those who do not trust themselves. That enigma is strictly peculiar to Christendom. There is nothing really humble about the abnegation of the Buddhist; the mild Hindoo is mild, but he is not meek. But there is something psychologically Christian about the idea of seeking for the opinion of the obscure rather than taking the obvious course of accepting the opinion of the prominent. To say that voting is particularly Christian may seem somewhat curious. To say that canvassing is Christian may seem quite crazy. But canvassing is very Christian in its primary idea. It is encouraging the humble; it is saying to the modest man, "Friend, go up higher." Or if there is some slight defect in canvassing, that is in its perfect and rounded piety, it is only because it may possibly neglect to encourage the modesty of the canvasser.

Aristocracy is not an institution: aristocracy is a sin; generally a very venial one. It is merely the drift or slide of men into a sort of natural pomposity and praise of the powerful, which is the most easy and obvious affair in the world.

It is one of the hundred answers to the fugitive perversion of modern "force" that the promptest and boldest agencies are also the most fragile or full of sensibility. The swiftest things are the softest things. A bird is active, because a bird is soft. A stone is helpless, because a stone is hard. The stone must by its own nature go downwards, because hardness is weakness. The bird can of its nature go upwards, because fragility is force. In perfect force there is a kind of frivolity, an airiness that can maintain itself in the air. Modern investigators of miraculous history have solemnly admitted that a characteristic of the great saints is their power of "levitation." They might go further; a characteristic of the great saints is their power of levity. Angels can fly because they can take themselves lightly. This has been always the instinct of Christendom, and especially the instinct of Christian art. Remember how Fra Angelico represented all his angels, not only as birds, but almost as butterflies. Remember how the most earnest mediaeval art was full of light and fluttering draperies, of quick and capering feet. It was the one thing that the modern Pre-raphaelites[51]

[51] Pre-raphaelite Brotherhood: A group formed about 1850 and including D. G. Rossetti, Holman Hunt and J. E. Millais, who wanted to return to the art forms and sincerity which they supposed to exist before the time of Raphael.

could not imitate in the real Pre-raphaelites. Burne-Jones[52] could never recover the deep levity of the Middle Ages. In the old Christian pictures the sky over every figure is like a blue or gold parachute. Every figure seems ready to fly up and float about in the heavens. The tattered cloak of the beggar will bear him up like the rayed plumes of the angels. But the kings in their heavy gold and the proud in their robes of purple will all of their nature sink downwards, for pride cannot rise to levity or levitation. Pride is the downward drag of all things into an easy solemnity. One "settles down" into a sort of selfish seriousness; but one has to rise to a gay self-forgetfulness. A man "falls" into a brown study; he reaches up at a blue sky. Seriousness is not a virtue. It would be a heresy, but a much more sensible heresy, to say that seriousness is a vice. It is really a natural trend or lapse into taking one's self gravely, because it is the easiest thing to do. It is much easier to write a good *Times* leading article than a good joke in *Punch*. For solemnity flows out of men naturally; but laughter is a leap. It is easy to be heavy: hard to be light. Satan fell by the force of gravity.

Now, it is the peculiar honour of Europe since it has been Christian that while it has had aristocracy it has always at the back of its heart treated aristocracy as a weakness—generally as a weakness that must be allowed for. If any one wishes to appreciate this point, let him go outside Christianity into some other philosophical atmosphere. Let him, for instance, compare the classes of Europe with the castes of India. There aristocracy is far more awful, because it is far more intellectual. It is seriously felt that the scale of classes is a scale of spiritual values; that the baker is better than the butcher in an invisible and sacred sense. But no Christianity, not even the most ignorant or perverse, ever suggested that a baronet was better than a butcher in that sacred sense. No Christianity, however ignorant or extravagant, ever suggested that a duke would not be damned. In pagan society there may have been (I do not know) some such serious division between the free man and the slave. But in Christian society we have always thought the gentleman a sort of joke, though

[52] Sir Edward Burne-Jones (1833–1898), Victorian painter and designer of stained-glass windows.

I admit that in some great crusades and councils he earned the right to be called a practical joke. But we in Europe never really and at the root of our souls took aristocracy seriously. It is only an occasional non-European alien (such as Dr. Oscar Levy,[53] the only intelligent Nietzscheite) who can even manage for a moment to take aristocracy seriously. It may be a mere patriotic bias, though I do not think so, but it seems to me that the English aristocracy is not only the type, but is the crown and flower of all actual aristocracies; it has all the oligarchical virtues as well as all the defects. It is casual, it is kind, it is courageous in obvious matters; but it has one great merit that overlaps even these. The great and very obvious merit of the English aristocracy is that nobody could possibly take it seriously.

In short, I had spelled out slowly, as usual, the need for an equal law in Utopia; and, as usual, I found that Christianity had been there before me. The whole history of my Utopia has the same amusing sadness. I was always rushing out of my architectural study with plans for a new turret only to find it sitting up there in the sunlight, shining, and a thousand years old. For me, in the ancient and partly in the modern sense, God answered the prayer, "Prevent us, O Lord, in all our doings." Without vanity, I really think there was a moment when I could have invented the marriage vow (as an institution) out of my own head; but I discovered, with a sigh, that it had been invented already. But, since it would be too long a business to show how, fact by fact and inch by inch, my own conception of Utopia was only answered in the New Jerusalem, I will take this one case of the matter of marriage as indicating the converging drift, I may say the converging crash of all the rest.

When the ordinary opponents of Socialism talk about impossibilities and alterations in human nature they always miss an important distinction. In modern ideal conceptions of society there are some desires that are possibly not attainable: but there are some desires that are not desirable. That all men should live in equally beautiful houses is a dream that may or may not be attained. But that all men should live in the same beautiful house is not a dream at all; it is a

[53] Dr. Oscar Levy (b. 1867) edited a complete edition of Nietzsche's works in eighteen volumes between 1909 and 1912.

nightmare. That a man should love all old women is an ideal that may not be attainable. But that a man should regard all old women exactly as he regards his mother is not only an unattainable ideal, but an ideal which ought not to be attained. I do not know if the reader agrees with me in these examples; but I will add the example which has always affected me most. I could never conceive or tolerate any Utopia which did not leave to me the liberty for which I chiefly care, the liberty to bind myself. Complete anarchy would not merely make it impossible to have any discipline or fidelity; it would also make it impossible to have any fun. To take an obvious instance, it would not be worth while to bet if a bet were not binding. The dissolution of all contracts would not only ruin morality but spoil sport. Now betting and such sports are only the stunted and twisted shapes of the original instinct of man for adventure and romance, of which much has been said in these pages. And the perils, rewards, punishments, and fulfilments of an adventure must be real, or the adventure is only a shifting and heartless nightmare. If I bet I must be made to pay, or there is no poetry in betting. If I challenge I must be made to fight, or there is no poetry in challenging. If I vow to be faithful I must be cursed when I am unfaithful, or there is no fun in vowing. You could not even make a fairy tale from the experiences of a man who, when he was swallowed by a whale, might find himself at the top of the Eiffel Tower, or when he was turned into a frog might begin to behave like a flamingo. For the purpose even of the wildest romance results must be real; results must be irrevocable. Christian marriage is the great example of a real and irrevocable result; and that is why it is the chief subject and centre of all our romantic writing. And this is my last instance of the things that I should ask, and ask imperatively, of any social paradise; I should ask to be kept to my bargain, to have my oaths and engagements taken seriously; I should ask Utopia to avenge my honour on myself.

All my modern Utopian friends look at each other rather doubtfully, for their ultimate hope is the dissolution of all special ties. But again I seem to hear, like a kind of echo, an answer from beyond the world. "You will have real obligations, and therefore real adventures when you get to my Utopia. But the hardest obligation and the steepest adventure is to get there."

VIII

THE ROMANCE OF ORTHODOXY

It is customary to complain of the bustle and strenuousness of our epoch. But in truth the chief mark or our epoch is a profound laziness and fatigue; and the fact is that the real laziness is the cause of the apparent bustle. Take one quite external case; the streets are noisy with taxicabs and motorcars; but this is not due to human activity but to human repose. There would be less bustle if there were more activity, if people were simply walking about. Our world would be more silent if it were more strenuous. And this which is true of the apparent physical bustle is true also of the apparent bustle of the intellect. Most of the machinery of modern language is labour-saving machinery; and it saves mental labour very much more than it ought. Scientific phrases are used like scientific wheels and piston-rods to make swifter and smoother yet the path of the comfortable. Long words go rattling by us like long railway trains. We know they are carrying thousands who are too tired or too indolent to walk and think for themselves. It is a good exercise to try for once in a way to express any opinion one holds in words of one syllable. If you say "The social utility of the indeterminate sentence is recognized by all criminologists as a part of our sociological evolution towards a more humane and scientific view of punishment," you can go on talking like that for hours with hardly a movement of the gray matter inside your skull. But if you begin "I wish Jones to go to gaol and Brown to say when Jones shall come out," you will discover, with a thrill of horror, that you are obliged to think. The long words are not the hard words, it is the short words that are hard. There is much more metaphysical subtlety in the word "damn" than in the word "degeneration."

But these long comfortable words that save modern people the toil of reasoning have one particular aspect in which they are especially ruinous and confusing. This difficulty occurs when the same long word is used in different connections to mean quite different things. Thus, to take a well-known instance, the word "idealist" has one meaning as a piece of philosophy and quite another as a piece of moral rhetoric. In the same way the scientific materialists have had just reason to complain of people mixing up "materialist" as a term of cosmology with "materialist" as a moral taunt. So, to take a cheaper instance, the man who hates "progressives" in London always calls himself a "progressive" in South Africa.

A confusion quite as unmeaning as this has arisen in connection with the word "liberal" as applied to religion and as applied to politics and society. It is often suggested that all Liberals ought to be freethinkers, because they ought to love everything that is free. You might just as well say that all idealists ought to be High Churchmen, because they ought to love everything that is high. You might as well say that Low Churchmen ought to like Low Mass, or that Broad Churchmen ought to like broad jokes. The thing is a mere accident of words. In actual modern Europe a freethinker does not mean a man who thinks for himself. It means a man who, having thought for himself, has come to one particular class of conclusions, the material origin of phenomena, the impossibility of miracles, the improbability of personal immortality and so on. And none of these ideas are particularly liberal. Nay, indeed almost all these ideas are definitely illiberal, as it is the purpose of this chapter to show.

In the few following pages I propose to point out as rapidly as possible that on every single one of the matters most strongly insisted on by liberalisers of theology their effect upon social practice would be definitely illiberal. Almost every contemporary proposal to bring freedom into the church is simply a proposal to bring tyranny into the world. For freeing the church now does not even mean freeing it in all directions. It means freeing that peculiar set of dogmas loosely called scientific, dogmas of monism, of pantheism, or of Arianism, or of necessity. And every one of these (and we will take them one by one) can be shown to be the natural ally of oppression. In fact, it is a remarkable circumstance (indeed not so very remarkable when one comes to think of it) that most things are the allies of oppression. There is only one thing that can never go past a certain point in its alliance with oppression — and that is orthodoxy. I may, it is true, twist orthodoxy so as partly to justify a tyrant. But I can easily make up a German philosophy to justify him entirely.

Now let us take in order the innovations that are the notes of the new theology or the modernist church. We concluded the last chapter with the discovery of one of them. The very doctrine which is called the most old-fashioned was found to be the only safeguard of the new democracies of the earth. The doctrine seemingly most unpopular was found to be the only strength of the people. In short, we found that the only logical negation of oligarchy was in the affirmation of original sin. So it is, I maintain, in all the other cases.

I take the most obvious instance first, the case of miracles. For some extraordinary reason, there is a fixed notion that it is more liberal to disbelieve in miracles than to believe in them. Why, I cannot imagine, nor can anybody tell me. For some inconceivable cause a "broad" or "liberal" clergyman always means a man who wishes at least to diminish the number of miracles; it never means a man who wishes to increase that number. It always means a man who is free to disbelieve that Christ came out of His grave; it never means a man who is free to believe that his own aunt came out of her grave. It is common to find trouble in a parish because the parish priest cannot admit that St. Peter walked on water; yet how rarely do we find trouble in a parish because the clergyman says that his father walked on the Serpentine?[54] And this is not because (as the swift secularist debater would immediately retort) miracles cannot be believed in our experience. It is not because "miracles do not happen," as in the dogma which Matthew Arnold recited with simple faith. More supernatural things are *alleged* to have happened in our time than would have been possible eighty years ago. Men of science believe in such marvels much more than they did: the most perplexing, and even horrible, prodigies of mind and spirit are always being unveiled in modern psychology. Things that the old science at least would frankly have rejected as miracles are hourly being asserted by the new science. The only thing which is still old-fashioned enough to reject miracles is the New Theology. But in truth this notion that it is "free" to deny miracles has nothing to do with the evidence for or against them. It is a lifeless verbal prejudice of which the original life and beginning was not in the freedom of thought, but simply in the

---

[54] A pond in Hyde Park, London.

dogma of materialism. The man of the nineteenth century did not disbelieve in the Resurrection because his liberal Christianity allowed him to doubt it. He disbelieved in it because his very strict materialism did not allow him to believe it. Tennyson, a very typical nineteenth-century man, uttered one of the instinctive truisms of his contemporaries when he said that there was faith in their honest doubt.[55] There was indeed. Those words have a profound and even a horrible truth. In their doubt of miracles there was a faith in a fixed and godless fate; a deep and sincere faith in the incurable routine of the cosmos. The doubts of the agnostic were only the dogmas of the monist.

Of the fact and evidence of the supernatural I will speak afterwards. Here we are only concerned with this clear point; that in so far as the liberal idea of freedom can be said to be on either side in the discussion about miracles, it is obviously on the side of miracles. Reform or (in the only tolerable sense) progress means simply the gradual control of matter by mind. A miracle simply means the swift control of matter by mind. If you wish to feed the people, you may think that feeding them miraculously in the wilderness is impossible—but you cannot think it illiberal. If you really want poor children to go to the seaside, you cannot think it illiberal that they should go there on flying dragons; you can only think it unlikely. A holiday, like Liberalism, only means the liberty of man. A miracle only means the liberty of God. You may conscientiously deny either of them, but you cannot call your denial a triumph of the liberal idea. The Catholic Church believed that man and God both had a sort of spiritual freedom. Calvinism took away the freedom from man, but left it to God. Scientific materialism binds the Creator Himself; it chains up God as the Apocalypse chained the devil. It leaves nothing free in the universe. And those who assist this process are called the "liberal theologians."

This, as I say, is the lightest and most evident case. The assumption that there is something in the doubt of miracles akin to liberality or reform is literally the opposite of the truth. If a man cannot

---

[55] From *In Memoriam*, poem 96:

> There lives more faith in honest doubt,
> Believe me, than in half the creeds.

believe in miracles there is an end of the matter; he is not particularly liberal, but he is perfectly honourable and logical, which are much better things. But if he can believe in miracles, he is certainly the more liberal for doing so; because they mean first, the freedom of the soul, and secondly, its control over the tyranny of circumstance. Sometimes this truth is ignored in a singularly naïve way, even by the ablest men. For instance, Mr. Bernard Shaw speaks with hearty old-fashioned contempt for the idea of miracles, as if they were a sort of breach of faith on the part of nature: he seems strangely unconscious that miracles are only the final flowers of his own favourite tree, the doctrine of the omnipotence of will. Just in the same way he calls the desire for immortality a paltry selfishness, forgetting that he has just called the desire for life a healthy and heroic selfishness. How can it be noble to wish to make one's life infinite and yet mean to wish to make it immortal? No, if it is desirable that man should triumph over the cruelty of nature or custom, then miracles are certainly desirable; we will discuss afterwards whether they are possible.

But I must pass on to the larger cases of this curious error; the notion that the "liberalising" of religion in some way helps the liberation of the world. The second example of it can be found in the question of pantheism—or rather of a certain modern attitude which is often called immanentism, and which often is Buddhism. But this is so much more difficult a matter that I must approach it with rather more preparation.

The things said most confidently by advanced persons to crowded audiences are generally those quite opposite to the fact; it is actually our truisms that are untrue. Here is a case. There is a phrase of facile liberality uttered again and again at ethical societies and parliaments of religion: "the religions of the earth differ in rites and forms, but they are the same in what they teach." It is false; it is the opposite of the fact. The religions of the earth do *not* greatly differ in rites and forms; they do greatly differ in what they teach. It is as if a man were to say, "Do not be misled by the fact that the *Church Times* and the *Freethinker*[56] look utterly different, that one is painted on vellum and the other carved on marble, that one is triangular and the other

[56] One the official organ of the Church of England, the other of the Society of Free Thought.

hectagonal; read them and you will see that they say the same thing." The truth is, of course, that they are alike in everything except in the fact that they don't say the same thing. An atheist stockbroker in Surbiton[57] looks exactly like a Swedenborgian[58] stockbroker in Wimbledon. You may walk round and round them and subject them to the most personal and offensive study without seeing anything Swedenborgian in the hat or anything particularly godless in the umbrella. It is exactly in their souls that they are divided. So the truth is that the difficulty of all the creeds of the earth is not as alleged in this cheap maxim: that they agree in meaning, but differ in machinery. It is exactly the opposite. They agree in machinery; almost every great religion on earth works with the same external methods, with priests, scriptures, altars, sworn brotherhoods, special feasts. They agree in the mode of teaching; what they differ about is the thing to be taught. Pagan optimists and Eastern pessimists would both have temples, just as Liberals and Tories would both have newspapers. Creeds that exist to destroy each other both have scriptures, just as armies that exist to destroy each other both have guns.

The great example of this alleged identity of all human religions is the alleged spiritual identity of Buddhism and Christianity. Those who adopt this theory generally avoid the ethics of most other creeds, except, indeed, Confucianism, which they like because it is not a creed. But they are cautious in their praises of Mahometanism, generally confining themselves to imposing its morality only upon the refreshment of the lower classes. They seldom suggest the Mahometan view of marriage (for which there is a great deal to be said), and towards Thugs and fetish worshippers their attitude may even be called cold. But in the case of the great religion of Gautama they feel sincerely a similarity.

Students of popular science, like Mr. Blatchford, are always insisting that Christianity and Buddhism are very much alike, especially

[57] Wimbledon is part of Greater London, Surbiton a few miles southwest of Wimbledon.

[58] Follower of Emmanuel Swedenborg (1685–1772), who claimed to have had personal experiences of divine revelation and reinterpreted the Scriptures in terms of them.

Buddhism. This is generally believed, and I believed it myself until I read a book giving the reasons for it. The reasons were of two kinds: resemblances that meant nothing because they were common to all humanity, and resemblances which were not resemblances at all. The author solemnly explained that the two creeds were alike in things in which all creeds are alike, or else he described them as alike in some point in which they are quite obviously different. Thus, as a case of the first class, he said that both Christ and Buddha were called by the divine voice coming out of the sky, as if you would expect the divine voice to come out of the coal-cellar. Or, again, it was gravely urged that these two Eastern teachers, by a singular coincidence, both had to do with the washing of feet. You might as well say that it was a remarkable coincidence that they both had feet to wash. And the other class of similarities were those which simply were not similar. Thus this reconciler of the two religions draws earnest attention to the fact that at certain religious feasts the robe of the Lama is rent in pieces out of respect, and the remnants highly valued. But this is the reverse of a resemblance, for the garments of Christ were not rent in pieces out of respect, but out of derision; and the remnants were not highly valued except for what they would fetch in the rag shops. It is rather like alluding to the obvious connection between the two ceremonies of the sword: when it taps a man's shoulder, and when it cuts off his head. It is not at all similar for the man. These scraps of puerile pedantry would indeed matter little if it were not also true that the alleged philosophical resemblances are also of these two kinds, either proving too much or not proving anything. That Buddhism approves of mercy or of self-restraint is not to say that it is specially like Christianity; it is only to say that it is not utterly unlike all human existence. Buddhists disapprove in theory of cruelty or excess because all sane human beings disapprove in theory of cruelty or excess. But to say that Buddhism and Christianity give the same philosophy of these things is simply false. All humanity does agree that we are in a net of sin. Most of humanity agrees that there is some way out. But as to what is the way out, I do not think that there are two institutions in the universe which contradict each other so flatly as Buddhism and Christianity.

Even when I thought, with most other well-informed, though un-scholarly, people, that Buddhism and Christianity were alike, there was one thing about them that always perplexed me; I mean the startling difference in their type of religious art. I do not mean in its technical style of representation, but in the things that it was mani-festly meant to represent. No two ideals could be more opposite than a Christian saint in a Gothic cathedral and a Buddhist saint in a Chinese temple. The opposition exists at every point; but perhaps the shortest statement of it is that the Buddhist saint always has his eyes shut, while the Christian saint always has them very wide open. The Buddhist saint has a sleek and harmonious body, but his eyes are heavy and sealed with sleep. The mediaeval saint's body is wasted to its crazy bones, but his eyes are frightfully alive. There cannot be any real community of spirit between forces that produced symbols so different as that. Granted that both images are extravagances, are perversions of the pure creed, it must be a real divergence which could produce such opposite extravagances. The Buddhist is looking with a peculiar intentness inwards. The Christian is staring with a frantic intentness outwards. If we follow that clue steadily we shall find some interesting things.

A short time ago Mrs. Besant,[59] in an interesting essay, announced that there was only one religion in the world, that all faiths were only versions or perversions of it, and that she was quite prepared to say what it was. According to Mrs. Besant this universal Church is simply the universal self. It is the doctrine that we are really all one person; that there are no real walls of individuality between man and man. If I may put it so, she does not tell us to love our neighbours; she tells us to be our neighbours. That is Mrs. Besant's thoughtful and suggestive description of the religion in which all men must find themselves in agreement. And I never heard of any suggestion in my life with which I more violently disagree. I want to love my neigh-bour not because he is I, but precisely because he is not I. I want to adore the world, not as one likes a looking-glass, because it is one's

[59] Annie V. Besant (1847–1933), who joined the Theosophical Society—a move-ment for the reconciliation of all religions, founded by Mme. Blavatsky in 1875—and became its president in 1907.

self, but as one loves a woman, because she is entirely different. If souls are separate love is possible. If souls are united love is obviously impossible. A man may be said loosely to love himself, but he can hardly fall in love with himself, or, if he does, it must be a monotonous courtship. If the world is full of real selves, they can be really unselfish selves. But upon Mrs. Besant's principle the whole cosmos is only one enormously selfish person.

It is just here that Buddhism is on the side of modern pantheism and immanence. And it is just here that Christianity is on the side of humanity and liberty and love. Love desires personality; therefore love desires division. It is the instinct of Christianity to be glad that God has broken the universe into little pieces, because they are living pieces. It is her instinct to say "little children love one another" rather than to tell one large person to love himself. This is the intellectual abyss between Buddhism and Christianity; that for the Buddhist or Theosophist personality is the fall of man, for the Christian it is the purpose of God, the whole point of his cosmic idea. The world-soul of the Theosophists asks man to love it only in order that man may throw himself into it. But the divine centre of Christianity actually threw man out of it in order that he might love it. The oriental deity is like a giant who should have lost his leg or hand and be always seeking to find it; but the Christian power is like some giant who in a strange generosity should cut off his right hand, so that it might of its own accord shake hands with him. We come back to the same tireless note touching the nature of Christianity; all modern philosophies are chains which connect and fetter; Christianity is a sword which separates and sets free. No other philosophy makes God actually rejoice in the separation of the universe into living souls. But according to orthodox Christianity this separation between God and man is sacred, because this is eternal. That a man may love God it is necessary that there should be not only a God to be loved, but a man to love him. All those vague theosophical minds for whom the universe is an immense melting-pot are exactly the minds which shrink instinctively from that earthquake saying of our Gospels, which declare that the Son of God came not with peace but with a sundering sword. The saying rings entirely true even considered as what it obviously is; the statement that any man who preaches real love is bound to beget hate. It is as true of democratic fraternity as a divine love; sham love ends in compromise and common philosophy; but real love has always ended in bloodshed. Yet there is another and yet more awful truth behind the obvious meaning of this utterance of our Lord. According to Himself the Son was a sword separating brother and brother that they should for an aeon hate each other. But the Father also was a sword, which in the black beginning separated brother and brother, so that they should love each other at last.

This is the meaning of that almost insane happiness in the eyes of the mediaeval saint in the picture. This is the meaning of the sealed eyes of the superb Buddhist image. The Christian saint is happy because he has verily been cut off from the world; he is separate from things and is staring at them in astonishment. But why should the Buddhist saint be astonished at things? — since there is really only one thing, and that being impersonal can hardly be astonished at itself. There have been many pantheist poems suggesting wonder, but no really successful ones. The pantheist cannot wonder, for he cannot praise God or praise anything as really distinct from himself. Our immediate business here, however, is with the effect of this Christian admiration (which strikes outwards, towards a deity distinct from the worshipper) upon the general need for ethical activity and social reform. And surely its effect is sufficiently obvious. There is no real possibility of getting out of pantheism any special impulse to moral action. For pantheism implies in its nature that one thing is as good as another; whereas action implies in its nature that one thing is greatly preferable to another. Swinburne, in the high summer of his scepticism, tried in vain to wrestle with this difficulty. In "Songs before Sunrise," written under the inspiration of Garibaldi and the revolt of Italy, he proclaimed the newer religion and the purer God which should wither up all the priests of the world:

> What doest thou now
> Looking Godward to cry
> I am I, thou art thou,
> I am low, thou art high,
> I am thou that thou seekest to find him, find
>   thou but thyself, thou art I.

Of which the immediate and evident deduction is that tyrants are as much the sons of God as Garibaldis; and that King Bomba[60] of Naples having, with the utmost success, "found himself" is identical with the ultimate good in all things. The truth is that the western energy that dethrones tyrants has been directly due to the western theology that says "I am I, thou art thou." The same spiritual separation which looked up and saw a good king in the universe looked up and saw a bad king in Naples. The worshippers of Bomba's god dethroned Bomba. The worshippers of Swinburne's god have covered Asia for centuries and have never dethroned a tyrant. The Indian saint may reasonably shut his eyes because he is looking at that which is I and Thou and We and They and It. It is a rational occupation: but it is not true in theory and not true in fact that it helps the Indian to keep an eye on Lord Curzon.[61] That external vigilance which has always been the mark of Christianity (the command that we should *watch* and pray) has expressed itself both in typical western orthodoxy and in typical western politics: but both depend on the idea of a divinity transcendent, different from ourselves, a deity that disappears. Certainly the most sagacious creeds may suggest that we should pursue God into deeper and deeper rings of the labyrinth of our own ego. But only we of Christendom have said that we should hunt God like an eagle upon the mountains: and we have killed all monsters in the chase.

Here again, therefore, we find that in so far as we value democracy and the self-renewing energies of the west, we are much more likely to find them in the old theology than the new. If we want reform, we must adhere to orthodoxy: especially in this matter (so much disputed in the counsels of Mr. R. J. Campbell[62]), the matter of insisting on the immanent or the transcendent deity. By insisting specially on the immanence of God we get introspection, self-isolation, quietism,

[60] Ferdinand II (1810–1859) was King of the two Sicilies when revolution broke out in Sicily in 1848. In the spring of 1849 he had subdued the country by the inhuman bombardment of its chief cities, which earned him the epithet "Bomba".

[61] Lord Curzon (1859–1925), Viceroy and Governor-general of India from 1898 to 1905.

[62] R. J. Campbell (1867–1956), a popular preacher and minister of the City Temple, London, was in the van of the "modernizers" of Christianity; his book on the subject, *The New Theology*, had appeared in 1907.

social indifference—Tibet. By insisting specially on the transcendence of God we get wonder, curiosity, moral and political adventure, righteous indignation—Christendom. Insisting that God is inside man, man is always inside himself. By insisting that God transcends man, man has transcended himself.

If we take any other doctrine that has been called old-fashioned we shall find the case the same. It is the same, for instance, in the deep matter of the Trinity. Unitarians (a sect never to be mentioned without a special respect for their distinguished intellectual dignity and high intellectual honour) are often reformers by the accident that throws so many small sects into such an attitude. But there is nothing in the least liberal or akin to reform in the substitution of pure monotheism for the Trinity. The complex God of the Athanasian Creed may be an enigma for the intellect; but He is far less likely to gather the mystery and cruelty of a Sultan than the lonely god of Omar or Mahomet. The god who is a mere awful unity is not only a king but an Eastern king. The *heart* of humanity, especially of European humanity, is certainly much more satisfied by the strange hints and symbols that gather round the Trinitarian idea, the image of a council at which mercy pleads as well as justice, the conception of a sort of liberty and variety existing even in the inmost chamber of the world. For Western religion has always felt keenly the idea "it is not well for man to be alone." The social instinct asserted itself everywhere as when the Eastern idea of hermits was practically expelled by the Western idea of monks. So even asceticism became brotherly; and the Trappists were sociable even when they were silent. If this love of a living complexity be our test, it is certainly healthier to have the Trinitarian religion than the Unitarian. For to us Trinitarians (if I may say it with reverence)—to us God Himself is a society. It is indeed a fathomless mystery of theology, and even if I were theologian enough to deal with it directly, it would not be relevant to do so here. Suffice it to say here that this triple enigma is as comforting as wine and open as an English fireside; that this thing that bewilders the intellect utterly quiets the heart: but out of the desert, from the dry places and the dreadful suns, come the cruel children of the lonely God; the real Unitarians who with scimitar in hand have laid waste the world. For it is not well for God to be alone.

Again, the same is true of that difficult matter of the danger of the soul, which has unsettled so many just minds. To hope for all souls is imperative; and it is quite tenable that their salvation is inevitable. It is tenable, but it is not specially favourable to activity or progress. Our fighting and creative society ought rather to insist on the danger of everybody, on the fact that every man is hanging by a thread or clinging to a precipice. To say that all will be well anyhow is a comprehensible remark: but it cannot be called the blast of a trumpet. Europe ought rather to emphasize possible perdition; and Europe always has emphasized it. Here its highest religion is at one with all its cheapest romances. To the Buddhist or the eastern fatalist existence is a science or a plan, which must end up in a certain way. But to a Christian existence is a *story*, which may end up in any way. In a thrilling novel (that purely Christian product) the hero is not eaten by cannibals; but it is essential to the existence of the thrill that he *might* be eaten by cannibals. The hero must (so to speak) be an eatable hero. So Christian morals have always said to the man, not that he would lose his soul, but that he must take care that he didn't. In Christian morals, in short, it is wicked to call a man "damned": but it is strictly religious and philosophic to call him damnable.

All Christianity concentrates on the man at the cross-roads. The vast and shallow philosophies, the huge syntheses of humbug, all talk about ages and evolution and ultimate developments. The true philosophy is concerned with the instant. Will a man take this road or that? —that is the only thing to think about, if you enjoy thinking. The aeons are easy enough to think about, any one can think about them. The instant is really awful: and it is because our religion has intensely felt the instant, that it has in literature dealt much with battle and in theology dealt much with hell. It is full of *danger*, like a boy's book: it is at an immortal crisis. There is a great deal of real similarity between popular fiction and the religion of the western people. If you say that popular fiction is vulgar and tawdry, you only say what the dreary and well-informed say also about the images in the Catholic churches. Life (according to the faith) is very like a serial story in a magazine: life ends with the promise (or menace) "to be continued in our next." Also, with a noble vulgarity, life imitates the serial and leaves off at the exciting moment. For death is distinctly an exciting moment.

But the point is that a story is exciting because it has in it so strong an element of will, of what theology calls free will. You cannot finish a sum how you like. But you can finish a story how you like. When somebody discovered the Differential Calculus there was only one Differential Calculus he could discover. But when Shakespeare killed Romeo he might have married him to Juliet's old nurse if he had felt inclined. And Christendom has excelled in the narrative romance exactly because it has insisted on the theological free will. It is a large matter and too much to one side of the road to be discussed adequately here; but this is the real objection to that torrent of modern talk about treating crime as disease, about making a prison merely a hygienic environment like a hospital, of healing sin by slow scientific methods. The fallacy of the whole thing is that evil is a matter of active choice whereas disease is not. If you say that you are going to cure a profligate as you cure an asthmatic, my cheap and obvious answer is, "Produce the people who want to be asthmatics as many people want to be profligates." A man may lie still and be cured of a malady. But he must not lie still if he wants to be cured of a sin; on the contrary, he must get up and jump about violently. The whole point indeed is perfectly expressed in the very word which we use for a man in hospital; "patient" is in the passive mood; "sinner" is in the active. If a man is to be saved from influenza, he may be a patient. But if he is to be saved from forging, he must be not a patient but an *impatient*. He must be personally impatient with forgery. All moral reform must start in the active not the passive will.

Here again we reach the same substantial conclusion. In so far as we desire the definite reconstructions and the dangerous revolutions which have distinguished European civilization, we shall not discourage the thought of possible ruin; we shall rather encourage it. If we want, like the Eastern saints, merely to contemplate how right things are, of course we shall only say that they must go right. But if we particularly want to *make* them go right, we must insist that they may go wrong.

Lastly, this truth is yet again true in the case of the common modern attempts to diminish or to explain away the divinity of Christ. The thing may be true or not; that I shall deal with before I end. But if the divinity is true it is certainly terribly revolutionary. That a good man may have his back to the wall is no more than we knew already; but that God could have His back to the wall is a boast for all insurgents for ever. Christianity is the only religion on earth that has felt that omnipotence made God incomplete. Christianity alone has felt that God, to be wholly God, must have been a rebel as well as a king. Alone of all creeds, Christianity has added courage to the virtues of the Creator. For the only courage worth calling courage must necessarily mean that the soul passes a breaking point—and does not break. In this indeed I approach a matter more dark and awful than it is easy to discuss; and I apologise in advance if any of my phrases fall wrong or seem irreverent touching a matter which the greatest saints and thinkers have justly feared to approach. But in that terrific tale of the Passion there is a distinct emotional suggestion that the author of all things (in some unthinkable way) went not only through agony, but through doubt. It is written, "Thou shalt not tempt the Lord thy God." No; but the Lord thy God may tempt Himself; and it seems as if this was what happened in Gethsemane. In a garden Satan tempted man: and in a garden God tempted God. He passed in some superhuman manner through our human horror of pessimism. When the world shook and the sun was wiped out of heaven, it was not at the crucifixion, but at the cry from the cross: the cry which confessed that God was forsaken of God. And now let the revolutionists choose a creed from all the creeds and a god from all the gods of the world, carefully weighing all the gods of inevitable recurrence and of unalterable power. They will not find another god who has himself been in revolt. Nay (the matter grows too difficult for human speech), but let the atheists themselves choose a god. They will find only one divinity who ever uttered their isolation; only one religion in which God seemed for an instant to be an atheist.

These can be called the essentials of the old orthodoxy, of which the chief merit is that it is the natural fountain of revolution and reform; and of which the chief defect is that it is obviously only an abstract assertion. Its main advantage is that it is the most adventurous and manly of all theologies. Its chief disadvantage is simply that it is a theology. It can always be urged against it that it is in its nature arbitrary and in the air. But it is not so high in the air but that great archers spend their whole lives in shooting arrows at it — yes, and their last arrows; there are men who will ruin themselves and ruin their civilization if they may ruin also this old fantastic tale. This is the last and most astounding fact about this faith; that its enemies will use any weapon against it, the swords that cut their own fingers, and the firebrands that burn their own homes. Men who begin to fight the Church for the sake of freedom and humanity end by flinging away freedom and humanity if only they may fight the Church. This is no exaggeration; I could fill a book with the instances of it. Mr. Blatchford set out, as an ordinary Bible-smasher, to prove that Adam was guiltless of sin against God; in manoeuvring so as to maintain this he admitted, as a mere side issue, that all the tyrants, from Nero to King Leopold,[63] were guiltless of any sin against humanity. I know a man who has such a passion for proving that he will have no personal existence after death that he falls back on the position that he has no personal existence now. He invokes Buddhism and says that all souls fade into each other; in order to prove that he cannot go to heaven he proves that he cannot go to Hartlepool.[64] I have known people who protested against religious education with arguments against any education, saying that the child's mind must grow freely or that the old must not teach the young. I have known people who showed that there could be no divine judgment by showing that there can be no human judgment, even for practical purposes. They burned their own corn to set fire to the church; they smashed their own tools to smash it; any stick was good enough to beat it with, though it were the last stick of their own dismembered furniture. We do not admire, we hardly excuse, the fanatic who wrecks this world for love of the other. But what are we to say of the fanatic who wrecks this world out of hatred of the other? He sacrifices the very existence of humanity to the non-existence of God. He offers his victims not to the altar, but

[63] Leopold II (1835–1909), King of the Belgians, who formed a company to exploit the region of the Congo in 1876. A commission of enquiry in 1904 confirmed rumors of barbarous treatment of the natives.

[64] A seaport and resort on the North Sea in the County of Durham.

merely to assert the idleness of the altar and the emptiness of the throne. He is ready to ruin even that primary ethic by which all things live, for his strange and eternal vengeance upon some one who never lived at all.

And yet the thing hangs in the heavens unhurt. Its opponents only succeed in destroying all that they themselves justly hold dear. They do not destroy orthodoxy; they only destroy political and common courage sense. They do not prove that Adam was not responsible to God; how could they prove it? They only prove (from their premises) that the Czar is not responsible to Russia. They do not prove that Adam should not have been punished by God; they only prove that the nearest sweater should not be punished by men. With their oriental doubts about personality they do not make certain that we shall have no personal life hereafter; they only make certain that we shall not have a very jolly or complete one here. With their paralysing hints of all conclusions coming out wrong they do not tear the book of the Recording Angel; they only make it a little harder to keep the books of Marshall & Snelgrove.[65] Not only is the faith the mother of all worldly energies, but its foes are the fathers of all worldly confusion. The secularists have not wrecked divine things; but the secularists have wrecked secular things, if that is any comfort to them. The Titans did not scale heaven; but they laid waste the world.

[65] A large London department store.

IX

AUTHORITY AND THE ADVENTURER

The last chapter has been concerned with the contention that orthodoxy is not only (as is often urged) the only safe guardian of morality or order, but is also the only logical guardian of liberty, innovation and advance. If we wish to pull down the prosperous oppressor we cannot do it with the new doctrine of human perfectibility; we can do it with the old doctrine of Original Sin. If we want to uproot inherent cruelties or lift up lost populations we cannot do it with the scientific theory that matter precedes mind; we can do it with the supernatural theory that mind precedes matter. If we wish specially to awaken people to social vigilance and tireless pursuit of practise, we cannot help it much by insisting on the Immanent God and the Inner Light: for these are at best reasons for contentment; we can help it much by insisting on the transcendent God and the flying and escaping gleam; for that means divine discontent. If we wish particularly to assert the idea of a generous balance against that of a dreadful autocracy we shall instinctively be Trinitarian rather than Unitarian. If we desire European civilization to be a raid and a rescue, we shall insist rather that souls are in real peril than that their peril is ultimately unreal. And if we wish to exalt the outcast and the crucified, we shall rather wish to think that a veritable God was crucified, rather than a mere sage or hero. Above all, if we wish to protect the poor we shall be in favour of fixed rules and clear dogmas. The *rules* of a club are occasionally in favour of the poor member. The drift of a club is always in favour of the rich one.

And now we come to the crucial question which truly concludes the whole matter. A reasonable agnostic, if he has happened to agree with me so far, may justly turn round and say, "You have found a practical philosophy in the doctrine of the Fall; very well. You have found a side of democracy now dangerously neglected wisely asserted in Original Sin; all right. You have found a truth in the doctrine of hell; I congratulate you. You are convinced that worshippers of a personal God look outwards and are progressive; I congratulate them. But even supposing that those doctrines do include those truths, why cannot you take the truths and leave the doctrines? Granted that all modern society is trusting the rich too much because it does not allow for human weakness; granted that orthodox ages have had a great advantage because (believing in the Fall) they did allow for human weakness, why cannot you simply allow for human weakness without believing in the Fall? If you have discovered that the idea of damnation represents a healthy idea of danger, why can you not simply take the idea of danger and leave the idea of damnation? If you see clearly the kernel of common sense in the nut of Christian orthodoxy, why cannot you simply take the kernel and leave the nut? Why cannot you (to use that cant phrase of the newspapers which I, as a highly scholarly agnostic, am a little ashamed of using), why cannot you simply take what is good in Christianity, what you can define as valuable, what you can comprehend, and leave all the rest, all the absolute dogmas that are in their nature incomprehensible?" This is the real question; this is the last question; and it is a pleasure to try to answer it.

The first answer is simply to say that I am a rationalist. I like to have some intellectual justification for my intuitions. If I am treating man as a fallen being it is an intellectual convenience to me to believe that he fell; and I find, for some odd psychological reason, that I can deal better with a man's exercise of free will if I believe that he has got it. But I am in this matter yet more definitely a rationalist. I do not propose to turn this book into one of ordinary Christian apologetics; I should be glad to meet at any other time the enemies of Christianity in that more obvious arena. Here I am only giving an account of my own growth in spiritual certainty. But I may pause to remark that the more I saw of the merely abstract arguments against the Christian cosmology the less I thought of them. I mean that having found the moral atmosphere of the Incarnation to be common sense, I then looked at the established intellectual arguments against the Incarnation and found them to be common nonsense. In case the argument should be thought to suffer from the absence of the ordinary apologetic I will here very briefly summarise my own arguments and conclusions on the purely objective or scientific truth of the matter.

If I am asked, as a purely intellectual question, why I believe in Christianity, I can only answer, "For the same reason that an intelligent agnostic disbelieves in Christianity." I believe in it quite rationally upon the evidence. But the evidence in my case, as in that of the intelligent agnostic, is not really in this or that alleged demonstration; it is in an enormous accumulation of small but unanimous facts. The secularist is not to be blamed because his objections to Christianity are miscellaneous and even scrappy; it is precisely such scrappy evidence that does convince the mind. I mean that a man may well be less convinced of a philosophy from four books, than from one book, one battle, one landscape, and one old friend. The very fact that the things are of different kinds increases the importance of the fact that they all point to one conclusion. Now, the non-Christianity of the average educated man to-day is almost always, to do him justice, made up of these loose but living experiences. I can only say that my evidences for Christianity are of the same vivid but varied kind as his evidences against it. For when I look at these various anti-Christian truths, I simply discover that none of them are true. I discover that the true tide and force of all the facts flows the other way. Let us take cases. Many a sensible modern man must have abandoned Christianity under the pressure of three such converging convictions as these: first, that men, with their shape, structure, and sexuality, are, after all, very much like beasts, a mere variety of the animal kingdom; second, that primeval religion arose in ignorance and fear; third, that priests have blighted societies with bitterness and gloom. Those three anti-Christian arguments are very different; but they are all quite logical and legitimate; and they all converge. The only objection to them (I discover) is that they are all untrue. If you leave off looking at books about beasts and men, if you begin to look at beasts and men then (if you have any humour or imagination, any sense of the frantic or the farcical) you will observe that the startling thing is not how like man is to the brutes, but how unlike he is. It is the monstrous scale of his divergence that requires an explanation. That man and brute are like is, in a sense, a truism; but that being so like they should then be so insanely unlike, that is the shock and the enigma. That an ape has hands is far less interesting to the philosopher than the fact that having hands he does next to nothing with them; does not play knuckle-bones or the violin; does not carve marble or carve mutton. People talk of barbaric architecture and debased art. But elephants do not build colossal temples of ivory even in a rococo style; camels do not paint even bad pictures, though equipped with the material of many camel's-hair brushes. Certain modern dreamers say that ants and bees have a society superior to ours. They have, indeed, a civilization; but that very truth only reminds us that it is an inferior civilization. Who ever found an ant-hill decorated with the statues of celebrated ants? Who has seen a bee-hive carved with the images of gorgeous queens of old? No; the chasm between man and other creatures may have a natural explanation, but it is a chasm. We talk of wild animals; but man is the only wild animal. It is man that has broken out. All other animals are tame animals; following the rugged respectability of the tribe or type. All other animals are domestic animals; man alone is ever undomestic, either as a profligate or a monk. So that this first superficial reason for materialism is, if anything, a reason for its opposite; it is exactly where biology leaves off that all religion begins.

It would be the same if I examined the second of the three chance rationalist arguments; the argument that all that we call divine began in some darkness and terror. When I did attempt to examine the foundations of this modern idea I simply found that there were none. Science knows nothing whatever about pre-historic man; for the excellent reason that he is pre-historic. A few professors choose to conjecture that such things as human sacrifice were once innocent and general and that they gradually dwindled; but there is no direct evidence of it, and the small amount of indirect evidence is very much the other way. In the earliest legends we have, such as the tales of Isaac and of Iphigenia, human sacrifice is not introduced as something old, but rather as something new; as a strange and frightful exception darkly demanded by the gods. History says nothing; and legends all say that the earth was kinder in its earliest time. There is no tradition of progress; but the whole human race has a tradition of the Fall. Amusingly enough, indeed, the very dissemination of this idea is used against its authenticity. Learned men literally say that this pre-historic calamity cannot be true because every race of mankind remembers it. I cannot keep pace with these paradoxes.

And if we took the third chance instance, it would be the same; the view that priests darken and embitter the world. I look at the world and simply discover that they don't. Those countries in Europe which are still influenced by priests, are exactly the countries where there is still singing and dancing and coloured dresses and art in the open-air. Catholic doctrine and discipline may be walls; but they are the walls of a playground. Christianity is the only frame which has preserved the pleasure of Paganism. We might fancy some children playing on the flat grassy top of some tall island in the sea. So long as there was a wall round the cliff's edge they could fling themselves into every frantic game and make the place the noisiest of nurseries. But the walls were knocked down, leaving the naked peril of the precipice. They did not fall over; but when their friends returned to them they were all huddled in terror in the centre of the island; and their song had ceased.

Thus these three facts of experience, such facts as go to make an agnostic, are, in this view, turned totally round. I am left saying, "Give me an explanation, first, of the towering eccentricity of man among the brutes; second, of the vast human tradition of some ancient happiness; third, of the partial perpetuation of such pagan joy in the countries of the Catholic Church." One explanation, at any rate, covers all three: the theory that twice was the natural order interrupted by some explosion or revelation such as people now call "psychic." Once Heaven came upon the earth with a power or seal called the image of God, whereby man took command of Nature; and once again (when in empire after empire men had been found wanting) Heaven came to save mankind in the awful shape of a man. This would explain why the mass of men always look backwards; and why the only corner where they in any sense look forwards is the little continent where Christ has His Church. I know it will be said that Japan has become progressive. But how can this be an answer when even in saying "Japan has become progressive," we really only mean, "Japan has become European"? But I wish here not so much to insist on my own explanation as to insist on my original remark. I agree with the ordinary unbelieving man in the street in being guided by three or four odd facts all pointing to something; only when I came to look at the facts I always found they pointed to something else.

I have given an imaginary triad of such ordinary anti-Christian arguments; if that be too narrow a basis I will give on the spur of the moment another. These are the kind of thoughts which in combination create the impression that Christianity is something weak and diseased. First, for instance, that Jesus was a gentle creature, sheepish and unworldly, a mere ineffectual appeal to the world; second, that Christianity arose and flourished in the dark ages of ignorance, and that to these the Church would drag us back; third, that the people still strongly religious or (if you will) superstitious — such people as the Irish — are weak, unpractical, and behind the times. I only mention these ideas to affirm the same thing: that when I looked into them independently I found, not that the conclusions were unphilosophical, but simply that the facts were not facts. Instead of looking at books and pictures about the New Testament I looked at the New Testament. There I found an account, not in the least of a person with his hair parted in the middle or his hands clasped in appeal, but of an extraordinary being with lips of thunder and acts of lurid decision, flinging down tables, casting out devils, passing with the wild secrecy of the wind from mountain isolation to a sort of dreadful demagogy; a being who often acted like an angry god — and always like a god. Christ had even a literary style of his own, not to be found, I think, elsewhere; it consists of an almost furious use of the *a fortiori*. His "how much more" is piled one upon another like castle upon castle in the clouds. The diction used *about* Christ has been, and perhaps wisely, sweet and submissive. But the diction used by Christ is quite curiously gigantesque; it is full of camels leaping through needles and mountains hurled into the sea. Morally it is equally terrific; he called himself a sword of slaughter, and told men to buy swords if they sold their coats for them. That he used other even wilder words on the side of non-resistance greatly increases the mystery; but it also, if anything, rather increases the violence. We cannot even explain it by calling such a being insane; for insanity is usually along one consistent channel. The maniac is generally a mono-maniac. Here we must remember the difficult definition of Christi-anity already given; Christianity is a superhuman paradox whereby two opposite passions may blaze beside each other. The one explana-tion of the Gospel language that does explain it, is that it is the sur-vey of one who from some supernatural height beholds some more startling synthesis.

I take in order the next instance offered: the idea that Christianity belongs to the Dark Ages. Here I did not satisfy myself with reading modern generalisations; I read a little history. And in history I found that Christianity, so far from belonging to the Dark Ages, was the one path across the Dark Ages that was not dark. It was the shining bridge connecting two shining civilizations. If any one says that the faith arose in ignorance and savagery the answer is simple: it didn't. It arose in the Mediterranean civilization in the full summer of the Roman Empire. The world was swarming with sceptics, and pan-theism was as plain as the sun, when Constantine nailed the cross to the mast. It is perfectly true that afterwards the ship sank; but it is far more extraordinary that the ship came up again: repainted and glittering, with the cross still at the top. This is the amazing thing the religion did: it turned a sunken ship into a submarine. The ark lived under the load of waters; after being buried under the débris of dynasties and clans, we arose and remembered Rome. If our faith had been a mere fad of the fading empire, fad would have followed fad in the twilight, and if the civilization ever re-emerged (and many such have never re-emerged) it would have been under some new bar-baric flag. But the Christian Church was the last life of the old society and was also the first life of the new. She took the people who were forgetting how to make an arch and she taught them to invent the Gothic arch. In a word, the most absurd thing that could be said of the Church is the thing we have all heard said of it. How can we say that the Church wishes to bring us back into the Dark Ages? The Church was the only thing that ever brought us out of them.

I added in this second trinity of objections an idle instance taken from those who feel such people as the Irish to be weakened or made stagnant by superstition. I only added it because this is a peculiar case of a statement of fact that turns out to be a statement of falsehood. It is constantly said of the Irish that they are impractical. But if we refrain for a moment from looking at what is said about them and look at what is *done* about them, we shall see that the Irish are not only practical, but quite painfully successful. The poverty of their country, the minority of their members are simply the conditions under which they were asked to work; but no other group in the British Empire has done so much with such conditions. The Nationalists were the only minority that ever succeeded in twisting the whole British Parliament sharply out of its path. The Irish peasants are the only poor men in these islands who have forced their masters to disgorge. These people, whom we call priest-ridden, are the only Britons who will not be squire-ridden. And when I came to look at the actual Irish character, the case was the same. Irishmen are best at the specially *hard* professions — the trades of iron, the lawyer, and the soldier. In all these cases, therefore, I came back to the same conclusion: the sceptic was quite right to go by the facts, only he had not looked at the facts. The sceptic is too credulous; he believes in newspapers or even in encyclopaedias. Again the three questions left me with three very antagonistic questions. The average sceptic wanted to know how I explained the namby-pamby note in the Gospel, the connection of the creed with mediaeval darkness and the political impracticability of the Celtic Christians. But I wanted to ask, and to ask with an earnestness amounting to urgency, "What is this incomparable energy which appears first in one walking the earth like a living judgment and this energy which can die with a dying civilization and yet force it to a resurrection from the dead; this energy which last of all can inflame a bankrupt peasantry with so fixed a faith in justice that they get what they ask, while others go empty away; so that the most helpless island of the Empire can actually help itself?"

There is an answer: it is an answer to say that the energy is truly from outside the world; that it is psychic, or at least one of the results of a real psychical disturbance. The highest gratitude and respect are due to the great human civilizations such as the old Egyptian or the existing Chinese. Nevertheless it is no injustice for them to say that only modern Europe has exhibited incessantly a power of self-renewal recurring often at the shortest intervals and descending to the smallest facts of building or costume. All other societies die finally and with dignity. We die daily. We are always being born again with almost indecent obstetrics. It is hardly an exaggeration to say that there is in historic Christendom a sort of unnatural life: it could be explained as a supernatural life. It could be explained as an awful galvanic life working in what would have been a corpse. For our civilization *ought* to have died, by all parallels, by all sociological probability, in the Ragnorak[66] of the end of Rome. That is the weird inspiration of our estate: you and I have no business to be here at all. We are all *revenants*; all living Christians are dead pagans walking about. Just as Europe was about to be gathered in silence to Assyria and Babylon, something entered into its body. And Europe has had a strange life— it is not too much to say that it has had the *jumps*—ever since.

I have dealt at length with such typical triads of doubt in order to convey the main contention—that my own case for Christianity is rational; but it is not simple. It is an accumulation of varied facts, like the attitude of the ordinary agnostic. But the ordinary agnostic has got his facts all wrong. He is a non-believer for a multitude of reasons; but they are untrue reasons. He doubts because the Middle Ages were barbaric, but they weren't; because Darwinism is demonstrated, but it isn't; because miracles do not happen, but they do; because monks were lazy, but they were very industrious; because nuns are unhappy, but they are particularly cheerful; because Christian art was sad and pale, but it was picked out in peculiarly bright colours and gay with gold; because modern science is moving away from the supernatural, but it isn't, it is moving towards the supernatural with the rapidity of a railway train.

But among these million facts all flowing one way there is, of course, one question sufficiently solid and separate to be treated briefly, but by itself; I mean the objective occurrence of the supernatural.

[66] In Scandinavian mythology, the day of the great battle between the gods and the powers of evil, when both are destroyed and the old order gives way to the new.

In another chapter I have indicated the fallacy of the ordinary supposition that the world must be impersonal because it is orderly. A person is just as likely to desire an orderly thing as a disorderly thing. But my own positive conviction that personal creation is more conceivable than material fate, is, I admit, in a sense, undiscussable. I will not call it a faith or an intuition, for those words are mixed up with mere emotion, it is strictly an intellectual conviction; but it is a *primary* intellectual conviction like the certainty of self or the good of living. Any one who likes, therefore, may call my belief in God merely mystical; the phrase is not worth fighting about. But my belief that miracles have happened in human history is not a mystical belief at all; I believe in them upon human evidences as I do in the discovery of America. Upon this point there is a simple logical fact that only requires to be stated and cleared up. Somehow or other an extraordinary idea has arisen that the disbelievers in miracles consider them coldly and fairly, while believers in miracles accept them only in connection with some dogma. The fact is quite the other way. The believers in miracles accept them (rightly or wrongly) because they have evidence for them. The disbelievers in miracles deny them (rightly or wrongly) because they have a doctrine against them. The open, obvious, democratic thing is to believe an old apple-woman when she bears testimony to a miracle, just as you believe an old apple-woman when she bears testimony to a murder. The plain, popular course is to trust the peasant's word about the ghost exactly as far as you trust the peasant's word about the landlord. Being a peasant he will probably have a great deal of healthy agnosticism about both. Still you could fill the British Museum with evidence uttered by the peasant, and given in favour of the ghost. If it comes to human testimony there is a choking cataract of human testimony in favour of the supernatural. If you reject it, you can only mean one of two things. You reject the peasant's story about the ghost either because the man is a peasant or because the story is a ghost story. That is, you either deny the main principle of democracy, or you affirm the main principle of materialism—the abstract impossibility of miracle. You have a perfect right to do so; but in that case you are the dogmatist. It is we Christians who accept all actual evidence—it is you rationalists who refuse actual evidence being constrained to do so by your creed. But I am not constrained by any creed in the matter, and looking impartially into certain miracles of mediaeval and modern times, I have come to the conclusion that they occurred. All argument against these plain facts is always argument in a circle. If I say, "Mediaeval documents attest certain miracles as much as they attest certain battles," they answer, "But mediaevals were superstitious"; if I want to know in what they were superstitious, the only ultimate answer is that they believed in the miracles. If I say "a peasant saw a ghost," I am told, "But peasants are so credulous." If I ask, "Why credulous?" the only answer is—that they see ghosts. Iceland is impossible because only stupid sailors have seen it; and the sailors are only stupid because they say they have seen Iceland. It is only fair to add that there is another argument that the unbeliever may rationally use against miracles, though he himself generally forgets to use it.

He may say that there has been in many miraculous stories a notion of spiritual preparation and acceptance: in short, that the miracle could only come to him who believed in it. It may be so, and if it is so how are we to test it? If we are inquiring whether certain results follow faith, it is useless to repeat wearily that (if they happen) they do follow faith. If faith is one of the conditions, those without faith have a most healthy right to laugh. But they have no right to judge. Being a believer may be, if you like, as bad as being drunk; still if we were extracting psychological facts from drunkards, it would be absurd to be always taunting them with having been drunk. Suppose we were investigating whether angry men really saw a red mist before their eyes. Suppose sixty excellent householders swore that when angry they had seen this crimson cloud: surely it would be absurd to answer "Oh, but you admit you were angry at the time." They might reasonably rejoin (in a stentorian chorus), "How the blazes could we discover, without being angry, whether angry people see red?" So the saints and ascetics might rationally reply, "Suppose that the question is whether believers can see visions—even then, if you are interested in visions it is no point to object to believers." You are still arguing in a circle—in that old mad circle with which this book began.

The question of whether miracles ever occur is a question of common sense and of ordinary historical imagination: not of any final physical experiment. One may here surely dismiss that quite brainless piece of pedantry which talks about the need for "scientific conditions" in connection with alleged spiritual phenomena. If we are asking whether a dead soul can communicate with a living it is ludicrous to insist that it shall be under conditions in which no two living souls in their senses would seriously communicate with each other. The fact that ghosts prefer darkness no more disproves the existence of ghosts than the fact that lovers prefer darkness disproves the existence of love. If you choose to say, "I will believe that Miss Brown called her *fiancé* a periwinkle or any other endearing term, if she will repeat the word before seventeen psychologists," then I shall reply, "Very well, if those are your conditions, you will never get the truth, for she certainly will not say it." It is just as unscientific as it is unphilosophical to be surprised that in an unsympathetic atmosphere certain extraordinary sympathies do not arise. It is as if I said that I could not tell if there was a fog because the air was not clear enough; or as if I insisted on perfect sunlight in order to see a solar eclipse.

As a common-sense conclusion, such as those to which we come about sex or about midnight (well knowing that many details must in their own nature be concealed) I conclude that miracles do happen. I am forced to it by a conspiracy of facts: the fact that the men who encounter elves or angels are not the mystics and the morbid dreamers, but fishermen, farmers, and all men at once coarse and cautious; the fact that we all know men who testify to spiritualistic incidents but are not spiritualists; the fact that science itself admits such things more and more every day. Science will even admit the Ascension if you call it Levitation, and will very likely admit the Resurrection when it has thought of another word for it. I suggest the Regalvanisation. But the strongest of all is the dilemma above mentioned, that these supernatural things are never denied except on the basis either of anti-democracy or of materialist dogmatism—I may say materialist mysticism. The sceptic always takes one of the two positions; either an ordinary man need not be believed, or an extraordinary event must not be believed. For I hope we may dismiss the argument against wonders attempted in the mere recapitulation of frauds, of swindling mediums or trick miracles. That is not an argument at all, good or bad. A false ghost disproves the reality of ghosts exactly as much as a forged banknote disproves the existence of the Bank of England—if anything, it proves its existence.

Given this conviction that the spiritual phenomena do occur (my evidence for which is complex but rational), we then collide with one of the worst mental evils of the age. The greatest disaster of the nineteenth century was this: that men began to use the word "spiritual" as the same as the word "good." They thought that to grow in refinement and uncorporeality was to grow in virtue. When scientific evolution was announced, some feared that it would encourage mere animality. It did worse: it encouraged mere spirituality. It taught men to think that so long as they were passing from the ape they were going to the angel. But you can pass from the ape and go to the devil. A man of genius, very typical of that time of bewilderment, expressed it perfectly. Benjamin Disraeli was right when he said he was on the side of the angels.[67] He was indeed; he was on the side of the fallen angels. He was not on the side of any mere appetite or animal brutality; but he was on the side of all the imperialism of the princes of the abyss; he was on the side of arrogance and mystery, and contempt of all obvious good. Between this sunken pride and the towering humilities of heaven there are, one must suppose, spirits of shapes and sizes. Man, in encountering them, must make much the same mistakes that he makes in encountering any other varied types in any other distant continent. It must be hard at first to know who is supreme and who is subordinate. If a shade arose from the under world, and stared at Piccadilly, that shade would not quite understand the idea of an ordinary closed carriage. He would suppose that the coachman on the box was a triumphant conqueror, dragging behind him a kicking and imprisoned captive. So, if we see spiritual facts for the first time, we may mistake who is uppermost. It is not enough to find the gods; they are obvious; we must find God, the real chief of the gods. We

[67] Standing beside Bishop Wilberforce, in a famous debate on Darwin's *Origin of Species* in 1864, Disraeli summarized the argument thus: "The question is this—is man an ape or an angel? My lord, I am on the side of the angels."

must have a long historic experience in supernatural phenomena — in order to discover which are really natural. In this light I find the history of Christianity, and even of its Hebrew origins, quite practical and clear. It does not trouble me to be told that the Hebrew god was one among many. I know he was, without any research to tell me so. Jehovah and Baal looked equally important, just as the sun and the moon looked the same size. It is only slowly that we learn that the sun is immeasurably our master, and the small moon only our satellite. Believing that there is a world of spirits, I shall walk in it as I do in the world of men, looking for the thing that I like and think good. Just as I should seek in a desert for clean water, or toil at the North Pole to make a comfortable fire, so I shall search the land of void and vision until I find something fresh like water, and comforting like fire; until I find some place in eternity, where I am literally at home. And there is only one such place to be found.

I have now said enough to show (to any one to whom such an explanation is essential) that I have in the ordinary arena of apologetics, a ground of belief. In pure records of experiment (if these be taken democratically without contempt or favour) there is evidence first, that miracles happen, and second that the nobler miracles belong to our tradition. But I will not pretend that this curt discussion is my real reason for accepting Christianity instead of taking the moral good of Christianity as I should take it out of Confucianism.

I have another far more solid and central ground for submitting to it as a faith, instead of merely picking up hints from it as a scheme. And that is this: that the Christian Church in its practical relation to my soul is a living teacher, not a dead one. It not only certainly taught me yesterday, but will almost certainly teach me to-morrow. Once I saw suddenly the meaning of the shape of the cross; some day I may see suddenly the meaning of the shape of the mitre. One fine morning I saw why windows were pointed; some fine morning I may see why priests were shaven. Plato has told you a truth; but Plato is dead. Shakespeare has startled you with an image; but Shakespeare will not startle you with any more. But imagine what it would be to live with such men still living, to know that Plato might break out with an original lecture tomorrow, or that at any moment Shakespeare might shatter everything with a single song. The man who lives in contact with what he believes to be a living Church is a man always expecting to meet Plato and Shakespeare to-morrow at breakfast. He is always expecting to see some truth that he has never seen before. There is one only other parallel to this position; and that is the parallel of the life in which we all began. When your father told you, walking about the garden, that bees stung or that roses smelt sweet, you did not talk of taking the best out of his philosophy. When the bees stung you, you did not call it an entertaining coincidence. When the rose smelt sweet you did not say "My father is a rude, barbaric symbol, enshrining (perhaps unconsciously) the deep delicate truths that flowers smell." No: you believed your father, because you had found him to be a living fountain of facts, a thing that really knew more than you; a thing that would tell you truth to-morrow, as well as to-day. And if this was true of your father, it was even truer of your mother; at least it was true of mine, to whom this book is dedicated. Now, when society is in a rather futile fuss about the subjection of women, will no one say how much every man owes to the tyranny and privilege of women, to the fact that they alone rule education until education becomes futile: for a boy is only sent to be taught at school when it is too late to teach him anything. The real thing has been done already, and thank God it is nearly always done by women. Every man is womanised, merely by being born. They talk of the masculine woman; but every man is a feminised man. And if ever men walk to Westminster to protest against this female privilege, I shall not join their procession.

For I remember with certainty this fixed psychological fact; that the very time when I was most under a woman's authority, I was most full of flame and adventure. Exactly because when my mother said that ants bit they did bite, and because snow did come in winter (as she said); therefore the whole world was to me a fairyland of wonderful fulfilments, and it was like living in some Hebraic age, when prophecy after prophecy came true. I went out as a child into the garden, and it was a terrible place to me, precisely because I had a clue to it: if I had held no clue it would not have been terrible, but tame. A mere unmeaning wilderness is not even impressive. But the garden of childhood was fascinating, exactly because everything had a fixed meaning which could be found out in its turn. Inch by inch I might discover what was the object of the ugly shape called a rake; or form some shadowy conjecture as to why my parents kept a cat.

So, since I have accepted Christendom as a mother and not merely as a chance example, I have found Europe and the world once more like the little garden where I stared at the symbolic shapes of cat and rake; I look at everything with the old elvish ignorance and expectancy. This or that rite or doctrine may look as ugly and extraordinary as a rake; but I have found by experience that such things end somehow in grass and flowers. A clergyman may be apparently as useless as a cat, but he is also as fascinating, for there must be some strange reason for his existence. I give one instance out of a hundred; I have not myself any instinctive kinship with that enthusiasm for physical virginity, which has certainly been a note of historic Christianity. But when I look not at myself but at the world, I perceive that this enthusiasm is not only a note of Christianity, but a note of Paganism, a note of high human nature in many spheres. The Greeks felt virginity when they carved Artemis, the Romans when they robed the vestals, the worst and wildest of the great Elizabethan playwrights clung to the literal purity of a woman as to the central pillar of the world. Above all, the modern world (even while mocking sexual innocence) has flung itself into a generous idolatry of sexual innocence—the great modern worship of children. For any man who loves children will agree that their peculiar beauty is hurt by a hint of physical sex. With all this human experience, allied with the Christian authority, I simply conclude that I am wrong, and the church right; or rather that I am defective, while the church is universal. It takes all sorts to make a church; she does not ask me to be celibate. But the fact that I have no appreciation of the celibates, I accept like the fact that I have no ear for music. The best human experience is against me, as it is on the subject of Bach. Celibacy is one flower in my father's garden, of which I have not been told the sweet or terrible name. But I may be told it any day.

This, therefore, is, in conclusion, my reason for accepting the religion and not merely the scattered and secular truths out of the religion. I do it because the thing has not merely told this truth or that truth, but has revealed itself as a truth-telling thing. All other philosophies say the things that plainly seem to be true; only this philosophy has again and again said the thing that does not seem to be true, but is true. Alone of all creeds it is convincing where it is not attractive; it turns out to be right, like my father in the garden. Theosophists for instance will preach an obviously attractive idea like re-incarnation; but if we wait for its logical results, they are spiritual superciliousness and the cruelty of caste. For if a man is a beggar by his own pre-natal sins, people will tend to despise the beggar. But Christianity preaches an obviously unattractive idea, such as original sin; but when we wait for its results, they are pathos and brotherhood, and a thunder of laughter and pity; for only with original sin we can at once pity the beggar and distrust the king. Men of science offer us health, an obvious benefit; it is only afterwards that we discover that by health, they mean bodily slavery and spiritual tedium. Orthodoxy makes us jump by the sudden brink of hell; it is only afterwards that we realise that jumping was an athletic exercise highly beneficial to our health. It is only afterwards that we realise that this danger is the root of all drama and romance. The strongest argument for the divine grace is simply its ungraciousness. The unpopular parts of Christianity turn out when examined to be the very props of the people. The outer ring of Christianity is a rigid guard of ethical abnegations and professional priests; but inside that inhuman guard you will find the old human life dancing like children, and drinking wine like men; for Christianity is the only frame for pagan freedom. But in the modern philosophy the case is opposite; it is its outer ring that is obviously artistic and emancipated; its despair is within.

And its despair is this, that it does not really believe that there is any meaning in the universe; therefore it cannot hope to find any romance; its romances will have no plots. A man cannot expect any adventures in the land of anarchy. But a man can expect any number of adventures if he goes travelling in the land of authority. One can find no meanings in a jungle of scepticism; but the man will find more and more meanings who walks through a forest of doctrine and design. Here everything has a story tied to its tail, like the tools or pictures in my father's house; for it is my father's house. I end where I began — at the right end. I have entered at least the gate of all good philosophy. I have come into my second childhood.

But this larger and more adventurous Christian universe has one final mark difficult to express; yet as a conclusion of the whole matter I will attempt to express it. All the real argument about religion turns on the question of whether a man who was born upside down can tell when he comes right way up. The primary paradox of Christianity is that the ordinary condition of man is not his sane or sensible condition; that the normal itself is an abnormality. That is the inmost philosophy of the Fall. In Sir Oliver Lodge's interesting new Catechism,[68] the first two questions were: "What are you?" and "What, then, is the meaning of the Fall of Man?" I remember amusing myself by writing my own answers to the questions; but I soon found that they were very broken and agnostic answers. To the question, "What are you?" I could only answer, "God knows." And to the question, "What is meant by the Fall?" I could answer with complete sincerity, "That whatever I am, I am not myself." This is the prime paradox of our religion; something that we have never in any full sense known, is not only better than ourselves, but even more natural to us than ourselves. And there is really no test of this except the merely experimental one with which these pages began, the test of the padded cell and the open door. It is only since I have known orthodoxy that I have known mental emancipation. But, in conclusion, it has one special application to the ultimate idea of joy.

It is said that Paganism is a religion of joy and Christianity of sorrow; it would be just as easy to prove that Paganism is pure sorrow and Christianity pure joy. Such conflicts mean nothing and lead nowhere. Everything human must have in it both joy and sorrow; the only matter of interest is the manner in which the two things are balanced or divided. And the really interesting thing is this, that the pagan was (in the main) happier and happier as he approached the

[68] Lodge (1851–1940), a physicist who tried to reconcile religion and science, wrote *The Substance of Faith Allied with Science: A Catechism for Parents and Teachers* in 1907.

earth, but sadder and sadder as he approached the heavens. The gaiety of the best Paganism, as in the playfulness of Catullus or Theocritus, is, indeed, an eternal gaiety never to be forgotten by a grateful humanity. But it is all a gaiety about the facts of life, not about its origin. To the pagan the small things are as sweet as the small brooks breaking out of the mountain; but the broad things are as bitter as the sea. When the pagan looks at the very core of the cosmos he is struck cold. Behind the gods, who are merely despotic, sit the fates, who are deadly. Nay, the fates are worse than deadly; they are dead. And when rationalists say that the ancient world was more enlightened than the Christian, from their point of view they are right. For when they say "enlightened" they mean darkened with incurable despair. It is profoundly true that the ancient world was more modern than the Christian. The common bond is in the fact that ancients and moderns have both been miserable about existence, about everything, while mediaevals were happy about that at least. I freely grant that the pagans, like the moderns, were only miserable about everything—they were quite jolly about everything else. I concede that the Christians of the Middle Ages were only at peace about everything—they were at war about everything else. But if the question turn on the primary pivot of the cosmos, then there was more cosmic contentment in the narrow and bloody streets of Florence than in the theatre of Athens or the open garden of Epicurus. Giotto lived in a gloomier town than Euripides, but he lived in a gayer universe.

The mass of men have been forced to be gay about the little things, but sad about the big ones. Nevertheless (I offer my last dogma defiantly) it is not native to man to be so. Man is more himself, man is more manlike, when joy is the fundamental thing in him, and grief the superficial. Melancholy should be an innocent interlude, a tender and fugitive frame of mind; praise should be the permanent pulsation of the soul. Pessimism is at best an emotional half-holiday; joy is the uproarious labour by which all things live. Yet, according to the apparent estate of man as seen by the pagan or the agnostic, this primary need of human nature can never be fulfilled. Joy ought to be expansive; but for the agnostic it must be contracted, it must cling to one corner of the world. Grief ought to be a concentration; but for the agnostic its desolation is spread through an unthinkable eternity. This is what I call being born upside down. The sceptic may truly be said to be topsy-turvy; for his feet are dancing upwards in idle ecstacies, while his brain is in the abyss. To the modern man the heavens are actually below the earth. The explanation is simple; he is standing on his head; which is a very weak pedestal to stand on. But when he has found his feet again he knows it. Christianity satisfies suddenly and perfectly man's ancestral instinct for being the right way up; satisfies it supremely in this; that by its creed joy becomes something gigantic and sadness something special and small. The vault above us is not deaf because the universe is an idiot; the silence is not the heartless silence of an endless and aimless world. Rather the silence around us is a small and pitiful stillness like the prompt stillness in a sick-room. We are perhaps permitted tragedy as a sort of merciful comedy: because the frantic energy of divine things would knock us down like a drunken farce. We can take our own tears more lightly than we could take the tremendous levities of the angels. So we sit perhaps in a starry chamber of silence, while the laughter of the heavens is too loud for us to hear.

Joy, which was the small publicity of the pagan, is the gigantic secret of the Christian. And as I close this chaotic volume I open again the strange small book from which all Christianity came; and I am again haunted by a kind of confirmation. The tremendous figure which fills the Gospels towers in this respect, as in every other, above all the thinkers who ever thought themselves tall. His pathos was natural, almost casual. The Stoics, ancient and modern, were proud of concealing their tears. He never concealed His tears; He showed them plainly on His open face at any daily sight, such as the far sight of His native city. Yet He concealed something. Solemn supermen and imperial diplomatists are proud of restraining their anger. He never restrained His anger. He flung furniture down the front steps of the Temple, and asked men how they expected to escape the damnation of Hell. Yet He restrained something. I say it with reverence; there was in that shattering personality a thread that must be called shyness. There was something that He hid from all men when He went up a mountain to pray. There was something that He covered constantly by abrupt silence or impetuous isolation. There was some one thing that was too great for God to show us when He walked upon our earth; and I have sometimes fancied that it was His mirth.

THE BLATCHFORD
CONTROVERSIES

1904

FOREWORD

Chesterton's Articles in the *Clarion*

Chesterton's part in the *Clarion* controversy is summarized in the Foreword to this volume. There it is pointed out that he soon got into the dispute provoked by the attacks on Christianity by the *Clarion's* editor, Robert Blatchford, and that he kept up a running controversy with Blatchford for nearly two years. It is not surprising, then, that George Haw invited him to contribute to the series of replies to Blatchford that he edited for the *Clarion* in 1904. In fact he was given a position of special prominence; listing the remaining contributors on June 24, Haw wrote: "And then, finally, Mr. G. K. Chesterton will wind up the discussion in one or two articles."

Actually Chesterton wrote three, which appeared in consecutive weeks: "Christianity and Rationalism" on July 22, "We Are All Agnostics Until—" on July 29 and "Mr. Blatchford's Religion" on August 5. When a selection of the articles was published by Macmillan under the title *The Religious Doubts of Democracy*, Chesterton's second one was retitled "Why I Believe in Christianity" and his third divided into "Miracles and Modern Civilisation" and "The Eternal Heroism of the Slums". The division seems a logical one, and the articles are reprinted here as they appeared in the book rather than as they appeared in the newspaper. Haw's introduction is also reprinted, since it describes the circumstances in which these papers in defense of Christianity were published and stresses, as Chesterton does, Blatchford's magnanimity in opening the columns of his paper to his adversaries.

David Dooley

INTRODUCTION

These papers in defence of Christianity appeared in the *Clarion* under the following circumstances: —

My friend, Mr. Robert Blatchford, the editor, after setting out his objections to the Christian Faith in a series of articles, which have since been widely circulated in book form under the title of *God and My Neighbour*[1] invited me to edit the case for the defence. Mr. Blatchford told me he was prepared to give the other side a fair hearing in the *Clarion*. Feeling that as he had led the attack, it was not for him to marshal the forces of "his friends the enemy," as he good-naturedly called us, he appealed to me to do that. He suggested that I deal with all articles and letters on the Christian side sent to the *Clarion* office, restricting the writers to a discussion of the two points, What they believed and Why they believed?

I assented, on condition that the scope of the discussion be widened to enable me to invite people of various denominations whom I knew to deal with some of the main questions raised in *God and My Neighbour*. Mr. Blatchford readily agreed that it would be better to ask selected writers than to depend on casual contributors.

Our writers range from working-men Socialists to the son of a peer and the daughter of an archbishop. They include journalists, authors, schoolmasters; Anglican and Nonconformist ministers and college professors; and a member of a former Government: all of whom find a common agreement in the essential truths of Christianity.

Every week for six months Mr. Blatchford gave us three of the best columns in the *Clarion*. During the whole of that time neither he nor any member of his staff interfered with the conduct of our case. We had a free and fair field all the time.

Mr. Blatchford is nothing if not straightforward and sincere. Nor does he mind his opponents being equally straightforward and

[1] Clarion Press, 72, Fleet Street, 6*d*.

sincere. We have said straight things, but not hard things, about his anti-Christian attitude; and, as becomes our belief, naught has been set down in malice.

The editor of the *Clarion* hopes to reply to our defence; but for a time, at least, Mr. Blatchford assures me that he personally will let the matter rest.

Many people have been sorely perturbed at the spirited onset Mr. Blatchford makes at our Faith; but I think we all agree that by giving such a long and patient hearing in his own columns to the arguments in refutation of those in *God and My Neighbour*, Mr. Blatchford has revealed a rare magnanimity. My own opinion is exactly that expressed by Mr. G. K. Chesterton, who, in the first of the papers he contributes to this series, uses words which the churches would do well earnestly to weigh as a solemn warning:—

"In the whole of this controversy," says Mr. Chesterton, "I have felt the force of one thing, which has really hit practical Christianity; I think it is a good argument; I think it is a terrible argument. It is that this controversy is being conducted in a non-Christian paper. It certainly is a fair point scored against a religion that the people who seem to be most interested in it are those who believe it to be a fraud. I think, therefore, that Mr. Blatchford's magnanimity, like all magnanimity, is profoundly philosophical and wise."

George Haw

LONDON, *July*, 1904

I

CHRISTIANITY AND RATIONALISM

My friend, Mr. George Haw, has asked me to state, in one or two articles, my general belief on the subject of Christianity, to be inserted in the *Clarion*. I will not pretend to any particular reluctance to do so; but I ought not to do it without first of all offering to Mr. Blatchford our gratitude, and something which is better than gratitude, our congratulations, upon the very magnanimous action which he has taken in thus putting his paper into the hands of his religious opponents. In doing so he has scored, in a generous unconsciousness, a real point.

Most of the awful revelations of Christian evil and ignorance do not, I am afraid, affect me in quite so serious a manner as they ought to. When I hear that a German professor has found the four-hundredth accurate origin of protoplasm, I try in vain to feel excitement; when I read that savages paint their faces green to please the ghosts (or what not), I have no feeling beyond a vague pleasure and sympathy. Both the German professor and the green-faced savage seem to me to be doing the same thing — that is, falling under the influence of that starry impulse which leads men to take a vast deal of trouble about quite useless things.

But such things do not make much difference to my view of Christianity. In the whole of this controversy I have felt the force of one thing, which has really hit practical Christianity; I think it is a good argument; I think it is a terrible argument. It is that this controversy is being conducted in a non-Christian paper. It certainly is a fair point scored against a religion that the people who seem to be most interested in it are those who believe it to be a fraud. I think, therefore, that Mr. Blatchford's magnanimity, like all magnanimity, is profoundly philosophical and wise.

Nor do I blame him, as some have done, for having discussed it at great length; as the subject is the nature of the Universe, it is necessarily as large as the Universe, and as rich as the Universe, and, I may add, as amusing as the Universe.

373

In fact, I fancy there must be such a thing as Immortality, merely that Mr. Blatchford and I may have time to discuss whether it is true.

Before I give an outline of my view, there is one other thing to be said in which I cannot avoid the personal note. I have begun to realise that there are a good many people to whom my way of speaking about these things appears like an indication that I am flippant or imperfectly sincere. Since, as a matter of fact, I am more certain of myself in this affair than I am of the existence of the moon, this naturally causes me some considerable regret; but I think I see the naturalness of the mistake, and how it arose in people far removed from the Christian atmosphere. Christianity is itself so jolly a thing that it fills the possessor of it with a certain silly exuberance, which sad and high-minded Rationalists might reasonably mistake for mere buffoonery and blasphemy; just as their prototypes, the sad and high-minded Stoics of old Rome, did mistake the Christian joyousness for buffoonery and blasphemy.

This difference holds good everywhere, in the cold Pagan architecture and the grinning gargoyles of Christendom, in the preposterous motley of the Middle Ages and the dingy dress of this Rationalistic century. And if Mr. Blatchford wishes to know why we should be surprised if the Duke of Devonshire walked about with one leg red and the other yellow (as a nobleman might have done in the thirteenth century), I can obligingly inform him that it is because of the decay of our faith. Nowhere in history has there ever been any popular brightness and gaiety without religion.

The first of all the difficulties that I have in controverting Mr. Blatchford is simply this, that I shall be very largely going over his own ground. My favourite text-book of theology is *God and My Neighbour*, but I cannot repeat it in detail. If I gave each of my reasons for being a Christian, a vast number of them would be Mr. Blatchford's reasons for not being one.

For instance, Mr. Blatchford and his school point out that there are many myths parallel to the Christian story; that there were Pagan Christs, and Red Indian Incarnations, and Patagonian Crucifixions, for all I know or care. But does not Mr. Blatchford see the other side of this fact? If the Christian God really made the human race, would not the human race tend to rumours and perversions of the Christian God? If the centre of our life is a certain fact, would not people far from the centre have a muddled version of that fact? If we are so made that a Son of God must deliver us, is it odd that Patagonians should dream of a Son of God?

The Blatchfordian position really amounts to this — that because a certain thing has impressed millions of different people as likely or necessary, therefore it cannot be true. And then this bashful being, veiling his own talents, convicts the wretched G. K. C. of paradox! I like paradox, but I am not prepared to dance and dazzle to the extent of Nunquam, who points to humanity crying out to a thing, and pointing to it from immemorial ages, as a proof that it cannot be there.

The story of a Christ is very common in legend and literature. So is the story of two lovers parted by Fate. So is the story of two friends killing each other for a woman. But will it seriously be maintained that, because these two stories are common as legends, therefore no two friends were ever separated by love or no two lovers by circumstances? It is tolerably plain, surely, that these two stories are common because the situation is an intensely probable and human one, because our nature is so built as to make them almost inevitable.

Why should it not be that our nature is so built as to make certain spiritual events inevitable? In any case, it is clearly ridiculous to attempt to disprove Christianity by the number and variety of Pagan Christs. You might as well take the number and variety of ideal schemes of society, from Plato's *Republic* to Morris' *News from Nowhere,* from More's *Utopia* to Blatchford's *Merrie England,* and then try and prove from them that mankind cannot ever reach a better social condition. If anything, of course, they prove the opposite; they suggest a human tendency towards a better condition.

Thus, in this first instance, when learned sceptics come to me and say, "Are you aware that the Kaffirs have a story of Incarnation?" I should reply: "Speaking as an unlearned person, I don't know. But speaking as a Christian, I should be very much astonished if they hadn't."

Take a second instance. The Secularist says that Christianity has been a gloomy and ascetic thing, and points to the procession of austere or ferocious saints who have given up home and happiness and macerated health and sex. But it never seems to occur to him that the very oddity and completeness of these men's surrender make it look very much as if there were really something actual and solid in the thing for which they sold themselves. They gave up all pleasures for one pleasure of spiritual ecstasy. They may have been mad; but it looks as if there really were such a pleasure. They gave up all human experiences for the sake of one superhuman experience. They may have been wicked, but it looks as if there were such an experience.

It is perfectly tenable that this experience is as dangerous and selfish a thing as drink. A man who goes ragged and homeless in order to see visions may be as repellent and immoral as a man who goes ragged and homeless in order to drink brandy. That is a quite reasonable position. But what is manifestly not a reasonable position, what would be, in fact, not far from being an insane position, would be to say that the raggedness of the man, and the homelessness of the man, and the stupefied degradation of the man proved that there was no such thing as brandy.

That is precisely what the Secularist tries to say. He tries to prove that there is no such thing as supernatural experience by pointing at the people who have given up everything for it. He tries to prove that there is no such thing by proving that there are people who live on nothing else.

Again I may submissively ask: "Whose is the paradox?" The frantic severity of these men may, of course, show that they were eccentric people who loved unhappiness for its own sake. But it seems more in accordance with commonsense to suppose that they had really found the secret of some actual power or experience which was, like wine, a terrible consolation and a lonely joy.

Thus, then, in the second instance, when the learned sceptic says to me: "Christian saints gave up love and liberty for this one rapture of Christianity," I should reply: "It was very wrong of them. But, having some notion of the rapture of Christianity, I should have been surprised if they hadn't."

Take a third instance. The Secularist says that Christianity produced tumult and cruelty. He seems to suppose that this proves it to be bad. But it might prove it to be very good. For men commit crimes not only for bad things, far more often for good things. For no bad things can be desired quite so passionately and persistently as good things can be desired, and only very exceptional men desire very bad and unnatural things.

Most crime is committed because, owing to some peculiar complication, very beautiful or necessary things are in some danger. For instance, if we wanted to abolish thieving and swindling at one blow, the best thing to do would be to abolish babies. Babies, the most beautiful things on earth, have been the excuse and origin of almost all the business brutality and financial infamy on earth.

If we could abolish monogamic or romantic love, again, the country would be dotted with Maiden Assizes. And if anywhere in history masses of common and kindly men become cruel, it almost certainly does not mean that they are serving something in itself tyrannical (for why should they?). It almost certainly does mean that something that they rightly value is in peril, such as the food of their children, the chastity of their women, or the independence of their country. And when something is set before them that is not only enormously valuable, but also quite new, the sudden vision, the chance of winning it, the chance of losing it, drive them mad. It has the same effect in the moral world that the finding of gold has in the economic world. It upsets values, and creates a kind of cruel rush.

We need not go far for instances quite apart from the instances of religion. When the modern doctrines of brotherhood and liberality were preached in France in the eighteenth century the time was ripe for them, the educated classes everywhere had been growing towards them, the world to a very considerable extent welcomed them. And yet all that preparation and openness were unable to prevent the burst of anger and agony which greets anything good. And if the slow and polite preaching of rational fraternity in a rational age ended in the massacres of September, what an *a fortiori* is here! What would be likely to be the effect of the sudden dropping into a dreadfully evil century of a dreadfully perfect truth? What would happen if a world baser than the world of Sade were confronted with a gospel purer than the gospel of Rousseau?

The mere flinging of the polished pebble of Republican Idealism into the artificial lake of eighteenth century Europe produced a splash that seemed to splash the heavens, and a storm that drowned ten thousand men. What would happen if a star from heaven really fell into the slimy and bloody pool of a hopeless and decaying humanity? Men swept a city with the guillotine, a continent with the sabre, because Liberty, Equality, and Fraternity were too precious to be lost. How if Christianity was yet more maddening because it was yet more precious?

But why should we labour the point when One who knew human nature as it can really be learnt, from fishermen and women and natural people, saw from his quiet village the track of this truth across history, and, in saying that He came to bring not peace but a sword, set up eternally His colossal realism against the eternal sentimentality of the Secularist?

Thus, then, in the third instance, when the learned sceptic says: "Christianity produced wars and persecutions," we shall reply: "Naturally."

And, lastly, let me take an example which leads me on directly to the general matter I wish to discuss for the remaining space of the articles at my command. The Secularist constantly points out that the Hebrew and Christian religions began as local things; that their god was a tribal god; that they gave him material form, and attached him to particular places.

This is an excellent example of one of the things that if I were conducting a detailed campaign I should use as an argument for the validity of Biblical experience. For if there really are some other and higher beings than ourselves, and if they in some strange way, at some emotional crisis, really revealed themselves to rude poets or dreamers in very simple times, that these rude people should regard the revelation as local, and connect it with the particular hill or river where it happened, seems to me exactly what any reasonable human being would expect. It has a far more credible look than if they had talked cosmic philosophy from the beginning. If they had, I should have suspected "priestcraft" and forgeries and third-century Gnosticism.

If there be such a being as God, and He can speak to a child, and if God spoke to a child in the garden, the child would, of course, say that God lived in the garden. I should not think it any less likely to be true for that. If the child said: "God is everywhere: an impalpable essence pervading and supporting all constituents of the Cosmos alike" — if, I say, the infant addressed me in the above terms, I should think he was much more likely to have been with the governess than with God.

So if Moses had said God was an Infinite Energy, I should be certain he had seen nothing extraordinary. As he said He was a Burning Bush, I think it very likely that he did see something extraordinary. For whatever be the Divine Secret, and whether or no it has (as all people have believed) sometimes broken bounds and surged into our work, at least it lies on the side furthest away from pedants and their definitions, and nearest to the silver souls of quiet people, to the beauty of bushes, and the love of one's native place.

Thus, then, in our last instance (out of hundreds that might be taken), we conclude in the same way. When the learned sceptic says: "The visions of the Old Testament were local, and rustic, and grotesque," we shall answer: "Of course. They were genuine."

Thus, as I said at the beginning, I find myself, to start with, face to face with the difficulty that to mention the reasons that I have for believing in Christianity is, in very many cases, simply to repeat those arguments which Mr. Blatchford, in some strange way, seems to regard as arguments against it. His book is really rich and powerful. He has undoubtedly set up these four great guns of which I have spoken. I have nothing to say against the size and ammunition of the guns. I only say that by some accident of arrangement he has set up those four pieces of artillery with the tails pointing at me and the mouths pointing at himself. If I were not so humane, I should say: "Gentlemen of the Secularist Guard, fire first."

But there is more to be said. Mr. Blatchford, for some reason or other (possibly want of space), has neglected to urge all the arguments for Christianity. And, oddly enough, the two or three arguments he has omitted to state are the really vital and essential ones. Without them, even the excellent four facts which he and I have respectively explained may appear superficially unintelligible.

Why will many of you not accept my four explanations? Obviously, in mere logic, they are as logical as Mr. Blatchford's. It is as reasonable, in the abstract, that a truth should be distorted as that a lie should be distorted; it is as reasonable, in the abstract, that men should starve and sin for a real benefit as for an unreal one. You will not believe it because you are armed to the teeth, and buttoned up to the chin with the great Agnostic Orthodoxy, perhaps the most placid and perfect of all the orthodoxies of men. You could sooner believe that Socrates was a Government spy than believe that he heard a voice from his God. You could more easily think that Christ murdered His mother, than that He had a psychic energy of which we know nothing. I approach you with the reverence and the courage due to a bench of bishops.

II

WHY I BELIEVE IN CHRISTIANITY

I mean no disrespect to Mr. Blatchford in saying that our difficulty very largely lies in the fact that he, like masses of clever people nowadays, does not understand what theology is. To make mistakes in a science is one thing, to mistake its nature another. And as I read *God and My Neighbour*, the conviction gradually dawns on me that he thinks theology is the study of whether a lot of tales about God told in the Bible are historically demonstrable. This is as if he were trying to prove to a man that Socialism was sound Political Economy, and began to realise half-way through that the man thought that Political Economy meant the study of whether politicians were economical.

It is very hard to explain briefly the nature of a whole living study; it would be just as hard to explain politics or ethics. For the more a thing is huge and obvious and stares one in the face, the harder it is to define. Anybody can define conchology. Nobody can define morals.

Nevertheless it falls to us to make some attempt to explain this religious philosophy which was, and will be again, the study of the highest intellects and the foundation of the strongest nations, but which our little civilisation has for a while forgotten, just as it has forgotten how to dance and how to dress itself decently. I will try and explain why I think a religious philosophy necessary and why I think Christianity the best religious philosophy. But before I do so I want you to bear in mind two historical facts. I do not ask you to draw my deduction from them or any deduction from them. I ask you to remember them as mere facts throughout the discussion.

1. Christianity arose and spread in a very cultured and very cynical world—in a very modern world. Lucretius was as much a materialist as Haeckel, and a much more persuasive writer. The Roman world had read *God and My Neighbour*, and in a weary sort of way thought it quite true. It is worth noting that religions almost always do arise

out of these sceptical civilisations. A recent book on the Pre-Mohammedan literature of Arabia describes a life entirely polished and luxurious. It was so with Buddha, born in the purple of an ancient civilisation. It was so with Puritanism in England and the Catholic Revival in France and Italy, both of which were born out of the rationalism of the Renaissance. It is so to-day; it is always so. Go to the two most modern and free-thinking centres, Paris and America, and you will find them full of devils and angels, of old mysteries and new prophets. Rationalism is fighting for its life against the young and vigorous superstitions.

2. Christianity, which is a very mystical religion, has nevertheless been the religion of the most practical section of mankind. It has far more paradoxes than the Eastern philosophies, but it also builds far better roads.

The Moslem has a pure and logical conception of God, the one Monistic Allah. But he remains a barbarian in Europe, and the grass will not grow where he sets his foot. The Christian has a Triune God, "a tangled trinity," which seems a mere capricious contradiction in terms. But in action he bestrides the earth, and even the cleverest Eastern can only fight him by imitating him first. The East has logic and lives on rice. Christendom has mysteries—and motor cars. Never mind, as I say, about the inference, let us register the fact.

Now with these two things in mind let me try and explain what Christian theology is.

Complete Agnosticism is the obvious attitude for man. We are all Agnostics until we discover that Agnosticism will not work. Then we adopt some philosophy, Mr. Blatchford's or mine or some others, for of course Mr. Blatchford is no more an Agnostic than I am. The Agnostic would say that he did not know whether man was responsible for his sins. Mr. Blatchford says that he knows that man is not.

Here we have the seed of the whole huge tree of dogma. Why does Mr. Blatchford go beyond Agnosticism and assert that there is certainly no free will? *Because he cannot run his scheme of morals without asserting that there is no free will.* He wishes no man to be blamed for sin. Therefore he has to make his disciples quite certain that God did not make them free and therefore blamable. No wild Christian doubt must flit through the mind of the Determinist. No demon must whisper to him in some hour of anger that perhaps the company promoter was responsible for swindling him into the workhouse. No sudden scepticism must suggest to him that perhaps the schoolmaster was blamable for flogging a little boy to death. The Determinist faith must be held firmly, or else certainly the weakness of human nature will lead men to be angered when they are slandered and kick back when they are kicked. In short, free will seems at first sight to belong to the Unknowable. Yet Mr. Blatchford cannot preach what seems to him common charity without asserting one dogma about it. And I cannot preach what seems to me common honesty without asserting another.

Here is the failure of Agnosticism. That our every-day view of the things we do (in the common sense) know, actually depends upon our view of the things we do not (in the common sense) know. It is all very well to tell a man, as the Agnostics do, to "cultivate his garden." But suppose a man ignores everything outside his garden, and among them ignores the sun and the rain?

This is the real fact. You cannot live without dogmas about these things. You cannot act for twenty-four hours without deciding either to hold people responsible or not to hold them responsible. Theology is a product far more practical than chemistry.

Some Determinists fancy that Christianity invented a dogma like free will for fun — a mere contradiction. This is absurd. You have the contradiction whatever you are. Determinists tell me, with a degree of truth, that Determinism makes no difference to daily life. That means that although the Determinist knows men have no free will, yet he goes on treating them as if they had.

The difference then is very simple. The Christian puts the contradiction into his philosophy. The Determinist puts it into his daily habits. The Christian states as an avowed mystery what the Determinist calls nonsense. The Determinist has the same nonsense for breakfast, dinner, tea, and supper every day of his life.

The Christian, I repeat, puts the mystery into his philosophy. That mystery by its darkness enlightens all things. Once grant him that, and life is life, and bread is bread, and cheese is cheese: he can laugh and fight. The Determinist makes the matter of the will logical and lucid: and in the light of that lucidiy all things are darkened, words have no meaning, actions no aim. He has made his philosophy a syllogism and himself a gibbering lunatic.

It is not a question between mysticism and rationality. It is a question between mysticism and madness. For mysticism, and mysticism alone, has kept men sane from the beginning of the world. All the straight roads of logic lead to some Bedlam, to Anarchism or to passive obedience, to treating the universe as a clockwork of matter or else as a delusion of mind. It is only the Mystic, the man who accepts the contradictions, who can laugh and walk easily through the world.

Are you surprised that the same civilisation which believed in the Trinity discovered steam?

All the great Christian doctrines are of this kind. Look at them carefully and fairly for yourselves. I have only space for two examples. The first is the Christian idea of God. Just as we have all been Agnostics so we have all been Pantheists. In the godhood of youth it seems so easy to say, "Why cannot a man see God in a bird flying and be content?" But then comes a time when we go on and say, "If God is in the birds, let us be not only as beautiful as the birds; let us be as cruel as the birds; let us live the mad, red life of nature." And something that is wholesome in us resists and says, "My friend, you are going mad."

Then comes the other side and we say: "The birds are hateful, the flowers are shameful. I will give no praise to so base an universe." And the wholesome thing in us says: "My friend, you are going mad."

Then comes a fantastic thing and says to us: "You are right to enjoy the birds, but wicked to copy them. There is a good thing behind all these things, yet all these things are lower than you. The Universe is right: but the World is wicked. The thing behind all is not cruel, like a bird: but good, like a man." And the wholesome thing in us says. "I have found the high road."

Now when Christianity came, the ancient world had just reached this dilemma. It heard the Voice of Nature-Worship crying, "All natural things are good. War is as healthy as the flowers. Lust is as clean as the stars." And it heard also the cry of the hopeless Stoics and Idealists: "The flowers are at war: the stars are unclean: nothing but man's conscience is right and that is utterly defeated."

Both views were consistent, philosophical and exalted: their only disadvantage was that the first leads logically to murder and the second to suicide. After an agony of thought the world saw the sane path between the two. It was the Christian God. He made Nature but He was Man.

Lastly, there is a word to be said about the Fall. It can only be a word, and it is this. Without the doctrine of the Fall all idea of progress is unmeaning. Mr. Blatchford says that there was not a Fall but a gradual rise. But the very word "rise" implies that you know toward what you are rising. Unless there is a standard you cannot tell whether you are rising or falling. But the main point is that the Fall like every other large path of Christianity is embodied in the common language talked on the top of an omnibus. Anybody might say, "Very few men are really Manly." Nobody would say, "Very few whales are really whaley."

If you wanted to dissuade a man from drinking his tenth whisky you would slap him on the back and say, "Be a man." No one who wished to dissuade a crocodile from eating his tenth explorer would slap it on the back and say, "Be a crocodile." For we have no notion of a perfect crocodile; no allegory of a whale expelled from his whaley Eden. If a whale came up to us and said: "I am a new kind of whale; I have abandoned whalebone," we should not trouble. But if a man came up to us (as many will soon come up to us) to say, "I am a new kind of man. I am the super-man. I have abandoned mercy and justice"; we should answer, "Doubtless you are new, but you are not nearer to the perfect man, for he has been already in the mind of God. We have fallen with Adam and we shall rise with Christ; but we would rather fall with Satan than rise with you."

III

MIRACLES AND MODERN CIVILISATION

Mr. Blatchford has summed up all that is important in his whole position in three sentences. They are perfectly honest and clear. Nor are they any the less honest and clear because the first two of them are falsehoods and the third is a fallacy. He says "The Christian denies the miracles of the Mahommedan. The Mahommedan denies the miracles of the Christian. The Rationalist denies all miracles alike."

The historical error in the first two remarks I will deal with shortly. I confine myself for the moment to the courageous admission of Mr. Blatchford that the Rationalist denies all miracles alike. He does not question them. He does not pretend to be agnostic about them. He does not suspend his judgment until they shall be proved. He denies them.

Faced with this astounding dogma I asked Mr. Blatchford why he thought miracles would not occur. He replied that the Universe was governed by laws. Obviously this answer is of no use whatever. For we cannot call a thing impossible because the world is governed by laws, unless we know what laws. Does Mr. Blatchford know all about all the laws in the Universe? And if he does not know about the laws how can he possibly know anything about the exceptions?

For, obviously, the mere fact that a thing happens seldom, under odd circumstances and with no explanation within our knowledge, is no proof that it is against natural law. That would apply to the Siamese twins, or to a new comet, or to radium three years ago.

The philosophical case against miracles is somewhat easily dealt with. There is no philosophical case against miracles. There are such things as the laws of Nature rationally speaking. What everybody knows is this only. That there is repetition in nature. What everybody knows is that pumpkins produce pumpkins. What nobody knows is why they should not produce elephants and giraffes.

There is one philosophical question about miracles and only one. Many able modern Rationalists cannot apparently even get it into their heads. The poorest lad at Oxford in the Middle Ages would have understood it. (Note. As the last sentence will seem strange in our "enlightened" age I may explain that under "the cruel reign of mediaeval superstition," poor lads were educated at Oxford to a most reckless extent. Thank God, we live in better days.)

The question of miracles is merely this. Do you know why a pumpkin goes on being a pumpkin? If you do not, you cannot possibly tell whether a pumpkin could turn into a coach or couldn't. That is all.

All the other scientific expressions you are in the habit of using at breakfast are words and winds. You say "It is a law of nature that pumpkins should remain pumpkins." That only means that pumpkins generally do remain pumpkins, which is obvious; it does not say why. You say "Experience is against it." That only means, "I have known many pumpkins intimately and none of them turned into coaches."

There was a great Irish Rationalist of this school (possibly related to Mr. Lecky), who when he was told that a witness had seen him commit murder said that he could bring a hundred witnesses who had not seen him commit it.

You say "The modern world is against it." That means that a mob of men in London and Birmingham, and Chicago, in a thoroughly pumpkiny state of mind, cannot work miracles by faith.

You say "Science is against it." That means that so long as pumpkins are pumpkins their conduct is pumpkiny, and bears no resemblance to the conduct of a coach. That is fairly obvious.

What Christianity says is merely this. That this repetition in Nature has its origin not in a thing resembling a law but a thing resembling a will. Of course its phase of a Heavenly Father is drawn from an earthly father. Quite equally Mr. Blatchford's phase of a universal law is a metaphor from an Act of Parliament. But Christianity holds that the world and its repetition came by will or Love as children are begotten by a father, and therefore that other and different things might come by it. Briefly, it believes that a God who could do anything so extraordinary as making pumpkins go on being pumpkins, is like the prophet, Habbakuk, *Capable de tout*. If you do not think it extraordinary that a pumpkin is always a pumpkin, think again. You have not yet even begun philosophy. You have not even seen a pumpkin.

The historic case against miracles is also rather simple. It consists of calling miracles impossible, then saying that no one but a fool believes impossibilites: then declaring that there is no wise evidence on behalf of the miraculous. The whole trick is done by means of leaning alternately on the philosophical and historical objection. If we say miracles are theoretically possible, they say, "Yes, but there is no evidence for them." When we take all the records of the human race and say, "Here is your evidence," they say, "But these people were superstitious, they believed in impossible things."

The real question is whether our little Oxford Street civilisation is certain to be right and the rest of the world certain to be wrong. Mr. Blatchford thinks that the materialism of nineteenth century Westerns is one of their noble discoveries. I think it is as dull as their coats, as dirty as their streets, as ugly as their trousers, and as stupid as their industrial system.

Mr. Blatchford himself, however, has summed up perfectly his pathetic faith in modern civilisation. He has written a very amusing description of how difficult it would be to persuade an English judge in a modern law court of the truth of the Resurrection. Of course he is quite right; it would be impossible. But it does not seem to occur to him that we Christians may not have such an extravagant reverence for English judges as is felt by Mr. Blatchford himself.

The experiences of the Founder of Christianity have perhaps left us in a vague doubt of the infallibility of courts of law. I know quite well that nothing would induce a British judge to believe that a man had risen from the dead. But then I know quite as well that a very little while ago nothing would have induced a British judge to believe that a Socialist could be a good man. A judge would refuse to believe in new spiritual wonders. But this would not be because he was a judge, but because he was, besides being a judge, an English gentleman, a modern Rationalist, and something of an old fool.

And Mr. Blatchford is quite wrong in supposing that the Christian and the Moslem deny each other's miracles. No religion that thinks itself true bothers about the miracles of another religion. It denies the doctrines of the religion; it denies its morals; but it never thinks it worth while to deny its signs and wonders.

And why not? Because these things some men have always thought possible. Because any wandering gipsy may have psychical powers. Because the general existence of a world of spirits and of strange mental powers is a part of the common sense of all mankind. The Pharisees did not dispute the miracles of Christ; they said they were worked by devilry. The Christians did not dispute the miracles of Mahomed. They said they were worked by devilry. The Roman world did not deny the possibility that Christ was a God. It was far too enlightened for that.

In so far as the Church did (chiefly during the corrupt and sceptical eighteenth century) urge miracles as a reason for belief, her fault is evident: but it is not what Mr. Blatchford supposes. It is not that she asked men to believe anything so incredible; it is that she asked men to be converted by anything so commonplace.

What matters about a religion is not whether it can work marvels like any ragged Indian conjurer, but whether it has a true philosophy of the Universe. The Romans were quite willing to admit that Christ was a God. What they denied was the He was the God—the highest truth of the cosmos. And this is the only point worth discussing about Christianity.

IV

THE ETERNAL HEROISM OF THE SLUMS

I have said it before, but it cannot be too often repeated, that what is the matter with Mr. Blatchford and his school is that they are not sceptical enough. For the really bold questions we have to go back to the Christian Fathers.

For example, Mr. Blatchford, in *God and My Neighbour*, does me the honour to quote from me as follows: "Mr. G. K. Chesterton, in defending Christianity, said, 'Christianity has committed crimes at which the sun might sicken in Heaven, and no one can refute the statement.'" I did say this, and I say it again, but I said something else. I said that every great and useful institution had committed such crimes. And no one can refute *that* statement.

And why has every great institution been criminal? It is not enough to say "Christians persecuted; down with Christianity," any more than it is enough to say, "A Confucian stole my hair-brush; down with Confucianism." We want to know whether the reason for which the Confucian stole the hair-brush was a reason peculiar to the Confucians or a reason common to many other men.

It is obvious that the Christian's reason for torturing was a reason common to hosts of other men; it was simply the fact that he held his views strongly and tried unscrupulously to make them prevail. Any other man might hold any other views strongly and try unscrupulously to make them prevail. And when we look at the facts we find, as I say, that millions of other men do, and have done so from the beginning of the world.

Mr. Blatchford quoted the one exception of Buddhism which never persecuted politically. This is, if ever there was one, an exception that proves the rule. For Buddhism has never persecuted, simply because it has never been political at all, because it has always despised material happiness and material civilisation. That is to say, Buddhism has never had an Inquisition for exactly the same reason that it has never had a printing-press, or a Reform Bill, or a *Clarion* newspaper.

But if Mr. Blatchford really thinks that the gory past of an institution damns it, and if he really wants an institution to damn, an institution which is much older, and much larger, and much gorier than Christianity, I can easily oblige him.

The institution called Government or the State, has a past more shameful than a pirate ship. Every legal code on earth has been full of ferocity and heartrending error. The rack and the stake were not invented by Christians; Christians only picked up the horrible cast toys of Paganism. The rack and the stake were invented by a bitter Rationalism older than all religions. The rack and stake were invented by the State, by Society, by the Social Ideal—or, to put it shortly, by Socialism. And this State or Government, the mother of all whips and thumbscrews, this is, if you please, the very thing which Mr. Blatchford and his socialistic following would make stronger than it has ever been under the sun. Strange and admirable delicacy. Delicacy which can have no further dealings with Christianity, because of the Massacre of Saint Bartholomew, but must rather invoke to purify the world a thing which has shown its soul in the torturing of Roman slaves for evidence, and in the artistic punishments of China.

I do not disagree with Mr. Blatchford for invoking the State. But then I do not think that the goriness of a thing's past disqualifies it from saving mankind. I, therefore, am consistent in thinking that Christianity is not disqualified. But Mr. Blatchford is not consistent, for he positively appeals to the greater sinner to save him from the lesser.

If only Mr. Blatchford would ask the real question. It is not, "Why is Christianity so bad when it claims to be so good?" The real question is, "Why are all human things so bad when they claim to be so good?" Why is not the most noble scheme a guarantee against corruption? If Nunquam will boldly pursue this question, will really leave delusions behind and walk across the godless waste, alone, he will come at last to a strange place. His sceptical pilgrimage will end at a place where Christianity begins.

Christianity begins with the wickedness of the Inquisition. Only it adds the wickedness of English Liberals, Tories, Socialists, and county magistrates. It begins with a strange thing running across human history. This it calls Sin, or the Fall of Man.

If ever I wish to expound it further, Mr. Blatchford's list of Christian crimes will be a most valuable compilation. In brief, however, Mr. Blatchford sees the sins of historic Christianity rise before him like a great tower. It is a star-defying Tower of Babel, lifting itself alone into the sky, affronting God in Heaven. Let him climb up it for a few years. When he is near to its tremendous top, he will find that it is one of the nine hundred and ninety-nine columns which support the pedestal of the ancient Christian philosophy.

Right or wrong, Christianity has her theory and her remedy for the world's evils. But what is Mr. Blatchford's remedy? Before him also lies the wilderness of human frenzy and frivolity. What is his remedy? I am not uttering (as anyone ignorant of the facts might fancy) a wild joke; I am stating the sober truth of the situation, when I say that Mr. Blatchford's remedy for all this is that nobody should be responsible for anything.

Never perhaps in the history of mankind has a serious malady been met by a more astounding cure. For Mr. Blatchford, remember, propounds it as a cure. Many have admitted Fatalism as a melancholy metaphysical truth. No one before him, as far as I know, ever took it round with a big drum as a cheery means of moral improvement. The problem is that men will not live up to ideals. The problem is that while Marcus Aurelius is breaking his heart for righteousness, his own son Commodus cares only for bloodthirsty pantomimes. The remedy is to tell Commodus that he cannot help it. The problem is that the purity of St. Francis cannot prevent the corruption of Brother Elias. The remedy is to tell Brother Elias that he is not to be blamed and Francis not to be admired. The problem is that a man will often choose a base pleasure rather than a hard generosity. The remedy is to tell him that the base pleasure has been chosen for him.

I know quite well, of course, that Mr. Blatchford tried to make this monstrous anarchy more tolerable to the intellect. He did it by saying that although people ought not to be blamed for their actions, yet they ought to be trained to do better. They ought, he said, to be given better conditions of heredity and environment, and then they would be good, and the problem would be solved. The primary answer is obvious. How can one say that a man ought not to be held responsible, but ought to be well trained? For if he "ought" to be well trained, there must be somebody who "ought" to train him. And that man must be held responsible for training him. The proposition has killed itself in three sentences. Mr. Blatchford has not removed the necessity for responsibility merely by saying that humanity, instead of being dealt with by the hangmen, ought to be dealt with by the doctors. For, upon the whole, and supposing that I required the services of either, I think I would sooner be dealt with by an irresponsible hangman than by an irresponsible doctor.

The second thing to say, of course, is that Mr. Blatchford offers nothing even remotely resembling an argument to show that he knows what conditions would produce good men, or that anybody knows. He cannot surely mean that mere conditions of physical comfort and mental culture produce good men; because manifestly they do not. Mr. Blatchford may have some secret receipt for virtue, making people live in trees, or shave their heads, or dine on some particular kind of lozenge, but he has not told anybody what it is.

The fact is very simple. It may be true that perfect conditions would produce perfect men. But it is much more obviously true that only perfect men could invent perfect conditions. If we make such a mess of our own lives, how can we be certain that we know the best soil for living things? If heredity and environment make it so necessary for us to commit theft and adultery, why should they not make it necessary for us to create conditions that will lead to theft and adultery? In the British Isles at this moment there exist, I imagagine, people in every conceivable degree of riches and poverty from insane opulence to insane hunger. Is any one of those classes morally exquisite or glaringly any better than the rest? And where so many modes of education fail, by what right does Mr. Blatchford assume his, whatever it is, to be infallible?

As for the great part of the talk of Mr. Blatchford about sin arising from vile and filthy environments, I do not wish to introduce into this discussion anything of personal emotion, but I am bound to say that I have great difficulty in enduring that talk with patience. Who in the world is it who thus speaks as if wickedness and folly raged only among the unfortunate? Is it Mr. Blatchford who falls back upon the old contemptible impertinence which represents virtue to be something upper-class, like a visiting card, or a silk hat? Is it Nunquam who denies the eternal heroism of the slums? The thing is almost incredible, but so it is. Nunquam has put as a coping stone upon his Temple, this association of vice with poverty, the vilest and the oldest and the dirtiest of all the stones that insolence has ever flung at the poor.

Man that is born of a woman has short days and full of trouble; but he is a nobler and a happier being than this would make him out. I will not deign to answer even Mr. Blatchford when he asks "how" a man born in filth and sin can live a noble life. I know so many who are doing it, within a stone's throw of my own house, in Battersea, that I care little how it is done. Man has something in him always which is not conquered by conditions. Yes, there is a liberty that has never been chained. There is a liberty that has made men happy in dungeons, as it may make them happy in slums. It is the liberty of the mind, that is to say, it is the one liberty on which Mr. Blatchford makes war. That which all the tyrants have left, he would extinguish. That which no gaoler could ever deny to a prisoner, Nunquam would deny. More numerous than can be counted, in all the wars and persecutions of the world, men have looked out of their little grated windows and said "at least my thoughts are free." "No, No," says the face of Mr. Blatchford, suddenly appearing at the window "your thoughts are the inevitable result of heredity and environment. Your thoughts are as material as your dungeons. Your thoughts are as mechanical as the guillotine." So pants this strange comforter, from cell to cell.

I suppose Mr. Blatchford would say that in his Utopia nobody would be in prison. What do I care whether I am in prison or no, if I have to drag chains everywhere. A man in his Utopia may have, for all I know, free food, free meadows, his own estate, his own palace. What does it matter? he may not have his own soul. Every thought that comes into his head he must regard as the click of a machine. He sees a lost child and with a spasm of pity decides to adopt it. Click! he has to remember that he has not really done it at all. He has a temptation to do some huge irresistible sin; he reminds himself that he is a man, that he can, if he likes, be a hero; he resists it. Click! he remembers that he is not a man and not a hero, but a machine, so made as to produce that result. He walks in wide fields under a splendid sunrise; he resolves on some vast magnanimity—Click! what is the good of sunrises and palaces? Was ever slavery like unto this slavery? Was ever man before so much a slave?

I know that this will never be. That is, I know that Mr. Blatchford's philosophy will never be endured among sane men. But if ever it is I will very easily predict what will happen. Man, the machine, will stand up in these flowery meadows and cry aloud, "Was there not once a thing, a church, that taught us we were free in our souls? Did it not surround itself with tortures and dungeons in order to force men to believe that their souls were free? If there was, let it return, tortures, dungeons and all. Put me in those dungeons, rack me with those tortures, if by that means I may possibly believe it again."

The text of this book has been set in Bembo by the Neumann Press of Long Prairie, Minnesota. Printed on Warren's Olde Style paper by Thomson Shore, Dexter, Michigan. Bound in kennet cloth by John H. Dekker & Sons. Cover and jacket design by Darlene Lawless.